W9-AQB-607

HQ 60 .M66 1998

Money, John, 1921-

ier

NEW ENGLAND INSTITUTE
OF TECHNOLOGY
LEARNING RESOURCES CENTER

Sin, Science, and the Sex Police

Authored or coauthored by John Money

Hermaphroditism: Inquiry into the Nature of a Human Paradox, 1952
The Psychologic Study of Man, 1957
A Standardized Road-Map Test of Direction Sense, 1965
Sex Errors of the Body and Related Syndromes, 1968/1994
Man and Woman, Boy and Girl, 1972/1996
Sexual Signatures, 1975
Love and Love Sickness, 1980
The Destroying Angel, 1985
Lovemaps, 1986
Venuses Penuses: Sexology, Sexosophy, and Exigency Theory, 1986
Gay, Straight, and In-Between, 1988
Vandalized Lovemaps, 1989
Biographies of Gender and Hermaphroditism, 1991
The Breathless Orgasm, 1991
The Kaspar Hauser Syndrome of "Psychosocial Dwarfism," 1992
The Adam Principle: Genes, Genitals, Hormones, and Gender, 1993
The Armed Robbery Orgasm, 1993
Reinterpreting the Unspeakable, 1994
Gendermaps, 1995
Principles of Developmental Sexology, 1997

Edited or coedited by John Money

Reading Disability: Progress and Research Needs in Dyslexia, 1962
Sex Research: New Developments, 1965
The Disabled Reader: Education of the Dyslexic Child, 1966
Transsexualism and Sex Reassignment, 1969
Contemporary Sexual Behavior: Critical Issues in the 1970s, 1973
Developmental Human Behavior Genetics, 1975
Handbook of Sexology, Volumes 1–7, 1977–1990
Traumatic Abuse and Neglect of Children at Home, 1980
Handbook of Human Sexuality, 1980
Handbook of Forensic Sexology, 1994

Essays
on Sexology
& Sexosophy

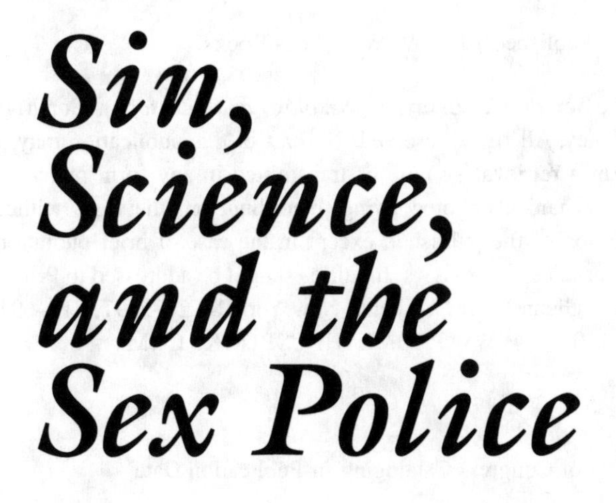

Sin, Science, and the Sex Police

JOHN MONEY

NEW ENGLAND INSTITUTE
OF TECHNOLOGY
LEARNING RESOURCES CENTER

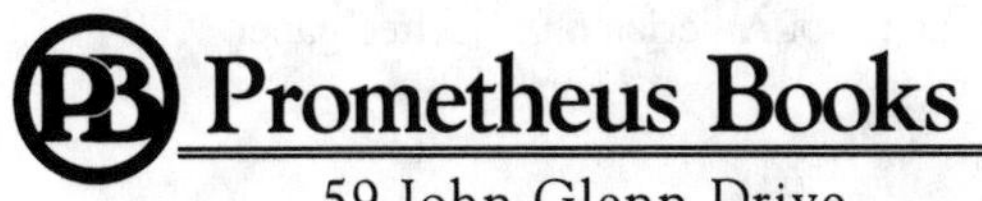

Prometheus Books
59 John Glenn Drive
Amherst, New York 14228-2197

3/99

#39897278

Dedicated to Professor Claude J. Migeon, M.D.,
my good friend and colleague in pediatrics,
endocrinology, and sexology.

Published 1998 by Prometheus Books

Sin, Science, and the Sex Police: Essays on Sexology and Sexosophy. Copyright © 1998 by John Money. All rights reserved. No part of this publication may be reproduced, stored in a retrieval system, or transmitted in any form or by any means, electronic, mechanical, photocopying, recording, or otherwise, without prior written permission of the publisher, except in the case of brief quotations embodied in critical articles and reviews. Inquiries should be addressed to Prometheus Books, 59 John Glenn Drive, Amherst, New York 14228–2197, 716–691–0133. FAX: 716–691–0137. WWW.PROMETHEUSBOOKS.COM

02 01 00 99 98   5 4 3 2 1

Library of Congress Cataloging-in-Publication Data

Money, John, 1921–
Sin, science, and the sex police : essays on sexology and sexosophy / John Money.
p.   cm.
Includes bibliographical references.
ISBN 1–57392–253–6 (alk. paper)
1. Sexology. 2. Sex—Philosophy. 3. Gender. 4. Pediatric psychoendocrinology. 5. Paraphilia. I. Title.
HQ60.M66   1998
306.7—dc21   98–37663
CIP

Printed in the United States of America on acid-free paper

Acknowledgments

The National Institute of Child Health and Human Development, Department of Health and Human Services, United States Public Health Service, has supported the author in psychohormonal research for forty-one years, currently under Grant number R25 HD-00325-41.

Thanks go to Sally A. Hopkins and William P. Wang for their industrious work on this book.

—John Money, Ph.D.
Professor Emeritus, Medical Psychology and Pediatrics
The Johns Hopkins University School of Medicine and Hospital
Baltimore, MD 21202–5327

Contents

Part Three. Ancestral Explanations

Part Four. Clinical Principles

Part Five. Pediatric Psychoendocrinology

Introduction

The computer and the science and technology of information—informatics—are of inestimable value to scholars for the retrieval of bibliographic data. Online bibliographic searches do not, however, retrieve data from further back than around 1970, nor from periodicals that are not on their index list. Their coverage of conference proceedings, review articles, and textbook chapters is spotty at best. The fate of most such writings is that they are irretrievable. Retrieval of everything attributable to a particular author is also not possible. In addition, the term *sexology* is not used by electronic-retrieval services. It is because of what gets omitted from retrieval services that, years ago, I adopted a policy of reissuing, in book form, readings collected from my own bibliography. There are three such books, all published by Prometheus Books. The first is titled *Venuses Penuses: Sexology, Sexosophy, and Exigency Theory* (1986). Its chapters are predominantly conceptual and theoretical in significance. The second volume is titled *The Adam Principle: Genes, Genitals, Hormones, and Gender: Selected Readings in Sexology* (1993). Its chapters are predominantly clinical and pediatric psychoendocrinological.

Its successor, the present volume, is titled *Sin, Science, and the Sex Police: Essays on Sexology and Sexosophy* (1998). This is a collection of more recent writings in five parts. The essays in Part One deal with theoretical sexology, and those in Part Two with developmental sexology. Part Three deals with evolutionary sexology and also with historically ancient sexological doctrines that still influence sexology today. Part Four deals with clinical principles and includes two chapters on the currently controversial issue of what to do with infant boys who undergo irreparable and total loss of the penis (ablatio penis) as a sequel to faulty circumcision or other accidents.

Part Five is virtually a book in itself. It summarizes a lifetime of clinical and research work in psychoendocrinology in the pediatric endocrine clinic at Johns Hopkins. It ranges quite widely beyond pediatric sexology per se to include behavior-genetics, retarded or precocious growth, IQ, and mental health, all in relation to hormones and to specific syndromes of hormonal deficiency or excess. As a compendium of pediatric psychoendocrinology, Part Five is unique and unrivaled in its field.

The term *commonplace,* when applied to a book, means that the book is a leading text of general application. This is a commonplace book, and one that has a wide range of appeal to scholars as well as to the general public interested in sex and sexuality from conception to maturity.

John Money, Ph.D.
Baltimore, Maryland
September 8, 1998

Part One

Theoretical Reviews

1

The Universals of Sexuality and Eroticism in a Changing World

Sexology's Scientific Status

Science lays claim to the reputation of knowing no national language. More precisely, it is basic science that claims this reputation, which is justified by the use of advanced mathematics as the universal language in which it speaks. The universality of basic science does not yet apply to sexology as it does, say, to molecular genetics or nuclear physics.

Sexology is still at the stage of being a phenomenological and descriptive science. Its mathematics are elementary contingencies based on frequency counts rather than absolute magnitudes. Its correlations all too often apply to variables that fail the test of a scientific classification, insofar as they are not mutually exclusive and exhaustively complete in their coverage. The rationale for their selection may be solely the availability of a test or rating scale that purports to measure them.

In many instances, variables in sex research represent value judgments that more properly belong to sexosophy, the philosophy of sex, rather than to sexology, the science of sex (Money, 1981). In conse-

---

Originally published in P. Kothari, ed., *Proceedings of the Seventh World Congress of Sexology* (Bombay: Indian Association of Sex Educators, Counsellors, and Therapists, 1986), pp. 1–11.

quence, they lead to generalizations that fail to have universal applicability, but reflect regional and cultural prejudices and relativities. For example, what is researched as pornography in one culture is legitimate entertainment in another.

Scholars from the scientifically undeveloped countries import basic science from the scientifically developed countries. Basic science migrates and acclimatizes well. Phenomenological science, by contrast, may find itself incompatible with the new cultural climate. Sexology is at risk in this respect, for it has absorbed the moral, religious, and legal climate of the culture of the West. It is profoundly influenced by its time and place of origin, and hence by ideas that, though they masquerade as universal principles, are in fact no more than contemporary vogues. For example, a "meaningful relationship" is not an eternal verity, but a very recent platitude that becomes absurd if one tries to differentiate it from a meaningless relationship, since all relationships have some sort of meaning.

India is the location of the Seventh World Congress of Sexology. Its theme is "Sexuality in a Changing World." This, therefore, is an auspicious occasion on which to examine sexology for some common denominators that apply to humankind as a whole, regardless of time and place.

Teleology and Mechanism

Sexology, like every science, has its theoretical underpinnings in the metaphysics of causality. Like other biological sciences, sexology is divided in allegiance to causality as teleological determinism and causality as mechanistic determinism. Teleological determinism in sexology derives from psychology. It is chiefly motivational determinism, conceptualized in terms of drives and needs, both conscious and unconscious; though evolutionary determinism also has a small niche as another manifestation of teleology in sexology.

Mechanistic determinism in sexology also derives from psychology. It has two major forms, namely associative determinism and organic determinism. Associative determinism is conceptualized as behavior modification, which is historically derived from stimulus-response theory, operant conditioning, and social-learning theory.

Organic determinism is conceptualized as being caused by the anatomy or physiology of the body, especially its pathology. It is biomedical, and is the province of the specialties subsumed under medicine, surgery, and radiology.

In the life sciences, the ancient metaphysical split between teleology and mechanism has undergone some conceptual attempts at unification, as indicated in such terms as *psychosomatic, psychobiology, sociobiology,* and *psychoneuroendocrinology.* With the familiarity of continued usage, however, the split re-emerges in these terms in the guise of mind/body dualism. In the mind/body split, teleology is assigned to the mind and mechanism to the body. One takes predominance over the other. Thus, *psychosomatic* implies that a psychologic determinant causes a somatic dysfunction. By contrast, *psychobiology* implies biologic determinants of psychologic functions. *Sociobiology* implies evolutionary biological determinants of social, psychological, or sociological behavior. *Psychoneuroendocrinology* implies neuroendocrine stimuli that determine psychologic responses. There may be some dissent to the aforesaid definitions of one-way interactions, but they do, nonetheless, prevail in idiomatic usage of the four terms.

In sexology, as in all the life sciences, the split between teleological and mechanistic determinism has an insidious and very fundamental influence. All of the formulations of sexology are, in the final analysis, derived from an assumption (more often covert than overt) of either teleological or mechanistic determinism. The two are mutually exclusive. Consequently, they lead to irreconcilable positions in sexology. Today's divergence between humanistic and experimental sexology is a clear-cut example. Humanistic sexology is teleologically based on motivation. Experimental sexology is mechanistically based in either physiology or stimulus-response behaviorism.

Five Universal Exigencies of Being Human

There is no Holy Grail that contains the reconciliation of teleology and mechanism. There is, however, a possible way of circumventing the adversarial relationship between the two by espousing neither principle exclusively, nor rejecting either in toto, but by following a third principle based in philosophical operationism instead. This is the principle of the universal exigencies of ontogeny that are preordained by phylogeny (Money, 1957).

There are five of these universal exigencies. They are to be pairbonded; troopbonded; abidant, or ecologically sustained; ycleped, or known for something; and foredoomed, or subject to unpredictable pathologies and finally to death.

Pairbondage. Pairbondage means being bonded together in pairs, as in the parent-child pairbond, or the pairbond of those who are lovers or breeding partners. In everyday usage, bondage implies servitude or enforced submission. Though pairbondage is defined so as not to exclude this restrictive connotation, it has also the larger meaning of mutual dependency and cooperation, and affectional attachment. Pairbondage has a twofold phyletic origin in mammals. One is mutual attachment between a nursing mother and her feeding baby, without which the young fail to survive. The other is mutual attraction between males and females, and their accommodation to one another in mating, without which a diecious or two-sexed species like our own fails to reproduce itself.

Male-female pairbonding is species-specific and individually variable with respect to its duration and the proximity of the pair. In human beings, the two extremes are represented by anonymous donor fertilization, on the one hand, versus lifelong allegiance and copulatory fidelity, on the other.

Troopbondage. Troopbondage means bondedness together among individuals so that they become members of a family or troop that continues its long-term existence despite the loss or departure of any one member. Human troopbondage has its primate phyletic origin in the fact that members of the troop breed not in unison but asynchronously, with transgenerational overlap and with age-related interdependency. In newborn mammals, the troopbonding of a baby begins with its pairbonding together with its mother as the phyletically ordained minimum unit for its survival and health. After weaning, it is also phyletically ordained for herding and troopbonding species that isolation from, and deprivation of the company of other members of the species or their surrogate replacements, is incompatible with health and survival. Nonhuman primate species are, in the majority of instances, troopbonders like ourselves.

Abidance. Abidance means sustentation, or continuing to remain, be sustained, or survive in the same condition or circumstance of living or dwelling. It is a noun formed from the verb *abide* (from the Anglo-Saxon root *bidan,* "to bide"). There are three forms of the past participle: *abode, abided,* and *abidden.*

In its present usage, abidance means to be sustained in one's ecological niche or dwelling place in inanimate nature in cooperation or competition with others of one's own species, as well as amongst other species of fauna and flora. Abidance has its phyletic origin in the fact that human primates are mammalian omnivores ecologically dependent for survival on air, water, earth, and fire, and on the products of these four, particularly those products that take the form of nourishment, shelter, and clothing. Human individuals or troops in an impoverished ecological niche that fails to provide sufficient food, water, shelter, and clothing do not survive.

Ycleptance. "Yclept" is an Elizabethan word, one form of the past participle of *clepe,* meaning to name, to call, or to style. *Ycleped* and *cleped* are two alternative past participles. Ycleptance means being classified, branded, labeled, stylized, or typecast. It has its phyletic basis in likeness and unlikeness of individual to group attributes. Human beings have named and typecast one another since before recorded time. The terms range from the haphazard informality of nicknames that recognize personal idiosyncrasies to the highly organized formality of scientific classifications or medical diagnoses that prognosticate our futures. The categories of ycleptance are many and diverse: sex, age, family, clan, language, race, region, religion, politics, wealth, occupation, health, physique, looks, temperament, and so on. We all live typecast under the imprimatur of our fellow human beings. We are either stigmatized or idolized by the brand names or labels under which we are yclept. They shape our destinies.

Foredoomance. "Doom," in Anglo-Saxon and Middle English usage, meant what is laid down, a judgment or a decree. In today's usage it also means destiny or fate, especially if the predicted outcome is adverse, as in being doomed to suffer harm, sickness, or death. A foredoom is a doom ordained beforehand. Foredoomance is the collective noun that, as here defined, denotes the condition of being preordained to die, and of being vulnerable to injury, defect, and disease. Foredoomance has its phyletic origins in the principle of infirmity and the mortality of all life forms. Some individuals are at greater risk than others because of imperfections or errors in their genetic code. Some are at greater risk by reason of exposure to more dangerous places or things. All, however, are exposed to the risk, phyletically ordained, that all life forms, from viruses and bacteria to insects and vertebrates, are subject to being displaced by and preyed upon by other life forms. Foredoomance applies to each one of us at first hand, in a primary way, and also in a derivative way insofar as it also applies to those we know. Their suffering grieves us, and their dying is our bereavement.

Sexology's Data Base

Among the five universals, pairbondage in all of its ramifications gives sexology its data base as a scientific specialty. However, without cross-reference to variables that belong in the categories of troopbondage, abidance, ycleptance, and foredoomance, sexology is incomplete as a basic science, and also as an applied social and therapeutic science.

Thus, whether in designing a research investigation, making an initial patient evaluation, or conducting a program of therapy, sexologists will find it intellectually efficacious to use the five universal exigencies as a template against which to check out variables that may have been either overlooked or included irrelevantly. To illustrate: I recall from ten years ago the case of a man with a history of transvestism since puberty. Rather suddenly, at age thirty, he became obsessed with sex reassignment. In the absence of a template against which to retrieve all potentially relevant information, nearly a year went by before it became evident that the transexual crisis coincided with a change in troopbonding. His household troop had been invaded, so to speak, by the man's chronically ill mother. She had a lifetime's history of mental illness. After her husband's death from cancer, she became overtly suicidal. Her son had no other alternative than to take his mother into his own home. The family pathology that ensued exacerbated the son's gender problem into a crisis for which he found no resolution except to leave home, ostensibly to become and to live as a woman.

Ten Constants of Pairbondage

Sexuality in a changing world is not static. Nor is it infinitely changeable. The extent of its change is phylogenetically stipulated within the constraints of our being a diecious species in which male-female bonding has flexible specifications. There are ten constants (Money and Ehrhardt, 1972) that are applicable to all systems of pairbondage, and upon which the differences between systems are elaborated. Each system is part of the historical heritage of the society that uses it and transmits it to its individual members. Among individuals, some adhere to the system as dogma, whereas others add their own revision to one or more of its specifications (Money, 1979). The ten constants are as follows:

Age: Each system specifies whether sexual partners will be age-matched or not. If not, then the tolerance limits of age disparity are specified. A child bride in one system is, in another system, regarded as a victim of child sexual abuse.

Physique: Conformity with the age specification may apply only at selected stages of physical maturation. Juvenile sexual partnering with agemates, positively endorsed as sexual rehearsal play in one system, is prohibited and abusively punished in another. Geriatric partnering is ridiculed in one system and necessary to survival in another.

Gender: Specifications as to when or where to pair with a member of the same sex, the other sex, both, or neither vary as to whom, within a system, they apply. In homosexual pairing, what one society prescribes as imperative in adolescence, another prohibits and punishes as sin, sickness, or offense. Teenaged pairing with ensuing pregnancy also is judged antithetically as either ideal or reprehensible, depending on how great a premium there is on young grandparenthood.

Kinship: Within a social system, kinship may be bestowed either genealogically or on the basis of totemic descent. Either way, the sexual pairing of two individuals may be enforced if they have the correct kinship relation and denied if they don't. The enforced marriage of first cousins in one system is prohibited as incest in another.

Caste or Class: The specification of within-clan pairing in marriage is, by extension, analogous to the specification of marriage to a person of the same caste, class, religion, race, or language group. A partnership that is stigmatized or penalized as miscegenation in one system may be tolerated or even romanticized in another.

Number: A system specifies how many sexual partnerships it permits or condones. If more than one partnership is tolerated, then the when, where, and with whom of the multiple partnerships is specified. What is punished as adultery in one system is institutionalized as errancy under the double standard in another.

Overlap: Multiple partnerships are either concurrent or sequential. Legal polygamy under one system is a crime under another system which may, nonetheless, permit serial divorce and remarriage. Concurrent partnerships may exist in isolation from one another or, conversely, may coexist in communal sharing of more than two partners together in group sex.

Span: Either single or multiple partnerships may be transient or long-lasting. A system that specifies monogamous pairing for life may either persecute nonconformists, or tolerate separation and divorce, or turn a blind eye to an affair, especially a transient one.

Privacy: The extent of the specification of privacy in a sexual pairing is total when it forbids any proceptive manifestation whatsoever in public. It is partial when certain proceptive interactions are restricted in public. Both kissing and genital eroticism, for example, may be specified as indecent or illegal in public. Alternatively, if kissing is tolerated and eroticism below the belt is not, then the latter is prosecuted as obscene and pornographic. Indeed, pornography can be defined as that which is depicted when a system's privacy specification regarding sexual pairing is disregarded. Even behind closed doors, the privacy rule may restrict a couple if the rule applies to the sounds of sexual intercourse as well as its sights.

Accessories: The specifications applied to the where and when of sexual pairing may be detailed and intrusive—and likewise the specifications of what to do sexually with the organs and limbs of the body, either plain or decorated with tattoo, scarification, mutilation, or ornamental accessories. A wedding band is an accessory that signals a change in what is permitted. Sexual toys may or may not be acceptable as erotic accessories, and the same applies to animals. It is, however, another accessory—namely the contraceptive device in its various forms—that incites divisive controversy as to whether it should or should not be used in a copulatory partnership.

For practicing sexologists, the foregoing ten constants are applicable sociologically to the comparative analysis of different or changing cultural, moral, religious, or legal systems of sexuality. In the clinic, they are applicable to the diagnostic analysis of couple mismatching and the formulation of therapeutic strategy.

Three Phases of Pairbondage

Whatever the historical and comparative changes that human pairbondage systems may undergo, they are superimposed on the three phenomenological phases of pairbondage. These three phases transcend not only cultures, but species also. They are: proception, acception, and conception.

In animal ethology, proception is often referred to as the mating dance. In human beings, and in some instances in animals, proception is also known as the courtship ritual. Courtship may last for years, months, days, hours, or minutes. In its explicitly genitoerotic manifestation, courtship changes its name to foreplay.

Saul Rosenzweig in 1973 used the term *proception* as the antonym of *contraception.* Frank Beach in 1976 independently used the term to refer to the stereotyped ritual of species-typical behavior that precedes reception and conception. He made the point that it does not suffice simply to refer to the female's receptivity and the male's intromission, because copulation is the culmination of the preliminary, or proceptive, ritual that precedes copulation and conception. Without the proceptive ritual, the penovaginal culmination may be unable to take place.

Beach and coworkers (1969) illustrated, in the case of the laboratory rat, the progression of proceptive behavior and its culmination in mutual acceptance of penovaginal intromission, followed by ejaculation of the male. They differentiated the following components of the total complex of mating behavior.

> *Ear Wiggle:* The female's head shakes vigorously in the lateral plane and the ears seem to vibrate.
>
> *Hop-and-Dart:* The female runs or hops rapidly away from the stimulus male and then comes to an abrupt stop.
>
> *Crouch:* The female assumes a motionless pose with legs slightly flexed and back held parallel to the floor.
>
> *Turn:* The female turns around when the male tries to mount.

Walk: When the male attempts to mount, the female walks away.

Flat: The female assumes a position in which the back is parallel to the floor, but neither the head nor the tail is elevated, as the male gets into the mounting position.

Arch I: The female raises both head and tail noticeably, but not maximally, and the male continues his mount.

Arch II: From the Arch I position, the female raises her head with marked neck flexion, and the tail is distinctly elevated or deviated laterally.

Male Mount: The male mounts the female directly from the rear, palpates and firmly clasps her sides with his forelegs, and executes vigorous pelvic thrusts.

Mount and Intromission Latency: After male and female are put together, this is the time that elapses until the first mount and first intromission, respectively.

Intromission Pattern: The male terminates mounting and thrusting with a definite and vigorous backward lunge which signals insertion of the penis into the vagina.

Ejaculation Pattern: The male achieves full insertion with the final pelvic thrust and holds it. He then releases his clasp of the female, typically elevating his forelegs slowly and dismounting in deliberate fashion without a backward lunge. There is a pause of four to five minutes before a second round commences.

Whereas rodents are veritable robots in their mating behavior, primates are more diversified. Human beings, in particular, have an extensive repertory of proceptive behavior from which a wide variety of programs can be assembled. The criteria of each program are stipulated socially by religion, law, or custom, and individually by habit, idiosyncrasy, or pathology, either singly or in combination. Any one person's program may be either reiterative and robotized or versatile and varied.

The wide-ranging variability of human mating behavior, coupled with moral sanctions against its scientific documentation in vivo, account for the difficulty of establishing a full scientific catalogue of the prevalence and social distribution of the components of men's and women's proceptivity. Marriage manuals, beginning with the *Kama Sutra,* give a historical and cultural perspective on idealized male and female proceptive and foreplay roles. Social-research surveys, beginning notably with the Kinsey reports, give a corresponding perspective on what men and women say that they actually do in these roles.

After the experience of being initially attracted to a partner, the major components of human proception are manifested by all members of the species, regardless of time and place. The following list is indebted in part to Perper (1985) and to Eibl-Eibesfeldt (Donahue, 1985).

—Establishing eye contact
—Holding the gaze
—Blushing
—Averting the gaze, eyelids drooping
—Shyly returning the gaze
—Squinting and smiling
—Vocal animation
—Vocal acceleration and breathiness
—Vocal loudness
—Vocal exaggeration of trivialities
—Laughter
—Rotating to face one another
—Moving closer to one another
—Wetting the lips
—Adjusting clothing to reveal bare skin
—Touching, as if inadvertently
—Mirroring each other's gestures
—Synchronizing bodily movements

In addition to these observable signs, those that are subjectively experienced are increased heart rate, breathing rate, perspiration, and butterflies in the stomach. Over a prolonged period of time, there may also be changes in eating, sleeping, dreaming, and fantasying.

Individual Lovemaps

Lovemap is a new term. It is defined as a developmental scheme or template in the mind and brain of the idealized lover and the projected sexuoerotic activity with that lover. Like a native language, a lovemap is not completed on the day of birth. It requires input from the social environment. The critical period for its development is not puberty, as is often assumed, but before the age of eight. Childhood sexuoerotic rehearsal play among agemates is profoundly important for the development of a normal, healthy lovemap. That is why sexologists neglect their scientific duty by not studying the sexuality and eroticism of childhood, and especially by not observing and cataloguing cross-cultural differences. It is especially important to compare, in adulthood, the outcome of childrearing that is sexuoerotically positive and free of taboo versus that which is negative and taboo-ridden.

What people say is not necessarily what they do—and when they might incriminate themselves, they do not necessarily tell the whole story. It is in the clinic that a person may have enough confidence and trust to be maximally self-revealing. Thus it is in the clinic that one learns most about the intimacies and intricacies of individual lovemaps, especially those that are not normophilic but strange and paraphilic.

Male/Female Differences

As has been the case for centuries, the sexuoerotic differences between men and women are tacitly assumed to outweigh the similarities. This insidious assumption underlies the stereotype that women are passive, submissive, and receptive in their sexuality, whereas men are active, assertive, and intrusive. In actuality, the stereotypes are interchangeable. Women can be overtly assertive, instead of only devious and seductive, in which case the term *quim* applies. The woman, taking the initiative, quims the man, using his penis as a quim stick or quim wedge, while he luxuriates in being taken and possessed. When, in turn, he takes the lead, he *swives* the woman. "To quim" and "to swive" are the once-obsolete terms, now revived, by which male and female copulatory parity are linguistically recognized in sexology (Money, 1982).

Quimming and swiving both apply to behavior that belongs to the proceptive phase of mating, as well as to its culmination in the second, or acceptive, phase when the sex organs mutually accept one another in coitus. The third, or conceptive, phase may or may not follow coital acception.

Four Grades of Gender Coding

The conceptive phase is the one in which the differences between men and women are irreducible, namely that women menstruate, gestate, and lactate, and men impregnate. In mammals these differences have been absolute since time immemorial. In the present era of in vitro fertilization and embryo transfer, they are on the eve of breaking down. In fact, the hormonal technology for an implanted extrauterine pregnancy in a male, with caesarean delivery, is already fairly well in place. The male-to-female transexual population will undoubtedly provide a first volunteer, even if there are no others. Nature herself has already shown how to dispense with the sexes in reproduction by creating parthenogenesis in lizards of the whiptail species (Crews, 1982) that are monecious or single-sexed.

Like rungs on a ladder, there are three grades of sex difference below the irreducible one (Money, 1980). The male/female differences to which they pertain are sex-derivative, sex-adjunctive, and sex-arbitrary.

Sex-derivative differences are chiefly hormone-mediated. They are exemplified in the androgen- and estrogen-determined sex differences in body build and function. Despite local variations in pedigree, they apply to all members of our species across cultures. The sex-adjunctive differences to which they give rise are, by contrast, culturally variable.

Sex-adjunctive differences apply chiefly to sex-coded work, play, education, and legal status. Cultures vary, for example, in the extent to which women's work roles are an adjunct of the constraints of pregnancy, breast feeding, and (in former times) of a brief life expectancy of thirty-five to forty years for both sexes. Women worked more closely to the hearth, while men roamed further afield, pursuing, defending, farming, and trading. The old traditions of sex-coded work, play, education, and legal status are now changing in response to changes initiated by the invention of contraception and family planning; the worldwide population explosion; the extension of the life span and the earlier onset of puberty; and the sex-interchangeable technological inventions of the computer age.

Sex-arbitrary differences pertain especially to culturally determined sex coding of clothing, cosmetics, ornamentation, forms of address, demeanor, and etiquette. Some of these arbitrary differences share in common the principle of male ostentation. They show the woman as a man's chattel and the showpiece of his power and wealth.

In a world that is changing, these arbitrary male/female differences also are changing.

Men and women, boys and girls, are becoming increasingly liberated from all the gender-coded stereotypes that have historically deprived them of the privilege of equality. The tide of change is already in motion worldwide. Though at present it is at an ebb tide, under the influence of a powerful wave of ultraconservative antisexualism it will change and flow again in synchrony with the inexorable changes of our changing world. It is appropriate, therefore, that the title of this congress, "Sexuality in a Changing World," should be applied to both sexes separately as well as together; and not only to men and women, but also to boys and girls. Let us not forget that sexuality is not static, but that it grows and develops from infancy and throughout childhood onward. The changing world of children demands a changing sexology of childhood and adolescence as well as of adulthood.

References

Beach, F. A. (1976). "Sexual attractivity, proceptivity, and receptivity in female mammals." *Hormones and Behavior* 7:105–38.

Beach, F. A., Noble, R. C., and Orndorff, R. K. (1969). "Effects of perinatal androgen treatment on responses of male rats to gonadal hormones in adulthood." *Journal of Comparative and Physiological Psychology* 68:490–97.

Crews, D. (1982). "On the origin of sexual behavior." *Psychoneuroendocrinology* 7:259–70.

Donahue, P. (1965). *The Human Animal: Who Are We? Why Do We Behave the Way We Do? Can We Change?* New York: Simon & Schuster.

Money, J. (1957). *The Psychologic Study of Man.* Springfield, IL: Charles C Thomas.

———. (1960). *Love and Love Sickness: The Science of Sex, Gender Difference, and Pair Bonding.* Baltimore: Johns Hopkins University Press.

———. (1962). "To quim and to swive: Linguistic and coital parity, male and female." *Journal of Sex Research* 15:173–76.

———. (1979). "Sexual dictatorship, dissidence and democracy." *International Journal of Medicine and Law* 1:11–20.

———. (1982). "Sexosophy and Sexology, Philosophy and Science: Two Halves, One Whole." In *Sexology: Sexual Biology, Behavior and Therapy* (Z. Hoch and H. I. Lief, eds.). Amsterdam: Excerpta Medica.

Money, J., and Ehrhardt, A. A. (1972). *Man and Woman, Boy and Girl: The Differentiation and Dimorphism of Gender Identity from Conception to Maturity.* Baltimore: Johns Hopkins University Press. Facsimile reprint edition, New York: Jason Aronson, 1996.

Perper, T. (1965). *Sex Signals: The Biology of Love.* Philadelphia: ISI Press.

Rosenzweig, S. (1973). "Human sexual autonomy as an evolutionary attainment, anticipating proceptive sex choice and idiodynamic bisexuality." In *Contemporary Sexual Behavior: Critical Issues in the 1970s* (J. Zubin and J. Money, eds.). Baltimore: Johns Hopkins University Press.

2

Sin, Science, Secret Police: Homosexuality

PART I: FROM SIN TO SCIENCE

Gender and Sex

Gender-identity/role, or G-I/R, is singular, not plural, but it is also two-dimensional, like two sides of the same coin (Money, 1985). Gender identity is self-revealed to others in words and behavior and is publicly known. Other people always know less than you yourself know about the totality of your gender identity, for they must construe it at second hand from the evidence of your gender role, whereas you have access to evidence at first hand.

G-I/R is more inclusive than sex. Your sex is your status as male or female, masculine or feminine (or intersexed), on the criterion of the external genitalia alone. Your G-I/R encompasses your status as male or female, masculine or feminine (or mixed), on the criterion of multiple

Originally published in Fernando J. Bianco and Rubén Hernández Serrano, eds., *Sexology: An Independent Field.* Proceedings of the Ninth World Congress of Sexology, Caracas, Venezuela, December 3–8, 1989 (Amsterdam–New York–Oxford: Excerpta Medica, 1990), pp. 41–49.

personal, societal, and legal premises, including sexuoerotic orientation. On the criterion of sexuoerotic orientation, your G-I/R may be bisexual or monosexual and, if monosexual, either homosexual or heterosexual.

Homosexual/Heterosexual Gender Identity

In the exact and literal sense, there was no language for a homosexual orientation or a homosexual gender identity (nor for a heterosexual one) until as recently as 1905. In that year, the sexologist Magnus Hirschfeld republished an 1869 Berlin newspaper article in which K. M. Kertbeny (also known as Benkert), an advocate of sexual-law reform, had originally coined the term *homosexual.*

A homosexual gender identity is not the same as a homosexual act. The Skyscraper Test demonstrates that a person who does not have a homosexual gender identity may perform a homosexual act. In the scenario of this test, you are caught in a Catch-22. On the edge of the parapet, atop the skyscraper, you are held hostage by a crazed paraphiliac with a gun. You are commanded by him: "Suck my thing or you go over." Which would you do? If you both were males and you chose to save your life, you would have committed a homosexual act, but you would not go home with a homosexual gender identity. Homosexuality is not socially contagious.

A homosexual gender identity has various manifestations and formats. Their common denominator is same-sex rather than other-sex erotic attraction and sexuoerotic pairing. At one extreme there is the comprehensive, full-time gender transposition that encompasses the entire gamut of male/female difference. Permanent and complete transposition from male to female is *gynemimesis* (woman miming), or the lady-with-a-penis syndrome. From female to male, it is *andromimesis* (man miming), or the man-despite-no-penis syndrome.

At the other extreme, there is the categorically limited gender transposition that, although long-lasting, is evidenced only as male-male or female-female sexuoerotic partnering. The gay macho football hero is a masculine example of this type of limited gender transposition, and the lesbian beauty-contest princess is a feminine example.

In the final analysis, *limerence* (Tennov, 1979) is the ultimate criterion of whether a gender identity is homosexual or heterosexual. Limerence means being in love, love-smitten, and perhaps lovesick. It is not planned. Neither is it begun or ended voluntarily. The definitive characteristic of a homosexual or heterosexual gender identity is whether the sex of the body morphology and of the external genital anatomy of the partner with whom one is capable of falling in love is, respectively, the same as or different than one's own. For the bisexual, either may qualify. Genetic, gonadal, and internal anatomical sex are irrelevant. All three may be discordant with external genital and body sex, as studies of hermaphroditism have conclusively shown (Money, 1988).

Science versus Sin

The movement to replace sin and crime with science to explain a homosexual gender identity had its beginnings in the embryology of the 1850s. It was then that the primordial hermaphroditism of the mammalian embryo was conclusively established (Adelmann, 1966). By 1864, Karl Heinrich Ulrichs, a jurist by training, had adapted this new scientific information in support of his attempt to explain that people like himself had a woman's mind trapped in a man's body (*anima muliebris virili corpore inclusa*) (Ulrichs, 1864; Kennedy, 1988).

The idea that a man's body might have a woman's hormones entrapped in it (and vice versa) has never actually been put into words. Nonetheless, it was implicit in Hirschfeld's recognition, early in the twentieth century, that the then-new science of endocrinology might provide a hormonal explanation for homosexuality. The earliest evidence came in 1912–13 from Steinach's "intentional reversal of sexual characteristics of both the body and behavior" of newborn guinea pigs by castrating them and then implanting heterotypic gonadal tissue—ovary in the place of testis and vice versa (see Steinach, 1940).

Sex Hormones and Homosexuality

The sex hormones were isolated in the 1920s, synthesized in the 1930s, and commercially marketed in the 1940s. Since then, attempts to diagnose and treat homosexual males hormonally have had no yield. Lesbians have been paid little attention.

Precision measurement of hormone levels and hormone uptake

within the body became possible only after the 1955 discovery of the radioimmunoassay technique (Yalow, 1978). The sum total of the evidence of research since then, despite sporadic inconsistencies, is that homosexual gender identity and heterosexual gender identity cannot be distinguished on the basis of hormone levels routinely measured in body fluids, nor on the basis of their being experimentally altered, as in the estrogen-feedback effect on the release of luteinizing hormone (Gooren, 1986).

Whereas the gonadal hormones are not the arbiters of sexuoerotic orientation at puberty and thereafter, in prenatal life they are active arbiters within the brain not of sexuoerotic orientation itself, but of its precursors. The animal experimental evidence is comprehensively reviewed in Sitzen (1988) and Money and Ehrhardt (1972). Epigrammatically stated, the intrinsic principle of male/female differentiation is "Eve first, then Adam."

The Bipotential Brain

Actual mapping of male/female sexological differences in neural structure and neurochemical function of the brain began at the end of the 1960s. The prime target zone has been the hypothalamus, and within it the preoptic area (POA) and adjacent anterior hypothalamic area. From animal experiments, it is well known that the POA is significant for the governance of mating behavior. It also plays a role in the release of fertility hormones (gonadotropin) from the nearby pituitary and in the manifestation of maternal behavior (Allen et al., 1989).

The size of the sexually dimorphic nucleus of the preoptic area (SDN/POA) is larger in males than in females (Gorski et al., 1978). In the case of the rat, the SDN/POA size difference originates perinatally under the influence of the steroidal sex hormone testosterone, either before or after its conversion to its metabolite, estradiol (Doehler et al., 1982). The SDN/POA in males becomes permanently diminished in size if the pregnant mother has been subjected either to malnutrition or environmental stress (Anderson et al., 1985).

In human beings, according to Swaab and Hofman (1988), the SDN/POA does not begin to become larger in boys than in girls until between two and four years of age. By this age, sensory and cognitional data on male/female differences enter the brain through the cerebral cortex, which transmits messages to the POA. In learning and remembering sensory and cognitional data, the brain may also expand its own dimorphism, microcellularly, in both structure and function. So far as is known, in human beings postnatal differentiation of G-I/R is sensoricognitionally, not hormonally, induced.

Male/female bipotentiality in the POA was demonstrated in an experiment by Nordeen and Yahr (1982). In newborn female rat pups, they implanted pellets of the steroidal hormone estradiol into the hypothalamus, in the region of the POA. The pellet had a masculinizing effect on subsequent mating behavior (i.e., mounting), but only if implanted on the right side. If a pellet was implanted on the left side, then the effect on subsequent mating behavior was not masculinizing but defeminizing (i.e., lordosis—the feminine copulatory crouching position—was suppressed).

With a pellet implanted on both sides, there exists the possibility of having exclusively masculine mating behavior in an animal with an otherwise female body. Similarly, with only a masculinizing pellet on the right and no implant on the left, there exists the possibility of having an animal that subsequently engages in mating behavior with either sex—that is, a bisexual animal.

Masculinization and feminization are not polar opposites. They may coexist. The opposite of feminization is defeminization. These are the four principles of sexually dimorphic differentiation. It is of great significance for sexological brain research that there are four and not only two principles of dimorphic differentiation: It means that masculine/feminine is not preordained as either/or, but may quite well be both-together. Hence, to paraphrase Ulrichs, to attempt to explain homosexuality as a woman's hypothalamus entrapped in a man's brain would be a futile exercise in either/or instead of both-together.

Except for one report, there are no data from the hypothalamus or elsewhere in the human brain to substantiate a difference that is contingent on sexuoerotic orientation as homosexual or heterosexual. The exception (Gooren, personal communication, May 1989) is the report of an autopsy study, as yet unpublished, released in February 1989 by Swaab in Amsterdam. He examined thirty brains bequeathed to research by men, fifteen straight and fifteen gay, before they died from AIDS. Statistically compared, the virus-exposed suprachiasmic nuclei from the POA of the anterior hypothalamus were larger if the brains had come from the gay men rather than from the straight men in the sample.

The ultimate verdict regarding the size of the suprachiasmic nucleus and its either/or correlation with both AIDS and sexuoerotic orientation as gay or straight is still awaited. It is extremely unlikely that the suprachiasmic nucleus alone will ever be proved responsible for all the known historical, cross-cultural, personal, and pathological variations of sexuoerotic orientation and gender identity as either heterosexual or homosexual, masculine or feminine.

PART II: FROM SCIENCE TO SECRET POLICE

Research Politics

Swaab's public announcement of his research stirred up a hornet's nest of political protest led by Dutch gay-rights activists and social scientists antagonistic to a biomedical instead of societal explanation of homosexuality. For them, Swaab's research represented a return to the "medical model" of homosexuality and to the era when homosexuality had been classified as a psychiatric disease.

If homosexuality is excluded from biomedical research, so too is its reciprocal, heterosexuality, and with it bisexuality as well. There is total negation of all scientific sex research implicitly concealed in the antiscientism of Swaab's critics. Moreover, it has the paradoxical effect of being acceptable to their foes, the unrelenting enemies of gay rights, namely the antisexual reactionaries of the Sexual Counterreformation.

Sexual Counterreformation

The Sexual Counterreformation, as I call it, is the contemporary societal response to sexual reformation that came into bloom during the era of the Sexual Revolution in the 1960s and 1970s. If one studies the record of history, there is to be found in it evidence of a tide that changes societal norms and policies in cycles of reformation and counterreformation.

Reformation begins as a sequel to the adoption in society of a newly discovered or newly borrowed cultural artifact. For example, the automobile and the airplane changed the norms and policies of population mobility. Reformation begins also as a sequel to big shifts in the demographics and distribution of people and of other living things in their ecology—as, for example, when the age or sex ratio changes, or when the population of a food species diminishes or increases.

The changed or reformed norms and policies of the Sexual Revolution were preceded by the discovery of two new cultural artifacts. One was penicillin, serendipitously discovered as a safeguard against the ravages of the two most dreaded sexually transmissible diseases, syphilis and gonorrhea. It became commercially available by the end of the 1940s. The other was the birth-control pill, a sequel to the synthesis and manufacture of the steroidal sex hormones in the 1930s and 1940s. The Pill became widely distributed by the 1960s. The Pill was not woman's first self-applied contraceptive, but it was the first that did not need planning so as to be synchronized with a specific act of copulation. Also, it was swallowed down the throat instead of being poked up the vagina.

Demographically, two noteworthy changes preceded the reformed norms and policies of the Sexual Revolution. One was a decrease in infant mortality and an increase in life expectancy, from forty-five to beyond seventy-five years of age, in the first half of the twentieth century. Another was a worldwide population explosion, so that people who would live longer as parents did not need to begin procreating early if they began their sex lives at a young age, nor to have an unrestricted and large number of offspring.

The Sexual Counterreformation began getting into gear by the end of the 1970s. It preyed upon the personal apprehension, doom, and dread that were the social heritage of ancient antisexual norms and policies. One of its early successes was a media blitz on genital herpes, spot-lighted as though the herpes virus had been previously unknown. Then a genuine unknown virus, first suspected in 1981, came on the scene: HIV (human immunodeficiency virus), the AIDS killer. From the Counterreformation pulpit, AIDS was heralded as God's vengeance on homosexuals.

Homosexuality is only one target of the Counterreformation. Others are well-known: sex education, teenaged pregnancy, abortion, fetal-tissue research, rape, date rape, wife abuse, child sexual abuse, sexual errancy of public figures, sexual addiction, and sexological survey research.

The ultimate target of the Sexual Counterreformation is women's emancipation. All of Counterreformatory policy is directed toward returning women to their erstwhile status quo of dependency upon men and subordination to patriarchal power and authority. Women who endorse this Counterreformatory policy sacrifice their own power. Men, by contrast, target some of their own kind as scapegoats, deprive them of their power and authority, and sacrifice them as victims, whereby they consolidate more power for themselves. In the pursuit of power, their own sacrifice is an impoverishment of their personal sex lives, as well as a vulnerability to falling prey to devious or behind-the-scenes sexual schemes.

Mobilization of support for the Sexual Counterreformation hinges partly on the fact that the very words that name the targets of Counterreformatory attack connote varieties of behavior that have a history of having been condemned and stigmatized as disreputable. By implication, only disreputable people would, under any circumstances, defend these targets against attack. If a reputable person did defend them, then that person's reputation would be soiled. Thus, no politician—not even a strong supporter of sex education in the age of AIDS—would dare to vote against a bill with such a title as "An Act to Protect Children against Exploitation from Pornography," despite a paragraph embedded in the bill making it a criminal offense to use any pictorial representations of naked genitalia in the sex education of anybody under the age of eighteen.

Secret Police of Sexology

The very insidiousness of the appeal to reputability dupes not only policy makers, but those whom they fund and employ. Researchers and therapists in sexology have been among those duped, along with thousands of others in the health-care industry who, lured by fresh sources of funding, have become practitioners of the newly organized specialty of victimology.

It is one of the tenets of victimology that there are sexual victims and sexual perpetrators—victims to treat, and perpetrators to punish and correct. Legally, no matter how loosely child sexual abuse is defined, perpetrators are criminal sex offenders. Anyone so accused, irrespective of deficient substantiating evidence, must be reported.

In effect, those obliged to report have been legislated into being the secret police of social service and health care. They are certified to practice the healing arts, and they think of themselves as healers in the Hippocratic tradition, not as the undercover spies and police informants which they have become. Their clients and patients—perpetrators and victims alike—are caught in the Catch-22 dilemma of being damned if they do say, and damned if they don't say, all that they know.

Victimology is one of the great sex-negating triumphs of the Sexual Counterreformation. It represents the criminalization of sex and the neutering of gender. It is a return to the adversarial system of the Inquisition and a forfeiture of the consensual system of medicine and science. It is a blot on the escutcheon of sexology. It punishes sexual illness instead of restoring sexual health. It dries up sexological research instead of expanding it. Under the threat of legal action, it affects all of us.

The decline of the Sexual Counterreformation will be contingent on technological innovation and demographic change. A current candidate on the technology list is the explicitly erotic videotape—privately produced, noncommercial, for home VCR use exclusively, and made possible by electronic miniaturization of the videocamera. A second candidate is the new French-developed contragestational drug RU–486, the so-called abortion pill (Baulieu, 1989).

Demographically, the longer the wait for an effective agent to control the AIDS epidemic, the greater will be the loss of population among AIDS-infected infants and young adults. This demographic change might, in turn, necessitate absolute explicitness in the exchange of sexual and erotic information between the generations. That would constitute a change in the direction of sexual reform.

The tide of history will change, and there will be a new era of Sexual Reformation in the twenty-first century—sooner, one hopes, than later.

References

Adelman, H. B. (1966). *Marcello Malpighi and the Evolution of Embryology.* Ithaca, NY: Cornell University Press.

Allen, L. S., Hines, M., Shryne, J. E., and Gorski, R. A. (1989). "Two sexually dimorphic cell groups in the human brain." *Journal of Neuroscience* 9(2):497–506.

Anderson, D. K., Rhees, L. W., and Fleming, D. E. (1985). "Effects of prenatal stress on differentiation of the sexually dimorphic nucleus of the preoptic area (SDN-POA) of the rat brain." *Brain Research* 332:113–18.

Baulieu, E. E. (1989). "Contragestion and other clinical applications of RU–486, an antiprogesterone at the receptor." *Science* 245:1351–57.

Doehler, K. D., Coquelin, A., Davis, F., Hines, H., Shryne, J. E., and Gorski, R. A. (1982). "Differentiation of the sexually dimorphic nucleus in the preoptic area of the rat brain is determined by the perinatal hormone environment." *Neuroscience Letters* 33:295–98.

Gooren, L. (1986). "The neuroendocrine response of luteinizing hormone to estrogen administration in heterosexual, homosexual and transsexual subjects." *Journal of Clinical Endocrinology and Metabolism* 63:583–88.

Gorski, R. A., Gordon, J. H., Shryne, J. E., and Southam, A. M. (1978). "Evidence for a morphological sex difference within the medial preoptic area of the rat brain." *Brain Research* 148:333–46.

Kennedy, H. (1988). *Ulrichs: The Life and Works of Karl Heinrich Ulrichs, Pioneer of the Modern Gay Movement.* Boston: Alyson.

Money, J. (1985). "Gender: History, theory and usage of the term in sexology and its relationship to nature/nurture." *Journal of Sex and Marital Therapy* 11:71–79.

———. (1990). "Agenda and Credenda of the Kinsey Scale." In *Homosexuality/Heterosexuality: Concepts of Sexual Orientation* (D. P. McWhirter, S. A. Sanders, and J. M. Reinisch, eds.). New York: Oxford University Press.

Money, J., and Ehrhardt, A. A. (1972). *Man and Woman, Boy and Girl: The Differentiation and Dimorphism of Gender Identity from Conception to Maturity.* Baltimore: Johns Hopkins University Press. Facsimile reprint edition, New York: Jason Aronson, 1996.

Nordeen, E. J., and Yahr, P. (1982). "Hemispheric asymmetries in the behavioral and hormonal effects of sexually differentiating mammalian brain." *Science* 218:391–93.

Sitzen, J. M. A., ed. (1988). *Handbook of Sexology, Volume 6: The Pharmacology and Endocrinology of Sexual Function.* Amsterdam–New York–London: Elsevier.

Steinach, E. (1940). *Sex and Life: Forty Years of Biological and Medical Experiments.* New York: Viking Press.

Swaab, D. F., and Hofman, M. A. (1988). "Sexual differentiation of the human hypothalamus: Ontogeny of the sexually dimorphic nucleus of the preoptic area." *Developmental Brain Research* 44:314–18.

Tennov, D. (1979). *Love and Limerence: The Experience of Being in Love.* New York: Stein and Day.

Ulrichs, K. H. (Numa Numantius). (1864). *Forschungen über das Räthsel der*

Mannmännlichen Liebe (*Inquiry into the Enigma of Man-to-Man Love*). Vol. 2, *"Inclusa": Anthropologische Studien über Mannmännliche Geschlechtsliebe, Naturwissenschaftlicher Theil: Nachweis das einer Classe von Mannlich gebauten Individuen Geschlechtsliebe zu Männern geschlechtlich angerboren ist* (*"Inclusa": Anthropological Studies of Man-to-Man Sexual Love, Natural Science Section: Proof of a Class of Male-bodied Individuals for whom Sexual Love for Men Is Sexually Inborn*). Leipzig: Selbstverlag der Verfassers (in Commission bei Heinrich Matthes).

Yalow, R. S. (1978). "Radioimmunoassay: A probe for the fine structure of biologic systems." *Science* 200:1236–45.

3

Agenda and Credenda of the Kinsey Scale

Historical and Cultural Relativity

The phenomenon that is today named homosexuality did not have that name until it was coined by K. M. Benkert, writing under the pseudonym of Kertbeny, in 1869 (Bullough, 1976). Although he applied the term *homosexuality* to both males and females, he defined it on the criterion of erectile failure:

> In addition to the normal sexual urge in men and women, Nature in her sovereign mood has endowed at birth certain male and female individuals with the homosexual urge, thus placing them in a sexual bondage which renders them physically and psychically incapable—even with the best intention—of normal erection. This urge creates in advance a direct horror of the Opposite sex, and the victim of this passion finds it impossible to suppress the feeling which individuals of his own sex exercise upon him. (p. 637).

Instead of the criterion of genital sexuality, as in homo*sexual,* Benkert could have used the criterion of falling in love, as in

Originally published in David P. McWhirter, Stephanie A. Sanders, and June Machover Reinisch, eds., *Homosexuality/Heterosexuality: Concepts of Sexual Orientation* (New York and Oxford: Oxford University Press, 1990), pp. 41–60.

homo*philic,* or the criterion of being attracted to those of the same sex, as in homo*genic.* Both terms were proposed by others, but *homosexual* won the day, probably because it was taken up in the early years of the twentieth century by Havelock Ellis (1942) and Magnus Hirschfeld (1948). Neither of these two writers recognized that the ethnocentricity of Benkert's definition of homosexuality as a sickness, though freeing it from being a sin or a crime, confines it too narrowly to pathological deviancy. It leaves no place for homosexuality as a status that is culturally ordained to be normal and healthy, as it is in societies that have, since time immemorial, institutionalized bisexuality. In bisexuality, homosexuality and heterosexuality may coexist concurrently, or they may be sequential, with a homosexual phase of development antecedent to heterosexuality and marriage. Concurrent bisexuality was exemplified in classical Athenian culture (Bullough, 1976). Sequential bisexuality is exemplified in various tribal Melanesian and related cultures.

There is a vast area of the world, stretching from the northwestern tip of Sumatra through Papua New Guinea to the outlying islands of Melanesia in the Pacific, in which the social institutionalization of homosexuality is shared by various ethnic and tribal people (Herdt, 1984; Money and Ehrhardt, 1972). More precisely, it is sequential bisexuality that is institutionalized in these societies. Their cultural tradition dictates that males between the ages of nine and nineteen no longer reside with their families but rather in the single longhouse in the village center where males congregate. Until the age of nineteen, the prescribed age of marriage, they all participate in homosexual activities. After marriage, homosexual activity either ceases or is sporadic.

The Sambia people (Herdt, 1981) of the eastern highlands of New Guinea are among those whose traditional folk wisdom provides a rationale for the policy of prepubertal homosexuality. According to this wisdom, a prepubertal boy must leave the society of his mother and sisters and enter the secret society of men in order to achieve the fierce manhood of a head-hunter. Whereas in infancy he must have been fed women's milk in order to grow, in the secret society of men he must be fed men's milk—that is, the semen of mature youths and unmarried men—in order to become pubertal and become mature himself. It is the duty of the young bachelors to feed him their semen. They are obliged to practice institutionalized pedophilia. For them to give their semen to another who could already ejaculate his own is forbidden, for it robs a prepubertal boy of the substance he requires to become an adult. When a bachelor reaches the marrying age, his family negotiates the procurement of a wife and arranges the marriage. He then embarks on the heterosexual phase of his career. He could not, however, have become a complete man on the basis of heterosexual experience alone. Full manhood necessitates a prior phase of exclusively homosexual experience. Thus, homosexuality is universalized and is a defining characteristic of head-hunting, macho manhood.

In Sambia culture, omission of rather than participation in the homosexual developmental phase would be classified as sporadic in occurrence, if it occurred at all, and would stigmatize a man as deviant. In our own culture, by contrast, it is homosexual participation that is classified as sporadic and stigmatized as a deviancy in need of explanation. For us, heterosexuality, like health, is taken as a verity that needs no explanation other than being attributed to the immutability of the natural order of things. Since heterosexuality needs no explanation, then in bisexuality the homosexual component alone needs explanation. Consequently, there has been no satisfactory place for bisexuality in theoretical sexology. The universalization of sequential bisexuality, as in the Sambia tradition, is unexplainable in homosexual theory that is based exclusively on the concept of homosexuality as sporadic in occurrence and pathologically deviant (Stoller and Herdt, 1985).

Institutionalized homosexuality, in serial sequence with institutionalized heterosexuality and marriage as among the Sambia and other tribal peoples, must be taken into account in any theory that proposes to explain homosexuality. The theory will be deficient unless it also takes heterosexuality into account. Culturally institutionalized bisexuality signifies either that bisexuality is a universal potential to which any member of the human species could be acculturated or that bisexuality is a unique potential of those cultures whose members have become selectively inbred for it. There are no data that give conclusive and absolute support to either alternative. However, genetically pure inbred strains are an ideal of animal husbandry, not of human social and sexual interaction. Therefore, it is likely that acculturation to bisexuality is less a concomitant of inbreeding than it is of the bisexual plasticity of all members of the human species. It is possible that bisexual plasticity may vary over the life span. Later in life, it may give way to exclusive monosexuality—or it may not.

Preference versus Status or Orientation

In the human species, a person does not prefer to be homosexual instead of heterosexual or to be bisexual instead of monosexual. Sexual preference is a moral and political term. Conceptually, it implies voluntary choice—that is, that one chooses or prefers to be homosexual instead of heterosexual or bisexual, and vice versa. Politically, sexual preference is a dangerous term, for it implies that if homosexuals choose their preference, then they can be legally forced, under threat of punishment, to choose to be heterosexual.

The concept of voluntary choice is as much in error here as in its application to handedness or to native language. You do not choose your native language as a preference, even though you are born without it. You assimilate it into a brain prenatally made ready to receive a native language from those who constitute your primate troop and who speak that language to you and listen to you when you speak it. Once assimilated through the ears into the brain, a native language becomes securely locked in—as securely as if it had been phylogenetically preordained to be locked in prenatally by a process of genetic determinism or by the determinism of fetal hormonal or other brain chemistries. So also with sexual status or orientation, which—whatever its genesis—also may become assimilated and locked into the brain as monosexually homosexual or heterosexual, or as bisexually a mixture of both.

A sexual status (or orientation) is not the same as a sexual act. It is possible to participate in or be subjected to a homosexual act or acts without becoming thereby predestined to have a homosexual status—and vice versa with heterosexuality. The Skyscraper Test exemplifies the difference between act and status. One of the versions of this test applies to a person with a homosexual status who is atop the Empire State Building and is pushed to the edge of the parapet by a gun-toting sex terrorist with a heterosexual status. Suppose the homosexual is a man and the terrorist a woman who demands that he perform oral sex with her or go over the edge. To save his life, he might do it. If so, he would have performed a heterosexual act, but he would not have changed to a heterosexual status. The same would apply if the tourist were a straight man and the terrorist a gay man. The tourist might perform a homosexual act, but would retain his heterosexual status, and so on.

By dramatizing the difference between act and status, the Skyscraper Test points to the criterion of falling in love as the definitive criterion of homosexual, heterosexual, and bisexual status. A person with a homosexual status is one who has the potential to fall in love only with someone who has the same genital and bodily morphology as the self. For a heterosexual, the morphology must be that of a person of the other sex. For the bisexual, it may be either.

It is not necessary for the masculine or feminine bodily morphology of the partner to be concordant with the chromosomal sex, the gonadal sex, or the sex of the internal reproductive anatomy. For example, a male-to-female, sex-reassigned transexual with the body morphology transformed to be female in appearance is responded to as a woman—and vice versa in female-to-male transexualism.

Discordance between the body morphology and other variables of sex occurs also in some cases of intersexuality. For example, it is possible to be born with a penis and empty scrotum and to grow up with a fully virilized body and mentality, both discordant with the genetic sex (46,XX), the gonadal sex (two normal ovaries), and the internal sexual structures (uterus and oviducts). Conversely, it is possible to be born with a female vulva and to grow up with a fully feminized body and mentality both discordant with the genetic sex (46,XY), the gonadal sex (two testes), and the internal sexual structures (vestigiated feminine Mullerian-duct structures and differentiated masculine Wolffian-duct structures). Clinical photographic examples of these and many other syndromes are reproduced in Money (1968, 1974).

The 46,XX intersexed man who falls in love with and has a sex life with a 46,XX normal woman is regarded by everyone as heterosexual, and so is his partner. The criterion of their heterosexuality is the sexual morphology of their bodies and masculinity or femininity of their mentality and behavior, not the sex of their chromosomes, gonads, or internal organs. The same principle applies conversely in the case of the feminized 46,XY intersexed woman whose sex life is with a normal 46,XY man.

Evolutionary Bisexuality

Any theory of the genesis of either exclusive homosexuality or exclusive heterosexuality must primarily address the genesis of bisexuality. Monosexuality, whether homosexual or heterosexual, is secondary and a derivative of the primary bisexual or ambisexual potential. Ambisexuality has its origins in evolutionary biology and in the embryology of sexual differentiation.

Ambisexuality has many manifestations in evolutionary biology. Oysters, garden worms, and snails, for example, are ambisexual. They are also classified as bisexual and as hermaphroditic. Many species of fish are capable of changing their sex from female to male or from male to female, in some species more than once (Chan, 1977). The change is so complete that the fish spends part of its life breeding as a male with testicles that make sperms and part as a female with ovaries that make eggs—an exceptionally thorough degree of sequential bisexuality.

A species of whiptail lizard from the Southwest, *Cnemedophorus uniparens,* offers a unique contribution to bisexual theory (Crews, 1982, 1987). This species has neither males nor females but is monecious and parthenogenic. Nonetheless, as judged by comparison with closely related two-sexed whiptail species, each individual lizard is able at different times to behave in mating as if a male and as if a female. The one in whom a clutch of eggs is ripening, ready to be laid in the sand for sun hatching, is mounted by a mate whose ovaries are in a dormant, nonovulatory phase. This enactment is believed to affect the hormonal function of the pituitary of the ovulating lizard and to facilitate reproduction. At a later date, their roles reverse.

In this parthenogenic reptilian species, the brain is bisexual or ambisexual, even though the pelvic reproductive anatomy is not. According to MacLean's evolutionary theory of the triune brain, the mammalian brain is made up of an evolutionarily ancient reptilian brain overlaid by a paleocortex that is shared by all mammals and is overlaid in turn by the neocortex, which is most highly evolved in the human species (MacLean, 1972). Thus, the behavioral bisexuality of parthenogenic whiptail lizards may provide a key to understanding the bisexual potential of mammalian species.

It has long been known that the mammalian embryo, in the early stages of its development, is sexually bipotential. The undifferentiated gonads differentiate into either testes or ovaries. Thereafter, the Eve principle triumphs over the Adam principle: Sexual differentiation proceeds to be that of a female unless masculinizing hormones are added, normally by being secreted by the fetal testes. One of the two masculinizing hormones from the fetal testes is actually a defeminizing hormone, MIH (Mullerian-inhibiting hormone). It has a brief life span during which it vestigiates the two Mullerian ducts and prevents them from developing into a uterus and fallopian tubes (oviducts). The other hormone, testosterone (or one of its metabolites), masculinizes. It presides over the two Wolffian ducts and directs their development into the male internal accessory organs, including the prostate gland and seminal vesicles.

Differentiation of the internal genitalia is ambitypic. That is to say, the male and female anlagen are both present to begin with, after which one set vestigiates while the other set proliferates. By contrast, differentiation of the external genitalia is unitypic. That is to say, there is a single set of anlagen that has two possible destinies, namely to become either male or female. Thus, the clitoris and the penis are homologues of each other, as are the clitoral hood and the penile foreskin. The tissues that become the labia minora in the female wrap around the penis in the male and fuse along the midline of the underside to form the tubular urethra. The swellings that otherwise form the divided labia majora of the female fuse in the midline to form the scrotum of the male.

The Adam principle as applied to hormonal induction of sexual dimorphism of the genitalia applies also to dimorphism of the brain and its governance of the genitalia and their functioning. According to present evidence, hormone-induced brain dimorphism takes place later than that of the genitalia and, depending on the species, may extend into the first few days or weeks of postnatal life. The primary masculinizing hormone is testosterone, though it is not necessarily used in all parts of the brain as such. Within brain cells themselves, as within cells of the pelvic genitalia, it may be reduced to dihydrotestosterone. Paradoxically, it may also exert its masculinizing action only if first aromatized into estradiol, one of the sex steroids that received its name when it was considered to be exclusively an estrogenic, feminizing hormone. In both sexes, estradiol is metabolized from testosterone, which in turn is metabolized from progesterone, of which the antecedent is the steroidal substance cholesterol, from which all the steroidal hormones are derived.

On the basis of animal experimental studies of the effects of prenatal brain hormonalization on subsequent sexually dimorphic behavior, it is now generally acknowledged that the converse of brain masculinization is not feminization but demasculinization. The converse of feminization is defeminization. It is possible for masculinization to take place without defeminization and for feminization to take place without demasculinization (Baum, 1979; Baum, Gallagher, Martin, and Damassa, 1982; Beach, 1975; Ward, 1972, 1984; Ward and Weisz, 1980; Whalen and Edwards, 1967). This means that the differentiation of sexual dimorphism in the brain is not unitypic, like that of the external genitalia, but ambitypic, like that of the internal genitalia. Ambitypic differentiation allows for the possible coexistence of both masculine and feminine nuclei and pathways, as well as the behavior they govern, in some if not all parts of the brain. The two need not have equality; one may be more dormant than the other. To illustrate, when cows in a herd are in season, the central nervous system functions in such a way as to permit cow to mount cow, whereas when a bull is present, the cow is receptive and the bull does the mounting. Mounting is traditionally defined as masculine behavior, but it would be more accurately defined as ambisexual since it is shared by both sexes. On the criterion of mounting, cows are bisexual insofar as they mount and are mounted. Bulls are less so insofar as they are seldom mounted.

The first evidence of the hormonal induction of sexual dimorphism in the brain was inferred from its effects on behavior. The first experiment was done by Eugen Steinach (1940) early in the twentieth century. He demonstrated that the mating behavior of female guinea pigs would be masculinized if they had been neonatally castrated and then given an implant of testicular tissue. The theoretical implications of Steinach's finding were too advanced for their time. They lay dormant until William C. Young confirmed the experiment in the 1950s (Young, Goy, and Phoenix, 1964). Since then there has developed a whole new science of hormone-brain-behavior dimorphism.

By the 1970s, it had become evident that hormone-mediated dimorphism of the brain was no longer an inference based on sexually dimorphic behavior but an actuality that could be neuroanatomically demonstrated directly in brain tissue. In 1969, Doerner and Staudt reported that the nuclear volume of nerve cells in the preoptic area and ventromedial nucleus in the rat hypothalamus was larger in females than in males and that androgen administered in late prenatal and early neonatal life would reduce the volume of these cells in both females and castrated males. In 1971, Raisman and Field reported their discovery of sexual dimorphism in the dendritic synapses of the preoptic area of the rat brain. Thus began a new era of research into the prenatal hormonal determinants of sex differences in the neuroanatomy of those regions of the brain that mediate mating behavior (see reviews by Arnold and Gorski, 1984; DeVoogd, 1986; De Vries, De Brun, Uylings, and Corner, 1984).

Confirmatory findings followed in quick succession. In rats, Gorski and his research colleagues found and named the sexually dimorphic nucleus of the preoptic area (SDN-POA) (Gorski, Gordon, Shryne, and Southam, 1978). The corresponding sexually dimorphic tissues in the human brain Gorski refers to as the interstitial nuclei of the anterior hypothalamus. The SDN-POA of male rats is bigger than that of females and becomes so under the influence of steroid hormone from the testes (testosterone or its metabolite, estradiol) during the critical period of the first few days after birth (Doehler et al., 1982). Also in rats, Breedlove and Arnold (1980) discovered sexual dimorphism in the number of motor neurons innervating the perineal muscles in rats; and it is during the critical period of the first few days that the larger number of these motor neurons in males is produced by the presence of steroid hormone from the testes (Breedlove, 1986).

In songbirds as well as in rats, the presence of testicular hormone during a brief critical period proved to be the determinant in the male brain of the neuroanatomy that governs song (Nottebohm and Arnold, 1976). In the zebra finch, testicular hormone exerts its masculinizing effect once and forever during the early critical period. There is no backtracking: The song pattern of the first spring singing season persists unchanged in subsequent years. In the canary, by contrast, the entire process is reactivated each spring, which allows the male to change his song and learn a new one each year instead of having only the one that he learned in the first year of life. An adult female, provided she is treated with steroid hormone, is able to learn a song for the first time as an adult. Learning the song first as a newly hatched nestling is not imperative. Male songbirds copy the song they hear in the nest even though they do not sing it until weeks later.

The findings with respect to canary song demonstrate a type of sexual dimorphism in which the ambisexual window is not forever closed after the neonatal critical period but is reopened annually. Thus, a canary of either sex may sing one year but not the next, depending on the degree of steroidal hormonalization of the sexually dimorphic brain in the springtime of each year. As a result, canaries have the possibility of being, as songsters, serially rather than concurrently bisexual.

Concurrent bisexuality would require two coexistent, dimorphic neuroanatomical systems, one subserving masculine and one feminine dimorphism of behavior—for example, mounting and lordosing, respectively. In rat experiments, Nordeen and Yahr (1982) found such a duality in the form of hemispheric asymmetry in the neighborhood of the sexually dimorphic nucleus of the preoptic area of the hypothalamus. They implanted pellets of the steroid hormone estradiol separately into the left and right sides of the hypothalamus of newborn female rat pups. The subsequent effect of the hormone on the left side was to defeminize (that is, to suppress lordosis) and on the right side to masculinize (that is, to facilitate mounting behavior) after the rats become mature.

The lateral distribution in the brain of masculine to the right and feminine to the left means that the two sides may develop to be either concordant (one masculinized and the other defeminized, or one feminized and the other demasculinized) or discordant (one masculinized and the other feminized, or one demasculinized and the other defeminized). Disparities may come into being on the basis of the amount of hormone needed by and available to each side, the timing of its availability to each side, the synchrony or dissynchrony of the hormonal programming on each side, and the pulsatility or continuity of the hormonal supply on each side. Thus, there are alternative ways in which one side could be rendered masculine and the other feminine to a sufficient degree to constitute bisexuality. Likewise, there are alternative ways in which the brain may be masculinized when the genitals are feminized, or vice versa, so as to constitute homosexuality.

These alternative ways of predisposing the brain to be either bisexual or homosexual can, in animals, be manipulated experimentally. They may also occur adventitiously as an unrecognized side effect of hormone imbalance secondary to nutritional, medicinal, or endocrine changes, including stress-derived changes, in the pregnant mother's bloodstream. Sleeping pills containing barbiturate, for example, may have a demasculinizing effect on the brain of the human fetus because the drug has been shown to have such an effect on male rat pups (reviewed in Reinisch and Sanders, 1982). Also in rats, maternal stress that alters maternal adrenocortical hormones may exert a prenatal demasculinizing effect on male pups that is subsequently evident in their bisexual and homosexual mating behavior (Ward, 1984).

The dramatic power of the steroid hormones in prenatal life to foreordain the sexual orientation and mating behavior of adult life has been illustrated in several laboratory species in experiments in which fetal females are hormonally masculinized or males demasculinized. The hormonal intervention may be timed so as to change the sex first of the external genitalia and then of the brain or to spare the external genitalia and change the brain only.

There is a remarkable film (Clarke, 1977; Short and Clarke, n.d.) that shows how the brains and behavior of ewe lambs, independently of their bodies, can be masculinized in utero by implanting the pregnant mother with testosterone at the critical period of gestation (day fifty and thereafter). The lamb grows up to be a lesbian ewe. Its brain is so effectively masculinized that its mating behavior, including mating rivalry and the proceptive courtship ritual (and also its urinating behavior), is exactly like that of a ram even though, at the same time, its own ovaries are secreting estrogen, not androgen. Moreover, the normal rams and ewes of the flock respond to the lesbian ewe's masculinized mating behavior as if it were that of a normal ram.

Sheep, cattle, swine (reviewed by D'Occhio and Ford, 1988), and other four-legged species are more or less hormonal robots, insofar as a masculine or a feminine mating pattern can be foreordained on the basis of regulating the prenatal hormonalization of the brain. Even among sheep, however, the final outcome will be influenced by whether the lamb grew up in a normal flock of ewes and rams or in a sex-segregated herd. Primates are even more influenced by the social conditions of growing up and are less subject to hormonal robotization (Goldfoot, 1977; Goldfoot and Neff, 1987; Goldfoot and Wallen, 1978; Goldfoot, Wallen, Neff, McBriar, and Goy, 1984; Phoenix and Chambers, 1982; Phoenix, Jensen, and Chambers, 1983).

Defining Criteria of Masculine and Feminine

A diecious species is one in which the male and female reproductive organs are housed in two separate and distinct individual beings. A monecious species is one that has the male and female organs housed in one individual being. Parthenogenic creatures, such as the whiptail lizards already mentioned, are a special instance of a monecious species, for their brains have two separate and distinct patterns of breeding behavior, though every member of the species has the same genital morphology and produces eggs exclusively. These eggs do not need to capture and join with a sperm in order to be fertile and produce young ones. Reproductively, the species is monomorphic. There are no sperm-bearing males. Without the dimorphism of male and female, there are therefore no females in the species. Nonetheless, so powerful is the dimorphism of language that it is all but inevitable that, when this same lizard—during an anovulatory phase—mounts another ovulatory lizard, the mounting behavior will be called masculine. The criterion of masculine in this instance is that it simulates the behavior of males in those whiptail species that are diecious and have sperm-bearing males as well as egg-bearing females.

In this example, one confronts the issue of the ultimate criterion of what is masculine, what is feminine, and what is bisexual. The workaday criterion is that if, in a diecious species, males do it, it is masculine, whereas if females do it, it is feminine. If both do it, it is sex-shared or bisexual. This criterion would be acceptable if it were applied with strict mathematical obedience to the statistical norm of what is manifested by males only, by females only, or by both. The statistical norm, however, insidiously yields to the ideological norm, which is not the norm of what males and females actually do but what they ought to do. Ideologically, what is masculine is what males ought to do, and what is feminine is what females ought to do, according to criteria that are assumed to be eternal verities but are actually culture-bound dogmas of history and the cultural heritage. Ideologically, there is practically no place for what is sex-shared or ambisexual. The very term *ambisexual* is seldom used, being replaced by the word *bisexual.* Bisexual does not imply that something is shared in common by both males and females but, with pejorative overtones, that something appropriate to one sex is incongruously manifested by a deviant member of the other sex. We are heirs to a long history of a cultural fixation on sex divergency rather than sex sharing.

This fixation has insidiously infected sexual science so as to ensure that its focus is on explaining sex difference, not sex similarity. The naming of the sex hormones when they were isolated in the 1920s and subsequently synthesized is an example. Androgen (from the Greek *andros,* "man") became the name for a male hormone, especially testosterone, secreted by testes. The female hormones were named estrogen (from the Greek *oistrous,* "gadfly"; and the Latin *oestrus,* or "the period of sexual heat") and progesterone (from the Latin *pro* + *gestatio,* "gestation," + *sterol,* as in "cholesterol," + *one*). The progesterone level is higher during pregnancy than in the nonpregnant state. Simply by being characterized as masculinizing and feminizing, the gonadal hormones have insidiously supported the idea of sex difference, whereas in fact all three hormones are sex-shared. Their ratio differs in males and females but not their occurrence. Moreover, as previously noted, the body synthesizes all three from cholesterol, the progression in both sexes being from progesterone to testosterone to estradiol.

One way out of the dilemma of relativity is to tolerate it. Thus, in genetics, one tolerates the stipulation that the genetic male is chromosomally XY and the female XX, despite the undisputed evidence that some males are XX, XXY, and XYY, not to mention a multiplicity of chromosomal mosaics; and females are likewise XY, XO, XXX, and mosaic. In traditional biology, one tolerates the stipulation that males bear sperm and females bear eggs, despite their relativity in hermaphroditic species in which the same individual bears both eggs and sperms. In comparative sexology, one tolerates the stipulation that having a penis is the criterion of being male and having a vulva is the criterion of being female, despite the relativity of intersexes or hermaphrodites. The XY/XX, sperm/egg, and penis/vulva criteria of male/female, respectively, impose a too rigid antithesis on the coding of what is male and what female in mating behavior by excluding the relativity of behavior that may be to some degree sex-shared.

In human sexology, one tolerates the penis/vulva criterion as a good enough approximation for stipulating that masculine is what males do and feminine is what females do. As an approximation, however, it is far from perfect because of the high degree of cultural relativity in the social stipulation of gender coding. The hazard of cultural relativity is that it is conducive to cultural chauvinism. The danger of cultural chauvinism for a science of sexology is that the stipulations of one culture (usually one's own, of course) will be universalized, and the cultural lessons of human gender diversity will be lost.

Sex and Gender

Although the terms *sex* and *gender* are carelessly used as synonyms, in fact they are not synonymous. They are also not antonyms, though they are frequently used almost as if they were. In one such usage, sex is defined as what you are born with, as male or female, and gender is what you acquire as a social role, from a social script. This usage lends support to a second one in which gender is sex without the dirty part that belongs to the genitalia and reproduction. This is the Barbie-doll usage, in which human beings are cast in the role of Barbie and Ken dolls molded with nothing between their legs, though blatantly sexy in shape and clothing.

It is the Barbie-doll definition of gender that made possible the political term *gender gap,* for which *sex gap* would be an unacceptable synonym because of its double meaning. In the politics of the women's movement, the separation of gender from sex was a godsend because it allowed sex differences in procreation to be set aside in the fight for gender equality in earning power and legal status.

Used strictly correctly, the word *gender* is conceptually more inclusive than the word *sex.* It is an umbrella under which are sheltered all the different components of sex difference, including the sex-genital, sex-erotic, and sex-procreative components. The need to find an umbrella term became for me an imperative in the early 1950s when I was writing about the manliness or womanliness of people with a history of having been born with indeterminate genital sex. They were hermaphrodites, and their genital sex was ambiguous. In some instances, they would grow up to live as women but would not have a woman's sex organs. In other instances, they would live as men without a man's sex organs. In the case of a man, by way of illustration, it made no sense to say that such a person had a male sex role when, in fact, he had no male external genitalia, could not urinate as a male, and would never be able to copulate as a male. No matter how manly he might otherwise be, his genital sex role was not that of a man. There was no word with which to name manliness despite the deficit of the very organs that are the criterion of being a man. That is why I turned to philology and linguistics and borrowed the term *gender* (Money, 1955). Then it became possible to say that the person had the gender role and also the gender identity of a man, but a deficient or partially deficient male sex role in his usage of the birth-defective sex organs. The new term also made it possible to formulate such statements as "a male gender role despite a female (46,XX) genetic sex." Without the term *gender,* one would get bogged down in statements such as this: "a male sex role, except that his sex role with the sex organs was not male and his genetic sex was female."

In popular and in scientific usage, gender role and gender identity have become separated, whereas they are really two sides of the same coin. Other people infer your private and personal gender identity from the public evidence of your gender role. You alone have intimate access to your gender identity. The acronym G-I/R (gender-identity/role) unifies identity and role into a singular noun.

There is no finite limit to the number of adjectives that may be used to qualify a G-I/R. One classification is into homosexual, bisexual, or heterosexual G-I/R. A homosexual G-I/R itself ranges widely from that of a full-time drag queen or gynemimetic (one who mimes women) to that of a stereotypically macho football hero or Marine Corps sergeant who has a masculine G-I/R except for the sex of the partner to whom he becomes erotically attracted and male-bonded in a love affair. Some people would say that the macho homosexual has a masculine G-I/R except for a homosexual-partner preference or object choice. The correct statement should be: masculine G-I/R except for the erotosexual and falling-in-love component.

Gender Coding

Reductionistic thinking as applied to gender coding is based on the split between sex and gender, according to which sex belongs to biology and gender to social science. For reductionists, biological means genetic, neuroanatomic, endocrinologic, or in some other way physiologic. Reductionist theory fails to recognize that there is a biology of learning and remembering, the effects of which may become permanently cemented into the brain. Reductionism adopts the common (though erroneous) assumption that what the brain assimilates it may always discard—that learning may always be undone by unlearning, or that memory may always be undone by forgetting.

Reductionist theory is popular on both sides of the fence that is falsely claimed to separate biology from social learning. It allows its proponents on either side to earn a living by ignoring each other's specialty knowledge, training, and certification. The bureaucracy of scholars is not well suited to interdisciplinary knowledge or to the concept of multivariate, sequential determinants that cross the boundaries of scientific specialties. Gender coding is both multivariate and sequential, and it is neither exclusively biological nor exclusively social but a product of both.

In the years of childhood, the gender-coded development of boys and girls invariably mirrors the masculine and feminine stereotypes of their social heritage. In the human species, there is no way in which to ascertain what culture-free masculinity and femininity would be like, for they are always packaged in culture, just as linguistic ability is always packaged in a native language. Primordial masculinity and femininity are unascertainable in their entirety. It is possible, however, to gender code and classify male/female differences into those that are sex-irreducible, sex-derivative, sex-adjunctive, and sex-adventitious. These four classes are hierarchical in their relationship, with sex-irreducible coding at the top.

Sex-irreducible differences are specific to reproduction: men impregnate, and women menstruate, gestate, and lactate. Ovulation is omitted insofar as gestation does not take place without it. Lactation might be omitted insofar as modern nutritional technology has made it possible (though not desirable) for maternal neonatal breast-feeding to be replaced by a formula-milk substitute.

Immutability of the procreative sex difference will undoubtedly remain as if absolute for most men and women forever. However, in light of contemporary experimental obstetrics, being pregnant is no longer an absolutely immutable sex difference. Twenty years ago, Cecil Jacobsen, geneticist, and the late Ray Hertz, endocrine oncologist, using the technique of embryo transplantation, got male baboons abdominally pregnant. In one case, six and a half months later, they delivered a live baby by caesarean section, two weeks premature. The experiment was designed to find out if pregnant women whose ovaries had to be removed because of ovarian cancer would be able to keep the pregnancy. Male baboons were used because males have no ovaries, and they demonstrated that a pregnancy can exist without ovarian hormones from the mother. "There is no question in my mind," Dr. Jacobsen recently stated, "that the hormones and stimuli required for normal fetal development are innate within the early embryo. Most developmental biologists are now coming round to that view. But back in the 1960s it was heresy" (Barsky, 1986).

Gender Cross-codification

It is necessary to have a conceptual term other than *paraphilia, perversion,* or *deviancy* for the name of whatever it is that makes homosexual different from heterosexual. In earlier writings, I used the term *gender transposition* to signify that, instead of complete concordance of all the components of either masculine or feminine, one or more is transposed so as to be, respectively, feminine or masculine. Gender transposition applies not only to homosexuality but to a range of phenomena that differ on the basis of the number of components involved and the persistence of their transposition (Table 3.1). In transexualism, for example, all the components of extrinsic gender coding are transposed (or cross-coded) relative to the criterion of the external genitalia, and the transposition is long-lasting—usually permanent.

Table 3.1
Gender Cross-Coding (Transposition)

	Continuous or Chronic	*Episodic or Alternating*
Total	Transexualism	Transvestophilia (fetishistic transvestism)
Partial unlimited	Gynemimesis or Andromimesis	Nonfetishistic transvestism
Partial limited	Male or Female Homophilia	Bisexualism

The term *gender transposition* carries no connotations as to causality, immutability, or penetrance, all three of which need to be specified on the basis of empirical data. However, the term has proved to be a stumbling block for those who have a strong antipathy to homosexual science, insofar as they believe that to classify homosexuality as a transposition is to stigmatize it as being abnormal. Their alternative is to classify homosexuality as a moral choice or preference for a same-sex partner, which in the vocabulary of psychoanalysis is a same-sex object choice.

Many social-science writers and sex therapists differentiate object choice, gender identity, and gender role. This enables them to say, for example, that a man is masculine in his gender identity and gender role but homosexual in orientation and object choice. The alternative is to say he has a masculine G-I/R (gender-identity/role) except for the sexuoerotic imagery and ideation of his love life and sex life in dreams and fantasies and in their translation into actual practices. This alternative formulation circumvents the scientific fallacy inherent in the term *object choice,* namely that heterosexuality and homosexuality have their origin in voluntary choice and are therefore already fully explained by fiat, without the superfluous addition of more research—which is the fallacy of scientific nihilism.

Terminologically, gender transposition and gender cross-coding are synonymous. However, cross-coding carries more the connotation of extrinsic and arbitrary social coding than the connotation of genetic coding, hormonal coding, or coding of any other less arbitrary intrinsic origin. Thus, it is possible that the term *gender cross-coding* will prove less of a stumbling block than will *gender transposition.* Gender cross-coding should not be construed as being exclusively socially programmed, however. It may be prenatally programmed as well, for example, by hormonal cross-coding, at least in part if not in toto.

One way of classifying gender cross-coding is the simple seven-point (0 to 6) scale devised by Kinsey and now commonly referred to as the Kinsey scale. It is a scale constructed on the assumption that exclusive heterosexuality (rated 0) and exclusive homosexuality (rated 6) are polar extremes on the same continuum. It is a ratio scale insofar as bisexual is rated as the ratio of heterosexual to homosexual, with the fifty-fifty ratio given a rating of 3. As in all ratios, the absolute scores of prevalence or intensity are forfeited. For example, a person who has had bisexual experience with more than five thousand different partners by age fifty, with never fewer than two partners daily and with frequent participation in bisexual group-sex parties, may get the same bisexual rating as another person who has had only two partners, one male and one female, and with a participation frequency no higher than twice a week.

Kinsey ratings are allocated on the basis of self-reported data on erotosexual imagery and ideation in fantasies and dreams as well as on actual erotosexual experiences. The Kinsey scale's criterion of homosexuality or heterosexuality is participation in a sexual act, actually and/or in imagery, without taking into account whether or not it is compatible with falling in love, homosexually, heterosexually, or both.

Because the Kinsey scale is a unidimensional ratio scale, a Kinsey rating does not take into account qualitative differences among the different categories, types, and syndromes of gender cross-coding. For example, a Kinsey rating does not disclose whether the person rated 6 is an exclusively homosexual drill sergeant, a full-time gynemimetic impersonator in the entertainment industry, a gay transvestophile, or a preoperative male-to-female transexual whose sexual partners are exclusively male.

It is possible, of course, to allocate a Kinsey rating to people who represent the qualitatively different manifestations of gender cross-coding. To do so, however, they must first be ascertained and classified as belonging to one subgroup or another. Table 3.1 presents such a classification.

To be empirically useful and scientific, a classification must be based on criteria that are exhaustive and mutually exclusive. That is, they must be able to accommodate all known cases or examples (and ideally all those remaining to be ascertained), and without overlap or ambiguity. Table 3.1 satisfies these conditions by classifying gender cross-coding according to the dual criteria of time (duration or persistence) and degree (penetrance or pervasiveness).

To avoid the pitfall of prematurely allocating causality, the classification of Table 3.1 expressly avoids any reference to psychogenic versus organogenic origin or etiology. Etiology in sexology can be established only by painstaking, laborious, empirical research, not by doctrinal revelation and not on the basis of diagnosis by exclusion, the trash-can method by which psychogenesis is all too often attributed. It is better to admit ignorance than to be pilloried for the folly of pretentious error. It is difficult to relinquish dogma. All present-day explanations of gender cross-coding are either social (nurture) or biological (nature) dogmas, unless they are presented with the proviso that they are incompletely substantiated.

There is no evidence that gender cross-coding is either all nature or all nurture in its origins. The forces of nature meet the forces of nurture in the course of development from embryonic life onward. When they meet at a so-called critical or sensitive period of some aspect of development, together they program what the outcome of that development will be. In fetal life, for example, thalidomide in the intrauterine environment falsely nurtures what nature is growing from buds to limbs, with the result that the limbs become permanently deformed. A corresponding example in postnatal life is Konrad Lorenz's now famous demonstration of how newly hatched ducklings became imprinted (nature) not to a mother duck but to him (nurture) provided he squatted and waddled during the critical posthatching period. Subsequently, they followed him, and forever failed to follow a duck, as mother.

The old paradigm was nature/nurture. The new paradigm is nature/critical period/nurture. The programming that takes place when nature and nurture interact at a critical period, whether in prenatal or postnatal life, may be irreversible and immutable.

Immutability is a key concept here. It is particularly relevant to gender cross-coding in the ideology of law, legislation, religion, and society, where the issue is not, as it is frequently assumed to be, innate versus acquired—that is, nature versus nurture—but immutability versus mutability.

As in the case of left-handedness, the immutability of any manifestation of gender cross-coding—for example, homophilic homosexuality—is not synonymous with whether its origin is ostensibly biological or not. In an earlier era, left-handedness was a deviation to be cured at school by tying the left hand behind the back and other punishments. The outcome was not right-handedness but poor writing, dyslexia, and delinquency in response to academic abuse. For society, it has been more expeditious not to punish but to tolerate left-handedness and to manufacture tools and artifacts to accommodate people with this status.

The lesson of left-handedness can be applied to gender crosscoding. It is more expedient and much less expensive for society to tolerate what it cannot change rather than to engage in trying to force a cure on what is already immutable. The false hope of curing left-handedness was based on the appearance of success in cases in which there was some degree of ambidexterity on which to capitalize. The counterpart in gender cross-coding is bisexuality that is wrongly classified as homosexuality. Most (if not all) the claimed cures of homosexuality prove, on more detailed investigation, to have been cases in which there was some degree of bisexuality on which to capitalize. It is in just such a case that the individual may experience a sense of the self divided and in conflict, for the resolution of which he or she seeks treatment to be monosexually one or the other, but not bisexually both together.

The homosexual person, like the bisexual or heterosexual, may be either normophilic or paraphilic. Paraphilia is independent of homosexuality or heterosexuality. If a paraphilia afflicts a heterosexual person, it is the paraphilia that needs treatment, not the heterosexuality. Likewise, it is the paraphilia and not the homosexuality that needs treatment when a homosexual person is paraphilically afflicted.

The canons of health and well-being do not discriminate between Kinsey 0 and Kinsey 6. They are disciplines of equal opportunity. They apply to us all.

Acknowledgment

This chapter was supported by USPHS Grant HD00325 and Grant 830-86900, William T. Grant Foundation.

REFERENCES

Arnold, A. P., and Gorski, R. A. (1984). "Gonadal steroid induction of structural sex differences in the central nervous system." *Annual Review of Neuroscience* 7:413–42.

Barsky, L. (1986). "Holy hormones . . . male pregnancy?" *Chatelaine* 59(8): 62–63, 123–24.

Baum, M. J. (1979). "Differentiation of coital behavior in mammals: A comparative analysis." *Neuroscience and Biobehavioral Reviews* 3:265–84.

Baum, M. J., Gallagher, C. A., Martin, J. T., and Damassa, D. A. (1982). "Effects of testosterone, dihydrotestosterone, or estradiol administered neonatally on sexual behavior of female ferrets." *Endocrinology* 111: 773–80.

Beach, F. A. (1975). "Hormonal modification of sexually dimorphic behavior." *Psychoneuroendocrinology* 1:3–23.

Breedlove, S. M. (1986). "Cellular analyses of hormone influence on motoneuronal development and function." *Journal of Neurobiology* 17:157–76.

Breedlove, S. M., and Arnold, A. F. (1980). "Hormone accumulation in a sexually dimorphic motor nucleus of the rat spinal cord." *Science* 210: 564–66.

Bullough, V. L. (1976). *Sexual Variance in Society and History.* New York: John Wiley and Sons.

Chan, S. T. H. (1977). "Spontaneous sex reversal in fishes." In *Handbook of Sexology* (J. Money and H. Musaph, eds.). New York: Excerpta Medica.

Clarke, I. J. (1977). "The sexual behavior of prenatally androgenized ewes observed in the field." *Journal of Reproduction and Fertility* 49:311–15.

Crews, D. (1982). "On the origin of sexual behavior." *Psychoneuroendocrinology* 7:259–70.

———. (1987). "Functional associations in behavioral endocrinology." In *Masculinity/Femininity: Basic Perspectives.* (J. M. Reinisch, L. A. Rosenblum, and S. A. Sanders, eds.). New York: Oxford University Press.

DeVoogd, T. J. (1986). "Steroid interactions with structure and function of avian song control regions." *Journal of Neurobiology* 17:177–201.

De Vries, C. J., De Brun, J. F. C., Uylings, H. B. M., and Corner, M. A., eds. (1984). *Sex Differences in the Brain: Relation between Structure and Function.* New York: Elsevier.

D'Occhio, M. J., and Ford, J. J. (1988). "Contribution of studies in cattle, sheep, and swine to our understanding of the role of gonadal hormones in processes of sexual differentiation and adult sexual behavior." In *Handbook of Sexology, Volume 7* (J. M. A. Sitsen, ed.). New York: Elsevier.

Doerner, C., and Staudt, J. (1969). "Perinatal structural sex differentiation of the hypothalamus in rats." *Neuroendocrinology* 5:103–106.

Doehler, K. D., Coquelin, A., Davis, F., Hines, M., Shryne, J. E., and Gorski, R. A. (1982). "Differentiation of the sexually dimorphic nucleus in the preoptic area of the rat brain is determined by the perinatal hormone environment." *Neuroscience Letters* 33:295–99.

Ellis, H. (1942). *Studies in the Psychology of Sex (Volumes 1 and 2).* New York: Random House.

Goldfoot, D. A. (1977). "Sociosexual behaviors of nonhuman primates during development and maturity: Social and hormonal relationships." In *Behavioral Primatology: Advances in Research and Theory, Volume 1* (A. M. Schrier, ed.). Hillsdale, NJ: Lawrence Erlbaum.

Goldfoot, D. A., and Neff, D. A. (1987). "On measuring behavioral sex differences in social contexts." In *Masculinity/Femininity: Basic Perspectives.* (J. M. Reinisch, L. A. Rosenblum, and S. A. Sanders, eds.). New York: Oxford University Press.

Goldfoot, D. A., and Wallen, K. (1978). "Development of gender role behaviors in heterosexual and isosexual groups of infant rhesus monkeys." In D. J. Chivers and J. Herbert (eds.). *Recent Advances in Primatology, Volume 1: Behaviour.* London: Academic Press.

Goldfoot, D. A., Wallen, K., Neff, D. A., McBrair, M. C., and Goy, R. W. (1984). "Social influences upon the display of sexually dimorphic behavior in rhesus monkeys: Isosexual rearing." *Archives of Sexual Behavior* 13:395–412.

Gorski, R. A., Cordon, J. H., Shryne, J. E., and Southam, A. M. (1978). "Evidence for a morphological sex difference within the medial preoptic area of the rat brain." *Brain Research* 148:333–46.

Herdt, G. H. (1981). *Guardians of the Flutes: Idioms of Masculinity.* New York: McGraw-Hill.

Herdt, G. H., ed. (1984). *Ritualized Homosexuality in Melanesia.* Berkeley: University of California Press.

Hirschfeld, M. (1948). *Sexual Anomalies: The Origins, Nature and Treatment of Sexual Disorders.* New York: Emerson Books.

Jackson, P., Barrowclough, I. W., France, J. T., and Phillips, L. I. (1980). "A successful pregnancy following total hysterectomy." *British Journal of Obstetrics and Gynaecology* 87:353–55.

MacLean, P. D. (1972). "A triune concept of the brain and behavior." In *The Hincks Memorial Lectures* (T. Boag, ed.). Toronto: Toronto University Press.

Money, J. (1955). "Hermaphroditism, gender, and precocity in hyperadrenocorticism: Psychologic findings." *Bulletin of The Johns Hopkins Hospital* 96:253–64.

———. (1968). *Sex Errors of the Body: Dilemmas, Education, Counseling.* Baltimore: Johns Hopkins University Press.

———. (1974). "Prenatal hormones and postnatal socialization in gender identity differentiation." *Nebraska Symposium on Motivation* 21:221–95.

———. (1987). "Propaedeutics of diecious G-I/R: Theoretical foundations for understanding dimorphic gender-identity/role." In *Masculinity/Femininity: Basic Perspectives* (J. M. Reinisch, L. A. Rosenblum, and S. A. Sanders, eds.). New York: Oxford University Press.

Money, J., and Ehrhardt, A. A. (1972). *Man and Woman, Boy and Girl: The Differentiation and Dimorphism of Gender Identity from Conception to Maturity.* Baltimore: Johns Hopkins University Press.

Nordeen, E. J., and Yahr, P. (1982). "Hemispheric asymmetries in the behavioral and hormonal effects of sexually differentiating mammalian brain." *Science* 218:391–93.

Nottebohm, F., and Arnold, A. P. (1976). "Sexual dimorphism in vocal control areas of the song-bird brain." *Science* 194:211–13.

Phoenix, C. H., and Chambers, K. C. (1982). "Sexual behaviour in adult gonadectomized female pseudohermaphrodite, female, and male rhesus macaques (*Macaca mulatta*) treated with estradiol benzoate and testosterone proprionate." *Journal of Comparative and Physiological Psychology* 96:823–33.

Phoenix, C. H., Jensen, J. N., and Chambers, K. C. (1983). "Female sexual behavior displayed by androgenized female rhesus monkeys." *Hormones and Behavior* 17:146–51.

Raisman, C., and Field, P. M. (1971). "Sexual dimorphism in the preoptic area of the rat." *Science* 173:731–33.

Reinisch, J. M., and Sanders, S. A. (1982). "Early barbiturate exposure: The brain, sexually dimorphic behavior, and learning." *Neuroscience and Biobehavioral Reviews* 6:311–19.

Short, R. V., and Clarke, I. J. (no date). *Masculinization of the Female Sheep.* Distributed by MRC Reproductive Biology Unit, 2 Forrest Road, Edinburgh, EH1 2QW, U.K.

Steinach, E. (1940). *Sex and Life: Forty Years of Biological and Medical Experiments.* New York: Viking.

Stoller, R. J., and Herdt, G. H. (1985). "Theories of origins of male homosexuality." *Archives of General Psychiatry* 42:399–404.

Ward, I. L. (1972). "Prenatal stress feminizes and demasculinizes the behavior of males." *Science* 175:82–84.

———. (1984). "The prenatal stress syndrome: Current status." *Psychoneuroendocrinology* 9:3–11.

Ward, I. L., and Weisz, J. (1980). "Maternal stress alters plasma testosterone in fetal males." *Science* 207:328–29.

Whalen, R. E., and Edwards, D. A. (1967). "Hormonal determinants of the development of masculine and feminine behavior in male and female rats." *Anatomical Record* 157:173–80.

Young, W. C., Goy, R. W., and Phoenix, C. H. (1964). "Hormones and sexual behavior." *Science* 143:212–18.

4

Propaedeutics of Diecious G-I/R: Theoretical Foundations for Understanding Dimorphic Gender-Identity/Role

Of the Flesh and of the Spirit: Nature and Nurture

The difference between male and female is something that everybody knows and nobody knows. Everybody knows it, proverbially, as an eternal verity. Nobody knows it, scientifically, as an absolute entity, for as day and night merge under the glare of the midnight sun, male and female merge under the scrutiny of empirical inquiry.

In the technical vocabulary of science, a monecious species of animal or plant is one in which male and female are accommodated in only one house (from the Greek *oikos,* "house"). In a diecious species, there are two houses, one for the male and one for the female. The single house has been cut or divided—etymologically, *sex* derives from the Latin *secare,* "to cut or divide." Thus, according to the wisdom of etymology, a male and female are defined, respectively, on the criterion of the morphology of the body in which they are housed. Beyond etymology, the great interest of science is in the live building materials that differentiate not only the construction of the two houses, but also the totality of their function.

Originally published in June Machover Reinisch, Leonard A. Rosenblum, and Stephanie A. Sanders, eds., *Masculinity/Femininity: Basic Perspectives* (New York: Oxford University Press, 1987), pp. 13–28.

In the prescientific thought of the era that preceded modern science, the constituents of sex were divided between the flesh and the spirit. The flesh was responsible for the animal nature of the sexes, and for their carnal desires that needed the purification of the spirit. The flesh represented the sin of passion; the spirit represented the purity of reason. Women were creatures of weakness and passion, men of power and rationality. These stereotypes have changed but have not become extinct.

The religious doctrine of the sin of the flesh versus the righteousness of the spirit underwent a scientific metamorphosis in the nineteenth century; it became the secular doctrine of nature versus nurture. In contemporary scholarship regarding sex difference, nature is equated with biology and nurture with what is taught and learned. Biology is of the flesh and immutable. Learning, if not of the spirit, is of the mind and mutable—ostensibly, what is learned can be unlearned, and unlearning takes place under the auspices of behavior modification or psychotherapy.

The faultiness of this line of reasoning is that there is a biology of learning and remembering. It is part of neuroscience. Although the biology of learning is only at the beginning of its development, its very existence is sufficient to demonstrate that the converse of biology is not social learning and memory. Logically, the converse of biology should be spiritualism and the astral body.

A New Paradigm: Nature/Critical Period/Nurture

The biology of learning includes learning that becomes imprinted and immutable. Thus, a new paradigm is needed to replace nature/nurture with a three-term principle: nature/critical period/nurture. The interaction of nature and nurture at a critical period may produce a permanent sequela that, in turn, may react at another critical period with a new facet of nurture. This principle has long been known in embryology. It is only slowly being applied to postnatal development.

Even nature is not inevitably immutable. The genes that govern heredity—the very epitome of nature—can be altered at a critical period by the intervention of nurture in the guise of gene splicing. The alteration then becomes permanent.

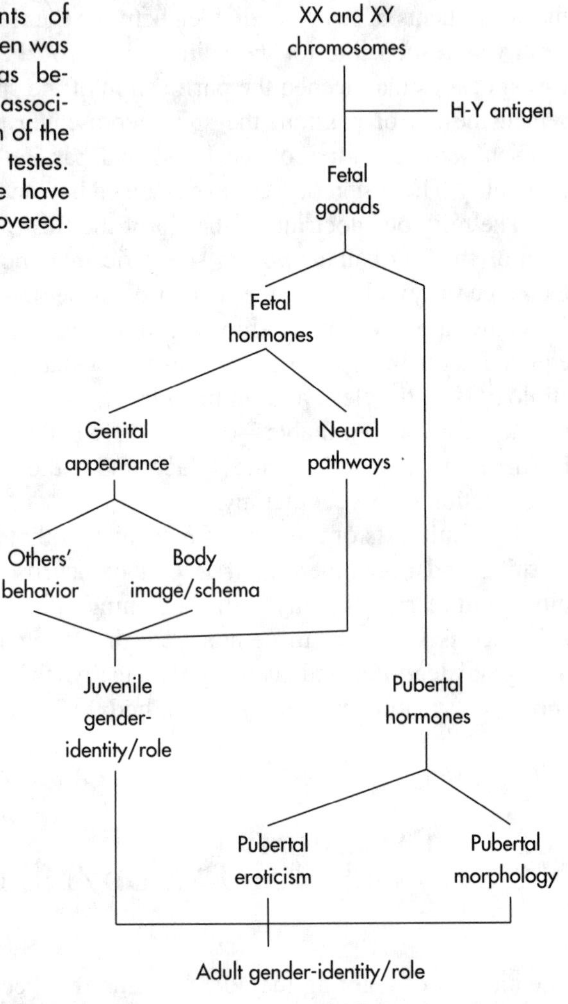

Figure 1. The multivariate and sequential determinants of G-I/R. When H-Y antigen was first discovered, it was believed to be invariably associated with differentiation of the gonadal anlagen as testes. Exceptions to this rule have subsequently been discovered.

There is something quaintly archaic in the application of a resurgent nature/nurture ideology to the science of sex difference. The hidden agenda of this archaism is political. Formulated in terms of reductionistic biology, nature is a political strategy of those committed to the status quo of sex differences. They use reductionist biology to maintain the biological inevitability of sex differences and to exclude the possibility of their being historically stereotyped. Conversely, neglect of biological determinism is the political strategy of the advocates of the political and social liberation of the sexes from historical stereotypes. I can attest to these strategies with an authority born of experience, for I have been attacked by nurturists for representing the absolutism of prenatal hormonal determinism, and by naturists for representing the relativism of social determinism.

Unification of the nature/nurture polarity can be found in the paradigm of native language. At birth, a baby must be equipped with a healthy human brain in order to develop a native language. But no genes program a native language. It must be programmed into the brain, socially, from the example of others who use it, and the programming must be done at a critical period of development.

As applied to sex difference, this paradigm means that some of the program of sex difference is phyletically designed and shared by most (if not all) members of the species, both male and female. This phyletically shared segment is not the whole program, however. The remainder is the ontogenetic program, designed by personal and sociocultural history specific to time and place. The great scientific challenge is to identify empirically the variety and number of phyletic and ontogenetic determinants, regardless of whether they are conventionally attributed to nature or nurture, and to uncover the mechanisms by which they underlie, overlie, and influence one another developmentally. This requires not a reductionist theory, but one that is both multivariate and sequential (Figure 1).

MULTIVARIATE SEQUENTIAL DETERMINISM

I designed Figure 1 originally for the *American Handbook of Psychiatry* (Money, 1974); it first appeared in print in Money and Ehrhardt (1972) and has since been used in several textbooks. Its purpose is to show that the adult status of gender-identity/role (G-I/R) is the culmination of a sequential and multivariate process. The multivariables range from prenatal to pubertal hormones, from body morphology to body image, and from prenatal hormonalization of the brain to postnatal assimilation of cultural stereotypes of male and female.

In ordinary, healthy people, the multiple variables of sex, both male and female, correlate perfectly with one another so that their potential independence of one another is not self-evident. This perfect correlation does not exist in syndromes of hermaphroditism. By reason of the discrepancies that exist in these syndromes, I could specify several of the variables of sex that are potentially independent of one another (Money, 1952, 1955; Money, Hampson, and Hampson, 1955).

In order of appearance, these variables were, as specified in 1955: chromosomal sex, gonadal sex, fetal hormonal sex, internal morphologic sex, and external morphologic sex. In postnatal life, the variables were, successively: assigned sex, sex of rearing (including clinical habilitation), and pubertal hormonal sex. Together, these variables were held responsible for the differentiation of gender role and orientation (identity) as male, female, or androgynous in the course of growing up. Since 1965, beginning with the 24th edition, *Dorland's Illustrated Medical Dictionary* has incorporated these variables into its definition of sex.

In 1955, the relationship of fetal sex hormones to the masculinization or feminization of brain and behavior was a branch of science that would not make its debut until the end of the decade.

Gender Role and Gender Identity

The term *gender role* first entered the literature and was defined in the previously cited articles (Money, 1955; Money et al., 1955). I found it not only expedient but also obligatory to coin this new term because, as a parallel to chromosomal sex or gonadal sex, a term such as *sex role sex* would make little sense. Moreover, because of the birth defect of the sex organs in hermaphroditism, the term *sex role* is needed to apply literally to the person's male or female capability with the sex organs in a sexual partnership. In traditional sex-role psychology, the term *sex role* refers to everything that differentiates male and female except the use of the sex organs.

As I originally defined it, *gender role* meant everything (literally everything, the erotosexual included) that a person says or does to indicate to the self or others his/her status as male, female, or ambiguous (androgynous). In any given case, this definition reciprocates an introspective, private self-definition, given to the self alone, with an observational and public definition arrived at by others on the basis of what they see, hear, touch, smell, or taste with respect to the person concerned.

This reciprocal definition did not take root. It split. The introspective part was renamed *gender identity.* In its most simplistic form, the term *gender identity* is defined by some who use it as the declaration "I am male" or "I am female."

The term for the observational part of the definition did not change, but the definition did: *gender role* became a social script or social stereotype to which an individual either did or did not conform.

In obedience to the nature/nurture cleavage, *gender* thus became allocated to nurture, and set off against *sex,* which became the property of nature. In this way, the vested interest of social science was left unperturbed. Social scientists claimed *gender role* for themselves. Media people and the general public followed suit, as in the political term *gender gap.* Thus the obligation to relate *gender role* to biology as well as to history and sociology was circumvented.

Biologists themselves have adopted the fashion of using the term *gender* outside of its former grammatical domain. But they use it chiefly as a harmless synonym for *sex*—as in referring to the gender of an animal. Going a step further, one biologist claimed to have found a hormonal determinant (testosterone) of gender identity at puberty (Imperato-McGinley, Guerrero, Gautier, and Peterson, 1974). And so the nature/nurture pincer tightens its grip!

The people most caught in the squeeze are those who deal with the gender-identity syndrome of transexualism, renamed gender dysphoria. Whereas, for the most part, they do not favor a social-science etiology for gender dysphoria, their hormonal data do not support the hypothesis that the testosterone level correlates with gender identity.

G-I/R: Heterosexual/Bisexual/Homosexual

My own present gender terminology forces the union of gender identity and gender role as two sides of the same coin, by using the acronym G-I/R for gender-identity/role. G-I/R has different components, one of which is erotosexual. Another is occupational, another recreational, and so on.

Erotosexually, a G-I/R may be heterosexual, bisexual (androgynous), or homosexual, or it may be transexual or transvestic. It also may or may not be paraphilic ("kinky"). It may or may not be congruous with the occupational component of G-I/R. Thus, one may, for example, say of a person that he has a homosexual G-I/R erotosexually, but not occupationally or recreationally. This avoids the conceptual diffuseness and contradiction inherent in saying that such a person has a male gender identity and a male gender role, but a homosexual preference or object choice.

Being homosexual (or bisexual or heterosexual) is not a preference or choice. It is a status—the status of having a G-I/R erotosexually concordant or discordant with the reproductive status of the genitalia, or an androgynous combination of both possibilities. The ultimate criterion of homosexual, bisexual, or heterosexual is not simply the sex of the partner with whom one's own sex organs are shared, but the sex of the partner toward whom one undergoes the experience of being love-smitten.

The person who falls in love with someone of the same genital morphology is erotosexually homosexual. He or she may procreate with a partner of the opposite sex, and may or may not appear to have an incongruous G-I/R at work and in other nonerotic, nonsexual contexts.

Sex-Irreducible G-I/R

Four grades of sexual dimorphism are found in G-I/R: sex-irreducible, sex-derivative, sex-adjunctive, and sex-arbitrary.

Among primates, the sex-irreducible difference is that males impregnate and females menstruate (which also usually means ovulate), gestate, and lactate. This division of reproductive labor holds throughout the diecious mammalian kingdom, but it does not invariably apply to diecious fishes. In many diecious fish species, an individual spends part of its lifetime breeding as a male and part breeding as a female (Chan, 1977), or vice versa. Some may alternate, more than once, their capability to produce both eggs and sperms. With each alternation is a concurrent capability of alternating the mating behavior of female and male. Both behavioral schemata are, by inference, on call in the brain and nervous system.

The concept of a brain that has encoded in it both the male and female schemata of behavior is especially well illustrated in a parthenogenetic species of whiptail lizard, *Cnemidophorus uniparens,* studied by Crews (1982). Being parthenogenetic, this species has no sex; all members of the species are clones. The clones hatch from eggs. When a lizard is in an ovulatory phase, it matches up with a nonovulatory clone, and together they simulate the behavior of mating seen in closely related diecious whiptail species. At a later phase, their roles may be reversed.

Once science uncovers the secret of the hermaphroditic versatility of sex-changing fish and parthenogenetic lizards, then on the criterion that today's science fiction becomes tomorrow's science, it will undoubtedly be applied to mammals. Thus, one can envisage a future when the sex-irreducible G-I/R will no longer be fixed and irreducible but, by a process equivalent to reverse embryogenesis, will be sex-reversible.

SEX-DERIVATIVE G-I/R

A male or female difference that is not sex-irreducible may nonetheless be derived from the difference that is irreducible. That is, it may have its origin in the same hormones that in prenatal life program the differentiation of the genitalia.

Fetal morphologic differentiation as male or female follows what may, on the basis of current knowledge, be known as the Adam/Eve principle. This principle signifies that regardless of its chromosomal sex, the primary destiny of the fetus is to become Eve, not Adam. Adam requires that something be added, namely MIH (Mullerian-inhibiting hormone) from the embryonic testes, to vestigiate the Mullerian ducts and prevent the growth of a uterus and fallopian tubes; and also testosterone, again from the testes, to induce development of the male organs.

If the testes fail to develop, a fetus will develop the genital morphology of a female, minus ovaries. An obvious sex-derivative by-product of such a deandrogenized development in the human fetus is that the baby will grow up to urinate in the sitting position. The reverse may also occur, so that an excessively androgenized 46,XX fetus with ovaries is born with a fully formed penis and empty scrotum.

When the latter condition is experimentally produced in animals, there is a species difference regarding the extent to which subsequent mating behavior will also be masculinized. The sheep has proved preprogrammed to be what I have called a hormonal robot. That is, the complete repertoire of its adult mating behavior is preprogrammed prenatally by a sex-hormonal effect on the brain. A film from Edinburgh by

Short and Clarke (no date) shows ewes impersonating rams at the first mating season. Their blood hormone levels at the time were normally female. They had been altered only in fetal life by the injection of testosterone into the pregnant mother. The timing was precisely calculated so that it was too late for the external genital morphology to be masculinized, but not too late for the sexual brain to be masculinized. Thus, the animal was preprogrammed to behave like a ram when old enough for first mating, and to be responded to as a male rival by other rams.

This same hormonal-robot effect is not seen in primates. It is also not encountered in human beings with clinical syndromes that induce prenatal masculinization. In its place is a greatly attenuated effect in the nature of a tendency or predisposition that will become incorporated into either a masculine or feminine G-I/R, in accordance with the vicissitudes of rearing as a boy or girl, respectively. The terminology I have used for these sex-derivative aspects in human beings is that they are sex-shared but threshold dimorphic. They are not dimorphic in the absolute sense of either male or female, but in the relative sense of being manifested with greater facility in one sex than the other. Parentalism is an example. Parentalism is sex-shared insofar as it is exhibited by the father as well as the mother, but is threshold dimorphic insofar as an infant or child evokes it more readily and more frequently in the mother than the father. For example, the sleeping mother is typically more sensitive to the stirrings of the neonate than is the sleeping father.

Nine Sex-Shared Threshold Dimorphisms

To date, nine phyletically basic behavioral dispositions have been isolated. Although they might appear as sexually dimorphic, they are actually sex-shared and dimorphic only in either threshold or frequency of manifestation. With the advent of new research, the list may well need to be revised.

First is kinetic-energy expenditure, which, in its more vigorous, outdoor, athletic manifestations, is typically more readily elicited and prevalent in males than in females, even before males reach the postpubertal stage of being, on the average, taller, heavier, and more lean and muscular than females.

Second is roaming and becoming familiar with or marking the boundaries of the roaming range. Whereas pheromonal (odoriferous) marking is characteristic of some small animals, in primates (including humans) vision takes the place of smell. The secretion of marker pheromones is largely under the regulation of male sex hormone and thus is more readily elicited in males than in females. The extent of a sex difference in the threshold for visual marking in primates is still conjectural.

Third is competitive rivalry and assertiveness for a position in the dominance hierarchy of childhood, which is more readily elicited in boys than in girls. A position of dominance may be accorded an individual without fighting or after a victory. Whereas fighting and aggressiveness per se are not sexually dimorphic despite a widespread scientific assumption that they are, sensitivity to eliciting stimuli may or may not be. An example of the latter is retaliation against a deserter or rival in love or friendship, which is not sex-specific.

Fourth is fighting off predators in defense of the troop and its territory, which, among primates, is typically more readily elicited in males than females.

Fifth is fighting in defense of the young, which is more readily elicited in females than males. Females are more fiercely alert and responsive to threats to their infants than are males in general.

Sixth is a provision of a nest or safe place for the delivery, care, suckling, and retrieving of the young. This variable may be associated with a greater prevalence of domestic neatness in girls than in boys, as compared with the disarray that is the product of, among other things, vigorous kinetic-energy expenditure.

Seventh is parentalism, exclusive of delivery and suckling. Retrieving, protecting, cuddling, rocking, and clinging to the young are more prevalent in girls' rehearsal play with dolls and/or playmates.

Eighth is sexual rehearsal play. Evidence from monkeys is that juvenile males elicit presentation responses in females, and juvenile females elicit mounting responses in males more readily than vice versa. The taboo on human juvenile sexual rehearsal play and its scientific investigation prohibits a definitive generalization regarding boys and girls at the present time.

Ninth is the possibility that the visual erotic image more readily elicits an initiating erotic response in males than in females, whereas the tactile stimulus more readily elicits a response in females. Here again, no definitive generalization can yet be made because of the effects of the erotic taboo and erotic stereotyping in our society.

Sex-derivative roles are, by definition, not sex-exclusive, but are sex-shared or interchangeable. Statistically there is overlap, so that extremely masculinized people of either sex resemble one another more closely than do men at either end of the scale of masculinization (and, conversely, women). In fact, men find it a severe hardship to be forced by cultural tradition into an ultramacho sex-derivative role to a degree beyond which they are, by disposition, ill-prepared.

SEX-ADJUNCTIVE G-I/R

Whereas sex-derivative is secondary to sex-irreducible G-I/R, sex-adjunctive G-I/R is tertiary. To illustrate: fetal androgen has a sex-irreducible effect in forming the male genitalia. It has also a sex-derivative effect in setting thresholds for certain constituents of behavior that are manifested more prevalently, or with more facility, in the play of boys than of girls. With puberty, androgen reasserts its sex-irreducible effect, although it can be attenuated or, by castration, interrupted. It governs the maturation of the male reproductive system, and also the growth of bone, fatty tissue, and muscle in such a way that males—on the average, and despite much overlap with females—are more muscularly powerful than females, on the basis of being taller and leaner. Thus, in all the millennia prior to the modern age of industrial, farming, and domestic labor-saving devices, it made sense for societies to have a sex-based division of labor.

This division of labor was, in ancient times, based on the greater mobility of the male as compared with the restricted mobility of the female while pregnant or breast-feeding. Women moved in closer proximity to the home base than men, and they were chiefly responsible for feeding not only their babies but all members of their troop. The men ranged more widely in hunting, fighting, and trading. This ancient division of labor survived the partial equalization of the sexes made possible first by the domestication of animals of transport. It is surviving less well the mechanization of transport by land, sea, and air, the invention of automated and computerized laborsaving devices, and the discovery of infant-feeding formulas, prepared baby foods, and ready-to-eat meals for the family.

The age-old division of labor has also been rendered anachronistic by the invention of contraception, which permits an abbreviated breeding period. Fewer births are needed because infant mortality is down, and a world already exploding with population needs a smaller next generation.

Added to these population dynamics is the dramatic increase in longevity from an average age of thirty-five in 1776 to around seventy or older today. Adulthood begins earlier, with the age of puberty having lowered by four months per decade for a century and a half or longer. These life-span changes mean that men and women have longer adult lives in which not to be enchained to the obligation of a sex-stereotyped division of labor in order to ensure that they will successfully launch a family in their formerly short life span. They have more years in which to do different types of work.

These tides of change that have set in motion the destereotyping of sex-adjunctive roles have also provoked a backlash. Most of the current feuding and political debate about equal rights for men and women rage around social, legal, and economic rights and restrictions of sex-adjunctive work roles and play roles.

Science has been drawn into this dispute. Funding for research on the psychology of sex differences, on closer scrutiny, turns out to be funding for research in sex differences in work or play. The current fashion is to research these differences in terms of aggression, delinquency, emotionality, learning disability, space-form perception, verbal ability, mathematical ability, and homosexuality in relation to sex differences in hormone levels, age of pubertal onset, and brain lateralization. All too often, the hidden assumption behind such research is that if a biological (physical or organic) correlate can be found, then the difference is one of real nature, and not of trivial nurture—an assumption that requires a blind adulation of biology. It is totally oblivious to the critical-period hypothesis and to the possibility that, in some instances, that which is postnatally learned becomes permanently encoded in the brain.

Sex-Arbitrary G-I/R

To a visitor from another planet, political and scientific feuding about sex-derivative G-I/R could well seem incomprehensible, but its incomprehensibility would be minor in comparison with that engendered by militancy over sex-arbitrary roles. Sex-arbitrary roles pertain to issues of sex-divergent body language, ornamentation, grooming, clothing, and etiquette. Often some sort of connection can be conjectured between sex-arbitrary and sex-adjunctive roles. For example, the former Polynesian custom of restricting the amount of tattoo a woman might have on her face as compared with that of a man ostensibly reflected her lesser bravery as a warrior. In fact, it signified her role as a lesser warrior who might fight only in defense of the tribal home territory when it was under attack by the enemy, whereas the male traveled far to maraud and initiate attack.

The ancient and widespread custom of the greater mobility of men has also been reflected in the footwear of women. Until the 1949 Communist revolution in China, families who aspired to wealth and prestige deformed the feet of their young daughters by binding them. These daughters were a living testament to their fathers' wealth, and also to that of their prospective husbands, because their deformed feet rendered them incapable of working competitively with men; henceforth, they could work only as courtesans or prostitutes. Today, in our own society, we have an adumbration of this custom of deformed feet in the fashion of high-heeled shoes for women which hobble their gait and enforce a method of locomotion that men may interpret as needing their support.

The contemporary American customs of feminine decoration can be traced to an earlier era in which aristocratic women were idle display models, exhibiting the wealth of their fathers or husbands. Now that women work and have their own wealth, women may opt to abandon cosmetic and jewelry decoration, or their male partners may opt to be decorated similarly. The furor in the 1960s regarding long hairstyles for males as well as females alienated many fathers from their own sons as effectively as if long hair were a badge of homosexual effeminacy, even though the new style also dictated a macho mustache and beard as a badge of masculinity. Here is certain evidence of the pervasive extent to which the superficialities of male and female permeate the average person's perception—or misperception—of irreducible masculinity and femininity. *Misperception* is the correct term: The average person, including the average scientist or physician, is not accustomed to differentiating the constituents of G-I/R that are not erotosexual from those that are.

Identification/Complementation

The constituents of G-I/R that are sex-arbitrary, and likewise those that are sex-adjunctive, become incorporated into the G-I/R totality by a joint process of assimilation and learning, namely identification and complementation. Identification is a familiar concept in psychology to signify learning that takes shape by copying, imitating, or replicating an example or model. In learning the sex-arbitrary conventions of couple dancing, for example, a girl identifies with a female dancer and a boy with a male dancer. The girl then complements her dancing to that of a male partner, and the boy to that of a female.

Complementation is not yet a familiar concept in psychology. I first became aware of the necessity of the concept on the basis of an account given to me by a father whose hermaphroditic child was sex-reassigned at the age of eighteen months. When she was three years old, the child made a boisterous game of copying her older brother's rock-and-roll dancing. Her father spent time with his two children when he arrived home from work. His impulse was to have his daughter dance with him as a partner more sedately. Initially she resisted, in favor of copying her big-shot brother. After a few evenings, when her brother became a rival for the father's attention, she was won over. The father's lesson to his son was that little boys copy their fathers, but dance with their mothers, and little girls copy their mothers, but dance with their fathers. He was aware of the role he was playing as a partial architect of G-I/R. The mother did not actually have to be there in person; she could have been symbolically represented as if present.

Complementation or identification each builds up its own representation or schema in the brain, and each becomes incorporated with its sex-derivative counterpart; but a sex-irreducible counterpart exists for only one of the pair, namely the identification schema coded "this is me." The complementation schema is coded "this is other," the reciprocal of "me." Complementation and identification schemas exist not only for gender, but also for age, social class, hierarchical authority, and so on.

The two gender schemata, male and female, exist compatibly in the brains of most people, one dominant over the other, their dual presence scarcely recognized. To encounter the duality, one needs a special syndrome—for example, transvestism of the type that is characterized by two names, two wardrobes, and two personalities, one male and one female (Money, 1974).

In some instances, this syndrome evolves to the point at which the complementation and identification schemata become permanently transposed (although the sex-irreducible constituent remains unchanged). Then the syndrome becomes one of the forms of transexualism. Eventually, the patient is likely to make an application for sex-reassignment.

The transposition phenomena include also the little-known syndrome of the woman with a penis, for which I have coined the term *gynemimesis.* This syndrome is close to transexualism, whereby the person lives and passes as a woman and takes female hormones, but does not apply for surgical sex-reassignment. In street argot, the syndrome is subsumed under the rubric "drag queen," which recognizes its relationship to extreme homosexual effeminacy of the G-I/R.

The counterpart argot for females is "butch dyke," for which the formal syndrome name is *andromimesis.* Although the andromimetic may apply for mastectomy, sex-reassignment genital surgery is not sought, and hormonal virilization is rare.

The more partial degrees of G-I/R transposition manifest themselves as the varied phenomenology of homosexual and bisexual G-I/R. These phenomena are not designated as syndromes. They are now officially classified as typological distinctions, analogous to left-handedness and ambidextrousness.

Masculinization and Defeminization Are Not Synonymous

The coexistence of identification and complementation schemata in the brain parallels the biphasic alternation of masculine and feminine in sex-changing fish and in parthenogenetic lizards, as previously mentioned. Another parallel is found in mammalian prenatal experiments demonstrating that masculinization of the fetal brain is not automatically synonymous with defeminization, nor is feminization with demasculinization (Ward, 1972, 1977; Ward and Weisz, 1980; Baum, 1979; Baum, Gallagher, Martin, and Damassa, 1982).

Applied to behavior, these experiments mean that prepotency of sexual mounting in an animal with a masculinized brain is compatible with a lesser potency of sexual crouching or presenting. Whether the one or the other will manifest itself will depend partly on the strength, insistence, timing, or context of the external evoking stimulus, and partly on the internal status of the arousal threshold.

Erotosexual Rehearsal Play

Juvenile erotosexual rehearsal play is one of the sex-shared/threshold dimorphic constituents of G-I/R in the sex-derivative category. It is subject also to some sex-adjunctive overlay, insofar as it can be affected by the sex ratio of the agemate play group.

The chief source of empirical data on juvenile erotosexual rehearsal play is the Wisconsin Regional Primate Center, where juvenile rhesus monkeys have been studied. Isolation-reared monkeys are deprived of play and grow up unable to perform their part in the strategy of mating (Goldfoot, 1977). Consequently, they do not reproduce their species. Males are more vulnerable to impairment as a consequence of play deprivation than are females.

Impairment is partly offset by as little as a half hour daily of agemate play. Given this opportunity, about one-third of the young ones became competent in foot-clasp mounting and in presenting, as male and female, respectively. Whereas the juveniles not deprived of play achieved such competency by the age of six to nine months, those permitted only a half hour of play a day did not achieve the same competency until as late as eighteen to twenty-four months of age. Despite their success, the retardation had a still later effect on their breeding success, for they had an abnormally low birth rate. The two-thirds of their unsuccessful age-mates continued to be unsuccessful as adults. They produced no offspring; they either did not mate or were incompetent when they attempted to do so.

Juvenile sexual rehearsal play and adult sexual interaction are also related to the sex ratio of playmates (Goldfoot, Wallen, Neff, McBrair, and Goy, 1984). In sex-segregated experiments, baby monkeys were reared with their mothers and with agemates of only their own sex. Males in the all-male group showed more rear-end presenting and less foot-clasp mounting than did those in the male/female group. Conversely, females in the all-female group showed a significant excess of foot-clasp mounting and a decrease of rear-end presenting. The conspicuous effect of segregated rearing on the aforesaid changes in sexual rehearsal play was an increase in heterotypical sexual play: males did more presenting and females more mounting than did their counterparts in the mixed-sex group.

The relationship of juvenile sexual rehearsal play to adult G-I/R in human beings has a history of insufficient research. It may well play an extremely influential role as a critical-period phenomenon wherein nature and nurture merge to establish future erotosexual health, male and female. Heterosexual rehearsal play, without question, establishes the primacy of the sex organs and their use as the definitive criterion of the difference between male and female. Children who grow up secure and confident in the immutability of this primary difference can be equally secure and confident in the mutability of other sex differences that are secondary and more or less arbitrary products of social and historical stereotyping. For them, adherence or nonadherence to these stereotypes is arbitrary or optional. Thus, they have the option of sex-sharing, free from the threat that male/female equality will somehow rob them of their quintessential identity and status as girl or boy, man or woman.

Acknowledgments

Supported by USPHS Grant HD00325 and funds from the William T. Grant Foundation.

References

Baum, M. J. (1979). "Differentiation of coital behavior in mammals: A comparative analysis." *Neuroscience and Biobehavioral Reviews* 3:265–84.

Baum, M. J., Gallagher, C. A., Martin, J. T., and Damassa, D. A. (1982). "Effects of testosterone, dihydrotestosterone, or estradiol administered neonatally on sexual behavior of female ferrets." *Endocrinology* 3:773–80.

Chan, S. T. H. (1977). "Spontaneous sex reversal in fishes." In *Handbook of Sexology* (J. Money and H. Musaph, eds.). Amsterdam: Excerpta Medica.

Crews, D. (1982). "On the origin of sexual behavior." *Psychoneuroendocrinology* 7:259–70.

Dorland's Illustrated Medical Dictionary (26th edition.). (1981). Philadelphia: Saunders.

Goldfoot, D. A. (1977). "Sociosexual behaviors of nonhuman primates during development and maturity: Social and hormonal relationships." In *Behavioral Primatology: Advances in Research and Theory, Volume 1* (A. M. Schrier, ed.). Hillsdale, NJ: Lawrence Erlbaum.

Goldfoot, D. A., Wallen, K., Neff, D. A., McBrair, M. D., and Goy, R. W. (1984). "Social influences upon the display of sexually dimorphic behavior in rhesus monkeys: Isosexual rearing." *Archives of Sexual Behavior* 13:395–412.

Imperato-McGinley, J., Guerrero, L., Gautier, T., and Peterson, R. E. (1974). "Steroid 5α-reductase deficiency in man: An inherited form of male pseudohermaphroditism." *Science* 186:1213–15.

Money, J. (1952). *Hermaphroditism: An Inquiry into the Nature of a Human Paradox.* Cambridge: Harvard University Library (Ann Arbor: University Microfilms, 1967).

———. (1955). "Hermaphroditism, gender, and precocity in hyperadrenocorticism: Psychologic findings." *Bulletin of The Johns Hopkins Hospital* 96:253–64.

———. (1974). "Intersexual and transexual behavior and syndromes." In *American Handbook of Psychiatry, Volume 3* (S. Arieti and E. B. Brady, eds.). New York: Basic Books.

———. (1974). "Two names, two wardrobes, two personalities." *Journal of Homosexuality* 1:65–70.

Money, J., and Ehrhardt, A. A. (1972). *Man and Woman, Boy and Girl: The Differentiation and Dimorphism of Gender Identity from Conception to Maturity.* Baltimore: Johns Hopkins University Press. Facsimile reprint edition, New York: Jason Aronson, 1996.

Money, J., Hampson, J. G., and Hampson, J. L. (1955). "An examination of some basic sexual concepts: The evidence of human hermaphroditism." *Bulletin of The Johns Hopkins Hospital,* 97:301–19.

Short, R. V., and Clarke, I. J. (no date). *Masculinization of the Female Sheep.* Distributed by R. V. Short, MRC Reproductive Biology Unit, 2 Forrest Road, Edinburgh EH1 2QW, Scotland, U.K.

Ward, I. L. (1972). "Prenatal stress feminizes and demasculinizes the behavior of males." *Science* 175:82–84.

———. (1977). "Exogenous androgen activates female behavior in noncopulating, prenatally stressed male rats." *Journal of Comparative and Physiological Psychology* 91:465–71.

Ward, I. L., and Weisz, J. (1980). "Maternal stress alters plasma testosterone in fetal males." *Science* 207:328–29.

5

Manhood and Womanhood in Conflict: Fin de Siècle Report

THE NEUTERING OF GENDER

Popular wisdom has long summed up the frustrations and exasperations of the man/woman relationship in the men's epigram: "Women—you can't live with them, and you can't live without them." The women's reciprocal, "Men—you can't live with them, and you can't live without them," is used less. The imbalance in usage is in itself an indication of the traditional imbalance in the overt versus covert, direct versus devious male/female power ratio.

Rectification of imbalance in overt power commenced in the eighteenth century with Mary Wollstonecraft's essay, *A Vindication of the Rights of Woman* (1792). The first wave of the women's movement accelerated after the mid-nineteenth century, its agenda being to secure voting rights for women. A century later, the second wave began. It is directed toward equal legal, vocational, and economic rights, and is more advanced in industrialized nations than in those of the Third World.

The social and political history of the male/female balance of human rights for the past half century is irrevocably bound to the lexical history of the word *gender.* Before 1955, *gender* was a philolog-

---

Written for the Third Asian Conference of Sexology, New Delhi, India, November 27–December 1, 1994.

ical and grammatical term. After 1955, it entered the language as a sexological term and rapidly became assimilated into the vernacular as an attribute of human beings, male and female. In its sexological sense it was first used in the *Bulletin of The Johns Hopkins Hospital* (Money, 1955) to encompass all those attributes that define a person's role in life as masculine or feminine, even if the sex organs are, by reason of accident or birth defect, missing, malformed, or incongruous with the other components of the gender role.

Since 1955, *gender* has assumed two additional meanings. One is as a synonym or substitute for *sex,* male or female. The other is as a partial substitute which signifies that sex is politically neutered or castrated, like the sex of the Barbie doll, as popular as ever on her thirtieth birthday in 1994. With her companion, Ken, she has nothing between the legs. Otherwise, the two are exaggeratedly feminine and masculine, respectively.

Politically neutered gender does not, of course, bring about politically equalized genital and procreative sex which are male/female reciprocal. Equalization would require that male and female genital and procreative sex could be homogenized, which is impossible. It is also impossible for masculine sexuality to be feminized—or conversely, for feminine sexuality to be masculinized. Even hormonal and surgical sex-reassignment in transexualism achieves that only partially.

In the first wave of the feminist movement, women's sexuality was sacrificed. Officially, the idealized Victorian lady had no carnal desire and lust. In the second and current wave, the pressure of sacrifice is on men. Men's sexuality is equated with carnal desire and lust, and women's with romantic love and affection. Men's sexuality is characterized increasingly as being synonymous with violence, rape, harassment in the workplace, child abuse, incest, pornography, and oppression of women.

Men's sexuality is under siege. Instead of an increase in sexual and erotic reciprocity between men and women, there is an incoming tide of alienation and distrust. For example, in her attack on men, polemicist Andrea Dworkin (1987) views acts of sexual intercourse as being pervaded with hatred, contempt, and force. This absurdity has been echoed even within the ranks of professional sexology, as in Andrea Parrot's statement that "any sexual intercourse without mutual desire is a form of rape. Anyone who is psychologically or physically pressured into sexual conduct is as much a victim of rape as the person who is attacked in the streets" (quoted in Gutmann, 1993).

The outcome of the attack on men's sexuality could be a backlash that would slow or reverse the momentum toward greater equality between the sexes. Or, conversely, it could be an increase in inequality in favor of the 51 percent female majority of the population who are women. The majority might select and sequester a few men as breeding studs; the remainder would be disposable.

That the male will become disposable is an unlikely outcome, however, insofar as men and women truly do undergo the experience of falling in love and becoming affectionately and lustfully pair-bonded. This is the experience of limerence (Tennov, 1974), which is phylogenetically built into our species.

In the absence of a mutually satisfactory reciprocity between males and females, children will be the ones who pay the price. Sexual and erotic discord in the adult generation induces an epidemic of developmental sexological pathologies in the juvenile generation. That epidemic is today part of the penalty exacted for the inequities between men and women that trace back to, and antedate, the nineteenth century. The penalty is exacted worldwide, not only in America and Europe.

Sexology's Nineteenth-Century Heritage

In the nineteenth century, medical sexology was still dominated by Tissot's eighteenth-century theory of degeneracy brought on by semen wastage. Simon André Tissot's treatise was first published in Latin in 1758. It went through multiple French and British editions prior to the first American edition (1832/1974), translated as *A Treatise on the Diseases Produced by Onanism.*

Although he wrote about the "social vice" of promiscuity and prostitution, Tissot was in fact in search of a way to control the epidemic of the "social disease" which had not yet been subdivided into syphilis and gonorrhea, as it would be after the discovery of germ theory in the 1870s. The theory of semen depletion is found in ancient Chinese medical teaching of the yin-and-yang principle, and in Indian Ayurvedic medical texts and oral traditions dating back two and a half thousand years and more. Semen depletion became the cornerstone of Tissot's thesis. In Ayurvedic teaching, semen is the most concentrated and powerful source of *sukra,* the vital spirit, and its depletion is a source of illness and eventual death.

Tissot correctly recognized the symptoms of syphilis and gonorrhea alone or in combination, and he correctly associated them with promiscuity in the patronage and performance of prostitution. He also recognized the symptoms in the affected offspring of prostitutes. His colossal intellectual error was to equate the loss of semen in the social vice of promiscuity with its loss in the secret vice of masturbation. This error released a two-hundred-year cascade of medical, moral, and religious antisexual mania. Masturbation was the chief culprit, but conjugal depletion of semen was an offender, too. The conjugal ideal was that sexual intercourse should be performed infrequently and only for procreation, not for pleasure.

By not having semen, women were viewed as having less vital spirit and less physical and mental energy than men. It was necessary for a wife to conserve not only her own quota of vital spirit, but also to be the guardian of her husband's supply by not consenting to sexual intercourse too often. This was her duty irrespective of her own enjoyment and orgasmic capability—witness the evidence of the recently discovered interview data of the late nineteenth-/early twentieth-century physician, Clelia Mosher (Mahood and Wenburg, 1980).

The self-appointed expert on the sexology of the Victorian woman was William Acton, a British surgeon known as an authority on venereal disease, prostitution, chastity, and masturbation (as well as honeybee copulation). He wrote in 1857, and in six later editions of his book until 1875, as follows:

> I should say that the majority of women, happily for them ["and for society," says the fifth edition] are not very much troubled with sexual feeling of any kind. What men are habitually, women are only exceptionally. . . . The best mothers, wives, and managers of households know little or nothing of sexual indulgences. Love of home, of children, of domestic duties, are the only passions they feel. As a general rule, a modest woman seldom desires any sexual gratification for herself. She submits to her husband, but only to please him; and but for the desire of maternity, would far rather be relieved from his attention (pp. 473–74).

Victorian sexological dogma met with strong approval in many home-doctor books, as well as books of sex and marriage hygiene written by doctors and endorsed by preachers. One extremely influential author in the latter part of the nineteenth century was John Harvey Kellogg, M.D., a great admirer of Acton. He was fanatical about semen conservation and the reduction of carnal desire, which he attributed to a carnivorous diet. To avoid meat on the menu of his Battle Creek Sanitarium, Kellogg substituted nut and cereal products. He developed and marketed breakfast cereals, including Kellogg's corn flakes, as lust suppressants and masturbation-preventative health foods.

The voice of antisexualism survived with vehemence into the twentieth century. One of its prestigious exponents was the famed Howard A. Kelly, M.D., founding professor of gynecology at the then-new Johns Hopkins University School of Medicine. The *Journal of the American Medical Association* (*JAMA*) had rejected a very enlightened and scientifically explicit article on female sexuality read in 1899 by Denslow Lewis, M.D., a professor of gynecology in Chicago. In the debate that followed in the American Medical Association (AMA), Kelly went on written record in 1900 as follows:

> I do not believe pleasure in the sexual act has any particular bearing on the happiness of life; that is the lowest possible view of happiness in married life. . . . Its discussion is attended with more or less filth and we besmirch ourselves by discussing it in public (quoted in Money, 1985).

Lewis defended a woman's right to undiluted sexual lust and orgasm. Three years earlier (1896), Alice B. Stockham, M.D., had idealized a more quiescent form of prolonged, nonorgasmic genital union which she named *karezza* (from the same root as *caress*). It was a new name for an ancient Tantric practice, and also for what John Humphrey Noyes (1872) termed "male continence." Noyes was leader of the Oneida Community in upstate New York, known for its practice of group marriage. For Victorian ladies, *karezza* combined the "exquisite exaltation" of genteel sex with the bonus of birth control—provided it was augmented, in case of necessity, by coitus interruptus.

Even though *karezza* had few adherents, it nonetheless carried the same message as did the defeat of Lewis in his AMA debate with Kelly and others, namely that the women's movement must put aside whatever unabashed demands women might have for sexual rights so that sexual rights would not confound and contaminate the demand for voting rights. Otherwise, suffragists would have Acton's "vile aspersions" cast upon them as loose women and harlots. To gain the vote, women were obliged to deprive themselves of the fulsomeness of their sexuality, at least insofar as their public utterances were concerned. A century later, the tables would be turned and men would have their sexuality under feminist attack.

Sexualization of Oppression

Sexuality made its first appearance in the feminist movement as a borrowing from the sexual-liberation movement. For example, Kate Millet wrote in her book *Sexual Politics* (1969):

> A sexual revolution would require an end of traditional sexual inhibitions and taboos, particularly those that most threaten patriarchal monogamous marriage: homosexuality, illegitimacy, and adolescent, premarital and extramarital sexuality. The negative aura with which sexual activities have generally been surrounded would necessarily be eliminated, together with the double standard and prostitution. The goal of revolution would be a permissive single standard of sexual freedom.

As it gained momentum in the 1970s, the feminist movement, although patterned after other liberation movements, had no explicitly identified equivalent of colonial oppressors—except that, as in Kate Millet's statement, oppression of women was attributed generically to institutionalized patriarchical domination. Then a change took place: Oppression became explicitly sexualized. Male domination was equated with male lust. The change was epitomized in Susan Brownmiller's book *Against Our Will* (1975), which paved the way for the reductio ad absurdum in which Andrea Dworkin equated all acts of sexual intercourse with acts of rape. "Violence is male," she wrote; "the male is the penis; violence is the penis" (Dworkin, 1979/1989). The same author also wrote:

> By thrusting into her, [the male] takes her over. His thrusting into her is taken to be her capitulation to him as conqueror; it is a physical surrender of herself to him; he occupies and rules her, expresses his elemental dominance over her, by his possession of her in the fuck (Dworkin, 1987, p. 63).

Radical extremism of the Dworkin type may have appealed to the sensation-hungry media and to a small faction of the man-hating lunatic fringe, but not to feminists who bore no grudge against men, nor to the men with whom they pairbonded. Ordinary people responded not to the rhetoric of metaphorical rape but to its counterpart, the rhetoric of criminal rape.

In radical feminism, rape was radically redefined by fiat as being not an act of sexual assault or coercion, but an act of male violence and aggression perpetrated against women. Demands for increased legal sanctions against not only stranger rape, but also against the newly decreed offenses of date rape and marital rape, were met by new legislation. Paradoxically, the feminist movement gave its opponents—namely antiliberationist women like Phyllis Schlafly with her Eagle Forum and archconservative men defending patriarchal authority—the first inch of the mile they would need to uphold the tradition that woman, the weaker sex, is dependent on man's power of protection. Women were surreptitiously being returned to the role of victims and martyrs—helpless, incompetent, and unable to fend for themselves.

Politicization of Pornography

The next inch of the return to victimhood and martyrdom was ceded in 1979 by Women Against Pornography, a subgroup from within the ranks of radical feminism. This organization has been conspicuously silent on what constitutes women's pornography, implying by its silence that there is no such commodity. Women Against Pornography have been sexologically naive in not knowing that normal female erotic arousal is predominantly tactile or haptic, whereas normal male erotic arousal is predominantly visual. Correspondingly, normal female pornography is predominantly narrative and romantic in imagery, whereas normal male pornography is predominantly pictorial and explicitly erotic in imagery.

Women Against Pornography have been sexologically naive also in not knowing that the full range and role of visual imagery in normal men's erotic arousal is not identical with what is depicted in commercial pornography, and that much of what is depicted is designed to appeal to specific audiences of sexual deviance.

Women Against Pornography could have been deliberately duped by antifeminist undercover agents assigned to deprive all women of independence by misleading them into fearing all masculine carnality and lust as dangerous. An alternative and more positive strategy would have been directed toward the improvement of the quality and appeal of the products of the pornography industry for not only male but also female viewers and audiences, which is now in fact happening to a certain extent.

The diverse types of imagery in commercial pornography are not universal but selective in their appeal. Gay men's pornography, for instance, does not appeal to straight men. Sadomasochistic pornography does not appeal to male viewers who are not already sadomasochistic, and the majority of males are not. Pornography does not convert ordinary, decent men into beasts who are dangerous to women.

The truth is that commercial pornography caters not to a random sample of ordinary people, but to selective samples of those who have one or another specific bias as to what is erotically arousing. The largest audience is biased toward specific sexual practices like oral sex and completely naked display that, although not deviant, are not engaged in at home, perhaps for religious, moral, or phobic reasons. Other, smaller audiences are separately biased toward one of the kinky (paraphilic or perverted) sexual scenarios that are unacceptable and an erotic turn-off to the partner at home.

Women Against Pornography failed to allow for the fact that, with no competition from big-budget filmmakers, commercial pornography seldom invests in the costly business of dramatically depicting genuine lovers, long-term relationships, authentic erotic ecstasy, and unfaked female orgasms. Instead, it does invest in low-budget, short-encounter sex which commonly depicts sexual scenarios of the disinhibited type that might be engaged in, not at home, but only with a paid partner, without romantic build-up and preliminary loveplay.

The images of commercial pornography that are paraphilically kinky or deviant appeal only to those people who have the same paraphilia. Sadism and masochism (S/M), already mentioned, are examples. Depictions of S/M leave non–S/M people cold. S/M, like all paraphilic sex, is not contagious; it cannot be caught from pictures or videos. S/M pornography does not incite non–S/M viewers into becoming sexual monsters.

Radical feminism is wrong in asserting that commercial pornography teaches males to denigrate women, to use them as sex objects, and to eroticize their power over women. That is putting the cart before the horse. If males have been conditioned since boyhood to denigrate, objectify, or sexually abuse females (a lesson that females learn to reciprocate), then men will be attracted to pornography that does the same—otherwise, not.

Women Against Pornography made a great tactical blunder in forming an alliance with the religiously political New Right, as represented in the U.S., at the time, by Jerry Falwell's Moral Majority and subsequently by Pat Robertson's Christian Coalition. This alliance was the equivalent of hauling the wooden horse of Troy into the citadel, filled this time with antifeminist fanatics only too eager to fight feminism with the weapon of antipornography. Women, they said, were too morally delicate to be exposed to men's pornography; they needed masculine power and authority to protect them from its evils, which the New Right—in collaboration with governmental policy and judicial censorship—would all too willingly provide.

At the same time that the New Right conspired to undermine sexual liberation and to suppress the freedom from censorship of sexual expression, it conspired also to help halt women's liberation and to bring about the eventual defeat of the Equal Rights Amendment on June 30, 1982.

REVIVAL OF SEDUCTION THEORY

In the 1960s, child abuse was rediscovered and renamed the battered-child syndrome. Abusive violence and neglect in childhood became extended to include child sexual abuse. This in turn raised the issue of Freud's abandonment of his prepsychoanalytic seduction theory, in which sexual abuse was an actuality in the childhood history (Masson, 1985). Freud's replacement for the seduction theory was the psychoanalytic theory of neurosis, in which childhood seduction occurred only in fantasy, the fantasy of the Oedipus complex.

There is no dispute that there are two versions of Freud's formulation of the cause of neurosis. In the 1885 version, the cause was childhood seduction, defined literally as a genital encounter with an older, possibly incestuous person. In the 1897 version, the cause became an oedipal fantasy of childhood seduction, maybe vivid enough to be subsequently recalled as actually having occurred.

Freud left no record explaining the change. Masson, attacking the Freudian establishment from within (he was director of the Freud

Archives), alleged the change to have been an expedient and fraudulent repudiation of the truth. A more likely explanation, however, is that the change was contingent on a great theoretical expansion toward which Freud had been groping, away from causality based on sporadically occurring and extrinsic happenstance, and toward causality based on universally occurring and intrinsic, phylogenetically determined intrapsychic development. Formulated as the theory of the Oedipus complex, the expanded version became the psychoanalytic theory of all of human nature, not only of neurosis.

Masson put the seal of approval on the deconstruction of Oedipal theory and filled the void thus created by reinstating seduction theory to explain the origin of neurotic and other psychopathological symptoms as the post-traumatic residual of a history of sexual abuse in childhood. The origin of the sexual abuser's own pathology, however, was left unexplained by Masson. Instead, the practice of sexual abuse was attributed—as it still is today—to the abuser's heretical choice of error and personal responsibility for his own criminality.

Victimology: The Criminalization of Sex

Jeffrey Masson and prior opponents of the medical model like Thomas Szasz (1961), Michel Foucault (1963/1973), and Ivan Illich (1976) are entrapped in an inherent Catch-22 of the new philosophy of constructionism and deconstructionism. The trap is that, ostensibly in the name of personal responsibility and freedom of choice, a person is released from the ideological tyranny of the medical system, only to be deprived of personal responsibility and freedom of choice under the ideological tyranny of the criminal-justice system. The headlines declare "Demedicalization, Freedom, and Responsibility," but the bottom line is "Criminalization, Totalitarianism, and Retribution."

Deconstruction of the medical model, by opening the way for new construction, has led to a proliferation of new entities based on the moral model of criminology. Among the new entities are sexual addiction, date or acquaintance rape, spouse rape, and sexual abuse of juveniles by juveniles. In the absence of any substantiating evidence, there is also alleged fetal and infant sacrifice and sexual abuse of children in satanic cult rituals.

The revival of Freud's seduction theory gave, with Masson's express blessing, a retroactive underpinning of prestige to the victimology movement. Victimology had been legitimized in the child-protection laws of the 1970s. Child-protection agencies are set up not within the health-care system, but the criminal-justice system. Respect for the sanctity of motherhood and the family, and for the right of parents to administer discipline, make it more difficult to prosecute violent abuse than sexual abuse. Hence, victimology has become biased toward sexual abuse. Its ideological principles and terminology are borrowed predominantly from the criminal-justice system. Instead of patients or clients, victimology has perpetrators of abuse and victims or survivors of abuse. Instead of diagnosis, it has validation of abuse by validators who practice disclosure therapy, which may include enforced disclosure of confabulatory memories, false accusations, and false confessions. Confabulations of sexual abuse are extracted from very young children with "anatomically correct" dolls as stage properties, the likes of which have been strictly prohibited as indecent in most children's prior experience.

In victimology, childhood sexual abuse is an etiological catch-all for many different symptoms. It is, by definition, invariably experienced as traumatic stress, and its outcome, although variable, is diagnosed as post-traumatic-stress disorder (PTSD). The symptoms may appear concurrently with the stress or be delayed in the onset, even for years. When the recollection is delayed, memories of abuse are said to have been "repressed" or the victim to have been "in denial." What appears to be recalled may prove to be confabulation. Multiple-personality disorder (MPD) is a frequent diagnosis. The validity of MPD is much disputed by its opponents, who attribute it to an iatrogenic (that is, a therapist's treatment-induced) origin. In cases of MPD, it may be noted in passing that it is common for one of the "alters" to have a gender role, masculine or feminine, discordant with that of the other or others.

Social Constructionism

Contemporary victimology theory incorporates Foucault's social constructionist theory not, as he had done, to expose the ideological relativity of the meaning of sexuality in history, but as a theory by which to deconstruct existing theories—especially so-called essentialist theories —of the origin of psychopathology. Essentialist theories are identified by social constructionists as biological and biomedical, and are vehemently opposed by them. Deconstruction of essentialist theory contains, however, an inescapable dilemma. The architect of any deconstructionist argument becomes the prophet of reconstruction only until the prophet is himself or herself deconstructed. The outcome is eventual academic chaos, which has led some scholars to designate social constructionism as the new, postmodern, intellectual obscurantism.

Social constructionism has divested itself of any explanations of human sexuality that utilize biological or medical conceptions. In doing so, it has put itself in the position, inadvertently or otherwise, of postulating that an individual is wholly responsible for his/her own sexuality. In other words, the expression of sexuality is a matter of voluntary choice, and so is its suppression. Unacceptable sexual behavior that medical scientists would call pathological, constructionists would either condone or criminalize. But the criminalization of sexual behavior does not lead to its rectification. Moreover, when criminalization is biased toward man-bashing, as currently it is, it certainly obscures the multiplex issues of manhood and womanhood in conflict, and of how to bring about a fair and equitable distribution of power and reciprocity of sexuality between men and women in the century ahead.

The paradox of constructionist man-bashing rhetoric is, in fact, that women are being reverted back again into the role of martyrdom, masochism, and inability to cope with men's sexuality. Constructionism is more effective in robbing men and women of equality than it is of recruiting them into relationships of nonexploitative reciprocality. Men's look-and-see, visual sexuality and women's touch-and-feel, haptic sexuality cannot be made identical, but they are able to function very well together reciprocally. What the twenty-first century needs is for men's and women's sexuality to be genuinely and concordantly mutual—not identical, not opposed, but mutually reciprocal. Success is within reach, but few are the arms that presently reach out to grasp it as the twentieth century comes to a close.

References

Acton, W. (1875). *The Functions and Disorders of the Reproductive Organs in Childhood, Youth, Adult Age, and Advanced Age, Considered in Their Physiological, Social, and Moral Relations* (6th edition). Philadelphia: Presley Blakiston.

Brownmiller, S. (1975). *Against Our Will: Men, Women and Rape*. New York: Simon & Schuster.

Dworkin, A. (1979). *Pornography: Men Possessing Women*. New York: Perigee. In paperback, New York: E.P. Dutton, 1989.

———. (1987). *Intercourse*. New York: Free Press.

Foucault, M. (1963). *The Birth of the Clinic: An Archaeology of Medical Perception*. (Translated from *Naissance de la Clinique: Une Archeologie du Regard Medical*. Paris: Presses Universitaires de France.) New York: Pantheon, 1973.

Gutmann, S. (1993). "Are all men rapists? The new Violence Against Women Act is sexual politics with a vengeance." *National Review* 45(16):44–47.

Illich, I. (1976). *Medical Nemesis: The Expropriation of Health*. New York: Pantheon.

Mahood J., and Wenberg, K. (1980). *The Mosher Survey: Sexual Attitudes of Forty-Five Victorian Women*. New York: Arno Press.

Masson, J. M. (1985). *The Assault on Truth: Freud's Suppression of the Seduction Theory*. New York: Penguin Books.

Millet, K. (1969). *Sexual Politics*. New York: Doubleday.

Money, J. (1955). "Hermaphroditism, gender and precocity in hyperadrenocorticism: Psychologic findings." *Bulletin of The Johns Hopkins Hospital* 96:253–64.

———. (1985). *The Destroying Angel: Sex, Fitness and Food in the Legacy of Degeneracy Theory, Graham Crackers, Kellogg's Corn Flakes and American Health History*. Amherst, NY: Prometheus Books.

Noyes, J. H. (1872). *Male Continence, or Self-Control in Sexual Intercourse*. Oneida, NY: Office of Oneida Circular. Facsimile reprint edition in *Sexual Indulgence and Denial: Variations on Continence* (C. Rosenberg and C. Smith-Rosenberg, eds.). New York: Arno Press, 1974.

Stockham, A. B. (1974). *Karezza: Ethics of Marriage*. Chicago: Stockham Publishing Co., 1896. Facsimile reprint edition in *Sexual Indulgence and Denial: Variations on Continence* (C. Rosenberg and C. Smith-Rosenberg, eds.). New York: Arno Press.

Szasz, T. (1961). *The Myth of Mental Illness: Foundations of a Theory of Personal Conduct*. New York: Hoeber-Harper.

Tennov, D. (1979). *Love and Limerence: The Experience of Being in Love*. New York: Stein and Day.

Tissot, S. A. (1832). *A Treatise on the Diseases Produced by Onanism. Translated from a New Edition of the French, with Notes and Appendix by an American Physician.* New York: Collins and Hannay. Facsimile reprint edition in *The Secret Vice Exposed! Some Arguments against Masturbation* (C. Rosenberg and C. Smith-Rosenberg, eds.). New York: Arno Press, 1974.

Wollstonecraft, M. (1792). *A Vindication of the Rights of Woman: With Strictures on Political and Moral Subjects.* Boston: Thomas and Andrews.

Part Two

Developmental Premises

6

Lovemaps/Loveblots

With early origins in forensics, sexology is a young science, barely a century old. Within sexology the concept of the lovemap (Money, 1986/1988) is only thirteen years old. My plan in this article is to explain the lovemap and then to examine some of its ramifications in forensic sexology.

During the 1970s, in the evolution of my thinking and teaching about the scientifically neglected phenomenon of falling in love and becoming pairbonded as lovers, the concept of the lovemap was preceded by the concept of the loveblot. The loveblot is a metaphor for the recipient onto whom one's love is projected. This recipient matches, at least in part, the highly specific and personalized prerequisites of one's idealized lover. I needed a term for the source of these highly specific and personalized prerequisites. *Lovemap* is the term I came up with. It met my criterion of sounding as though it belongs in the English vernacular. Upon first encounter, it is for many people self-defining. Its debut in print was in an abstract for the published proceedings of a meeting held in Sydney, Australia, in 1981, and is here reproduced as follows:

Synoptic Statement

In the human species, a lovemap is analogous to a native language. Both are conceptual entities that comprise ideation, imagery and behav-

---

Previously unpublished.

ioral practices. A lovemap is a mental template. It governs the erotosexual imagery that in fantasy and/or practice will permit a person to be erotosexually aroused or turned on. Only then can the genitalia follow through and perform their full role, culminating in orgasm.

As in the case of a native language, a lovemap in a human being requires a healthy human brain properly differentiated and developed prenatally. Just as in the case of language, the content of the human brain's lovemap is not preprogrammed prenatally, whereas in species lower in the phylogenetic scale—for example, rodents and sheep—such programming takes place prenatally under the influence of hormones, and expresses itself postnatally after puberty. In primates, and specifically in human beings, the brain's lovemap requires postnatal, exteroceptive input through the special senses. Long before puberty, it expresses itself developmentally in play rehearsals. If heterosexual play is prohibited, prevented and punished, then development of the lovemap becomes subverted, distorted and in error. Such error expresses itself in full at puberty. When extreme, it is classified among the erotosexual dysfunctions as a paraphilia (known legally as perversion or deviation).

Whether heterosexually typical or paraphilically atypical, a lovemap, once established in prepuberty, is as native as a native language, and it cannot be eradicated, even though it should fall into disuse. In many instances, it cannot be forced into disuse, regardless of the negative consequences of its manifestations in practice.

In everyday idiom, it is said that someone falls in love, even at first sight, with someone else—a live person, usually, not a photograph, painting, or sculpture. That person may be defined metaphorically as a loveblot. By analogy with an inkblot in a Rorschach test, a loveblot is a person who serves as a stimulus onto whom one projects the imagistic content of one's own lovemap. This projection is enabled to take place because there is some degree of correspondence between the person-as-loveblot and the image of the lover and love affair embodied in one's own idealized lovemap. Then ensues the omnipotence of the concept that love conquers all. This is a false concept except when, like the two sides of the same coin, the lovemaps of the two persons are reciprocally perfect matches, blemishes and all. Then each person is a reciprocally matching loveblot for the lovemap of the other.

When each lover reciprocates and fulfills the imagery of the other, then the erotosexual pairbonding of falling in love is likely to be very long-lasting, regardless of whether the match is orthodox and typical or unorthodox and atypical. For example, when a male-to-female impersonator (or gynemimetic) falls in love with a man who has the syndrome of gynemimetophilia, that is of being able to fall in love and to pairbond only with a lady with a penis, then the relationship may indeed be prolonged, even until death claims one partner first. There are many analogous relationships that are insufficiently studied in sex research. They are also insufficiently known and helped in sex therapy, for one or both of the partners may be accused as a sexual offender and imprisoned as a criminal (Money, 1981, p.11).

Lovemap Defined

In dictionary format, today's definition of lovemap is as follows:

> *lovemap:* a developmental representation or template, synchronously existent in the mind and in the brain, depicting the idealized lover, the idealized love affair, and the idealized program of sexuoerotic activity projected in private imagery and ideation or in observable performance, either alone or accompanied.

Lovemaps are an example of both cognitive mapping and brain mapping. One may anticipate that, with advances in the technology of brain imaging, today's meager knowledge of the development and functional representation of lovemaps in the brain will be greatly expanded. The concept of cognitive brain mapping applies more broadly than to lovemaps alone. Thus there are, for example, gendermaps, languagemaps, foodmaps, agemaps, and other maps still to be recognized and empirically demonstrated.

There are two criteria as to what is normal in lovemap development, one statistical and the other ideological. The statistical criterion, by which the norm is mathematically defined in terms of the mean and standard deviation, signifies what the majority of people conform to, regardless of the ideological criterion. The ideological criterion, by which the norm is more or less arbitrarily defined in terms of moral, religious, or legal doctrine, signifies what the majority of people are required to conform to by those who exercise the power to enforce conformity.

Every society has its own ideology, usually of ancient vintage, to which lovemaps are expected to conform. One of the noteworthy features of the lovemap ideology in our own society is the proposition that lovemap development will be spontaneously error-free if it is left untended. If, however, there is any sign of the juvenile sexual rehearsal play that is prerequisite to normal lovemap development in primate species, then punishment and humiliation should be meted out. The outcome of this faulty ideology is that it generates errors in lovemap development that remain unrecognized and uncorrected until they become fixated in adolescence and young adulthood. The error may be fixated by way of the principle of opponent-process learning, in which negative becomes converted to positive (Solomon, 1980). The fixation of error generates a lovemap that may be ideologically forbidden or criminal.

There are three categories of error in lovemap development, namely underinclusive (hypophilic or hyposexual), overinclusive (hyperphilic or hypersexual), and incongruously inclusive (paraphilic). The signs of hypophilia are sexuoerotic apathy and inertia and also those impairments of function that Masters and Johnson called sexual inadequacies. The signs of hyperphilia are excesses in frequency and/or intensity of sexuoerotic functions. Hyperphilia is commonly trivialized as lack of moral restraint. The signs of paraphilia are those that historically have been and often still are condemned as deviant, perverted, criminal, or kinky.

Paraphilia Defined

In dictionary format, the definition of a paraphilia is as follows (Money, 1986):

> *paraphilia:* a condition occurring in men and women of being compulsively responsive to and obligatively dependent on an unusual and personally or socially unacceptable stimulus, perceived or in the ideation and imagery of fantasy, for optimal initiation and maintenance of erotosexual arousal and the facilitation or attainment of orgasm (from the Greek *para-*, "altered" + *-philia,* "love"). Paraphilic imagery may be replayed in fantasy during solo masturbation or intercourse with a partner. In legal terminology, a paraphilia is a perversion or deviancy; in the vernacular, it is bizarre or kinky sex.

There are forty-odd named paraphilias, the exact number being dependent on the breakdown into subtypes and on whether each compound or multiplex paraphilia is given its own name or not.

When lovemaps go developmentally awry, it would appear, on the basis of such evidence as is presently available, that in girls the predominant outcome is hypophilic, whereas in boys it is paraphilic. In both outcomes there is a split between affectionate love above the belt and carnal lust below. In hypophilia, the expression of affectionate love (as in courtship) is not impaired, whereas the expression of carnal lust may be not only impaired (as in vaginal-penetration phobia, for example), but also virtually nonexistent. In paraphilia, by contrast, carnal lust continues to exist, preserved deviously in the paraphilia but dissociated from the expression of affectionate love. Typically, the recipient of the paraphile's affectionate love is not the same person as the recipient of his/her carnal lust. Hyperphilia, although it may exist as a quantitative entity only, is commonly associated with paraphilia.

Insofar as it belongs to a sexuoerotic minority of people, a paraphilic lovemap may be statistically abnormal without automatically qualifying as noxious and pathological, but rather as innocuous. A paraphilia is noxious and pathological when it is fixated and imperative in its demands, in which case engagement in the paraphilia resembles an addiction in its compulsive persistence and resistance to change. An innocuous paraphilia, by contrast, is more flexible, more optional, and less insistently obligatory. The measure of a paraphilia's pathology includes its harmfulness not only to the self, but also to possible participants.

Paraphilias that qualify diagnostically as pathological do not automatically qualify as being illegal, whereas those that qualify as illegal are classified as pathological. Five of the nine paraphilias listed by name and number in the new DSM-IV (APA, 1994) are prosecutable by law. These five are: 302.4 Exhibitionism; 302.89 Frotteurism; 302.2 Pedophilia; 302.84 Sexual Sadism; and 302.82 Voyeurism. The other four are 302.81 Fetishism; 302.83 Sexual Masochism; 302.3 Transvestic Fetishism; and 302.9 Not Otherwise Specified. Although seven additional paraphilias are mentioned by name under 302.9, the total falls far short of the forty-odd paraphilias defined in Money (1988), and omits such forensically relevant paraphilias as raptophilia (paraphilic rape, which is omitted for reasons of political correctness) and asphyxiophilia (accidental autoerotic death from self-strangulation; Boglioli et al., 1991; Money et al., 1991).

Paraphilic Stratagems

A paraphilia constitutes a ruse or stratagem whereby carnal lust is developmentally rescued from the threat of extinction by being enchained to a phylism—that is, to a phylogenetically determined building block of behavior (Money, 1983) that usually serves a different function. For example, in pedophilia, the phylism of lover-lover bonding becomes enchained to the phylism of parent-child bonding (Money, 1990).

The paraphilic ruses or stratagems are classifiable in a taxonomy of seven grand stratagems. They are expressed in terms of the transgression, sinfulness, or defilement of carnal lust, which is antithetical to the saintly spirituality of affectional love, as follows.

The *sacrificial/expiatory stratagem* requires reparation or atonement for the defiling sin of carnal lust by way of penance and sacrifice.

The *marauding/predatory stratagem* requires that, insofar as saintly lovers ought not to consent to the defilement of carnal lust, a partner in lust must be stolen, abducted, or coerced by force.

The *mercantile/venal stratagem* requires that defiling carnal lust be traded, bartered, or purchased, insofar as saintly lovers ought not to engage consensually in its free exchange.

The *fetishistic/talismanic stratagem* spares the saintly lover from the defilement of carnal lust by substituting a token, fetish, or talisman instead.

The *stigmatic/eligibilic stratagem* requires that the partner in carnal lust be, metaphorically, a pagan infidel, disparate in religion, race, color, nationality, social class, or age from the spiritual and saintly lovers of one's own social group.

The *solicitational/allurative stratagem* displaces carnal lust away from genital copulation onto the preliminaries of the invitation and display of courtship, and thus saves the saintly partner from the carnal defilement of genital union.

The *understudy/subrogation stratagem* requires one to rescue and deliver another person from suffering and defilement as the victim of carnal lust by nobly and altruistically taking that other person's place.

Sexosophy and Sexology

The dysfunction between the criteria of what constitutes pathology versus what constitutes illegality in the paraphilias reflects the disjunction between sexology and sexosophy. *Sexology* is the science of sex and, like all the sciences, is empirical. *Sexosophy* is the philosophy of sex and, like all philosophies, is ideological. In today's judicial practices, priority is ceded to forensic sexosophy, not forensic sexology.

In conformity with the overall premise of the criminal-justice system, forensic sexosophy is predicated on the doctrine of free will, moral choice, and personal responsibility for illegal sexual behavior. Technically, it is possible to plead not guilty by reason of insanity (under the M'Naghten Rules), or by reason of gross mental retardation or irresistible impulse. There is no guarantee, however, that these defenses will be sustained, even if they are supported by unequivocal and demonstrable evidence of deteriorative brain disease, traumatic brain injury, temporal-lobe epilepsy, or genetic error.

The judicial doctrine of personal responsibility for sex offenses effectively dispenses with forensic sexological services related to scientific causal explanations of sex-offending paraphilic behavior. The only scientific sexology that the law is effectively able to use is that which contributes to the identification of an offender—for instance, as in differentiating accidental, autoerotic paraphilic death from homicide, or in comparing DNA in biological samples from suspects with those found on victims of sexual assault, murder, or abuse.

Gender Coding

Lovemaps are gender coded. They can be classified as heterosexual, homosexual, or bisexually somewhere in between. Developmentally, the progression is from bipotentiality toward either heterosexual or homosexual monopotentiality, either of which may be, in the years of adulthood, either partial or total.

Beginning in fetal life, gender coding of the brain for masculinization or feminization is superimposed on the original bipotential state. The fetal and neonatal brain is gender coded hormonally. The default position is for feminization. Masculinization requires the addition of a masculinizing principle, namely masculinizing hormone. This proposition is supported by an abundance of animal experimental evidence (Sitsen, 1988; Tobet and Fox, 1992; Ward, 1992), and human clinical evidence (Money, 1993). It has also been demonstrated microscopically with neuroanatomical evidence (McEwen, 1992; Swaab et al., 1992).

Brain hormonalization prenatally and neonatally is not exclusively the determinant of gender coding in mammals, although it predominates in the four-legged species. Among primates, gender coding is also a function of postnatal sociosensory coding, and especially so in the human species. The rudiments of human gendermaps are laid down prenatally, but the finished product is dependent also on sociosensory experiences encountered and transacted postnatally, initially through the skin senses and then predominantly through the ears and eyes, by way of cognitive assimilation, conditioning, and indoctrination. Thus, gendermap determinants are multivariate and sequential, not univariate and abrupt.

The same principle of multivariate and sequential determinism applies also to lovemap development. However, the prenatal determinants have not yet been empirically teased out, except in the most general sense of a vulnerability factor. Thus, boys with a supernumerary Y chromosome (the 47,XYY syndrome) are more at risk for developing a paraphilic lovemap than are 46,XY boys (Money et al., 1975). Postnatally, a history of traumatic abuse and neglect, irrespective of chromosome count, adds another vulnerability factor (Money, Annecillo, and Lobato, 1990).

Essentialism/Constructionism

The concept of multivariate sequential determinism is still oversimplified by many people into the nature/nurture dichotomy (which should be expanded into nature/critical period/nurture), recently renamed the essentialist/constructionist dichotomy and so given a new lease on life. Essentialists are biomedical demons in the cosmogony of social constructionists, whose high priest is the late French historian, Michel Foucault. Foucault (1973, 1978) exposed various biomedical doctrines as being scientific masquerades to justify exploitation of the powerless by the power elite. Thus he deconstructed the medicalization of sex in the nineteenth century as a power play of the elite to deprive the people of sexual freedom and responsibility.

Foucault and his social-science and humanist followers are committed to the principle that the expression of one's sexuality is a moral choice that should not be politically dictated. Hence their stringent resistance to the principle of genetic, hormonal, neuroanatomical, or any other biological determinants of sexuality. They are particularly resistant to the concept of biologically based gender differences, male or female, homosexual or heterosexual. They look the other way if reminded that differences attributable to learning—especially learning that takes place at a critical period of development—become part of the biology of the brain.

Foucault's social constructionism has roots in dialectical materialism and in what was called, in the 1920s and 1930s, the sociology of knowledge. It makes tolerable sense when used to explain major social movements and institutions. In the social sciences, however, Foucault's disciples have gone one step further. They use social constructionism to explain all of human nature, including the social construction of paraphilias and the stigmatization of deviance. Social constructionism allows no place for biological and phylogenetic heritage. There are no fixed criteria, only relativistic and arbitrary ones.

Seduction Theory Recycled

Social-constructionist doctrine serendipitously gained an unforeseen increment of popularity when Jeffrey Masson published his book, *The Assault on Truth* (1985). In this book, Masson accused Freud of suppressing his 1895 seduction theory of neurosis in favor of his 1897 psychoanalytic oedipal theory. In the seduction theory, sexual abuse was a childhood actuality; in oedipal theory, a childhood fantasy only.

As an argument of Masson's book, seduction theory was recycled, almost overnight, to fill the theory gap in the new specialty of victimology. Victimology has grown out of the rediscovery of abusive violence in the battered-child syndrome (Kempe et al., 1980). Violence soon gave way to sexual abuse and incest as the priority focus of victimology, especially in the media. The new vogue is to attribute all manner of symptoms in adulthood to sexual abuse in childhood.

An entire new therapeutic industry has grown up around the concept of multiple-personality disorder (MPD) caused by repressed memories of sexual abuse in childhood. These memories allegedly can be recovered in adulthood with the help of therapists, some of dubious training, who call themselves validators. In many instances, abuse is alleged to have taken place in vile and secret satanic cult rituals, of which no substantiating evidence has yet been found (Lanning, 1992).

False accusations of satanic rituals require that some women be cast in the role of witches and some men in the role of demonic monsters. Thus does the history of heresy-hunting revive itself. This revival confronts forensic sexologists with a major problem that few admit or face up to. Part of this failure is attributable to the fact that society is presently gripped by a counterreformationist zeal against the Sexual Revolution of the 1960s and 1970s, against the women's equal-rights movement, and against the HIV/AIDS epidemic. In the present era of medical-insurance cutbacks and managed care, it is easy to join the reimbursed elite of false accusers and to be persuaded of one's own self-righteousness as a heresy-hunter.

In victimology, Foucault's social constructionism has proved itself to be a self-fulfilling prophesy. It has socially constructed itself into being a new sexosophical elite, a cadre of heresy-hunters who function as undercover agents for the sex-abuse police.

Prevention and Treatment

Biomedically instead of criminologically, forensic sexology as science has a great deal of catching up to do with respect to the prevention and treatment of paraphilias (Krivacska and Money, 1994). Properly defined, the prevention of paraphilia, in the sense of eliminating the development of paraphilia in all infants and children of the next generation, is an epidemiological problem in the public-health forensics of the future. It will necessitate an increased understanding of the etiology of paraphilia. Forensic prevention in the sense of complete elimination of a syndrome from someone who already has it cannot yet be guaranteed for all persons with a paraphilia. Rather, by analogy, the treatment of paraphilia resembles the treatment of temporal-lobe epileptic attacks (which paraphilic fugue states resemble), namely by suppressing the recurrence of symptoms pharmacologically. In 1966, Depo-Provera (medroxyprogesterone acetate) was the first pharmaceutical product to be used successfully in the treatment of a paraphilic sex-offender (Money, 1970). More recently, other psychoactive medications have been sporadically tried with success. What forensic sexology needs next is a concerted and systematic research program that will include clinical therapeutic trials.

REFERENCES

American Psychiatric Association. (1994). *Diagnostic and Statistical Manual of Mental Disorders,* 4th edition. Washington, DC: American Psychiatric Press.

Boglioli, L. R., Taff, M. L., Stephens, P. J., and Money, J. (1991). "A case of autoerotic asphyxia associated with multiplex paraphilia." *American Journal of Forensic Medicine and Pathology* 12:64–73.

Foucault, M. (1973). *The Birth of the Clinic: An Archaeology of Medical Perception.* (Translated from *Naissance de la Clinique: Une Archeologie du Regard Medical.* Paris: Presses Universitaires de France, 1963). New York: Pantheon.

———. (1978). *The History of Sexuality, Volume 1: An Introduction.* New York: Random House.

Kempe, C. H., Silverman, F. N., Steele, B. F., Droegemuller, W., and Silver, H. K. (1980). "The battered-child syndrome." In *Traumatic Abuse and Neglect of Children at Home* (G. J. Williams and J. Money, eds.). Baltimore: Johns Hopkins University Press.

Krivacska, J. J., and Money, J., eds. (1994). *Handbook of Forensic Sexology.* Amherst, NY: Prometheus Books.

Lanning, K. V. (1992). *Investigator's Guide to Allegations of "Ritual" Child Abuse.* Quantico, VA: National Center for the Analysis of Violent Crime.

Masson, J. M. (1985). *The Assault on Truth: Freud's Suppression of the Seduction Theory.* New York: Penguin Books.

Masters, W. H., and Johnson, V. E. (1970). *Human Sexual Inadequacy.* Boston: Little, Brown.

McEwen, B. S. (1992). "Steroid hormones: Effect on brain development and function." *Hormone Research* 37 Suppl. 3:1–10.

Money, J. (1981). "Lovemaps, loveblots, imagery and pairbonding." In *Education, Research, and Therapy in Sexuality: Proceedings of the 2nd National Conference of the Australian Association of Sex Educators, Researchers and Therapists* (M. J. Baker and S. F. Abraham, eds). Sydney: Australian Association of Sex Educators, Researchers, and Therapists.

———. (1983). "New phylism theory and autism: Pathognomonic impairment of troopbonding." *Medical Hypotheses* 11:245–50.

———. (1986). *Lovemaps: Clinical Concepts of Sexual/Erotic Health and Pathology, Paraphilia, and Gender Transposition in Childhood, Adolescence, and Maturity.* New York: Irvington. Paperback edition, Amherst, NY: Prometheus Books, 1988.

———. (1988). *Gay, Straight, and In-Between: The Sexology of Erotic Orientation.* New York: Oxford University Press.

———. (1990). "Pedophilia: A specific instance of new phylism theory as applied to paraphilic lovemaps." In *Pedophilia: Biosocial Dimensions* (J. R. Feierman, ed.). New York: Springer-Verlag.

———. (1993). *The Adam Principle: Genes, Genitals, Hormones, and Gender—Selected Readings in Sexology.* Amherst, NY: Prometheus Books.

Money, J., Annecillo, C., and Lobato, C. (1990). "Paraphilic and other sexological anomalies as a sequel to the syndrome of child-abuse (psychosocial) dwarfism." *Journal of Psychology and Human Sexuality* 3:117–50.

Money, J., Wainwright, G., and Hingsburger, D. (1991). *The Breathless Orgasm: A Lovemap Biography of Asphyxiophilia.* Amherst, NY: Prometheus Books.

Money, J., Wiedeking, C., Walker, P., Migeon, C., Meyer, W., and Borgaonkar, D. (1975). "47,XYY and 46,XY males with antisocial and/or sex-offending behavior: Antiandrogen therapy plus counseling." *Psychoneuroendocrinology,* 1:165–78.

Sitsen, J. M. A., ed. (1988). *Handbook of Sexology, Volume 6: The Pharmacology and Endocrinology of Sexual Function* (J. Money and H. Musaph, series eds.). Amsterdam: Elsevier.

Solomon, R. L. (1980). "The opponent-process theory of acquired motivation." *American Psychologist* 35:691–712.

Swaab, D. F., Gooren, L. J. G., and Hofman, M. A. (1992). "The human hypothalamus in relation to gender and sexual orientation." *Progress in Brain Research* 93:205–17.

Tobet, S. A. and Fox, T. O. (1992). "Differences in neuronal morphology influenced hormonally throughout life." In *Handbook of Behavioral Neurobiology, Volume 11: Sexual Differentiation* (A. A. Gerall, H. Moltz, and I. L. Ward, eds.). New York: Plenum Press.

Ward, I. L. (1992). "Sexual behavior: The product of perinatal hormonal and prepubertal social factors." In *Handbook of Behavioral Neurobiology, Volume 11: Sexual Differentiation* (A. A. Gerall, H. Moltz, and I. L. Ward, eds.). New York: Plenum Press.

7

Gendermaps and Lovemaps

Introduction

Sexology needs concepts and terms that bridge the presently existing gap between biological and sociological sexology. Hence the coinage of the terms *gendermap* and *lovemap*. The lovemap is gender coded. Both maps, like the native-language map, are multivariate and sequential in origin. The paradigm of their development is not nature/nurture, but nature/critical period/nurture. Eventually they become fixated in the mindbrain and change very little, if at all. The gendermap codes for masculine, feminine, or androgynous, and for hetero-, homo-, or bisexual orientation. The lovemap codes for normophilia versus paraphilia, hypophilia, or hyperphilia. Normal and abnormal are defined either statistically or ideologically. The two great principles whereby children assimilate gendermap and lovemap norms and stereotypes are bipolar, namely identification and complementation. Opponent-process learning is the principle of repolarization whereby negative becomes positive, avoidance becomes attraction, and aversive becomes addictive. In this way, gendermaps and lovemaps become pathologized.

Written for the 1992 Shanghai Conference of Sexology, Shanghai, China, September 12–16, 1992. Published only in Spanish as "Mapas del genero y mapas del amor: Nuevos conceptos en sexología." *Revista Latinoamericana de Sexologia* VII: 271–77, 1993.

TERMINOLOGY

A person's gendermap is a template that exists synchronously in the brain and the mind. The same applies to a person's lovemap. Whereas the lovemap is less inclusive than the gendermap, the lovemap is always gender coded as male, female, or to some degree androgynous.

> *gendermap:* a developmental representation or template synchronously in the mind and brain depicting the details of one's gender-identity/role (G-I/R). It includes the lovemap but is larger, insofar as it incorporates whatever is gender coded vocationally, educationally, recreationally, sartorially, and legally as well as in matters of etiquette, grooming, body language, and vocal intonation.

> *lovemap:* a developmental representation or template synchronously in the mind and brain depicting the idealized lover, the idealized love affair, and the idealized program of sexuoerotic activity projected in imagery or actually engaged in with the lover.

The gendermap and lovemap have a history of growth and development from very simple beginnings to very complex outcomes. They are multivariately and sequentially determined. Explanations of their genesis are in terms of temporal sequences, not causal sequences.

Conceptually, gender is more inclusive than sex. It is a conceptual umbrella under which are assembled all the male/female differences (and similarities also), not only those that are arbitrary and conventional, but also those that are procreative and phylogenetically determined.

GENDER BIPOTENTIALITY

The sequence of gender differentiation is from bipotential to monopotential. In the earliest stage of embryonic life, gonadal bipotentiality is resolved under the influence of the Testis-Determining Factor (TDF) on the short arm of the Y chromosome, within which is encoded the gene named SRY for Sex-Determining Region of the Y chromosome. In the absence of this genomic influence, the gonad differentiates as an ovary.

Hormonal secretions from the embryonic testis resolve the bipotentiality of the internal reproductive anatomy. Mullerian-inhibiting hormone (MIH) prevents the Mullerian ducts from developing into female internal organs. Testosterone, the chief androgenizing hormone, develops the Wolffian ducts into internal male organs. Subsequently, testosterone and its derivative, dihydrotestosterone, masculinize the bipotential anlagen of the external organs into scrotum, penis, penile sheath, and foreskin, which otherwise become labia majora, clitoris, labia minora, and clitoral hood, respectively.

Testosterone also plays a role in resolving bipotential sexual coding of the brain in late fetal and early postnatal life. Within the nuclei of many brain cells, testosterone does its masculinizing work by way of an apparent paradox—namely by being converted first to estradiol. Sexual coding of the brain for female procreative functioning requires only the absence of testosterone. In the posterior region of the hypothalamus, sexual coding mediates chiefly the neuroregulation of pituitary hormones essential to procreation, whereas in the anterior region of the hypothalamus, sexual coding mediates the behavior of courtship and mating. In human beings, imagery and ideation may be included. There is usually some degree of residual bipotentiality so that male and female sexual behavior are not absolutely dimorphic, but shared.

Within the first three postnatal months, there is in male (but not in female) human babies a transient surge of testosterone in the bloodstream equivalent to that of puberty. Its effect on gender bipotentiality in the brain remains to be ascertained. In newborn rats, it has been shown that the concentration of serotonin in the hypothalamus is higher in females than males; and also that an increase in neonatal serotonin has a demasculinizing effect. Serotonin counteracts the long-term sequelae, namely masculinized mating behavior experimentally induced in newborn female rats by injecting them with testosterone. Synergism between testosterone and serotonin, so far as is presently known, has no equivalent or counterpart in the juvenile years before puberty, either in rats or human beings.

Juvenile Gender Coding

After the earliest years of infancy, gender coding of the human brain away from bipotentiality toward masculine or feminine monopotentiality is no longer directly mediated by hormonal or other neurotransmitter substances in the brain. Instead, it is mediated by informational input from the social environment through the senses—haptic, olfactory, and to some extent gustatory at first, and then predominantly auditory and visual. In other words, from late infancy onwards, boys assimilate and express boyhood, and girls girlhood, in conformity with the societal ideology and the stereotypes of the community and culture in which they live. They do so in conformity with two great principles, identification and complementation.

Identification means becoming identified with, imitating, and copying people of the same declared sex as one's own, whether parent, other relative, older sibling, or agemate. Complementation means reciprocating with a parent, other relative, older sibling, or agemate that which has been attained through identification. Thus, the little girl flirts with her daddy, and her little brother plays escort to his mommy. Identification and complementation continue throughout childhood and beyond. One manifestation of peer-group identification and complementation is in juvenile sexual rehearsal play, a developmental phenomenon common to the young of primate species. In addition to coital positioning, prepubertal rehearsal play may include penovaginal intromission.

In the developmental coding of the gendermap in childhood, bipotentiality is resolved into bipolarity. The positive pole codes for "me," for who I am, boy or girl. The negative pole codes for "not me," for who I am not, girl or boy, respectively. At each pole there is a map or schema of what is coded there, one labeled feminine and the other masculine. Everybody—boy and girl, man and woman—has both maps, one depicting "me," and the other depicting "thee." If the two maps change places, then the individual has a gender disorder. One map may displace the other, as in full-blown transexualism, or both may coexist in alternation as a phenomenon of dual personality, one masculine and one feminine. Another possibility is that the two maps may merge into some degree of androgyny or bisexuality.

Under ordinary circumstances of development, one expects concordance between the prenatal and the postnatal coding of an individual's gendermap. In addition, one expects that the gendermap will be concordant with the natal sex of the external genitalia. Under circumstances in which the gendermap is discordant with the natal sex of the external genitalia, the source of discordancy may lie in either the prenatal or the postnatal coding of the gendermap, or in both combined.

Lovemaps

In addition to being gender coded, a lovemap develops so as to be sexuoerotically either normophilic, hypophilic, hyperphilic, or paraphilic. The criteria of normophilia are not absolute but ideological and transculturally variable. Hypophilia signifies troublesome insufficiency or incompleteness of sexuoerotic arousal and genital function, up to and including orgasm. Hyperphilia signifies a vexatious excess of sexuoerotic arousal and genital function in either duration or frequency. Paraphilia signifies that sexuoerotic arousal and orgasmic climax are contingent on a rehearsal in imagery and ideation of eccentric or bizarre practices or rituals that may also be carried out in actual behavior. The formal definition of paraphilia is as follows.

> *paraphilia:* a condition occurring in men and women of being compulsively responsive to and obligatively dependent on an unusual and personally or socially unacceptable stimulus, perceived or in the ideation and imagery of fantasy, for optimal initiation and maintenance of erotosexual arousal and the facilitation or attainment of orgasm (from the Greek *para-*, "altered" + *-philia,* "love"). Paraphilic imagery may be replayed in fantasy during solo masturbation or intercourse with a partner. In legal terminology, a paraphilia is a perversion or deviancy; in the vernacular, it is bizarre or kinky sex.

Not enough is known about the concatenation of factors responsible for the shaping of a lovemap into a paraphilic one. Allowance must be made for a vulnerability or risk factor present in some but not all boys and girls. Boys with an extra Y chromosome (the 47,XYY syndrome), for example, have such a risk factor.

It is in the postnatal biography of paraphilias, however, that one looks for early evidence of the genesis of a paraphilic lovemap. There it is common to find early traumatization of the developing lovemap, particularly at around eight years of age. Any kind of traumatic suffering, including abusive neglect and injurious violence (nonsexual as well as sexual), may be implicated. So too may exposure to sexual or erotic pursuits out of synchrony with the developmental sexological age. The most frequent traumatization, however, is from the quandary —popularly known as the Catch-22—of being damned if you do and damned if you don't confess to having obtained forbidden sexual knowledge, or to having engaged in prohibited sexual behavior, consensual or otherwise, especially in childhood sexual rehearsal play.

The outcome of being caught in a Catch-22 may be, according to the opponent-process theory of Richard Solomon, that negative converts to positive. In other words, aversion converts to addiction, after which one repeats ad infinitum that which was once forbidden, prohibited, and punished, no matter how dangerous or self-sabotaging. This is the formula whereby a normophilic lovemap converts to a paraphilic one. Triumph is snatched from the jaws of tragedy and carnal lust is preserved, but at the cost of its separation from affectional love.

It is possible for a paraphilia that is classified as deviant in one society to be institutionalized as ideologically acceptable in another. For example, in Western (but not in Muslim) advertising, it is ideologically acceptable to depict models in lingerie and for viewers to be fetishistically aroused by the undergarments on the model. By contrast, the depiction of a naked woman would be condemned as pornographic. Another example, forbidden in the West but formerly fashionable in China, is the paraphilia for tiny feet, deformed by binding, known as the "golden lotus." This paraphilia served also as a strategy of social control. It subordinated footbound women of the upper class to permanent dependence on wealthy fathers, husbands, or pimps, and required less wealthy men to work harder and earn more to gain access, if possible, to a prostitute with bound feet with which to satisfy their paraphilia. In the West, the counterpart to bound feet are the stiletto heels on the shoes of a dominatrix who uses them as weapons on wealthy customers. They pay handsomely for the masochistic privilege of being jabbed. The fetishistic attraction of high heels on women's street shoes is socially so completely acceptable that they are not defined as fetishes.

Understanding paraphilias is integral to understanding the sexology of not only the individual, but also of the society in which that individual lives. To understand the politics and sociology of any society, one must understand also the ideological sexology, better named the *sexosophy,* of that society, as manifested in the gendermaps and lovemaps that it selectively endorses or rejects.

8

The Concept of Gender-Identity Disorder

LEXICAL HISTORY OF GENDER

Thirty-nine years ago, there was no concept of gender-identity disorder in adulthood, nor in childhood and adolescence. In fact, there was no concept of gender as a human attribute. As an attribute of nouns and pronouns, gender was the intellectual property of grammarians and philologists almost exclusively. Only rarely had the term been used as a synonym for a person's sex as male or female. The *Oxford English Dictionary* (OED) in its original edition quotes from a letter written in 1709 by Lady M.W. Montagu to Mrs. Wortley: "Of the fair sex . . . my only consolation for my being of that gender has been the assurance it gave me of never being married to any one among them." The ensuing quotation is from the *Daily News,* July 17, 1896: "As to one's success in the work one does, surely that is not a question of gender either."

Another quotation that escaped the lexigraphical sleuthing of the OED was brought to my attention in 1980 by Russell W. S. Reid, M.D. It is from "The Pig-Faced Queen of the Dominion of Women," a con-

Written for the International Conference on Gender Identity and Development in Childhood and Adolescence, St. George's Hospital Medical School, London, England, March 13–16, 1992. First published in Spanish in *Revista Latinoamericana de Sexologia* VII:221–40, 1993; in German in *Zeitschrift für Sexualforschung* 7:20–34, 1994; and in English in *Journal of Sex and Marital Therapy* 20:763–77, 1994.

temptuously satirical and scurrilous short story by the Right Honorable E. H. Knatchbull-Hugessen, M.P., one of seven published simultaneously in London and New York in 1874 under the title, *Queer Folk.* The quotation reads as follows:

> They were not long in discovering that their mission upon earth was neither to be pig-faced nor single. Three eligible suitors appeared, who, although of the male gender, were gentle as possible in their behaviour before they were married, and, strange to say, never beat, bullied, or teased their wives afterwards. Clara, Bertha, and Mathilde, never claiming rights which Nature had denied them, found that privileges of their sex were willingly conceded to them by their husbands, and that they really enjoyed quite as much influence and authority as they could desire.

The second edition (1989) of the OED adds a new definition under *gender,* namely its modern (especially feminist) use as a euphemism for the sex of a human being, often intended to emphasize the social and cultural—as opposed to the biological—distinctions between the sexes. The first quotation, dated 1963, is from Alex Comfort's *Sex in Society*: "The gender role learned by the age of two years is for most individuals almost irreversible, even if it runs counter to the physical sex of the subject."

In March 1991, Mr. William P. Wang, a research associate in my office, received a reply from Peter M. Gilliver, Senior Assistant Science Editor for the OED, saying that: "In the third edition of the *Oxford English Dictionary,* to be published sometime early next century, Dr. Money's article will be consulted when the entries for *gender* and related terms come up for revision." The article to be consulted is "Gender: History, Theory and Usage of the Term in Sexology and Its Relationship to Nature/Nurture" (Money, 1985).

This 1985 history traces the origin and first definition of the term *gender role* to 1955, when it appeared in *The Bulletin of The Johns Hopkins Hospital* in a research report entitled "Hermaphroditism, Gender and Precocity in Hyperadrenocorticism: Psychologic Findings" (Money, 1955). The relevant passage is as follows:

> The cases of contradiction between gonadal sex and sex of rearing are tabulated together with data on endogenous hormonal sex and gender role. The term *gender role* is used to signify all those things that a person says or does to disclose himself or herself as having the status of boy or man, girl or woman, respectively. It includes, but is

> not restricted to, sexuality in the sense of eroticism. Of the seventeen people represented in the table, all but three disclosed themselves in the gender role fully concordant with their rearing though contradicted by their gonads. Gonadal structure per se proved a most unreliable prognosticator of a person's gender role and orientation as man or woman; assigned sex proved an extremely reliable one (p. 254).

Even today I am still in possession of the heavy oak desk, vintage 1912, its grain hidden behind worn turquoise paint, at which in 1955 I toiled, night after night, in a small office between the elevators on the third floor of Adolph Meyer's Phipps Psychiatric Clinic. My challenge was to find order in the chaos of five years' worth of data on the psychology and sexology of hermaphroditism, for which the conceptual terminology of the day was inadequate.

I could not write about the male sex role of a hermaphrodite who lacked the genitalia of a male with which to perform a male sex role even though, reared and living as a male, he was taken for granted in everyday occupational, recreational, and social life as a man in a man's role. In addition, I could not follow the practice of traditional sex-role psychology and write that, like Ken, the male Barbie doll with nothing between the legs, he had a male sex role.

With respect to genital, copulatory sex, the type of hermaphrodite of whom I was writing was deprived of an adequate set of male genitalia, and so was deprived of a full-fledged sex role as a male. For him, as for his female counterpart, I needed a term that did not then exist. Thus did *gender role* come into being. I was able to write that he had, overall, the gender role of a male, but with an impairment limited to that segment of it which constituted the specific genital and erotic sex role of a man—and correspondingly for his female counterpart.

In a second 1955 paper, I expanded the foregoing definition of gender role as follows:

> Gender role is appraised in relation to the following: general mannerisms, deportment and demeanor; spontaneous topics of talk in unprompted conversation and casual comment; content of dreams, daydreams and fantasies; replies to oblique inquiries and projective tests; evidence of erotic practices and, finally, the person's own replies to direct inquiry (Money et al., 1955).

I had then, as I do now, a philosophical commitment to the principle of defining gender role phenomenologically, and also to the principle of defining it as a unitary, not a dichotomous, phenomenon, irrespective of what might be postulated regarding its determinants. As a unitary phenomenon, it is defined as belonging to oneself, within, and as manifesting itself to others, without.

In the language of the theater, a gender role is not a script handed to an actor, but a role incorporated into the actor who, metamorphosed by it, manifests it in person. An actor does not simply learn a role, he/she assimilates and lives it. So also with gender role: A child assimilates and lives it, is inhabited by it, has it as a belonging, and manifests it to others phenomenologically in word and deed. There is no one cause of a gender role. It develops under the influence of multiple parameters, sequentially over time, from prenatal life onwards. Nature alone is not responsible, nor is nurture alone; they work together, hand in glove.

For the first six or seven years after its introduction in 1955, the term *gender role* did not take hold in the vernacular, but began to do so in the biomedical literature. By the middle 1960s, the logistic of dichotomization had also commenced to take hold, as manifested in the merging of the concept of gender with the intrapsychic concept of identity to form the new term *gender identity.*

I trace my initial acquaintance with this new term to communication at the time with Evelyn Hooker, the psychologist now famed for her pioneering studies in Los Angeles that led to the official depathologization of homosexuality. According to a personal communication (1984) with the late Robert Stoller, there was a psychoanalytic gender-identity study group at the University of California at Los Angeles (UCLA) medical center during this same period, the middle 1960s. By the time Stoller published his book, *Sex and Gender,* in 1968, this group had been formalized as the Gender Identity Research Clinic at UCLA.

In the OED, the earliest reference to gender identity is a quotation from the Spring 1969 issue of the *Erickson Educational Foundation (EEF) Newsletter,* Vol. 2 (erroneously identified as Vol. 1 in the OED), No. 1, page 1, as follows: "The Erickson Educational Foundation has been called upon to function in gender identity areas needing service not otherwise supplied." This was, in fact, the second time that the term *gender identity* had appeared in the *EEF Newsletter.* The first was in the Spring 1968 issue, Vol. 1, No. 1, page 1, as follows:

> **A Changing of Sex by Surgery Begun at Johns Hopkins**
>
> This *New York Times* headline Nov. 21, 1966, was one of many that startled the American public. The Gender Identity Clinic at this

major medical center had quietly started work with transsexuals and the related cases of the Hermaphrodite and the Klinefelter syndrome. EEF helped support the committee, cooperating with John Money, Ph.D., Associate Professor of Medical Psychology and Pediatrics, as well as the surgical team at Johns Hopkins.

The clinic had for a couple of years before 1966 been unofficially referred to as the "sex-change clinic." Under my influence, it was officially named the Gender Identity Clinic. Although the clinic's official name was compatible with allowing it to become a center for manifold syndromes related to gender identity, it failed to become such a center. One consequence was that, in general usage, *gender identity* became rather too closely identified with *transexualism,* a term which, although coined (and spelled with one *s*) in 1949 by Cauldwell, entered the vernacular only after the publication in 1966 of Harry Benjamin's book, *The Transsexual Phenomenon.*

Pediatrics and Gender Role

The term *gender role* has always belonged in pediatrics and child development. It owes its existence to children born with hermaphroditically ambiguous genitalia and enrolled in the psychohormonal research unit of The Johns Hopkins Pediatric Endocrine Clinic, in which their development was being followed longitudinally.

The study of gender-role development in children with a birth defect of the genitalia had begun in 1950. It was ten years later that the study was expanded to include boys born without a birth defect of the genitalia but who, early in the juvenile years, were showing signs of gender-role incongruity. In popular parlance, they were "sissy boys": Their interests and mannerisms conformed to their idealized stereotype of the gender role of girls, and their ideation and imagery—body imagery included—was of being a girl. The medical student who used his elective research time to assist in the study of these boys was Richard Green. He was a coauthor, in 1960, of the first pediatric paper in which the term *gender role* appeared. It was entitled "Incongruous Gender Role: Nongenital Manifestations in Prepubertal Boys."

THE CLEAVING OF GENDER

In pediatric and ephebiatric usage, as well as in adult usage in the 1960s, the "genius of the language" (as it is known in philology) took charge of the concept of gender and butchered it. The first cleavage was to separate sex from gender and to allocate sex to biology and gender to social science. In the doctrines of simplistic textbooks, *sex* is defined as biological and what you're born with, and *gender* as social and what you acquire. Thus is the sanctity of the nature/nurture dichotomy retained in place.

The second challenge was to split gender identity from gender role, and to allocate gender identity to the workings of the mind, and gender role to the workings of society.

The doctrine of gender identity as a phenomenon of the mind is reduced, in some simplistic texts, to assertions of "I am male" or "I am female" that may or may not agree with gender role or even with orientation, which may be homosexual or heterosexual. To reinforce the doctrine of gender identity as belonging to psychology and psychiatry, gender-identity disorder eventually became renamed as a state of mind, namely gender dysphoria (Fisk, 1974), even though gender dysphorics themselves say they are dysphoric about their sex, not their gender.

The doctrine of gender role as a phenomenon of society has been reinforced as a domain of political, epistemological, social, and philosophical history by declaring gender an arbitrary construction deserving of nothing less than total deconstruction. Social deconstructionists do not hesitate to merge role with identity in their assault on gender. Everything must go!

This divvying up of gender between biology and social science, nature and nurture, essentialism and constructionism, identity and role, intrapsychic gender dysphoria and extrapsychic gender deviance brings with it enormous doctrinal carnage. (Or perhaps it is the other way round, and doctrinal carnage demanded a divvying up.) The scholarly divisions are not self-contained, independent entities separated by fixed boundaries. On the contrary, the boundaries overlap and are open to sometimes unseemly doctrinal dispute that detracts from the credibility of our science and the respect accorded to our professional and scholarly endeavors.

Doctrinal dispute exerts a heavy toll on those who serve and on those whom they serve, who are, in this instance, children and adolescents with disordered gender identity. Confronted with doctrinal dispute, the professional caregiver becomes an adherent either of a particular faction or of no faction at all. Either way, he/she encounters a void where there should be a theoretical consensus.

To illustrate the lack of theoretical consensus, here is an example: The social constructionist/deconstructionist faction maligns the medical model of the gender-dysphoria faction and proclaims, in effect, that all manifestations of gender identity—and with it, of erotic orientation—are the products of personal moral choice. No other causal explanation is needed; scientific research is irrelevant. Gender-identity disorder is a fiction perversely constructed by adherents of the medical model. Either it does not exist or it, too, is a moral choice. In the latter case, its prescribed treatment is moral-modification therapy which, carried to its ultimate extreme, becomes the exorcism of demons.

Glossary of Gender Terms

I shall now take the responsibility of disclosing where I stand in the thirty-ninth year since 1955 with respect to a theory of gender-identity disorder in childhood and adolescence. Here, to put first things first, is a brief glossary of terms (Money, 1988).

> *gender:* one's personal, social, and legal status as male or female, or mixed, on the basis of somatic and behavioral criteria more inclusive than the genital criterion and/or erotic criterion alone.

The grammatical and syntactical need of a singular noun with which to circumvent the duality of "gender identity and gender role" is met by telescoping them into the unity of an acronymic noun, G-I/R.

> *G-I/R (gender-identity/role):* gender identity is the private experience of gender role, and gender role is the public manifestation of gender identity. Both are like two sides of the same coin and constitute the unity of G-I/R. Gender identity is the sameness, unity, and persistence of one's individuality as male, female, or androgynous, in greater or lesser degree, especially as it is experienced in self-awareness and behavior. Gender role is everything that a person says

> and does to indicate to others or to the self the degree that one is either male or female or androgynous; it includes but is not restricted to sexual and erotic arousal and response (which should not be excluded from the definition).

In deference to the nomenclature of the DSM-III-R, henceforth I continue to use the term *gender-identity disorder,* even though it should be understood to mean G-I/R disorder.

The next two definitions are formulated so as to be compatible with the idea of development as a series of temporal sequences that may or may not be causal sequences.

> *gender coding:* combined genetic coding, hormonal coding, and social coding of a person's characteristics of body, mind, and/or behavior as either exclusively male, exclusively female, or nonexclusively androgynous relative to a given, and in some instances arbitrary, criterion standard.

> *gender cross-coding:* gender coding in which there is discordance between the natal anatomical sex and one or more of, in particular, the behavioral variables of male and female.

These next two definitions are compatible with the formulation of gender disorder as a developmental transposition or crossover phenomenon, irrespective of etiology.

> *gender transposition:* the switching or crossing over of attributes, expectancies, or stereotypes of G-I/R from male to female, or vice versa, either serially or simultaneously, temporarily or persistently, in small or large degree, and with insignificant or significant repercussions and consequences.

> *gender dysphoria:* the state, as subjectively experienced, of incongruity between the genital anatomy and the G-I/R, particularly in the syndromes of transexualism and transvestism.

Gender and Causality

To observe phenomena in either temporal sequence or spatial contiguity and then to formulate a causal contingency is a phylogenetically ancient heritage of the human mind, and one with a high degree of prepotency. To convert a hypothesis or theory of causal contingency into a proof of causality is an assignment of such magnitude that few achieve it. Proofs of causality in psychology and sexology are few and far between. I have no proven cause of gender-identity disorder in childhood and adolescence, and I do not adhere to any dogma of causality. My policy, over the years, has been to have a developmental template or grid (Figure 1), with labeled markers showing where, from conception onward, causality has been suspected and found, and where the most promising high-yield locations for new research may be staked out (Money and Ehrhardt, 1972).

Genetic Coding and Gender Disorder

No one knows what to expect, in the twenty-first century, from the sequencing of the human genome on the origins of gender-identity disorder. Meanwhile, genetics research has had no direct light to shed on the subject. The most that may presently be expected from genes is that they may create an as yet unknown vulnerability factor or predisposition that will, however, require augmentation from other sources before it can express itself. There may, for example, be such a vulnerability factor fortuitously distributed with a supernumerary X or Y chromosome in males, namely the 47,XXY (Klinefelter) syndrome, and the 47,XYY (supernumerary Y) syndrome (Money, 1980). Concordance studies of homosexuality in male twins may point to a vulnerability factor associated with identical male twinning, but the statistical evidence remains inconclusive (Buhrich et al., 1991).

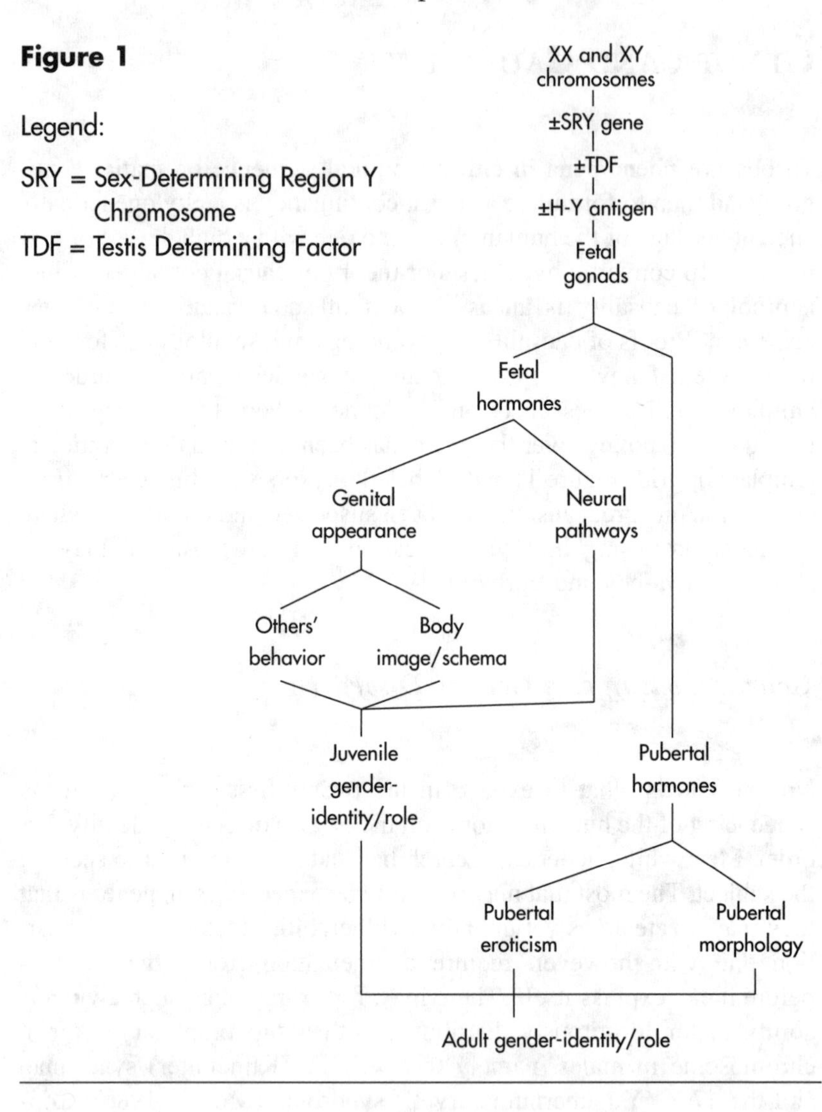

Prenatal Hormonal Coding and Gender Disorder

In the case of prenatal hormonal sex coding of the brain, there is incontrovertible evidence from experimental work with four-legged mammals that gender identity, as inferred from the complete mating ritual, can be masculinized or demasculinized by manipulating the prenatal hormonal environment during a critical period of fetal differentiation.

By way of illustration, there is a sheep movie made at the veterinary school in Edinburgh some fifteen years ago (Short and Clarke, undated; Clarke, 1977). A pregnant ewe, carrying a female fetus, had a pellet of testosterone subcutaneously implanted on day fifty of the pregnancy. Whereas the baby's genital anatomy had already differentiated as female and was not affected by the pellet of male hormone, the undifferentiated sexual brain responded by becoming masculinized. If I commit the scientific sin of anthropomorphism (which I am about to do), then I can say that the gender identity of the animal was also masculinized and that, when the first mating season came around, it thought it was a ram, despite still having two ovaries that secreted female hormones. Moreover, the other members of the flock—rams and estrous ewes alike—also thought it was a ram and reacted to it as such. It went through the complete preliminary mating ritual and mounted a ewe in heat. Its urinary posture was also that of a male.

Subhuman primates resemble prenatally programmed hormonal robots far less than do sheep, and in human primates the resemblance is least of all. Prenatal hormonalization does to some extent program the sexual differentiation of the human brain, however, laying down a template on which the gender identity in all of its complexity will progressively be organized and brought to completion.

The apposite illustration here is that of an uncontrived "experiment of nature," namely the hermaphroditic syndrome of congenital virilizing adrenal hyperplasia (CVAH), which is the human counterpart of the contrived sheep experiment above. CVAH has its origin in a recessive gene which, if present in both the sperm and the egg, accedes to a malfunction of the adrenocortical glands in fetal life and thenceforth so that they secrete not cortisol, but a precursor hormone possessing the androgenic power of masculinization. If the fetus is female, after its internal genitalia have differentiated as female, the androgenic hormone masculinizes the external genitalia.

In an extreme case of hermaphroditism of the CVAH type, the baby will be born with an empty scrotum instead of labia majora, and a normally formed penis instead of a clitoris with clitoral hood and labia minora. In some such cases, the masculinization of prenatal life is not interrupted at birth, but the baby is assigned as a boy and given the endocrine and surgical care concordant with being reared as a boy. His gender identity differentiates from childhood through adulthood as masculine, sexuoeroticality included, despite his chromosomal status as 46,XX and his natal gonadal status as ovarian.

In the counterpart to such a case, the masculinization of prenatal life is interrupted at birth and the baby, assigned as a girl, is given the endocrine and surgical care concordant with being reared as a girl. Her gender identity differentiates from childhood through adulthood as feminine, but with an overlay of characteristics that are popularly stereotyped as masculine and are known as tomboyish. In addition, her sexuoeroticality differentiates with around a fifty-fifty chance of being partly or wholly lesbian.

CVAH cases like the foregoing, with two ovaries and a penile urethra, are very rare as compared with the far more prevalent cases in which there is not a penile urethra but a hypospadiac urethra opening at the base of a grossly hypertrophied clitoris. In the majority of such cases, the baby is assigned and reared as a girl and given concordant endocrine and surgical care. There are now two long-term follow-up studies which have shown the incidence of a partial or complete lesbian sexuoeroticality to be elevated at between 40 percent and 50 percent (Money et al., 1984; Dittman et al., 1991). Conversely, 50 percent or more of women with a CVAH diagnosis and treatment history differentiate a gender identity that is feminine and sexuoerotically heterosexual.

Evaluated in the context of animal experiments and of other varieties of hermaphroditism, the foregoing CVAH data are consistent with the proposition that, in the human species, the differentiation of gender identity (or G-I/R) as masculine, feminine, or mixed cannot be directly attributed to the history of prenatal hormonalization in prenatal life. The principle of gender coding in the brain is such that when it begins in prenatal life, the coding is hormonally programmed, whereas when it is brought to completion in postnatal life, the coding is socially programmed through the senses. Prenatal and postnatal gender coding of the brain may be either concordant or discordant; if discordant, either one may override the other.

In the case of gender-identity disorder in children with no birth defect of the sex organs, today's technology precludes the retrospective ascertainment of the prenatal history of brain hormonalization. There are some cases in which it is on record in the mother's pregnancy history that she was administered hormonal or other medication that might have affected the fetal brain. There is only a sporadic, not a consistent, relationship between such a maternal history and the development of gender-identity disorder in the offspring. Large-scale statistical surveys of the offspring of mothers who took hormones or hormone-like medications while pregnant and those who did not have not yielded a harvest of offspring with gender-identity disorders.

The present state of knowledge regarding the prenatal hormonal history and gender-identity disorder in childhood is that it has not been proven contributory, but cannot be ruled out as noncontributory. It should, therefore, be retrieved to whatever extent possible and kept on record for future research.

Gendermaps

The analogy between gender identity (G-I/R) and native language begins, in prenatal life, with precoding of the brain in preparation for what will follow, and it continues in postnatal life with further development and maturation being contingent on brain coding through the senses from social sources.

The coding of language in the brain is bipolar. The positive pole codes for language that is idiomatic, syntactical, and shared reciprocally. The negative pole codes for language forms that do not match the usage of others and so fail to be communicational.

The developmental coding of gender identity (G-I/R) in the brain is also bipolar. The positive pole codes for "me," for what I am, boy or girl, and the other codes for "not me," for what I am not, girl or boy, respectively. At each pole there is a map or schema of what is coded there. At one pole the map is labeled feminine, and at the other masculine. Everybody—boy and girl, man and woman—has both maps, one depicting "me" and the other depicting "thee." Gender-identity disorder is a signal that the "me" and "thee" gendermaps have, in greater or lesser degree, become crisscrossed. One may displace the other, or both may coexist in alternation (a dual-personality phenomenon), or one may merge into the other, either transiently or long-term and either partially or (much less likely) completely.

Under ordinary circumstances of development, one expects concordance between the prenatal and postnatal coding of an individual's gendermap. In addition, one expects that the gendermap will be concordant with the natal sex of the external genitalia. Under circumstances in which the gendermap is discordant with the natal sex of the external genitalia, the source of discordancy may lie in either the prenatal or the postnatal coding of the gendermap, or in both combined.

Postnatal Coding and Gender Disorder

Irrespective of what is and is not politically correct in gender polemics, people do use the morphology of the external genitalia as the criterion of sex. Having announced a newborn baby as boy or girl, those whose cultural heritage is that of Christendom then proceed—usually with considerable diligence—to keep the irreducible insignia of boyhood and girlhood hidden, and their use in normal sexuoerotic rehearsal play tabooed and abusively punished.

The nonhidden insignia of boyhood and girlhood are not immutable but, like haircut and clothing styles, arbitrary and elective. Even proper names and pronouns are not immutably fixed. This is the backdrop that lends a certain degree of credence in early childhood to the idea that sex change of the body is as plausible as sex change of the body image (Money, 1993). For most children, if the idea materializes at all, it is in play-acting only. There are very few in whom girl-to-boy or boy-to-girl conversion becomes a persistent, unrelenting, and often desperate fixation or monomania which, if brought to professional attention, will be diagnosed as gender-identity disorder of childhood.

Healthy differentiation of the gendermap in infancy and the juvenile years is, like much else in pediatric health, subject to developmental disruption if the environment is pathogenic. There has been no systematic survey of the environmental pathogens that may have a disruptive impact on the developing gendermap. One particular pathogen—this one within the intrafamilial environment—came to my notice for the first time several years ago (Money, 1984). It pertained to a morbid sexological relationship between the parents. I made a notation, at the time, as follows:

> I am dictating a note to put on record a new hypothesis or formula regarding the role of the father in the genesis of feminism in a son's G-I/R (gender-identity/role). This is the formula: the father covertly courts his son's allegiance, in place of what he finds missing in his wife, and casts him in the role of a wife substitute, if not for the present, then for the future. The son, for his part, may solicit his father's allegiance as a formula for keeping him in the household, and for preventing a parental separation. If the father has already gone, or even if he had died, the son's gender transposition may serve to solicit his dad's miraculous return. His life becomes a living fable of

> the boy who will become daddy's bride, for the evidence is plentiful that a daddy can be counted on to return to the home that his wife keeps ready for him (Money, 1988, p. 82).

I nowadays narrate this story as a parable with which to inform the parents of a child with a gender-identity disorder that, although they did not schedule themselves for sexological evaluation, the future of the child's gender identity may well ultimately depend on what they can say about themselves, sexologically, and on what happens to their relationship. It is not just a gender-identity disorder that needs attention, but a three-way relationship that needs to be repaired.

Pubertal Hormonal Gender Coding

Ever since the classification of the sex hormones early in the twentieth century as male and female—androgenic, estrogenic, and progestogenic—there has been a persistent hankering to relate them not only to masculinity and femininity, but also to homosexuality and heterosexuality. Hence the pop-science yearning to find a correlation after puberty between a hormonal imbalance and homosexuality, transexuality, and perhaps transvestism. The serious-science findings are that there is no correlation at any age between gender identity and the measurable levels of hormones circulating in the bloodstream. Children with a diagnosis of gender-identity disorder do not have abnormal levels of circulating hormone prepubertally. The same applies also postpubertally when the expected outcome is not a gender-identity disorder but, in the preponderance of cases, a nondisordered homosexual gender identity and, in a small minority, a nondisordered heterosexual gender identity.

Glossary of Gender Terms, *Continued*

> *gendermap:* a developmental representation or template synchronously in the mind and brain depicting the details of one's G-I/R. It includes the lovemap but is larger, insofar as it incorporates whatever is gender coded vocationally, educationally, recreationally, sartorially, and legally as well as in matters of etiquette, grooming, body language, and vocal intonation. See also *lovemap.*

lovemap: a developmental representation or template synchronously in the mind and brain depicting the idealized lover, the idealized love affair, and the idealized program of sexuoerotic activity projected in imagery or actually engaged in with the lover.

gender-identity disorder: a condition in which there is discordancy, either partial or complete, between the natal sex of the external genitalia on the one hand, and the gender coding of the brain on the other hand. Gender coding of the brain is hormonal in prenatal life and sociosensory in postnatal life. The disorder is characterized phenomenologically by an unrelenting and often desperate or monomaniacal fixation on being a member of the nonnatal sex.

Conclusion

What's in a name? That which we call gender-identity disorder by any other name would be justly known. With apologies to Shakespeare, that simply isn't so. The future historian of sexology and sexological medicine in the second half of the twentieth century will need to know that gender-identity disorder did not, like AIDS, suddenly emerge after mid-century. Instead, what did emerge was a new name for a new concept, gender identity, which brought about a reformulation in how we think about sex and its disorders.

This reformulation diffused far beyond the confines of medicine, where it began, and permeated the policies and politics of sex in society at large. It did so to such an extent that the social history of our era cannot be written without naming gender, gender role, and gender identity as organizing principles.

Bibliography

Benjamin, H. (1966). *The Transsexual Phenomenon: A Scientific Report on Transsexualism and Sex Conversion in the Human Male and Female.* New York: Julian Press.

Buhrich, N., Bailey, J. M., and Martin, N. G. (1991). "Sexual orientation, sexual identity, and sex-dimorphic behaviors in male twins." *Behavior Genetics* 21:75–96.

Cauldwell, D. O. (1949). "Psychopathia transexualis." *Sexology* 16:274–80.

Clarke, I. J. (1977). "The sexual behavior of prenatally androgenized ewes observed in the field." *Journal of Reproduction and Fertility* 49:311–15.

Dittman, R.W., Kappes, M. E., and Kappes, M. H. (1993). "Sexual behavior in adolescent and adult females with congenital adrenal hyperplasia." *Psychoneuroendocrinology* 17:153–70.

Fisk, N. M. (1974). "Gender dysphoria syndrome: The how, what, and why of a disease." In *Proceedings of the 2nd Interdisciplinary Symposium on Gender Dysphoria Syndrome* (D. R. Laub and P. Gandy, eds.). Stanford, CA: Division of Reconstructive and Rehabilitation Surgery, Stanford University Medical Center.

Green, R., and Money, J. (1960). "Incongruous gender role: Nongenital manifestations in prepubertal boys." *Journal of Nervous and Mental Disease* 130:160–67.

Knatchbull-Hugessen, E. H. (1874). *Queer Folk: Seven Stories.* London and New York: Macmillan.

Money, J. (1955). "Hermaphroditism, gender and precocity in hyperadrenocorticism: Psychologic findings." *Bulletin of The Johns Hopkins Hospital* 96:253–64.

———. (1980). "Genetic and chromosomal aspects of homosexual etiology." In *Homosexual Behavior: A Modern Reappraisal* (J. Marmor, ed.). New York: Basic Books.

———. (1984). "Gender transposition theory and homosexual genesis." *Journal of Sex and Marital Therapy* 10:75–82.

———. (1985). "Gender: History, theory and usage of the term in sexology and its relationship with nature/nurture." *Journal of Sex and Marital Therapy* 11:71–79.

———. (1988). *Gay, Straight, and In-Between: The Sexology of Erotic Orientation.* New York: Oxford University Press.

———. (1993). "Body-image syndromes in sexology: Phenomenology and classification." *Journal of Psychology and Human Sexuality* 6(3):31–48.

Money, J., and Ehrhardt, A. A. (1972). *Man and Woman, Boy and Girl: The Differentiation and Dimorphism of Gender Identity from Conception to Maturity.* Baltimore: Johns Hopkins University Press. Facsimile reprint edition, New York: Jason Aronson, 1996.

Money, J., Hampson, J. G., and Hampson, J. L. (1955). "An examination of some basic sexual concepts: The evidence of human hermaphroditism." *Bulletin of The Johns Hopkins Hospital* 97:301–19.

Money, J., Schwartz, M., and Lewis, V. G. (1984). "Adult erotosexual status and fetal hormonal masculinization and demasculinization: 46,XX congenital virilizing adrenal hyperplasia and 46,XY androgen-insensitivity syndrome compared." *Psychoneuroendocrinology* 9:405–14.

Short, R. V., and Clarke, I. J. (no date). *Masculinization of the Female Sheep.* Distributed by MRC Reproductive Biology Unit, 2 Forrest Road, Edinburgh, EH1 2QW, United Kingdom.

Stoller, R. (1968). *Sex and Gender: On the Development of Masculinity and Femininity.* New York: Science House.

9

The Development of Paraphilia in Childhood and Adolescence

TERMINOLOGY

In the United States, the age of childhood's end was changed from sixteen to eighteen years by an act of Congress in 1984. In pediatric practice, childhood generally extends up to the changes of puberty and the onset of adolescence. Adolescence, by convention, ends at eighteen to twenty years, although it has been extended up to the twenty-fifth year in some actuarial statistics.

This chapter addresses the development of paraphilias in childhood through adolescence and into adulthood. Although paraphilias are generally regarded as adult phenomena, they have their antecedents in childhood. In prepuberty, a paraphilia is best characterized as a protoparaphilia; it comes into full bloom in adolescence and adulthood.

To assure consensus of understanding, there are four formal definitions that follow. Except for *gendermap,* which is a new term, these definitions are taken from Money (1988), which can be consulted for additional definitions as required.

Originally published in *Child and Adolescent Psychiatric Clinics of North America* 2: 463–75, 1993, with Galdino F. Pranzarone as coauthor.

Paraphilia (from the Greek *para-,* "altered" + *-philia,* "love"; or "love beyond the usual"): a condition occurring in men and women of being compulsively responsive to and obligatorily dependent on an unusual and personally or socially unacceptable stimulus, perceived or in the ideation and imagery of fantasy, for optimal initiation and maintenance of sexuoerotic arousal and the facilitation or attainment of orgasm. Paraphilic imagery may be replayed in fantasy during solo masturbation or intercourse with a partner. Its antonym is *normophilia.*

The term *sexuoerotic* is used instead of "sexual" and "erotic" so as to provide a singular noun, *sexuoeroticism.* Sexuoeroticism is a unity that combines events occurring between the legs with events occurring between the ears. The singular term is a reminder that one aspect should not be considered without cognizance of the other.

Normophilia (from the Greek *norma-,* "carpenter's square rule" + *-philia,* "love"): the condition that is antipodean to paraphilia. In normophilia, there is no obligatory and immutable dependency on a fixated partner, object, or ritualized activity. The possible range of acceptable and sexuoerotically arousing activities is greater in a normophilic than in a paraphilic person. The criteria of normophilia are not absolute but are statistically, transculturally, and ideologically variable. The ideological norm is imposed by those in power, be it parent, peer, clergy, or police.

Gendermap: a developmental representation or template existing synchronously in the mind and brain (mindbrain) depicting the details of one's gender-identity/role (G-I/R)—the self-identification as male or female and the culture's expectation of behavior for a male or female. The gendermap includes the lovemap (defined below), but is broader insofar as the gendermap also incorporates whatever is gender coded vocationally, educationally, recreationally, sartorially, and legally as well as in matters of etiquette, grooming, body language, and vocal intonation.

Lovemap: a developmental representation or template existing synchronously in the mind and brain (mindbrain) depicting the idealized lover, the idealized love affair, and the idealized program of sexuoerotic activity projected in imagery or actually engaged in with the lover.

The lovemap is subsumed within the gendermap and comprises its sexuoerotic component. The lovemap is always gender-identity coded as male, female, or to some degree androgynous. The lovemap may be heterophilic, homophilic, or biphilic in its partner specification. It is usually quite specific as to details of the physiognomy, build, race, color, and demeanor of the ideal lover and may also specify the ideal lover's athletic and academic achievements, financial status, and so on. A person's lovemap, like native language, accent, face, or fingerprints, bears the mark of that person's unique individuality.

Lovemap Development

Human sexuoerotic diversity coded in the lovemap is analogous to the varieties of native language; the acquisition of both require the preparatory development in embryonic and fetal life of a brain that is both healthy and human. The detailed coding and configuration of a native-language map, a gendermap, and a lovemap are mediated by and contingent on informational input from the social environment through the senses—olfactory, gustatory, haptic, and predominantly auditory and visual. Input into lovemap development occurs from the first pairbonding with the mother or caregiver, possibly under the governance of the hormone oxytocin (Insel, 1992; Pedersen, Caldwell, Jirikowski, and Insel, 1992), through the limerent pairbonding affairs of the adolescent period and later. In adulthood, gendermap and lovemap coding in the mindbrain is complete and relatively immutable. Once a lovemap has formed, it is, like a native-language map, extremely resistant to change. If changes should occur, as is possible in the years of senescence or after intracranial neuropathy or head injury, they do so chiefly by a malfunction in decoding and playback of what has already been encoded.

Lovemap development is multivariate and sequential from conception, when the genetic code is set down, through infancy, childhood, prepuberty, and adolescence into adulthood. The issue is not one of nature versus nurture, but of nature and nurture converging and interacting at a critical period of development, leaving persistent or immutable sequelae in the mindbrain lovemap. Development first begins with the differentiation of what will become the gendermap, which will eventually include the lovemap as one of its components. Lovemap genesis is presently understood only in terms of temporal sequences, not causal sequences.

Lovemap development, as normophilic, hypophilic, hyperphilic, or paraphilic, is concurrent with the development of the gendermap as masculine or feminine. Hypophilia signifies troublesome insufficiency or incompleteness of sexuoerotic arousal and genital function up to and including orgasm. Colloquially, the hypophilic syndromes may be called the Masters and Johnson disorders of sexuoerotic inadequacy (Gosselin and Wilson, 1980). Hyperphilia signifies a vexatious excess of sexuoerotical arousal and genital function in either duration or frequency. Hyperphilic syndromes are poorly named; they include nymphomania, satyriasis, and erotomania (the Clérambault-Kandinsky syndrome). Hyperphilia is also a secondary characteristic of many of the paraphilic syndromes. There is no evidence that paraphilia is preformed or ready-made in the mindbrain at birth, except perhaps as a predisposition.

When the lovemap develops so as to not be normophilic, it may then be considered to have been marred, distorted, or damaged. Such a damaged lovemap is then referred to as a vandalized lovemap (Money and Lamacz, 1989). Hypophilia, hyperphilia, and paraphilia are manifestations of a vandalized lovemap, the details of which are the outcome of displacements, deletions, or inclusions of sexuoerotic elements in the developmental coding of the lovemap from infancy through prepuberty and later. Paraphilic miscoding or vandalization of a lovemap involves a stratagem for wresting triumph from tragedy—in this case, the triumph of saving carnal lust from the tragedy of its extinction or threat of extinction in the wake of either acute or prolonged sexuoerotic trauma. Each stratagem, of which there are seven all told, works by dissociating carnal lust from affectional love.

Juvenile Sexual Rehearsal Play (JSRP)

A cross-species examination of primate juvenile sexual rehearsal play (JSRP) reveals parallels to the human experience. The role of JSRP seems essential as an antecedent to normophilic lovemap development.

In comparison with sheep, whose mating behavior is governed in large part by hormonal preprogramming of the brain before birth

(Clarke, 1977), the mating maps or lovemaps of primates at birth are relatively unfinished.

In the young rhesus monkey (*Macaca mulatta*), play which includes JSRP is an essential precursor of successful mating in adulthood. Rhesus monkeys deprived of JSRP by being reared in social isolation grow up unable to position themselves for copulation, and so fail to reproduce their kind (Harlow and Harlow, 1962; Harlow and Mears, 1979). In contrast, among monkeys that were not totally isolated but allowed a playtime as short as half an hour a day, one-third were successful in adult mating, but they were slow achievers and poor breeders with a low birthrate (Goldfoot, 1977).

The sexual behavior of bonobos (*Pan paniscus*), also known as pygmy chimpanzees, is closer to that of human beings than is that of other primates (deWaal, 1989). As in the human female, a female bonobo's sexuality is independent of her ovulatory cycle. Very young bonobos are seen to engage in extensive JSRP with each other, both homosexually and heterosexually (Sitsen, 1988). These observations, together with comparable JSRP data on immature common chimpanzees (*Pan troglodytes*), orangutans (*Pongo pygmaeus abelii*), and wild mountain gorillas (*Gorilla gorilla beringei*), support the thesis that JSRP is a species-typical antecedent for the behavioral development of normophilia in the great apes (Nadler, 1987).

The contingency between normophilic lovemap development and JSRP in human children follows the nonhuman primate pattern illustrated above. Ethnographic evidence from societies that do not place taboos on children's sexuoerotic development supports the cross-species evidence. In the majority (if not all) of the children in these taboo-free societies, the lovemaps are normophilic and heterosexual (Money and Ehrhardt, 1972). In some of these cultures, paraphilias may even be nonexistent, as indeed appeared to be the case in aboriginal Arnhem Land (Money, Cawte, Bianchi, and Nurcombe, 1970). Taken together, the nonhuman primate and transcultural human data suggest the essential role of JSRP for normophilia.

Lovemap Matching and Mismatching

During the developmental years of JSRP, appropriate matching of the lovemaps of playmates for age synchrony and image reciprocity has a healthy developmental outcome more often than does mismatching. One of the primary criteria of matching, insofar as one can judge from the available evidence of comparative ethnography and comparative primate ethology as aforementioned, is age synchrony. This means that early JSRP takes place predominantly between infants or juveniles whose lovemaps are developing in synchrony. Primate young may learn from the sexual activities of older juveniles, or of adolescents and adults, but they do so from the periphery, with or without playful participation, rather than by reciprocating as an equal in status with the older partner. Synchrony of lovemap age in reciprocal sexuoerotic rehearsal play continues through the juvenile years, but may be less strictly adhered to with the approach of puberty.

Age-discrepant sexuoerotic interaction between children is, for the most part, rare, unless one of the children involved has experienced overt sexual activity as in incest, or is exposed to adult patterns of sexuoerotic expression. Being the younger partner in a pedophilic relationship with a wide age discrepancy between the two partners is a setup for a Catch-22 dilemma (discussed below). Similarly, being the younger partner in an incest relationship can produce the same dilemma. The child may then, when older, reiterate what had happened by repeating it in interaction with a younger friend or relative—for instance, as when a ten-year-old boy, reversing roles, engages in sexual activity with his five-year-old cousin. This behavior does not qualify as authentic paraphilic rapism, although erection, penetration, and climax without ejaculation may have occurred.

The other criterion of lovemap matching in all primate JSRP is male/female image reciprocity. In the earliest years, however, male and female positioning is sex-shared and not sex-discriminant. That is to say, males and females may substitute for one another in cavorting around and playing at presenting and mounting. Homosexual and heterosexual practice serve the same function at the outset. In nonhuman as well as human primates, heterosexual pairing progressively predominates.

Lovemap Vandalization

Lovemap development is vulnerable to vandalism by diverse traumas and stresses in childhood that need not necessarily be explicitly sexual. For example, in a sample of patients with the Kaspar Hauser syndrome

(N = 16; Money, 1992) of psychosocial dwarfism induced by child abuse and neglect, the incidence in adulthood of sexuoerotic disorders, including paraphilia, was 69 percent (N = 11; Money, Annecillo, and Lobato, 1990).

When the precipitating trauma or stress is identifiably sexual, it is classifiable into four categories, namely: (1) explicit neglect of attention to sexual learning and to healthy JSRP; (2) abusive punishment and humiliation of children for engaging in JSRP; (3) premature induction of children into JSRP out of synchrony with the developmental age; and (4) coercion of children into age-discrepant sexual rehearsal play, with or without inflicting bodily injury (Money and Lamacz, 1989). Each of these child-rearing policies fails to recognize JSRP as a statistically normal primate phenomenon and are thus effective in inducing lovemap pathology. They lend themselves to the production of Catch-22 entrapments.

Catch-22s and Opponent-Process

At about age eight, children grasp the significance of the double-entendre in jokes and puns. They also grasp the significance of the no-win entrapment of the Catch-22, in which you're damned if you do and damned if you don't take action. Sexologically, it is a Catch-22 to confess or to not confess to having obtained forbidden sexual knowledge, or to having engaged in prohibited sexual behavior, consensually or otherwise. This is especially true in JSRP. Children entrapped in such a dilemma face the threat of severe sanctions. To quit JSRP would bring ostracism and agemate rejection. Not to quit brings the risk of parental discovery and reprisal. To ask for help may bring about both consequences. Sexual experimentation is thus a minefield of Catch-22s, namely either/or propositions with no compromise in between.

In the sexological development of childhood, the Catch-22s of sexual information or pursuits generate unspeakable monsters which, being unspeakable, are monstrously traumatizing, in many instances more so than the actual occurrence of the JSRP or other sexual activity which must be kept hidden in silence. The more intense the societal sanctions against what a child knows, has pursued, or has been coercively imposed upon sexuoerotically, the more intense the power of the unspeakable monster, as in the case of incest, for example. For a girl of eleven who becomes the coerced lover of her father, the Catch-22 is to tell, say, the mother, who will possibly call her daughter a liar, or to tell the authorities and have her family torn apart. On the other hand, to say nothing is to endure the continuance of incest. The same may apply to a boy.

The penalties and penances that the adult world imposes on children for being entrapped in a sexual Catch-22 constitute, albeit paradoxically, the most prevalent manifestation of child sexual abuse and neglect, and are also the major source of errancy in lovemap development.

According to opponent-process theory (Solomon, 1980), the outcome of being caught in a Catch-22 is that negative and aversive stimuli and situations convert to positive and appetitive. In other words, initial aversion converts to addiction, after which one repeats ad infinitum that which was once forbidden, prohibited, and punished, no matter how dangerous or self-sabotaging. With the development of a paraphilic lovemap, experiences which once were horrible and unthinkable flip-flop and begin to enthrall. If the flip-flop is into masochism, then the pain of being paddled and whipped, which others would avoid, becomes transmogrified into erotic ecstasy.

As paradoxical as it appears, corporal punishment may affect the genitals and their sensations by producing arousal. In boys, the evidence is visible, for they get a panic erection. The best explanation of this reaction is in terms of an arousal of the autonomic nervous system, which generalizes the response to bodily insult from being noxious to being sexuoerotic.

A letter from a student in India, in a British-style school with a tradition of corporal punishment, demonstrates an opponent-process transformation in the lovemap (Money, 1987):

> . . . During my schoolhood in a Christian missionary Anglo-Indian Institute in Calcutta we were (all boys) often caned on our upturned, upraised buttocks by the headmaster (with his attractive wife sometimes looking on and passing humiliating, sarcastic comments). Needless to say, this brutalized our lovemaps and in certain cases brought about orgasms and a sickening addiction to the rod and a good whipping.
>
> . . . I was nine when the canings began, and seventeen when I left school. For the others it may have started earlier, slightly. I got sexual feelings from around the age twelve, especially if she was watching. We usually collected five or six cuts of the cane, but once I got eighteen. . . .

> . . . This addiction has resulted in certain friends hiring Anglo-Indian prostitutes to spank them. One is going through a divorce because his wife can't stand an emotional, sexual cripple pervert, and leper (her words, not mine)! . . . Men should be trained in auto-eroticism and to accept their buttocks/derriére and anus as means to pleasure themselves . . . (pp. 273–74).

This account indubitably demonstrates the formula wherein tragedy becomes triumph. Aversive pain becomes addictive pleasure. Lust is reconciled with hurt and humiliation by the paradoxical erotization of suffering into the ecstasy of orgasmic masochism. The price of this reconciliation is the severance of lust from pairbonded love. It is typical of paraphilia that the affectional-love partner (madonna) and the carnal-lust partner (whore) are not the same person. This is why it is more accurate to say that paraphilias are affectional-love disorders rather than carnal-lust or sex disorders.

To be smitten with a paraphilia is to be fixated on the partner and the paraphernalia of the paraphilia. Fixation is an essential feature of the formula whereby a normophilic lovemap converts to a paraphilic one. Triumph is snatched from the jaws of tragedy, and carnal lust is preserved, but at the cost of its separation from affectional love.

Not enough is known about the concatenation of factors that go into the development of a paraphilically vandalized lovemap to make diagnostic predictions about which boy or girl, if exposed to similar vandalizing experiences, will or will not emerge with a paraphilia. There are no effective diagnostic tests. An allowance must be made, as aforesaid, for a vulnerability factor, such as an intracranial neuropathy or history of head injury. There is no established contingency between paraphilia and hormonal functioning. Pedigree genetics are noncontributory; however, chromosomal genetics may be contributory, notably in the supernumerary Y syndrome (47,XYY) in males (Money, 1991). A facility or propensity to experience the opponent-process phenomenon (Solomon, 1980) also may be contributory.

As with any injury, a vandalized lovemap attempts to heal itself and function sexuoerotically. Nevertheless, in the process it becomes scarred, skewed, and misshapen. Some of the sexuoerotic features of the lovemap become, as aforesaid, omitted, some become displaced, and some become replaced by substitutes that would not otherwise be included. Omission of sexuoerotic features more likely transforms an ordinary heterosexual lovemap into a hypophilic one, whereas displacements and inclusions of sexuoerotic features more often transform it into a paraphilic or hyperphilic one, sometimes concurrently.

The paraphilic transformation and stratagem seems at the time to be a satisfactory compromise. It disassociates lust from its place alongside love in the lovemap and relocates it. In the long run, however, this relocation proves to be a compromise that is too costly. In a paraphilic lovemap, lust is attached to fantasies and practices that are forbidden, disapproved, ridiculed, or penalized. In extreme cases, the penalty is death.

Taxonomy of Paraphilia

The human species is phyletically designed in such a way as to permit many variations in the basic sexuoerotic imagery of mammalian mating. Whether normophilic, hypophilic, hyperphilic, or paraphilic—heterophilic or homophilic—mating is subdividable into three phases: proceptive (attraction and courtship), acceptive (bodily and genital union), and conceptive (conception, gestation and parturition). Proceptivity in humans may be manifested as a species-shared stereotypical ritual of courtship and behavior usually called "foreplay." However, human proceptivity exists not only as behavior, but also as the rehearsal of that behavior in the totality of imagery and ideation found in dreams, daydreams, fantasies, and thoughts projected from an individual's lovemap. This projection can be ascertained not only through observation, but also through verbal report.

Paraphilias are preeminently anomalies of proceptivity rather than acceptivity. In paraphilia, sexuoerotic functioning becomes particularly biased or skewed with respect to the ideation and imagery of the proceptive phase, that is, the arousal phase of sexuoeroticism. Paraphilia signifies that sexuoerotic arousal and orgasm are contingent on a rehearsal in imagery and ideation of eccentric or unusual practices or rituals that may also be carried out during masturbation or in actual behavior with a partner. No absolute criterion standard exists by which to separate paraphilia as a personal, harmless, and playful eccentricity from paraphilia as a social nuisance or a noxiously morbid or lethal syndrome, as is the case in some extreme forms of paraphilic sadism. In current biomedical usage, paraphilia has largely displaced the terms "perversion" and "deviancy." In legal usage, the term "perversion" still persists. In the vernacular, the synonyms are "kinky" or "bizarre" sex. Some—but not all—paraphilias are criminalized. Of the forty-plus paraphilias which have been identified and defined (Money, 1986, 1988; Money and Lamacz, 1989), only a minority come under the jurisdiction of the law. For example, being paraphilically dependent upon being administered an enema for sexuoerotic arousal and orgasm (klismaphilia) is not a criminal sex-offense.

Males are likely to become proceptively aroused predominantly through vision, and females predominantly through the sense of touch. This sex difference is very likely phyletically determined. Paraphilically, its significance is that paraphilic imagery in males is highly visile, whereas in females it is highly tactile. Another possibly related sex difference, not yet adequately explained, is that paraphilias are more often reported in males than in females, whereas in females hypophilias, especially anorgasmia, predominate.

Some paraphilic manifestations are thematically simplex, and others are thematically duplex or multiplex. The latter are compounded with features of two or more simplex paraphilias merged into one complex whole. Paraphilias may occur concurrently with heterophilia, or with the gender transpositions of transvestism, transexualism, or homophilia. Whereas transvestophilia (fixation on cross-dressing for sexuoerotic arousal and orgasm) is one of the paraphilias, transexualism and homophilia alone are not considered paraphilic.

The forty-plus paraphilias that have been identified are categorized under seven grand stratagems. The term *stratagem* is used rather than "strategy" because a stratagem has the quality of a ruse or trickery. It deceives and circumvents the enemies of lust regardless of the cost, which may turn out to be exorbitant. The taxonomy of the stratagems that follow delineates what may happen to human beings phyletically as a species so that the outcome is a paraphilic lovemap. The taxonomy does not, however, delineate the personal ontogeny of paraphilic lovemap formation. The seven grand stratagems are as follows:

The *sacrificial/expiatory stratagem* requires reparation or atonement for the sin of lust by way of penance and sacrifice.

The *marauding/predatory stratagem* requires that, insofar as saintly lovers do not consent to the sin of lust, a partner in lust must be stolen, abducted, or coerced by force.

The *mercantile/venal stratagem* requires that sinful lust be traded, bartered, or purchased and paid for, insofar as saintly lovers do not engage consensually in its free exchange.

The *fetishistic/talismanic stratagem* spares the saintly lover from the sin of lust by substituting a token, fetish, or talisman instead.

The *stigmatic/eligibilic stratagem* requires that the partner in lust be, metaphorically, a pagan infidel, disparate in religion, race, color, nationality, social class, or age from the saintly lovers of one's own social group.

The *solicitational/allurative stratagem* protects the saintly lover by displacing sinful lust from the act of copulation in the acceptive phase to an invitational gesture or overture in the proceptive phase.

The *understudy/subrogation stratagem* requires one to rescue and deliver another person from suffering the defilement of lust by nobly and altruistically taking that other person's place.

For a complete exposition of the stratagems, see Money (1986, 1988) and Money and Lamacz (1989).

Clinical Retrospective Studies

Evidence for the childhood origins of paraphilia may be derived from retrospective clinical studies. A childhood biographical history of the development of a paraphilic lovemap may be reconstructed retrospectively from personal recall. Ideally, such experiences should be authenticated with evidence, such as confirmation from the recall of others. In forensic matters, authentication is imperative; retrieved memories are invariably subject to omission, distortion, and confabulation. Additional information may be found fortuitously preserved in the pediatrician's record and confirmed in subsequent long-term follow-up. The clinic thus provides preliminary evidence from which to develop hypotheses for future investigation. However, the association between socioerotic events and paraphilic syndromes signifies only what is antecedent and subjectively construed and is therefore not necessarily causal.

With surprising regularity, one finds in the biographies of paraphiles that events experienced as sexuoerotically traumatic are reported as having occurred at or around the developmental age of eight. This period in a child's life emerges as a crucial time for the incorporation of a paraphilic omission, intrusion, or displacement into the developing lovemap which consequently may distort or vandalize it, as seen in the following examples.

In one case, a woman told of abuse at age six by her stepmother who had beaten her hands until they were "blood red and swelled up" in order to extract a confession of masturbation. When the child was eight, the stepmother found the girl masturbating in the bathtub and accused her of being a "bad little girl" with the boys at school. The stepmother then brought in a needle and thread, pricked the girl's labia, drew blood, and said she would sew them up if she ever caught her doing it again. When the girl was eleven, the stepmother died of cancer. Shortly thereafter, she was sexually abused by her father until her menses began. At age thirteen, she ran away from the domestic trauma at home and entered into collusional relationships and two marriages in which she manifested the paraphilic syndrome of masochistic-abuse martyrdom. She in effect then stage-managed her own oppression and suffering at the hands of her partners (Money, 1981).

Antecedents occurring even earlier than age eight may be implicated in paraphilic fetishism. Fetishism is an example of an inclusion—namely of the fetish—into a lovemap so that there exists a fixation upon the specific object or material. Without the fetish, sexuoerotic arousal and orgasm are impaired. Fetish objects are typically associated with infantile tactile or olfactory stimuli from the human body. Fetishes are called hyphephilic when they are akin in tactile quality to human skin or hair. When they are akin to human odors, they are designated as olfactophilic.

Gosselin and Wilson (1980) found that of their sample of rubber fetishists, the majority reported first awareness of sexuoerotic arousal to rubber between the ages of four to ten years (N = 100, Mdn = 8.5 yrs.). Rubber does not, of course, evoke sexuoerotic arousal in the majority of young children. Sargent (1988), a rubber fetishist and professional psychotherapist, recalled that his earliest memory was of a woman playing with his penis by stroking it with soft rubber panties and her long dark hair. As a child of two or so, he enjoyed the skin of his face, stomach, and penis coming into contact with the rubber sheet placed under the cotton one. He was able to date a gift of rubber animals received on his third birthday.

Prospective Clinical Studies

The logistics and costs of studying the development of paraphilia prospectively from infancy onward in a randomly selected sample of children have, as of the present time, effectively ensured a dearth of early developmental-incidence data from the population at large. Through lack of identifying markers, it is not now possible to assemble an at-risk infantile or juvenile sample for a long-term outcome study. The most reasonable alternative approach is to record data on the sexuoerotic development of children who have a variety of pediatric diagnoses which necessitate longitudinal follow-up. Applying this strategy, Money, Annecillo, and Lobato (1990) documented a relationship between the Kaspar Hauser syndrome of abuse dwarfism in infancy and childhood, and a syndrome of paraphilia in adolescence and later (see above). The same research strategy applied to a large clinical sample of children with an endocrine and/or congenital sex-organ defect yielded seven biographies in which the postpubertal emergence of a paraphilia could be related to prepubertal vandalization of the lovemap. In each case the child became trapped in a Catch-22 pertaining to the secret of his or her diagnosis and treatment. Each experienced some degree of stigmatization in childhood. The paraphilias that appeared in the seven cases were, apart from one case of pedophilia, variants of masochism (Money and Lamacz, 1989).

Treatment

In the pharmacologic approach to the clinical treatment of paraphilia, medroxyprogesterone acetate (Depo-Provera) has been extensively and effectively utilized (Lehne, 1988). The rationale for using an antiandrogen is that it is able to lower the circulating androgen titers to the level of prepuberty. There is a corresponding reduction in the frequency and intensity of paraphilic fantasies and urges. For the male paraphile, treatment with Depo-Provera gives him the opportunity to gain more effective governance over the expression of his paraphilia. In some patients, the effect of Depo-Provera is augmented if used in conjunction with lithium carbonate, which in other patients has proved beneficial when used alone. Whereas Depo-Provera has provided relief for adolescents whose paraphilic ideation, imagery, and behavior are problematic, the use of Depo-Provera has not been tried in juveniles. An alternative antiandrogenic hormone is cyproterone acetate (Androcur), used in Europe and Canada, but not yet cleared by the FDA (Food and Drug Administration) for use in the U.S.A.

In addition to pharmacologic therapy with antiandrogenic hormone, some psychoactive drugs have been anecdotally reported to be therapeutically successful in the treatment of paraphilias in adulthood. These drugs include lithium carbonate (Cesnik and Coleman, 1989), buspirone (BuSpar; Federoff, 1992), fluoxetine hydrochloride (Prozac; Bianchi, 1990; Perilstein, Lipper, and Friedman, 1991), and, by verbal report, carbamazepine (Tegretol), clozapine (Clozaril), and goserelin (Zoladex). Some psychiatrists also prescribe thioridazine (Mellaril), a phenothiazine and major tranquilizer that may induce impotence and suppress ejaculation as side effects (Money and Yankowitz, 1967). Recent reports on the relationship of oxytocin to sexuoerotic phenomena and its relatedness to the pairbondance of lovers and the mother-infant bond (Insel, 1992; Pedersen, Caldwell, Jirikowski, and Insel, 1992) suggest the experimental use of oxytocin and, possibly, oxytocin antagonists for the treatment of paraphilia. For the pharmacologic treatment of sexual disorders overall, see Sitsen (1988). Pharmacologic therapy, to be maximally effective, should always be accompanied by talking therapies or counseling.

Training therapies are those with an ancient history that derives from the reward-and-punishment training used by animal trainers, and a recent history that derives from conditional reflexology and operant conditioning. Training therapies are subsumed under the generic name of behavior modification and biofeedback. Their aim is to eliminate or modify symptoms. Their use for the treatment of paraphilias is predominantly found in correctional institutions. Their efficacy over the very long term has not been tested, however. As applied to males, a highly controversial and unproved version of behavior modification entails the timing of rewards and punishments to coincide with changes in penile tumescence in response to erotic pictures or stories. The penis is harnessed into a plethysmograph which records changes in its dimensions.

Apart from institutional detention or foster-home placement, the most common intervention for the treatment of juvenile and adolescent protoparaphilia or paraphilia is some form of talking therapy—either individual, family, or group therapy. For very young children, play therapy is also used. Free-associative (psychoanalytic) or nondirective psychotherapy is, however, not compatible with the psychopathology of the paraphilia and is ineffectual. In conversational dialogue, however, protoparaphilic or paraphilic juveniles and adolescents are able to be talkative, even voluble, provided they do not encounter a finger-wagging response of blame and judgmentalism. They do not know why they do what they do and are often quite interested in trying to figure it out. Since no one has a complete answer to the question of why, only talking about it does not necessarily produce a higher likelihood of success than simply waiting for spontaneous remission and then offering rehabilitative support. Talking is of help in the reorganization of a life, especially after the disruption of a period of detention. Ultimately, however, one looks forward to advances in molecular neuroscience and neuropsychopharmacology to provide changes in the sexuoerotic malfunction of paraphilia so that talking treatments can be successfully superimposed.

The treatment of the individual alone is often not as efficacious as treatment within the family in the form of family therapy, or within a consortium of his peer relationships; the "group" in group therapy is a consortium of people with the same or similar diagnosis.

Self-help groups that provide supportive rehabilitative environments or opportunities for troopbonding of individuals with shared dilemmas and interests do not exist for juveniles or adolescents who are developing or have developed a paraphilia. Support groups that do exist are informal and semi-underground networks of adults who have identified one another as sharing a common paraphilia. The oldest of these organizations are for transvestophiles, but similar organizations are known to exist for apotemnophiles (those who have a sexuoerotic fixation on the stumps of amputees), rubber fetishists (Gosselin and Wilson, 1980), klismaphiles (whose fixation is on enemas), sadomasochists (some of whom are fixated on genital mutilation), and pedophiles. One threat to these self-help support groups is that their mail, phone, and computer bulletin-board services are scanned by the criminal-justice system. Thus it is virtually impossible for older paraphilies to underwrite help or offer support to adolescents and juveniles undergoing the same sufferings as they themselves once did.

Prevention

The extent to which sexology professionals can get involved in advancing research on paraphilias and providing preventive and protective services for juveniles and adolescents is, today, severely limited by lack of funding. In addition, public opinion favors criminalization rather than medicalization of paraphilia.

The ultimate culprit responsible for paraphilia in the lovemap is the powerful antisexualism found in the taboos to which our society is heir. Antisexual taboos commit a society to the obliteration in childhood of the very sexuoeroticism that it prescribes in adulthood as normal and necessary. A new and frightening antisexual initiative is seen in the attempt to criminalize JSRP and to punish and incarcerate juvenile offenders. In the professional-victimology literature, a new category of criminal deviant has emerged: the very young juvenile sexual offender or child perpetrator. The child perpetrator literature fails, however, to adhere to established tenets of scientific inquiry. It also attempts to pathologize species-typical childhood sexual rehearsal play (Nadler, 1987). In actuality, it surreptitiously reflects a backlash response to the sexual emancipation of the 1960s and early 1970s, the era of the so-called sexual revolution. This new trend toward treating all JSRP as criminal behavior, if successful, will ironically achieve a pathological outcome opposite from that intended. Developing lovemaps will be vandalized by the trauma of the well-meaning but ill-informed guardians of children's welfare. Thus, rather than diminishing the incidence of paraphilia, such misguided social policies may well expand it exponentially from one generation to the next.

The sexual taboo can also be held responsible for the failure of medical institutions to establish specialty clinics in pediatric and ephebiatric (adolescent) sexology. As a consequence, there is no agreed-upon body of scientific and medical knowledge by which to gauge whether a child's lovemap is developing normophilically or paraphilically. Correspondingly, there is no agreed-upon method of effective corrective intervention in the developmental years of childhood. There is also no public-health policy for the ultimate eradication of paraphilias in society. Both the prevention and the correction of lovemap errors during childhood are still at the trial-and-error stage.

REFERENCES

Bianchi, M.D. (1990). "Fluoxetine treatment of exhibitionism." *American Journal of Psychiatry* 147:1089–90.

Cesnik, J. A., and Coleman, E. (1989). "Use of lithium carbonate in the treatment of autoerotic asphyxia." *American Journal of Psychotherapy* 43:277–86.

Clarke, I. J. (1977). "The sexual behavior of prenatally androgenized ewes observed in the field." *Journal of Reproductive Fertility* 49:311–15.

de Waal, F. (1989). *Peacemaking Among Primates.* Cambridge–London: Harvard University Press.

Fedoroff, J. P. (1992). "Buspirone hydrochloride in the treatment of an atypical paraphilia." *Archives of Sexual Behavior* 21(4):401–406.

Goldfoot, D. A. (1977). "Sociosexual behaviors of nonhuman primates during development and maturity: Social and hormonal relationships." In *Behavioral Primatology, Advances in Research and Theory* (A. M. Schrier, ed.). Hillsdale, NJ: Lawrence Erlbaum.

Gosselin C., and Wilson, G. (1980). *Sexual Variations.* New York: Simon & Schuster.

Harlow, H. F., and Harlow, M. K. (1962). "Social deprivation in monkeys." *Scientific American* 207(5):136–46.

Harlow, H. F., and Mears, C. (1979). *The Human Model: Primate Perspectives.* Washington, DC: Winston.

Insel, T. R. (1992). "Oxytocin—A neuropeptide for affiliation: Evidence from behavioral, receptor autoradiographic, and comparative studies." *Psychoneuroendocrinology* 17:3–35.

Lehne, G. K. (1988). "Treatment of sex offenders with medroxyprogesterone acetate." In *Handbook of Sexology, Volume 6: The Pharmacology and Endocrinology of Sexual Function* (J. M. A. Sitsen, ed.). Amsterdam: Elsevier.

Masters, W. H., and Johnson, V. E. (1970). *Human Sexual Inadequacy.* Boston: Little, Brown.

Money, J. (1981). "Paraphilia and abuse martyrdom: Exhibitionism as a paradigm for reciprocal couple counseling combined with antiandrogen." *Journal of Sex and Marital Therapy* 7:115–23.

———. (1986). *Lovemaps: Clinical Concepts of Sexual/Erotic Health and Pathology, Paraphilia, and Gender Transposition in Childhood, Adolescence, and Maturity.* New York: Irvington. Paperback edition, Amherst, NY: Prometheus Books, 1988.

———. (1987). "Masochism: On the childhood origin of paraphilia, opponent-process theory, and antiandrogen therapy." *Journal of Sex Research* 23:273–75.

———. (1988). *Gay, Straight, and In-Between: The Sexology of Erotic Orientation.* New York: Oxford University Press.

———. (1991). *Biographies of Gender and Hermaphroditism in Paired Comparisons: Clinical Supplement to the Handbook of Sexology.* Amsterdam: Elsevier.

———. (1992). *The Kaspar Hauser Syndrome of "Psychosocial Dwarfism": Deficient Statural, Intellectual, and Social Growth Induced by Child Abuse.* Amherst, NY: Prometheus Books.

Money J., Annecillo, C., and Lobato, C. (1990). "Paraphilic and other sexological anomalies as a sequel to the syndrome of child-abuse (psychosocial) dwarfism." *Journal of Psychology and Human Sexuality* 3:117–50.

Money J., Cawte, J. E., Bianchi, G. N., and Nurcombe, B. (1970). "Sex training and traditions in Arnhem Land." *British Journal of Medical Psychology* 43:383–99.

Money J., and Ehrhardt, A. A. (1972). *Man and Woman, Boy and Girl: The Differentiation and Dimorphism of Gender Identity from Conception to Maturity.* Baltimore: Johns Hopkins University Press. Facsimile reprint edition, New York: Jason Aronson, 1996.

Money J., and Lamacz, M. (1989). *Vandalized Lovemaps: Paraphilic Outcome of Seven Cases in Pediatric Sexology.* Amherst, NY: Prometheus Books.

Money, J., and Yankowitz, R. (1967). "The sympathetic-inhibiting effects of the drug Ismelin on human male eroticism, with a note on Mellaril." *Journal of Sex Research* 3:69–82.

Nadler, R. D. (1987). "Behavioral dimorphisms in the sexual initiative of great apes." In *Masculinity/Femininity: Basic Perspectives* (J. M. Reinisch, L. A. Rosenblum, and S. A. Sanders, eds.). New York: Oxford University Press.

Okami, P. (1992). "Child perpetrators of sexual abuse: The emergence of a problematic deviant category." *Journal of Sex Research* 29:109–30.

Pedersen, C. A., Caldwell, J. D., Jirikowski, G. F., and Insel, T. R., eds. (1992). *Oxytocin in Maternal, Sexual, and Social Behaviors.* New York: New York Academy of Sciences.

Perilstein, R. D., Lipper, S., and Friedman, L. J. (1991). "Three cases of paraphilias responsive to fluoxetine treatment." *Journal of Clinical Psychiatry,* 52:169–70.

Sargent, T. O. (1988). "Fetishism." In *The Sexually Unusual: A Guide to Understanding and Helping* (D. M. Dailey, ed.). New York–London: Harrington Park Press.

Sitsen, J. M. A., ed. (1988). *Handbook of Sexology, Volume 6: The Pharmacology and Endocrinology of Sexual Function.* Amsterdam: Elsevier.

Small, M. F. (1992). "What's love got to do with it? Sex among our closest relatives is a rather open affair." *Discover* 13(6):46–51.

Solomon, R. L. (1980). "The opponent-process theory of acquired motivation: The costs of pleasure and the benefits of pain." *American Psychology* 35:691–712.

Part Three

Ancestral Explanations

10

Homosexualization of the Visual Release of Lust

NATURE NEEDS NURTURE

Renamed essentialism versus social constructionism, the egregious rivalry between doctrines of nature versus nurture as causes of homosexuality (and, therefore, of heterosexuality) is as alive and well in the present era of genes and the genome as it was in the pre-Darwinian era of the Enlightenment. In that eighteenth-century era, the nature of human nature was sought in the noble savage and in such renowned and mysterious cases as the "Wild Boy," Victor of Aveyron (Itard, 1962), and Kaspar Hauser of Nuremburg (Money, 1992).

The rivalry between nature and nurture in explanations of sexual orientation is a rivalry that has no right to exist. Nature does not exist in a vacuum, nor does nurture. The genome cannot be unfurled except within the preordained limits of the genomic environment. Instead of yesterday's paradigm that nature and nurture are adversaries, today's new paradigm is that nature needs nurture.

According to the old paradigm, nature is equated with biological and nurture with societal explanations of the cause of homo-, hetero-, and bisexuality. In the ultimate analysis, however, all explanations of sexuality, no matter where they begin, reach their destination along a

Unpublished manuscript, accepted for publication in *Medical Hypotheses*: In press, 1999.

final common pathway in the brain. The brain is the central organ for the coding of sexuality, no matter whether the data to be coded originate phylismically (i.e., species-determined; Money, 1990) or environmentally, singly or in combination, simultaneously or sequentially. In this sense, sexuality is always biological; there is a biology of learning as well as of genes and hormones (Money, 1997).

Homosexual/Heterosexual Criteria

There is a certain panache attached to neuroanatomical, genetic, and prenatal hormonal explanations of male/female and homosexual/heterosexual differences in sexual orientation (LeVay, 1991, 1996; Hamer et al., 1993; Hu et al., 1995; Swaab, Gooren, and Hofman, 1992). Whatever their merits, such explanations fail to pin down the meaning of the term *sexual orientation* with empirical precision. They do not specify exactly what is being coded in the brain that makes sexual orientation different in males and females and in heterosexuals and homosexuals. Sexuality is too multivariate to be coded at one particular brain locus, by a single set of genes, or a single prenatal hormonal determinant.

In everyday usage and in the sexological literature, the criterion of homosexual and heterosexual is the genital anatomy of the partner in a sexual encounter. If each sexual partner has a penis, then their sexual activity is male homosexual. If each has a vulva, then their sexual activity is lesbian. If one has a penis and the other a vulva, then their activity is heterosexual.

Defining homosexuality on the criterion of the sexual anatomy of the partner is legalistic. It does not consider the situational or chronological circumstances of the sexual engagement. Moreover, it does not differentiate a homosexual act from a homosexual person. Nor does it differentiate the feminoid from the viriloid homosexual male, nor the masculinoid from the uxorioid lesbian. The corresponding terms in the gay vernacular are, respectively, "sissy" and "queen" versus "butch" and "leather queen," and "butch" or "diesel dyke" versus "lipstick lesbian."

The viriloid male homosexual and the uxorioid lesbian may conform to the socially prescribed criteria of masculinity and femininity, respectively, including the begetting of children. They may, in fact, be bisexual rather than exclusively homosexual. What they share in common with, respectively, feminoid male homosexuals and uxorioid lesbians, is this: Their lust response is released by a stimulus emanating from a partner who has the same sexual body morphology as their own. In heterosexuals, the lust response is released by a stimulus emanating from a partner whose sexual body morphology is other than their own.

Stimuli That Release Lust

According to the evidence of evolutionary sexology, the stimulus that emanates from an established or potential partner and releases a lust response could be either olfactory, contrectative (haptic or tactual), or visual. Smell as a chemical attractant is typical of subprimate mammals. The attractant odor or pheromone is secreted from the estrual vagina and is picked up, at a distance, in the vomeronasal organ within the male's nose. Among primates, the nose leaves off where the eyes take over. In the human species, the eyes are the primary distance receptors of the stimuli of lust, with the contrectative skin senses being a close follow-up.

The stimulus image that releases a human lust response may be the perceived image of a live person, or a printed or electronic representation of a live person. It may be the image of a fictive person produced in fantasy or it may be a memory image. The features of the image may be of someone well known or of a stranger. For bisexual people, the features and body morphology of the image may sometimes be male and sometimes female. For exclusively homosexual males or lesbians, the features and body morphology of the image is, respectively, male or female only.

The sexual body morphology of the image that stimulates the release of a lust response constitutes a defining characteristic of homosexual, heterosexual, and bisexual orientation in the human species. It goes together with another defining characteristic, namely the sexual body morphology of the partner with whom one is able to fall in love and become love-smitten.

The defining characteristic of exclusive heterosexuality and exclusive homosexuality is that the sexual body morphology of the lust-arousing image does not change, whereas in the bisexual it is interchangeable. Once the exclusively homosexual or heterosexual image enters the brain it becomes immutably lodged there, a property that belongs to the brain. The stages, from embryonic life onward, by which it becomes immutable constitute a fertile field for future sexological research and explanation.

Fetal/Neonatal Brain Coding

According to the precepts of ethological theory, the brain is developmentally precoded with an innate recognition and releasing mechanism in response to certain categories of stimuli subsequently encountered at a critical age and stage of life. The stimulus-response bond that becomes imprinted in the brain then is long-lasting. According to these precepts, the sexual brain is innately precoded as either male or female to recognize the image of a potential partner's sexual body morphology (or a part thereof) as the attractant that releases the response of lust. In heterosexuality, innate precoding is for the body morphology other than one's own; in homosexuality, the same as one's own; and in bisexuality, a ratio of the two. The source of the transposition in homosexuality may be prenatal hormonal which, in turn, may be gene-regulated. However, no explanation is, as yet, adequately complete.

One possible explanation is that the developmental embryonic strategies responsible for the differentiation of the male and female pelvic procreative anatomy include distant neuroanatomical connections within the brain. Further, in the case of the heterosexual, these brain connections include also connections with the visual cortex and with a visual schema of the sexual body morphology of the other sex. In the case of the homosexual, the visual schema is of the same sex as one's own.

There is a general principle of embryonic sexual differentiation, namely that female differentiation has primacy over male (Money, 1995). Thus the brain of the fetal female would be coded for the future release of lust in response to the stimulus image of the male. To suppress this coding in the fetal male's brain and to replace it with a female image as a lust attractant necessitates the superimposition of an additional, not yet ascertained developmental determinant—possibly androgen. Should that superimposition be complete, then the ultimate outcome is an exclusively heterosexual male. Should it be only partial, then the outcome might be bisexual. Should the superimposed determinant have failed for whatever reason, then the outcome would be exclusive male homosexuality.

In the lust coding of the brain of the developing female fetus, an incomplete overlay of the masculinizing determinant, regardless of its source, may have a bisexual outcome, whereas the outcome of a complete overlay would be exclusive lesbianism. In the exclusively heterosexual female, there would be no overlay at all.

The power of a visual lust image to release a lust response is shared by, but is not identically the same in, men and women. Men are relatively more dependent on the eyes as the organs of lust arousal from a distance than women are. Women, by contrast, are more dependent on the closer contrectative (haptic and tactual) skin senses than men are. What their eyes perceive, men approach and woo. Women display and invite, then hold and enfold. These differences are manifest not only in heterosexual but also in homosexual relationships. When they are reciprocally discordant, a power struggle is likely to ensue and the relationship, heterosexual or homosexual, is imperiled. The ramifications of sight versus touch account for a good deal of disparity between the homosexual male and lesbian woman with respect to the durability of paired relationships.

The fact that women are more dependent on the contrectative senses than on vision may also be the source of the feminist doctrine that lesbianism is a voluntary choice and a political statement. With the eyes closed, male and female touch may be more neutral and less easy to distinguish than male and female visual appearance. Proportionately more women than men in the general population may consider themselves bisexual, whereas more men than women consider themselves as exclusively homosexual or, conversely, as exclusively heterosexual.

From the viewpoint of evolutionary sexology, it would be strange if the procreativity of the human species did not have a phylismically ordained stimulus for the release of lust, namely the image of the sexual body morphology and touch of a potential partner. These two lust-release phylisms, the one visual and the other contrectative, are the irreducible base on which the full sexuality of lust has multiple overlays, including overlays that are psychodynamic in origin. With all of its overlays in place, the sexuality of lust is subject to a high degree of individual variability, idiosyncrasy, and indeed eccentricity, as for example in the paraphilias (Money, 1988).

The multivariate and sequential determinants of the many faces of lust in all of their complexity have not yet been fully traced and catalogued scientifically. Homosexual and heterosexual lust both have many faces and they also wear many masks.

DEFINITIONS

contrectation: erotic stimulation by fondling, handling, touching, and fingering.
feminoid: feminine, although not female.
masculinoid: masculine, although not male.
pheromone: an odoriferous secretion that acts as a chemical attractant or repellent between members of the same species or other species.
phylismic: phylogenetically coded; common to all members of a species and not unique to a specific individual.
phylism: one of the rudimentary building blocks of behavior that belong to all members of the species and are phylogenetically transmitted, not ontogenetically inculcated.
uxorioid: conventionally feminine except for same-sex attraction (e.g., an uxorioid lesbian).
viriloid: conventionally masculine except for same-sex attraction (e.g., a viriloid gay male).
vomeronasal organ: a sense organ situated bilaterally on the vomer (nasal septum) that may respond to pheromones directly, bypassing the sense of smell.

REFERENCES

Hamer, D. H., Hu, S., Magnuson, V. L., Hu, N., and Pattatucci, A. M. L. (1993). "A linkage between DNA markers on the X chromosome and male sexual orientation." *Science* 261:321–27.

Hu, S., Pattatucci, A. M. L., Patterson, C., Li, L., Fulker, D. W., Cherny, S. S., Kruglyak, L., and Hamer, D. H. (1995). "Linkage between sexual orientation and chromosome Xq28 in males but not in females." *Nature Genetics* 11:248–57.

Itard, J. M. G. (1962). *The Wild Boy of Aveyron* (G. Humphrey and M. Humphrey, trans.). Englewood Cliffs, NJ: Prentice-Hall.

LeVay, S. (1991). "A difference in hypothalamic structure between heterosexual and homosexual men." *Science* 253:1034–37.

———. (1996). *Queer Science: The Use and Abuse of Research into Homosexuality.* Cambridge, MA: MIT Press.

Money, J. (1988). *Gay, Straight, and In-Between: The Sexology of Erotic Orientation.* New York: Oxford University Press.

———. (1990). "Pedophilia: A specific instance of new phylism theory as applied to paraphilic lovemaps." In *Pedophilia: Biosocial Dimensions* (J. R. Feierman, ed.). New York: Springer-Verlag.

———. (1992). *The Kaspar Hauser Syndrome of "Psychosocial Dwarfism": Deficient Statural, Intellectual, and Social Growth Induced by Child Abuse.* Amherst, NY: Prometheus Books.

———. (1995). *Gendermaps: Social Constructionism, Feminism, and Sexosophical History.* New York: Continuum.

———. (1997). *Principles of Developmental Sexology.* New York: Continuum.

Swaab, D. F., Gooren, L. J. G., and Hofman, M. A. (1992). "The human hypothalamus in relation to gender and sexual orientation." *Progress in Brain Research* 93:205–17.

11

Hypothesis of Song, Sex, and Speech

In early twentieth-century comparative sexology, the only role assigned to the mammalian female in mating was to be receptive to the male. Periodically or seasonally, she became copulatively attractive to the male by reason of the hormonally induced vaginal odor or pheromone of being in estrus (that is, in heat). In the laboratory, estrus and receptivity toward the male could be induced by sequential hormonal injection of estrogen and progesterone. This simplistic view of receptivity changed when, in 1976, Frank Beach introduced the new term *proceptivity* in a publication titled "Sexual attractivity, proceptivity, and receptivity in female mammals."

In this paper, Beach focused sexological attention on the proceptive phase of the courtship ritual or display, also known as the mating dance and, in the human species, as flirtation as well as foreplay. Proceptivity precedes and is prerequisite to the phase of penovaginal union. To illustrate: the urban dog marks his domain by dribbling urine on upright markers, and at the same time sniffs the ground for the urine of a bitch in heat. An odoriferous sex attractant or pheromone in his own urine advertises his presence to rival males and also to estrual females ready to copulate. The male dog's nose is exquisitely sensitive at detecting and discriminating odors even at a distance. Neighborhood dogs, with tails held upright and muzzles forward, track down the

---

Originally published as "Evolutionary sexology: The hypothesis of song and sex." *Medical Hypotheses* 48:399–402, 1997.

source of the pheromonal odor of a bitch in heat, and nuzzle and smell her hindparts. Then ensues a "you-may/you-may-not" doggie dance in which the female, crouching on forepaws, allows one of the males to make a prancing approach, from which she coyly backs off, then turns and runs away. Many times repeated, this approach-and-chase procedure concludes with her accepting or receiving one of the males as her copulatory partner. He reciprocates, so that the two accept or receive one another in genital union. She crouches or lordoses, and he mounts. The other males disperse, leaving the couple to remain tied in the copulatory lock until his penile bulb detumesces.

This stereotyped proceptive and acceptive-receptive canine mating ritual is exhibited by dogs everywhere, and thus is phylogenetically ordained independently of individual (ontogenetic) history (Money, 1996). Like the mating rituals of other four-legged mammals, filmed in sheep for example by Short and Clarke (undated), it is carried out as if by a biogenic robot. The mating rituals of subhuman primates, especially the great apes, are less biorobotic and more diversified, but much less so than those of human primates. No other species equals the human species in the diversity and multiplicity of personalized mating rituals, as exemplified in erotic fantasies, for example, and in the paraphilias, some of which are highly idiosyncratic.

Paraphilias in ideation, imagery, and practice range from trivial and entertaining to morbid and lethal. In the law and in psychoanalysis, paraphilias are known as perversions, and on the street as kinky sex. Paraphilia is the official biomedical term in DSM-IV (1994). There are forty-odd paraphilias (Money, 1986, 1988). The total number is contingent upon whether a general category, like fetishism, is subdivided and named according to the fetish object, and upon whether a multiplex paraphilia is named as a single syndrome with multiple components or subdivided into multiple syndromes compounded together.

An example of a commonly occurring paraphilia is sadomasochism, whereas an uncommon one is klismaphilia, in which erotic arousal and performance are contingent on receiving an enema. One of the playful paraphilias is narratophilia, obligatory erotic or dirty talk between a usually straight-laced couple as an aid to erotic arousal. At the opposite extreme, two of the most pathological paraphilias are serial assaultive rape and serial lust murder. Paraphilias are rated as pathological on the criterion of the degree of their exclusivity, fixatedness, and compulsive autonomy.

In the mind and the brain, sexuoeroticism—paraphilic or otherwise—is represented as a lovemap, which is defined as follows:

> *Lovemap:* a developmental representation synchronously existent in the mind and the brain (the mindbrain) depicting the idealized lover, the idealized love and sexual affair, and the idealized program, solo or partnered, of sexuoerotic activity projected in private imagery and ideation or in observable performance.

Somewhere along the evolutionary way, human lovemaps were emancipated from the restrictive confines of being biorobotic to become developmentally diversified and idiosyncratic instead. This emancipation constitutes a theoretical challenge for evolutionary sexology. It does not necessarily bestow a procreative advantage; on the contrary, it may to some degree bestow even the reverse. In the pathology of some of the paraphilias, for example, procreation may be limited or nil, as in lust murder. How then might one account for the existence of evolutionary emancipation from biorobotism in human lovemaps?

In answer to this question, the evolutionary hypothesis proposed in this essay is that emancipation of the lovemap was, eons ago, part of an emancipation of all the mindbrain's biorobotic maps, and that this emancipation was essential for, and coincident with, the evolution of the speechmap for human language. The speechmap is defined as follows:

> *Speechmap:* a developmental representation synchronously existent in the mind and the brain (the mindbrain) depicting the generic principles of linguistic dialogue, syntactical reasoning, and numerical logic, as well as the idiom of one's own language or languages. In multilingualism, each language has a corresponding speechmap and can be translated from one to the other.

Developmentally, in the human species, the lovemap and the speechmap (and also all other mindbrain maps—e.g., the foodmap) are multivariately and sequentially coded and have a high degree of personalized heterogeneity. In subhuman species, by contrast, each type of mindbrain map is phyletically ordained to develop ontogenetically so that it is replicated from one individual to another. The locus of maps in the subhuman brain is presumably in the paleocortex, whereas in the human species mindbrain maps are represented to a much greater degree in the neocortex as well.

In subhuman mammals, the mindbrain's lovemap governs the sequence of sexual attraction, courtship (proception), and copulation in a highly predictable and stereotypic fashion. Synchrony between female hormonal periodicity, on the one hand, and the timing and frequency of copulation, on the other, is a basic principle of quadrupedal mammalian sexology. Quadrupedal locomotion allows the male nose and its vomeronasal organ to have easy access to the smell and taste of the female's genitals and to pheromones generated in the vagina concurrently with ovulation when the female is behaviorally in heat. These smell and taste stimuli, in turn, incite the male to make reciprocal responses that lead to copulation.

Among primates, the bonobo *(Pan paniscus)*, formerly known as the pygmy chimpanzee, is the only species in which the diversity of usage of the sex organs resembles that of the human species (Kano, 1990, 1992; de Waal, 1988, 1989, 1990, 1996). Otherwise, the human species is sexuoerotically unique among primates in the following three evolutionary ways.

First, human beings are emancipated from quadrupedal to bipedal locomotion, and thus from having the nose and the genital organs on the same plane as they are in quadrupeds that are sexually aroused by smell, and also from exclusively dorsoventral to ventroventral (missionary) copulatory positioning as well. Second, they are emancipated from regular hormonal and pheromonal cyclicity to sporadic periodicity in mating. Third, they are emancipated from the nose in favor of the eyes, augmented cutaneously, as the organs of sexuoerotic attraction and arousal.

These three evolutionary emancipations expanded to include a fourth emancipation, namely emancipation from the phyletically fixed soundmaps of communicative hoots, yowls, clicks, whistles, squeals, barks, snarls, chatters, screams, grunts, and yells. Instead, communication would become more versatile by the inclusion of crooning, cooing, humming, and chanting with rhythmic and syllabic intonation, melody, phrasing, and mimicry of audible sounds, all of which are features of musical songmaps.

Still today, subhuman primates and other mammals on land and in the ocean, together with fish (Lobel, 1991), retain nonmusical soundmaps, whereas only human beings have musical soundmaps, for which the apt name is songmap. Nonmusical soundmaps held little evolutionary promise of human speech, with its verbal dialogue, syntactical reasoning, and numerical reasoning. Perhaps, therefore, the primordial origins of human language ought not to be sought exclusively in the mindbrain map for warnings, alarms, threats, food alerts, and other vocal signals, but also in the songmap. Then follows the corollary that human language began as a protomusical love song—maybe also a lullaby! Like the mating invitation of a songbird, the love song would have been at first a song without words, a song of solicitation and allure. If the human species were not a singing species, it may never have evolved into a talking species. The songmap is the evolutionary bridge that connects the lovemap and the speechmap.

According to contemporary research, music and language are differently mapped in the human mindbrain, and also differently represented in the left and right hemispheres. Both are closely tied to the lovemap. Song and dance are ingredients of sexuoerotic attractivity and arousal worldwide, especially in the culture of adolescence. We may not fall in love when we sing, but we certainly sing and wax poetic when we fall in love.

Lovemap: Phyletic Essentials

To recapitulate: in the evolution of human language, the lovemap is related in the mindbrain to the language map (speechmap) by way of the songmap. Evolution of the speechmap required a degree of mindbrain flexibility and versatility not present in the various mindbrain maps of the prelinguistic mammalian brain. Emancipation of the lovemap opened the way to a range of sexuoerotic diversity so wide that it easily masks the bare essentials of what is phyletically coded into the human lovemap solely to guarantee perpetuation of the species. These bare essentials are three in number; the names coined for them are *haptoerotic, morphoerotic,* and *gnomoerotic*. The age of hormonal puberty is the chronological pivot toward which the development of all three has been in rehearsal, and after which they go into full production on center stage.

Haptoerotic

Haptoerotic (from the Greek *haptikos,* "to grasp or touch" + *Eros,* the god of love) means genitoerotic stimulation and response related to touch and the cutaneous senses. Haptoeroticism, especially in the early years of puberty, may be a sequel to frictional movement (for example, of clothing), with or without accompanying erotic imagery or ideation. It may also be autoerotically induced, as in digital or some other technique of masturbation, with or without erotic ideation and imagery. Haptoeroticism has a kinship with tickling and massage in being qualitatively different when self-performed than when performed by a partner. With a partner, haptoerotic arousal typically begins with body surfaces in juxtaposition, while engaged in pressing, stroking, rubbing, licking, or sucking, and progressing to intromission. Phyletically, the bare essentials of intromission are that something is put somewhere, not only that the penis is put in the vagina or that the vagina engulfs the penis. The fingers may take the place of the penis, and the mouth or anus may take the place of the vagina. The inserter does the mounting and thrusting, and the recipient does the presenting (crouching or lordosis in nonhuman mammals) and engulfing. Mounting and thrusting are predominantly a male practice, and presenting and engulfing predominantly a female practice, but they are not absolutely fixed as male or female, respectively, but are to some degree sex-interchangeable, as can be demonstrated in contrived animal experiments. Literally, therefore, they should be characterized as ambisexual.

Morphoerotic

Morphoerotic (from the Greek *morpho-*, "form," + *Eros,* the god of love) means genitoerotic stimulation and response related to the image, depiction, or appearance of a particular shape or form. Although morphoerotic idiosyncrasies are myriad and extremely varied, what they share in common is that, in the heterosexual majority of the population, males are turned on by the female morphology or some detail of it, and females are turned on by the male morphology or some detail of it. Regardless of male homosexual subtyping as feminal versus virile and of lesbian subtyping as masculate versus femme, in the homosexual minority of the population natal males are turned on by the male morphology, and natal females by the female morphology. In the bisexual minority, males and females are turned on by both morphologies.

Morphoeroticism corresponds to olfactoeroticism in the lower mammalian species. Phylogenetically, they are ordained to be ruled by the nose; thus the male dog's nose is exquisitely sensitive to the genital odor of the bitch in heat. By contrast, morphoeroticism in the human species is ophthalmoerotic. Phylogenetically, our species is ordained to be ruled by the eyes, more predominantly so in the male than the female. No research has yet been directed toward ascertaining how or when the developing lovemap in the mindbrain is equipped with ophthalmoerotic receptors that release sexuoerotic responsivity when activated by the matching morphoerotic image of, in monosexuality, male or female, and in bisexuality, both male and female.

Hypothetically, the ophthalmoerotic image could be transcribed directly into the lovemap from a male/female determining segment of the genome. More likely, the transcription would be developmentally progressive by way of hormonal modulation in fetal or neonatal life, followed by a subsequent overlay of sensorial and social imprinting in infancy and childhood.

Whatever the ultimate explanation might be, the sex of the human morphoerotic image as male or female indisputably differentiates heterosexual from homosexual genitoerotic stimulation and response. What the sex of the image will be commonly declares itself contemporaneously with puberty and with the first love-smitten infatuation or limerent attraction. It appears in erotic dreams as well as waking reveries and fantasies, and in response to cognitional stimuli.

Gnomoerotic

Gnomoerotic (from the Greek *gnome,* "thought, judgment, opinion," + *Eros,* the god of love) means genitoerotic stimulation and response related to ideation and imagery—that is, to what one personally recognizes, knows, and can report narratively to be sexual and erotic. Under primordial conditions of troopliving, human juveniles—like the juveniles of contemporary subhuman primates in the wild—would assimilate knowledge of sex by exposure to the copulation of adolescents and elders and by participating in juvenile sexual rehearsal play. Contemporary children who have restricted access to explicit sexual knowledge are destined, therefore, to develop lovemaps that are restricted and susceptible to error. Thus the sexuoerotic versatility of the human mindbrain may actually become a liability insofar as it allows for the improvisation and imprinting of lovemap pathology.

One pathological outcome is the multiplicity of paraphilic stratagems, each one formed when a nonsexuoerotic phylism is pried loose from its locus of origin and coopted into the service of sexuoerotic arousal. Pain, for example, when pried loose from injurious hurt, may be put into the service of masochistic sexuoerotic ecstasy.

Evolutionary sexology may provide a theory to explain why the human species is, phylogenetically, a species susceptible to paraphilic and other sexuoerotic variations, but it does not provide a theory to explain why some individuals are ontogenetically more susceptible than others. For that explanation, it may be necessary to search the genome for an alteration of the genetic code that marks a person susceptible to dissociative error in the coding of the lovemap. That search may be like looking for a needle in a haystack, but it is not totally without feasibility in the present era of sequencing the human genome.

References

American Psychiatric Association. (1994). *Diagnostic and Statistical Manual of Mental Disorders, Fourth Edition.* Washington, DC: American Psychiatric Association.

Beach, F.A. (1976). "Sexual attractivity, proceptivity, and receptivity in female mammals." *Hormones and Behavior* 7:105–38.

de Waal, F.B.M. (1988). "The communicative repertoire of captive bonobos (*Pan paniscus*) compared to that of chimpanzees." *Behaviour* 106(3/4): 183–251.

———. (1989). *Peacemaking Among Primates.* Cambridge, MA: Harvard University Press.

———. (1990). "Sociosexual behavior used for tension regulation in all age and sex combinations among bonobos." In *Pedophilia: Biosocial Dimensions* (J. R. Feierman, ed.). New York: Springer-Verlag.

———. (1996). *Good Natured.* Cambridge, MA: Harvard University Press.

Goodman, S. (1996). "Fish say the darndest things." *National Wildlife* 34(2):48–55.

Kano, Y. (1990). "The bonobos' peaceable kingdom." *Natural History* 11: 62–71.

———. (1992). *The Last Ape: Pygmy Chimp Behavior and Ecology.* Stanford, CA: Stanford University Press.

Lobel, P. (1991). "Mating stratagies of coastal marine fishes." *Oceanus* 34:19–26.

Money, J. (1986). *Lovemaps: Clinical Concepts of Sexual/Erotic Health and Pathology, Paraphilia, and Gender Transposition in Childhood, Adoles-*

cence, and Maturity. New York: Irvington. Paperback edition, Amherst, NY: Prometheus Books, 1988.

———. (1988). *Gay, Straight, and In-Between: The Sexology of Erotic Orientation.* New York: Oxford University Press.

———. (1997). *Principles of Developmental Sexology.* New York: Continuum Publishers.

Short, R.V., and Clarke, I.J. (no date). *Masculinization of the Female Sheep.* Distributed by MRC Reproductive Biology Unit, 2 Forrest Road, Edinburgh, EH1 2QW, United Kingdom.

12

Paleodigms and Paleodigmatics

Definitions and Examples

Paleodigm and *paleodigmatics* are two newly coined terms, here defined for the first time:

> *Paleodigm:* an ancient example or model of a concept, explanation, instruction, idea, or notion, preserved in the folk wisdom of mottos, proverbs, superstitions, incantations, rhymes, songs, fables, myths, parables, revered writings, sacred books, dramas, and visual emblems (from the Greek *paleo,* "ancient" + *deigma,* "example," derived in turn from *deiknyai,* "to show").
>
> *Paleodigmatics:* the organized body of knowledge and theory of paleodigms.

Folk wisdom penetrates the idiom of our everyday language. We assimilate its paleodigmatic meanings, make them our own, and then—though we may fail to recognize what we are doing—put them to our own use.

Take, for example, the paleodigm of a child being sacrificed by a parent. It is found in the biblical story of Abraham sacrificing Isaac, in

Originally published in *American Journal of Psychotherapy* 43:15–24, 1989.

which the sacrifice is discontinued before being consummated in death. It is found also in the very basis of the Christian religion (John 3:16), insofar as God the father so loved the world that he gave his only begotten son to die on the cross so that sinners might believe and not perish, but have everlasting life.

The paleodigm of salvation by sacrifice is of ancient, almost certainly pre-Biblical origin. Geographically, it is widely diffused. In Greek mythology, it appeared as the story of Andromeda, daughter of the Ethiopian king, Cepheus, and his wife Cassiopea. Andromeda was rescued by Perseus from the rock where she had been chained as a sacrifice to the sea monster from whom the people sought deliverance.

There are modern day stand-ins for Abraham and for Cepheus and Cassiopea. Some of them do progressively sacrifice their child and ultimately terminate its life. Others are suspected or confronted before the sacrifice is completed and while the child is still alive. They are then uncannily resourceful at camouflaging what they are doing and explaining away the evidence, no matter how convincingly it implicates them. That is why they themselves are said to have Munchausen's syndrome by proxy when the history of sacrifice, not yet completed, is finally authenticated, as in the following case reported from a British hospital (Southall, Stebbens, Rees, et al., 1987).

Case 1

A twenty-month-old boy, the third child of a twenty-two-year-old mother, had been admitted because of a series of sudden and unexplained attacks of suffocation. Four more attacks in the hospital were diagnostically without explanation, so the boy was linked to diagnostic monitors and put in a special observation room. The next attack occurred when the special nurse briefly left the boy alone with his mother. The child was resuscitated and tested. The results raised suspicions. The mother refused to have her constant vigil relieved by a replacement. To prevent the child's sudden death, a consultative committee decided to coopt the security police, and hidden video cameras were installed in the child's hospital room.

For sixteen hours the cameras recorded nothing untoward in the mother's bedside behavior. Then, after moving her chair away and lowering the railing of the baby's bed, she placed a tee shirt close to the baby's face. Five minutes later, she stuffed the shirt into the baby's mouth and nose, and held his head down forcibly. The baby struggled violently until the nursing staff, having been alerted, intervened.

The published report indicated that the mother admitted that this was not the only occasion that she had suffocated her baby. She was sentenced to three years on probation with psychiatric treatment recommended. The only information of potential explanatory value was the mother's own history of having herself been an abused child.

This case is only one of dozens that have appeared in the pediatric literature since 1976, the year in which the term *Munchausen's syndrome by proxy* was coined (Money and Werlwas, 1976; Money, 1986a) and applied diagnostically to parental child abusers, so that their behavior became classified not only as criminological, but also as medical and pathological.

Munchausen's Syndrome by Proxy

Medical "impostoring" was eponymously (and somewhat facetiously) named *Munchausen's syndrome* by Richard Asher (1951). The name is derived from Rudolf E. Raspe's account of Baron Munchausen's *Narrative of his Marvellous Travels and Campaigns in Russia,* first published in London in 1785. The book was progressively enlarged in many subsequent editions, so that Hieronymous Karl Friedrich von Munchausen became in literature, even more than in life, a symbol of mendacious exaggeration and imposture. A diagnosis of Munchausen's syndrome is given to those patients whose illness is an imposture and whose symptoms are self-induced. A diagnosis of Munchausen's syndrome by proxy is given when the symptoms are not self-induced, but are induced in another person. In pediatrics, the other person is a child who may be brought in by the parents who have induced the ailment. In pediatrics or in adult medicine, the outcome of medical imposture may be lethal.

The correct diagnosis of Munchausen's syndrome by proxy leads to an accurate prognosis and, above all, to expeditious and efficacious treatment, namely removal of the child from the custody of the parent or guardian who is the medical impostor. Diagnosis, however, does not provide insight into the origin and irrationality of medical impostoring. Paleodigmatics does not provide a full explanation of the etiology of

Munchausen's syndrome by proxy in a parent or other provider of child care, but to construe the irrationality of injuring or killing one's own child in terms of the paleodigm of sacrifice and redemption does make it a bit more comprehensible.

Syndrome of Abuse Dwarfism

Case 2

I first deciphered the quasi-religious principle of sacrifice camouflaged in Munchausen's syndrome by proxy in connection with the case of a boy of sixteen who had the physique age, mental age, and social age of a child of eight (Money, 1977; Money, Annecillo, and Hutchinson, 1985). He was severely dwarfed in stature because his pituitary gland had failed to secrete growth hormone. His diagnosis was the syndrome of abuse dwarfism, so named because the failure to grow physically, mentally, and socially was caused by extreme child abuse from the age of three onwards, until he was rescued at the age of sixteen. After the rescue, the pituitary resumed secretion of growth hormone and there was a significant, though incomplete, degree of physical, mental, and social catch-up growth.

The story of abuse could be told by the boy himself and confirmed by relatives, but they could not explain why it had happened. The information from which an explanation could be deduced was gradually produced by relatives over a period of months. The parents themselves were in prison; they also had no reasonable explanation. As pieced together, the biography of a child abuser belonged chiefly to the mother, with the biography of the father being one of mostly passive collusion.

The mother was, in fact, his stepmother. His natal mother and her paramour, his father of conception, had died in an auto crash when he was a baby. He was three years old when his deceased mother's husband, his legal father, remarried. The new wife had had four children of her own. The oldest, a daughter, had been born out of wedlock when the mother was a teenager. The next three were children of her first marriage. These three, but not the oldest daughter, were given up for adoption after the marriage failed. At that time the mother had been clinically diagnosed as depressed but she did not pursue treatment.

In middle teenage, this woman's personality had reputedly undergone a rapid change. From a well-behaved religious girl, she had become a rebellious delinquent. The change had followed hospitalization for third-degree burns suffered when her robe had caught on fire, apparently accidentally. While she was in the hospital, her grandmother, devoutly religious, prepared her for final absolution in anticipation of the last rites by disclosing to her the secret of her birth. Her natal father was not the same man as the father of her siblings, she being their half-sister. She herself had been born out of wedlock. Her grandmother's husband, the man she knew as her grandfather, was actually her natal father. Knowing this incest secret traumatized and reshaped her life.

At the time she remarried, she was well thought of in the neighborhood and had no reputation for cruelty or abusiveness toward children. She quit working to become a full-time homemaker. Her husband needed her not only as a wife, but also as a mother to his four children. He was a hard-working wage earner who could not run his household as a single parent. He had no reputation as a child abuser in his former marriage.

Of the four children, it was the youngest, the three-year-old boy, who became the sacrificial lamb. Like his stepmother, he also had been born out of wedlock. It was his destiny to become a stand-in for herself, an atonement to redeem her from the original sin of incest in which she had been conceived and with which she was forever tainted. Intellectually, of course, she did not make this connection, nor did her husband. The enormity of the deprivation and cruelty she meted out on the child was beyond her own explanation, as well as her husband's. Self-righteously, she justified herself as being generous toward him by keeping him at home instead of putting him away in an institution for the hopelessly retarded.

Opponent-Process

In the ideal morality of child care, the majority opinion is that parents are the ones who should sacrifice themselves for their children, and not that children should be sacrificed for their parents. The reversal represents a manifestation of the principle of opponent-process (Solomon,

1980), whereby negative becomes repolarized as positive and aversive becomes repolarized as addictive. For example, a daredevil sky-diver changes from being terror-stricken initially to being ecstatically euphoric subsequently. The switch may, according to one hypothesis, be accompanied by a flood of endorphin, the endogenous opiate, released from brain cells. Quite literally, the sky-diver becomes high, or quasi-manic, as if from the "rush" of a drug.

The opponent-process principle applies also to the sexual syndromes that are collectively known as the paraphilias (formerly, the perversions). The defining principle of paraphilia is that it constitutes a stratagem whereby lust is rescued from total obliteration when love and lust become separated or dissociated from one another in the cerebral and mental organization known as the *lovemap* (Money, 1986b). According to the terms of the split, love is relegated to the realm of romance and affection. It may be expressed not only privately but also in public where it is licit, provided it is not in overt conjunction with lust. Lust itself is relegated to the realm of carnality and defilement. It may express itself only by way of an underhanded or clandestine stratagem which, in some instances, is illicit and a criminal offense. In addition, lust's stratagem in paraphilia requires that the copartner in the expression of lust not be the same person as the copartner in the expression of love.

The lust-preserving stratagem of a paraphilia comes into being as a product of opponent-process insofar as the very stratagem that preserves lust is the one that previously was lust-aversive. For example, the stratagem of erotic bondage and being beaten has become lust-positive for the masochist, whereas it had previously been lust-negative in that same person's life until the opponent-process flip-flop took place.

The stratagems of paraphilia number at least forty. The precise count depends on whether or not minor variations are subdivided and counted separately. Regardless of the total count of the paraphilic stratagems, they can be distributed into seven overall categories or grand stratagems. Within each grand stratagem is the hidden code of a paleodigm, and it is from this paleodigm that the grand stratagem is named (Money, 1984, 1986b, 1988).

Seven Paraphilic Paleodigms

Sacrifice and Expiation: In paraphilia, as in the child abuse of Munchausen's syndrome by proxy, this grand stratagem encodes the paleodigm of sin and its expiation or atonement through sacrifice. In this case, the sin is the experience of lust in genitoerotic arousal and orgasm. The ultimate in paraphilic sacrifice is serial lust murder. Its converse or antipode is the self-arranged risk of one's own accidental autoerotic death, by self-asphyxiation, for example, or by accidental self-electrocution. Alternatively, the risk of one's own erotic death may be self-stage-managed with another actor or actors coopted to perform in what may conclude as an accidental erotic homicide. Another form of paraphilic sacrifice is the punishment inflicted or received in a sadomasochistic performance.

Marauding and Predation: This grand stratagem encodes the paleodigm of capturing and possessing another human being by force, entrapment, or abduction. In military history, when victorious armies raped the women of the enemies they had defeated, rape was defined not as the sexual coercion of the female, but as the misappropriation of another man's property, for she belonged to either her father or her husband. In contemporary usage, the heterosexual meaning of the term *rape* has been changed to signify vaginal penetration insisted upon after a female—who may be a wife, paramour, or date—says no to a male (rape of a male by a female is rarely considered). Rape defined in this way bears only peripheral relationship to the clinical syndrome named *raptophilia* (the Latin derivative) or *biastophilia* (the Greek derivative). In the syndrome of raptophilia, the raptophile's genitoerotic arousal and, eventually, the orgasm are contingent on having a partner who, as a captive, is forced to yield sexually under threat of assault and injury.

Mercantilism and Venality: This grand stratagem encodes the paleodigm of obtaining goods or services by bartering and trade, of which a specific instance is the payment of the bride price or the payment of the dowry in an arranged marriage. A mercantile or venal paraphilia is one in which the paraphile's genitoerotic arousal and orgasm are contingent on making some form of payment. In the orgasm trade, lust is a commodity, bought and sold independently of love and affection.

Fetishism and Talismanism: This grand stratagem encodes the paleodigm of being in possession of an object or artifact that has extraordinary power of causality, which enables its possessor to control events and to make the otherwise impossible come to pass. A paraphilic fetish or talisman is an object or artifact that, as a stimulus of genitoerotic arousal and orgasm, substitutes for the person who is its owner. There are two categories of paraphilic fetishes and talismans. One comprises the touchy-feely or hyphephilic artifacts that are derived from human-body contact, especially with skin and hair. The other comprises the tasty-smelly or olfactophilic artifacts that are derived from human body tastes and smells, especially sweaty and crotch smells.

Stigmatism and Eligibility: This grand stratagem encodes the paleodigm of love at first sight, the irresistible attraction that draws an observer toward an erstwhile stranger even at a distance, as if the meeting had been inevitably predestined by an inexplicable fate. Some people explain it as due to the chemistry of love. Since there are, as yet, no laboratory tests for the brain's chemistries of love, it is more down to earth to explain the attraction as the observer's sudden recognition that there is something about the stranger that exactly mirrors the imagery and ideation of his or her brain's own *lovemap* (Money, 1986b). The observer is love-stricken. If the stranger responds by being love-stricken also, then the reciprocal match holds promise of becoming the proverbial marriage made in heaven. It is the romantic alternative to an arranged marriage in which the partners are matched by a broker or by the elders of their family and kin. Though the qualities that trigger love at first sight are not necessarily discordant with family ideals, they may be so. Then they derive their power from what they signify as a repudiation and defiance of family ideals. Thus, the heir to a politically conservative fortune may be able to be smitten in love only if his/her lover meets the eligibility requirements of belonging not only to an ethnic stock that is socially anathema to the heir's family, but also to a radical political faction or religious cult which is equally anathema.

Solicitation and Allure: This grand stratagem encodes the paleodigm of what is known in the animal kingdom as assortative, conspecific mating while being in season or in heat. It may take the form of a mating dance or courtship display, the gestures of which are an overt presentation of the sex organs as an invitation to copulate. Except in live shows and movies for erotic entertainment, in the human species the mating dance is more likely to be a debutante ball or disco dance than a display of the naked genitalia. Solicitation and allurement become paraphilic when, instead of being invitational and preliminary to bilateral eroto-sexual involvement, they are engaged in unilaterally and themselves constitute the trigger on which orgasm is dependent. Thus, the person being solicited or allured needs only to look and thus is spared the defilement of genital contact. Despite this fact, people fear that both the paraphilic exhibitionist and the peeping Tom (voyeur) will also be a rapist; but paraphilic rape (raptophilia) belongs in the category of marauding and predation, and rarely overlaps with paraphilic solicitation and allure.

Subrogation and Understudyship: This grand stratagem encodes the paleodigm of rescue and deliverance by one who nobly and altruistically takes the place of someone else who would otherwise suffer and be a victim. A paraphilic subrogate or understudy is one whose lust becomes released only if, by taking on the role of someone else as sexual partner, he or she emancipates that person from the duty and obligation of being in that role. For example, there are some instances of paraphilic adultery in which the role of at least one of the adulterous pair is to rescue the other's spouse from having to perform sexually. There are also some instances of paraphilic incest in which the same stratagem applies. It may apply also in association with commercial prostitution, in which case the choice of prostitution as a career is paraphilic as well as monetary. Subrogation or understudy paraphilias may be heterosexual, homosexual, or mixed.

Nosological Application and Intervention

The syndromes of paraphilia are not the exclusive domain of sexual paleodigms—witness the syndrome of anorexia nervosa. Fasting to achieve spiritual purity is the paleodigm encoded in this syndrome. Impurity for the anorexic patient is very frequently (if not always) the impurity of lust. It is not necessary for the anorexic patient, male or female, to know in advance that self-starvation to achieve purity from lust actually reduces the subjective experience of lust and sexual desire, and induces hormonal changes that eventually suppress fertility and, in the female, menstruation.

In anorexia nervosa, self-starvation has profound effects on the endocrine system and its regulation of fertility and procreation. Similarly, in the syndrome of abuse dwarfism, the experience of deprivation and abuse have profound effects on the endocrine system and its regulation of statural growth and intellectual and social maturation. Both syndromes serve as a reminder that paleodigmatic theory is not one-sidedly a theory of nurture versus nature, nor of mind over matter. Rather, it is a three-term theory, in which the middle term is *critical period,* as in:

nature/critical period/nurture
mind/critical period/matter

Nature and nurture (or mind and matter) work together, hand in glove, during a critical period of development or existence, and produce an outcome that may be temporary and mutable or persistent and immutable. Somatically and behaviorally, in any given instance the full range of the outcome, as well as its mutability-immutability ratio with or without the intervention of treatment, needs to be ascertained empirically, not declared by fiat.

Therapeutically, one of the assets of paleodigmatic theory is that a paleodigm allows a patient to explain what otherwise appears to be a personal-health mystery, and to do so without experiencing the explanation as self-accusatory, insulting, or unfairly judgmental. When the paleodigm has religious connotations, the way is opened for more effective pastoral counseling, provided the counselor has been schooled in paleodigmatics.

The full range of syndromes to which paleodigmatic theory might apply will need to be ascertained empirically. As a general rule, it would appear that they are those syndromes in which the symptoms correlate with a given set of life circumstances and encounters in which the patient becomes either entrapped or excluded, irrespective of the degree to which either entry or escape may have been optional or coercively imposed. Panic attacks replete with somatic alterations are a prime example. They are epitomized in such paleodigmatic colloquialisms as being "scared shitless," having the "piss scared out of" oneself, turning "as white as a sheet," having "butterflies in the stomach," and so on. Phobic attacks are another example. They are epitomized in such paleodigmatic sayings as being "scared to death," "scared stiff," "stopped dead in one's tracks," "having one's hands turn cold and clammy," and so on.

Despite some conceptual resemblance, paleodigms differ from the archetypes of Jungian psychology and likewise from the innate releasing mechanisms of ethology. The difference is that paleodigms are not postulated to exist in the realm of, respectively, the collective unconscious or the phylogenetic heritage, but in the realm of actual cultural and philological history. Philologically, paleodigms exist in diverse forms, from myth to metaphor. Metaphor is used as a therapeutic principle in Ericksonian psychotherapy.

Metaphor and paleodigm both exemplify an epistemic principle of logic which, although prescientific and naive, is used everywhere, namely the logic of reasoning by analogy and attributing identicality to resemblance. Metaphors are potentially infinite in number. Paleodigms, by contrast, must by definition be limited in number by reason of their antiquity. Thus, eventually it should be possible to catalogue all of the paleodigms that relate to health and pathology.

Insofar as talking therapy may be capable of influencing behavior in any given paleodigmatic syndrome, then the change effected by talking works in conjunction with, not in opposition to, whatever somatic, pharmacologic, radiologic, or other methods of therapeutic intervention may be beneficial.

Theoretically, paleodigmatic explanations are phenomenological rather than causal. They spell out an otherwise unrecognized sequential relationship of two entities—the one, an individual's assimilation of an ancient paleodigm, and the other, that same individual's translation of that paleodigm into practice—without construing that there is a connection between the two. The causal explanation of how that connection selectively takes root in the mind and the brain of one individual and not another will be contingent on future advances in the developmental and biographical mind/brain sciences. It will be contingent on future advances also in the evolutionary mind/brain sciences, for paleodigms may themselves be primevally and circuitously derived from behavioral phylisms (Money, 1981, 1983) that are endogenous to our species on the basis of our phylogenetic history and evolution.

Summary

A paleodigm—a term newly coined from the Greek *paleo,* "ancient" + *deigma,* "example"—is an example of prescientific folk wisdom that encodes cause-and-effect explanations in, for instance, a saying or story, the significance of which penetrates the idioms of our everyday language. Paleodigms influence behavior, and pathologically bizarre and irrational behavior, in some instances, becomes somewhat more comprehensible if its paleodigmatic significance can be deciphered. There are cases of Munchausen's syndrome by proxy, for example, in which a parent's abuse and sacrifice of a child serves to expiate and atone for that parent's own self-perceived sin. Paraphilias are, inter alia, paleodigmatic syndromes. They exemplify seven different paleodigms. Paleodigmatic syndromes like abuse dwarfism and anorexia nervosa, insofar as they involve major shifts in endocrine and other somatic functions, show that paleodigmatic explanations are not, per se, etiologically complete. Paleodigmatic theory has not only diagnostic, but also prognostic and therapeutic applicability.

References

Asher, R. (1951). "Munchausen's syndrome." *Lancet* 1:339–41.

Money, J. (1977). "The syndrome of abuse dwarfism (psychosocial dwarfism or reversible hyposomatotropinism): Behavioral data and case report." *American Journal of Diseases of Children* 131:508–13.

———. (1981). "Paraphilias: Phyletic origins of erotosexual dysfunction." *International Journal of Mental Health* 10:75–109.

———. (1983). "New phylism theory and autism: Pathognomonic impairment of troopbonding." *Medical Hypotheses* 11:245–50.

———. (1984). "Paraphilias: Phenomenology and classification." *American Journal of Psychotherapy* 38:164–79.

———. (1986a). "Munchausen's syndrome by proxy: Update." *Journal of Pediatric Psychology* 11:583–84.

———. (1986b). *Lovemaps: Clinical Concepts of Sexual/Erotic Health and Pathology, Paraphilia, and Gender Transposition in Childhood, Adolescence, and Maturity.* New York: Irvington. Paperback edition, Amherst, NY: Prometheus Books, 1988.

———. (1988). *Gay, Straight, and In-Between: The Sexology of Erotic Orientation.* New York: Oxford University Press.

Money, J., Annecillo, C., and Hutchinson, J. W. (1985). "Forensic and family psychiatry in abuse dwarfism: Munchausen's syndrome by proxy, atonement, and addiction to abuse." *Journal of Sex and Marital Therapy* 11:30–40.

Money, J., and Werlwas, J. W. (1976). "*Folie à deux* in the parents of psychosocial dwarfs: Two cases." *Bulletin of the American Academy of Psychiatry and the Law* 4:351–62.

Solomon, R. L. (1980). "The opponent-process theory of acquired motivation." *American Psychologist* 35:691–712.

Southall, D. P., Stebbens, V. A., Rees, S. V., et al. (1987). "Apnoeic episodes induced by smothering: Two cases identified by covert video surveillance." *British Medical Journal* 294:1637–41.

13

Kama Sutra: Women's Sexology versus Semen-Conservation Theory in Sanskrit Teachings

AROUSAL AND ORGASM IN AYURVEDIC TEACHING

The purpose of the first part of this chapter is to present a brief review of arousal and orgasm according to the sexology of Ayurvedic medicine as found in the teachings of the *Caraka Samhita* and the *Kama Sutra,* and to consider the relationship of these ancient teachings to those of modern sexology.

Caraka Samhita

The most ancient source of contemporary Ayurvedic sexology is the *Caraka Samhita* (*The Collection of Caraka,* the physician, also spelled *Charaka*), which is variously dated from between 600 B.C.E. and 100 C.E. in origin (Ray and Gupta, 1965), and which, in the intervening centuries, has been added to by many commentators. Quotations from

Originally published in Marc Kessler, Stephen E. Goldston, and Justin M. Joffe, eds., *The Present and Future of Prevention: In Honor of George W. Albee, Ph.D.* (Newbury Park, CA: Sage Publications, 1992), pp. 214–24, with Venkat N. Joshi and K. Swayam Prakasam as coauthors.

the *Caraka Samhita* have been preserved in the Bower manuscript, the origin of which is dated between the second and fourth centuries C.E. (Hoernle, 1987; see also *Kama Sutra* Editorial Board, 1949).

In the advice given by Caraka, there is overlap between what is efficacious for arousal and for the production of progeny. Both are considered exclusively from the point of view of the male. For the male, the best aphrodisiac is said to be a female in whose presence all of his senses are aroused. She is beautiful, youthful, endowed with auspicious features, submissive, obedient, and never boring.

To augment sexual arousal in the absence of such a partner, Caraka recommended fifty different aphrodisiac potions compounded of herbs and various nutritional components. The same potions enable a man to function sexually up to the age of seventy years.

Caraka recognized that inadequacy of arousal in some cases may be the responsibility not of the female partner, but of the male's dependency or fixation on a specific stimulus of the type that today might be characterized as paraphilic. He mentioned in particular *irshyaka* and *samskaravahi. Irshyaka* (*irshya* = envy, jealousy) signifies that a male's arousal, erection, and orgasm with his own partner is dependent upon the stimulus of watching the copulation of another couple. *Samskaravahi* (*samskara* = to improve; *vahi* = practice) signifies that arousal may improve with the help of various auxiliary practices. The practices themselves were not specified by Caraka; however, they are mentioned by name in the *Susruta Samhita* (*The Collection of Susruta*) as follows:

Sougandhika (*su* = good; *ghandha* = smell) signifies that a male's arousal and erection is dependent on the stimulus of smelling the vagina of his partner.

Asekya (swallow) signifies that a man's arousal, erection, and orgasm with his own female partner is dependent on the stimulus of first being able to suck another man's penis so as to taste and swallow his semen, and thus to incorporate some of the power of his *sukra* (vital fluid).

Kumbhika (catamite; anal penetration) signifies that a man's arousal, erection, and orgasm with his own female partner is dependent on the stimulus of his first being able to have another male penetrate him in anal intercourse.

Caraka recognized in young men the fantasy of being able to maintain "stiffness of the organ without discharge for the whole night." He prescribed a concoction for erectile constancy that had, if nothing else, the merit of a placebo. It consisted of well-pounded pepper seeds (*Piper longum*) fried in oil and ghee, mixed with sugar and honey, stirred in milk, and eaten on rice of the *shah sastika* (sixty-day) variety.

For those disposed to premature ejaculations, Caraka's follower, Cakradatta, recommended diverting the mind by rolling in the mouth a device made of the seed of the *Caesalpinia crista* vine. The enucleated shell of the seed was partially filled with mercury and covered with gold or silver so as to be smooth to hold in the mouth during sexual intercourse.

Kama Sutra

Ayurvedic sexological teaching is far less extensive and explicit in the *Caraka Samhita* than in the *Kama Sutra.* In Sanskrit, *Kama Deva* is the Love God. Hence, *Kama* signifies erotic love. The literal meaning of *Sutra* is *thread* or *cord,* as used for binding, and hence a collection of principles or precepts. Thus *Kama Sutra* is translated as the *Precepts of Love.* The *Kama Sutra* consists of teachings of great antiquity that were compiled and edited by Vatsyayana (1982). The precise age of Vatsyayana's compilation is uncertain. Attributions range from 200 B.C.E. (Haeberle, 1978) to the fourth century C.E. (Anand, 1958; Kothari and Brahmbhatt, 1985).

Compared with the *Caraka Samhita,* the *Kama Sutra* is a manual not of potions, prowess, and fertility, but of the art of love and sexual intercourse with a wife, a courtesan, or the wife of another. Vatsyayana departs from Caraka in giving consideration to the erotic pleasure of the woman as well as of the man, and to the reciprocal dependence of the pleasure of each on the pleasure of the other.

Enigmatically, Vatsyayana fails to mention the practice of the family-arranged marriage and the possibility of reciprocal incompatibility between two partners as a concomitant of this ancient system. The only type of erotic incompatibility he mentions, without specifying how to either avoid or correct it, is quantitative:

> It is obvious that the need for sexual intercourse and desire varies with each person. For the sake of analysis it is perhaps best to divide people into three groups according to their [small, medium, or intense] sexual appetite and passion.

Vatsyayana circumvents individual differences and deficits in erotic arousal by adopting from the ancient precepts known as the *Chatushshasti* (*The Sixty-Four*) the device of addressing couples who, already erotically compatible, are prepared to engage in varieties of loveplay prior to genital union and orgasm.

In the *Kama Sutra* there are five categories of loveplay: embraces and caresses, the kiss, scratches and marks made with the fingers, love bites, and hitting and the accompanying sounds. Within each of these classes there are as many as eight varieties, each with its own name. For example, in the category of embraces and caresses, the fifth variety is described thus:

> When a woman clasps her lover as closely as a serpent twined around a tree, and pulls his head towards her waiting lips, if she then kisses him making a light kissing sound, "soutt, soutt" and looks at him long and tenderly, her pupils dilated with desire, this posture is known as the Clasp of the Serpent.

There is no fixed order or duration for the various acts of loveplay, as exemplified in the following general piece of advice:

> The first time one performs the act of love, kisses, scratches, bites and other such caresses should be used with moderation and the whole act of love should not last long. But on following occasions, on the contrary, all moderation should be thrown aside, the act should be prolonged for as long as possible, and to make the fires of desire burn even more brightly, all manner of caresses, cries and other stimulants to love should be used. The kiss should be imprinted on the following parts of the body: the forehead, the eyes, the cheeks, the throat, the chest, the breasts, the lips, and the interior of the mouth.

For both partners, all of the acts of loveplay engage the tactile or haptic (contact) sensory channels, and to some extent kinesthesia (motion and muscle sense). The *Kama Sutra* is virtually silent with respect to erotic visual stimuli and visual arousal as a prelude, in either the male or the female, to the engagement of tactile arousal in loveplay. In consequence, there is no reference to either similarity or difference between men and women with respect to visual and tactile arousal.

The counterparts of the varieties of loveplay are the various positions, each with its own name, for penovaginal coition. The position singled out for special consideration is for the "Woman Who Plays the Role of the Man," which she might do if she "sees her lover is exhausted by prolonged intercourse, even before he has reached his climax." Alternatively: "She may also undertake to adopt the position normally held by the man in intercourse just to satisfy his curiosity or because she feels a need for variety."

Compared with foreplay and coital positions, orgasm itself is treated only briefly in the *Kama Sutra.* A threefold classification applies to both sexes: "those who reach their climax very quickly; those who need a certain amount of time; and those who are exceedingly slow." A special consideration applies only to women:

> If a woman is pleased and satisfied, her body relaxes, she closes her eyes, forgets all modesty, and shows an increasing desire to unite the two organs as closely as possible, and she reaches her climax at the same time as her lover. Women do not generally come with the same force as men. Men simply assuage their desire; while women, with their basically puritan temperaments, feel a certain pleasure during the act. But, it is impossible for them to define this pleasure, or to say exactly what it is. The proof lies in the fact that after the orgasm the man voluntarily ceases the coitus, while this is not the case with women. Yet, it is well known that women enjoy the sexual act being prolonged, and if a man arrives at his climax too quickly, they feel angry and frustrated. Some of the ancient Masters interpret this as proof that a woman has as strong an orgasm as a man.

Orgasm achieved by means of *Auparishtaka* (oral intercourse) is recognized as being provided by men of the type who are today known as *hijras,* and "who disguise themselves as women and lead the life of courtesans." Men of good reputation are advised against being their clients.

Without being censured, *Auparishtaka* is recognized also as an orgasmic practice engaged in by two women, and by a man with a woman.

Anal penetration is named "Inferior Intercourse," and is attributed to "the people of southern lands." Anal sex with or without orgasm is not elsewhere mentioned in the *Kama Sutra.*

DISCUSSION

Despite its overall sketchiness and brevity, the *Caraka Samhita* recognizes the significance of the visual image for erotic arousal in men, even to the point of recognizing some men's dependence on watching the copulation of another couple. By contrast, the more sophisticated and far more detailed *Kama Sutra* neglects the eyes in favor of the skin for the initiation of erotic arousal. It neglects also to mention the visual imagery of fantasies and dreams, including the wet dreams or masturbation fantasies that initiate a boy's erotic arousal to orgasm at puberty.

One might almost dare to propose that only a woman author would have given such disproportionate representation to tactile versus visual arousal, insofar as females of the human species are phyletically ordained to be less dependent on vision for erotic arousal than are males, and more dependent on touch. If a learned woman of the courtesan class had indeed written the *Kama Sutra,* perhaps as a manual to instruct young men of the wealthy and leisured classes, she may have been obliged to hide her authorship behind the masquerade of a male name in order to have her work accepted in a male-dominant social hierarchy.

Alternatively, if the author of the *Kama Sutra* was, as most people have believed, a male from the fourth-century Golden Age of the Gupta Kingdom (Thomas, n.d.), he may have been instructing both the cultured courtesans and their wealthy, pleasure-seeking, youthful partners from the ruling classes. Among them, he may have assumed, preliminary visual arousal could be taken for granted.

Whatever the explanation for the lack of attention to visual erotic arousal in the *Kama Sutra,* the repercussions of its omission continue to be felt in contemporary sexology insofar as the *Kama Sutra* in translation has long been a model for European and American sexology. For well over a century, it was the only completely explicit celebration of erotic technique in Western sexological literature. Its influence can be recognized in, for example, Van de Velde's immensely influential and revolutionary *Ideal Marriage* (published in England in 1928), with its greater attention to the tactile stimulation of foreplay and coital positioning than to preparatory visual stimulation and imagery.

A similar preponderance was evident earlier in the twentieth century in Albert Moll's (1912, pp. 22, 26) four-stage analysis of voluptuous pleasure into its onset or ascending limb, the equable voluptuous sensation, the acme, and the rapid decline. This four-stage analysis reappeared in Masters and Johnson (1966) under new names: the excitement, plateau, orgasmic, and resolution phases. In this analysis, visual stimulation is reduced to a minimum in favor of a focus on physiological changes.

If the period of copulatory union in which two bodies accept each other and eventually achieve orgasm is called acceptive, then the period that precedes it is proceptive, and it may be followed by a conceptive period (Money, 1980, p. 73). Visual arousal imagery belongs predominantly to the proceptive period. Its preponderance in the male has long been a source of erotic misunderstanding between men and women. Lacking either a social or a professional policy of prevention, this misunderstanding between men and women results from a conception of tactile and visual arousal as mutually exclusive instead of reciprocal or mutually inclusive. By law and religion, in many communities narrative and visual depictions of the imagery of visual arousal are declared pornographic and illicit, even though they depict not paraphilic, hypophilic, or hyperphilic anomalies, but heterosexual normalcy.

Negative reactions to the imagery of visual arousal are not only mandated through law and religion but also exacerbated by parental attitudes toward visual arousal in the sexological development of childhood. The latter poses potentially harmful consequences in the prevention, in childhood, of the development of sexological anomalies. When, for example, a mother punishes and humiliates a newly pubertal son after finding *Playboy* and other heterosexual visual masturbation images under his mattress, she is, instead of preventing anomalies of subsequent sexological functioning, achieving exactly the reverse—namely provoking them.

Negating the explicit depiction of the visually erotic and stigmatizing all of it as pornography that exploits women as sex objects has been the bane of the feminist movement—something many feminists themselves now openly admit. Instead of preventing misunderstanding and alienation between the sexes, it has had the opposite effect of promoting it. There was no greater political mistake and misunderstanding of the essential healthiness of male visual erotic arousal than when militant feminists joined forces with the antisexual male chauvinists of the fundamentalist religious New Right. Preventing the negative effect of that error is a major task ahead.

The proceptive period has been far less researched than either the acceptive or conceptive period. Proceptive research, since it involves erotic arousal imagery, is often equated with pornography and prohibited. Thus, discovery of the prevention and cure of proceptive disorders—some of which are legally sex-offending and criminal—is also prohibited.

There is no occasion more propitious than the present to reverse the calendar past the *Kama Sutra* to the earlier era of the *Caraka Samhita,* and to learn anew the lesson of respect for visual erotic imagery and its pathologies. Then it will become possible to direct research in child development toward prevention of the paraphilic pathologies of visual erotic arousal that, today, constitute a major sexological challenge in public health.

Theory of Semen Conservation in Ancient Ayurvedic and Modern Sexology

The purpose of this section is to show the similarity between the ancient Ayurvedic theory of semen conservation and modern European and American sexological doctrines and nineteenth-century masturbation panic.

There is no exact date for the earliest Ayurvedic teachings. The first named teachers are Agnivesa and Susruta, who are said to have lived as early as 1500 B.C.E. Though the exact century is disputed (Ray and Gupta, 1965), at some time between 600 B.C.E. and 100 C.E. the traditional knowledge was edited and systematized in two texts, Agnivesa in the *Caraka* (or *Charaka*) *Samhita* and Susruta in *Susruta Samhita* (*samhita* = collection). The former deals mainly with medicine and the latter mainly with surgery. These two collections became the basis for Ayurvedic texts that are still used today. The oldest surviving written text (Hoernle, 1987) dates from between the second and fourth centuries C.E. It is found in what is known as the Bower manuscript, and consists of quotations from the *Caraka* in a Buddhist medical compilation, the *Navanitaka.* Bower discovered the manuscript in 1890 in Kuchar, in far western China, north of Kashmir.

Sukra Conservation in Ayurvedic Doctrine

Contemporary Ayurvedic sexological teaching derives from the *Caraka Samhita* and from its basic principle that general health in both sexes and at all ages depends on conservation of the life-giving power of the vital fluid, the *sukra. Sukra* is defined as essential for the healthy functioning of all the body; it is essential also for mental health, which includes intelligence and memory. In the *Caraka* it is characterized as pervading the body "like juice in sugar cane" or "oil in sesame seed." Although the source of its power is basically nutritional in origin, it might be augmented by herbal or other drugs, especially those reputed to be aphrodisiacs. Whereas the necessity of conserving *sukra* applies to both sexes, it has been given greater significance in males, insofar as *sukra* is quite specifically identified with semen, the most important of the vital fluids.

Wastage or depletion of semen has, since ancient times, been attributed to an excessive frequency of ejaculatory orgasm. According to Vagbhata, a fourth-century C.E. redactor of the *Samhitas,* in summer there should be only one ejaculation a week and in winter the frequency may be daily. The total ejaculations for one year should be no more than 168.

Sukra might be lost not only in the depletion of semen from an excessive frequency of orgasms, but also from an excess of fasting, physical exercise, mental work, grief, fear, anger, jealousy, and other negative mental states. Women as well as men might lose *sukra,* except that in vaginal secretion it is depleted less than in the ejaculation of semen. Thus males, more than females, need to protect themselves from wasting *sukra* through an excessive frequency of orgasm, or they may become vulnerable to a loss of resistance to all illnesses and to a decrease of well-being, sexological and otherwise.

Prescriptions for Potency and Fertility

To maintain a healthy level of *sukra,* as well as to restore a depleted level, the *Caraka* offers fifty prescriptions. They are specified as being for both potency and fertility, each of which is not consistently differentiated from the other. All fifty prescriptions are given under the general heading of aphrodisiacs. According to today's criteria, they fall into three categories: dietary, medicinal, and psychological. Quantities and frequencies are not given precisely. Some of the contents and specifications are fanciful by contemporary standards, whereas others are not.

In the dietary prescriptions, a unifying principle may be discerned, namely to supplement the intake of protein. For example, eggs or powdered black lentil, mixed with milk and ghee and to which licorice might be added, would be taken morning and evening. The Ayurvedic menu is not exclusively vegetarian; thus, soups made from various animal meats are also prescribed. A fish-containing prescription translates as follows:

> Pounded fish meat flavored with asafoetida gum, rock salt and coriander leaves should be mixed with flour and cooked in ghee to make pupalika cakes. [These cakes] are bulk-promoting, strengthening, and exhilarating. They increase charm, ensure progeny, promote semen profusely (Sharma, 1983).

The Ayurvedic herbal pharmacopoeia of the *Caraka* has been augmented successively since the thirteenth century. Approximately one hundred herbs were recommended for maintenance of *sukra* and restoration of its depletion. Some of these herbs are known to contain a pharmacologically active principle, among which are *Cannabis sativa* (Indian hemp, bangh, or hashish), *Papaver somnifera* (opium), and *Strychnos nuxvomica* (strychnine).

The third method for restoring *sukra* depletion is named in the *Caraka* as *satvavajaya* (mind control). This method is directed toward reduction of stress and anxiety. One recommended procedure has been translated as follows:

> The youthful person who performs sexually with women under the sign of the bull is free from fear and disorders, takes diet with ghee and milk, cohabits frequently, and has strong determination. He confides with his close friends and colleagues who are successful in endeavors, companionable, expert in arts, equal in psychic condition, similar in age, and endowed with excellence of family. They are also noble, kind, moral, joyful, free from pain and anxiety, similar in ideals, sincere, dear, and sweet-spoken. He gets stimulated by massage, anointing, and bathing; by receiving perfumes, garlands, and adorations; by having a comfortable house, bed and chairs, and

> untorn favorite clothes. In addition he is stimulated by the chirping of favorite birds and the tinkling of ornaments of women, and by gentle pressing of the body by a favorite woman (translation in Sharma, 1983).

Semen Conservation in Western Medical Doctrine

Ayurvedic principles and the practice of *sukra* conservation are still widely accepted in the traditional medicine of India, both by Ayurvedic professionals and the village people who seek their services. The doctrine of *sukra* conservation is not confined to India, however. Since time immemorial, it has been widely diffused geographically. It has had a long philosophical history in Europe, insofar as it is embedded in the sexology of the Bible and the church. In the context of degeneracy theory, the doctrine of semen conservation became incorporated into eighteenth-century European medical theory by the Swiss physician Simon André Tissot (1728-1797). His *Treatise on the Diseases Produced by Onanism* (1974) was first published in 1758. The basic tenet of Tissot's theory was that debility, disease, and death are the outcome of degeneracy induced by semen loss. Tissot was much concerned with halting the spread of syphilitic and gonorrheal degeneracy. In that era, these two diseases together constituted a single "social disease," known to be associated with promiscuity.

> The two great cornerstones of degeneracy theory are the secret vice and the social vice, masturbation and prostitution, respectively. Both wasted the vital fluid, semen, which was believed to be made from the most precious drops of the blood. Both also overstimulated and drained the nervous system with the erethism of concupiscent thoughts and carnal desire. Like his predecessors long before him, Tissot knew that one of the effects of castration of the male is the drying up of the semen. From this he drew the momentously wrong conclusion that all the devirilizing effects of castration could be attributed to the loss of this vital fluid. Then, by one more step of logic, he concluded that similar degenerative effects could be prevented by conservation of the semen. The missing proposition in this logic, still undiscovered in Tissot's day, is that postcastrational

degeneration of virility is caused not by loss of semen, but of male sex hormone secreted from the testes (Money, 1988).

Tissot's doctrine of degeneracy and semen conservation became widely adopted. In the nineteenth century, it became the basis of the antimasturbation hysteria in European and American medicine. The methods recommended for the "cure" of masturbation and the conservation of semen were dietetic, gymnastic (fresh air, physical exercise), moral (abstinence), and religious (prayer). The overlap between these and Ayurvedic methods is in the area of diet. However, whereas vegetarianism is Ayurvedically optional, it became imperative for Graham, Kellogg, and other followers of Tissot, who believed that carnivorous eating of flesh produced carnal desire (Money, 1985).

Ayurvedic/Western Comparison

Semen-conservation theory in Ayurvedic medicine is compatible with the promotion or restoration of healthy functioning, whereas in Western medicine it continues to exert a sexually and erotically nihilistic effect. Its nihilism waned after the advent of germ theory in the 1870s and the beginning of the age of medical science. Today, however, there is a resurgence of antisexualism in modern American medicine. It is a counterreformation in response to the reforms of the so-called sexual revolution of the 1960s and 1970s. Ostensibly, the counterreformation is directed at the prevention of moral decay, but it has itself become a moral danger that calls for prevention before it advances further toward the revival of the Inquisition—witness the new societal hysteria regarding satanism as a source of child sexual abuse.

The antisexual movement of the 1980s and 1990s received serendipitous assistance from the HIV epidemic. Prevention of HIV infection does not necessitate semen conservation per se, but it absolutely necessitates extremely selective care as to where semen goes. The greatest of all the challenges of prevention in today's sexology is the discovery of a means of preventing death from AIDS.

In India today, there are two legacies of semen-conservation theory. One is the Ayurvedic legacy of *sukra* conservation, which has an orgasm-positive approach in its prescriptions for the maintenance of health. The other is the allopathic legacy of Victorian and contemporary American antisexualism, derived from Tissot's semen-conservation theory. Its prescriptions for the maintenance of health are orgasm-negative. For the future of sexology in India and the West, it is desirable that the orgasm-positive ideals of Ayurvedic teaching replace the orgasm-negative ideals of contemporary Western antisexualism.

REFERENCES

Anand, M. R. (1958). *Kama Kala: Some Notes on the Philosophical Basis of Hindu Erotic Sculpture.* Geneva: Editions Nagel.

Caraka Samhita Editorial Board. (1949). *The Caraka Samhita.* Jamnagar, India: Jamnagar Shree, Gulabkunverba Ayurvedic Society.

Haeberle, S. J. (1978). *The Sex Atlas: A New Illustrated Guide.* New York: Seabury.

Hoernle, A. F. R., ed. (1987). *The Bower Manuscript: Facsimile Leaves, Nagari Transcript. Romanised Transliteration and English Translation with Notes* (3 vols., facsimile of 1893 ed.). New Delhi: Aditya Prakashan.

Kothari, P., and Brahmbhatt, R. (1985). "*Kama Sutra:* Ancient and yet modern." In *Proceedings of the Seventh World Congress of Sexology.* Bombay: Indian Association of Sex Educators, Counsellors, and Therapists.

Masters, W. H., and Johnson, V. E. (1966). *Human Sexual Inadequacy.* Boston: Little, Brown.

Moll, A. (1912). *The Sexual Life of the Child.* New York: Macmillan.

Money, J. (1980). *Love and Love Sickness: The Science of Sex, Gender Difference, and Pairbonding.* Baltimore: Johns Hopkins University Press.

———. (1985). *The Destroying Angel: Sex, Fitness, and Food in the Legacy of Degeneracy Theory, Graham Crackers, Kellogg's Corn Flakes, and American Health History.* Amherst, NY: Prometheus Books.

———. (1988). *Lovemaps: Clinical Concepts of Sexual/Erotic Health and Pathology, Paraphilia, and Gender Transposition in Childhood, Adolescence, and Maturity.* Amherst, NY: Prometheus Books.

Ray, P., and Gupta, H. (1965). *Charaka Samhita: A Scientific Synopsis.* New Delhi: National Institute of Sciences of India.

Sharma, P. V. (1983). *Caraka Samhita: Agnivesa's Treatise Refined and Annotated by Caraka and Redacted by Drdhabla.* Varanasi: Chowkhambha Orientalia.

Thomas, P. (no date). *Kama Kalpa or the Hindu Ritual of Love: A Survey of the Customs, Festivals, Rituals, and Beliefs Concerning Marriage,*

Morals, Women, the Art and Science of Love, and Sex Symbolism in Religion in India from Remote Antiquity to the Present Day. Bombay: Taraporevala Sons.

Tissot, S. A. (1974). *A Treatise on the Diseases Produced by Onanism. Translated from a New Edition of the French, with Notes and Appendix by an American Physician.* New York: Collins and Hannay, 1832. Facsimile reprint edition in *The Secret Vice Exposed! Some Arguments against Masturbation* (C. Rosenberg and C. Smith Rosenberg, eds.). New York: Arno.

Van de Velde, T. H. (1928). *Ideal Marriage: Its Physiology and Technique.* London: Heinemann.

Vatsyayana. (1982). *Kama Sutra* (M. R. Anand and L. Dave, eds.). Atlantic Highlands, NJ: Humanities Press.

14

Semen-Conservation Theory vs. Semen-Investment Theory, Antisexualism, and the Return of Freud's Seduction Theory

SEMEN-CONSERVATION THEORY

Semen, the vital fluid of procreation, has a mythological and metaphysical history of great antiquity in the propositions and practices of folk medicine. Modern medicine to this day is influenced by the age-old theory of semen conservation.

Semen-conservation theory existed in oral tradition for perhaps millennia before it was recorded in the earliest medical writings, reputedly more than two and a half millennia ago, of China and Ayurvedic India. Its antithesis, semen-investment theory, by contrast remained an oral tradition in tribal New Guinea until it was first committed to writing early in the twentieth century (Van Baal, 1966; Money and Ehrhardt, 1972; Herdt, 1981, 1984).

Semen-conservation theory has a history of assimilation into the doctrines of the world's major religions and hence has affected the sexual practices of billions of people. By contrast, semen-investment theory, whereby semen is released as a public service, has a history of having affected the sexual practices of not billions but at most millions

---

Written for the 17th Annual Meeting of the International Academy of Sex Research, Barrie, Ontario, Canada, August 6–10, 1991. Originally published in *Journal of Psychology and Human Sexuality* 4(4):31–46, 1991.

of tribal peoples in New Guinea and neighboring Melanesia, and to an increasingly diminishing extent.

Semen-Investment Theory

Among the Sambia people of New Guinea, prior to the recent encroachment of white Australian culture, the basic tenets of semen-investment theory were as follows. Whereas in infancy a boy's survival was contingent on the ingestion of woman's milk, his development into manhood at puberty was contingent on the ingestion of men's milk. Moreover, it was prerequisite to the perpetuation of the species that a boy ingest a lifetime's supply of the fluid. It was a moral obligation of postpubertal males, prior to the tribal marriage age of nineteen, to ensure tribal continuity by feeding their semen to the younger boys who, from the age of seven or eight, resided with them in the long house, the bachelors' quarters in the center of the village. There, free from the effeminating influence of women, girls, and infants, boys were subjected to the rigors of training for fierce, head-hunting warriorhood. Their initiations included the ritual of sucking a ceremonial flute, after which they sucked men's milk from men's penises on a nightly basis. When they in turn became mature, they donated their own milk to a younger boy, never to one who already produced his own—that would have been a major transgression. According to the folk-biology of the Sambian people, semen is not wasted by being given to the young, but is recycled from generation to generation, thus accounting for male fertility. In this respect, semen-investment theory resembles the modern scientific principle of the continuity of germ plasm and the theory of gene investment for the perpetuation of the kinship.

Onanism

As a sexual doctrine of Christendom, the antithesis of semen conservation is not semen investment but semen wastage, epitomized in the Biblical story of Onan. Onan's sin was his failure to obey the law of the levirate, whereby, on behalf of his deceased brother, he should have had a child by the brother's widow. Instead, Onan practiced premature withdrawal.

> And Er, Judah's firstborn, was wicked in the sight of the Lord, and the Lord slew him. And Judah said unto Onan, Go in unto thy brother's wife, and marry her, and raise up seed to thy brother. And Onan knew that the seed should not be his; and it came to pass when he went in unto his brother's wife, that he spilled it on the ground, lest that he should give seed to his brother. And the thing which he did displeased the Lord: wherefore he slew him also (Genesis 38:7–10).

Although the sin of Onan was not masturbation, his name became an eponym for that practice. It was under the name of onanism that semen-conservation theory became incorporated into eighteenth-century medical theory.

Early in the eighteenth century, an anonymous sermonizing tract was published in London under the title of *Onania; or the Heinous Sin of Self-Pollution, and all its Frightful Consequences, in both sexes, Considered. With Spiritual and Physical Advice to Those, who have already injur'd themselves by this Abominable Practice.* The first American edition appeared in Boston in 1724 (Anonymous, 1724/1974).

Onania became a source book for the Swiss physician Simon André Tissot, who in 1758 published in Latin his volume on *Onanism: Dissertation on Maladies Produced by Masturbation.* French and English translations followed. The first American edition (Tissot, 1832/1974) was titled *Treatise on the Diseases Produced by Onanism.*

Degeneracy Theory

Tissot medicalized semen-conservation theory by fusing it with degeneracy theory. According to his explanation, health would degenerate into debility, disease, and death as a consequence of failure to conserve semen. Tissot identified the two sources of failure as the social vice and the solitary vice. There is an epidemiological logic in Tissot's attribution of degeneracy to the social vice of prostitution, for the symptomology of the degeneracy which he described is the symptomology of syphilis and gonorrhea. In the eighteenth century, these two infections were named as one, the "social disease." In Tissot's day, the scourge of the social disease was the counterpart to what is today the scourge of AIDS. Although Tissot did not actually say so, he was in search of an explanation for the spread of the social disease, as well as a method for containing it. He was on the right track with respect to those who lost semen in the course of indiscriminately and promiscuously practicing the social vice. By contrast, he made one of the most momentous intellectual errors of modern medicine by equating the solitary or secret vice of masturbation with the social vice as a source of semen loss and of the symptoms of degeneracy. His error ushered in a frenzy of masturbation phobia and fanatical antisexualism that, after two and a half centuries, is far from having dissipated.

Antisexualism

In nineteenth-century America, the cult of antisexualism became a medical mania. In the 1830s, the Reverend Sylvester Graham emerged as a high priest of the cult. He preached food, fitness, abstinence, and fashion (loose-fitting clothing for women) as the cornerstones of health. His book, *A Lecture to Young Men* (1834/1974), influenced a century of Christian medical writings on the virtues of abstinence. Today he is most well known for graham crackers, a legacy of his vegetarian emphasis on the nutritional virtue of whole-grain flour.

In the 1870s, one of Graham's successors emerged as a new high priest of medical antisexualism. He was John Harvey Kellogg, M.D., a vehement enemy of masturbation and fanatical zealot of abstinence and health foods. He was born in 1852, in Battle Creek, Michigan, into the then newly formed Seventh Day Adventist faith. His medical education was sponsored by his church and he became superintendent of its Health Reform Institute (later the Battle Creek Sanitarium) at age twenty-four. He was against eating meat, as he attributed carnal desires to carnivorous eating. He invented the process of flaking cereals as meat substitutes for breakfast. His corn flakes were first marketed in 1898 as, in effect, an antimasturbation food! To conserve his own semen, he did not consummate his marriage. On his honeymoon he wrote *Plain Facts for Old and Young, Embracing the Natural History and Hygiene of Organic Life* (1888/1974). The many editions of his home-doctor books spread the gospel of antisexualism with a plausible mix of biology and practical medical advice. Their advice on pregnancy and home delivery ensured that they circulated widely among isolated pioneer women from North America to the South Pacific. At the turn of the century, Kellogg won additional fame as an abdominal surgeon. Whereas he kept abreast of new developments in medical biochemistry, he rejected germ theory from its inception in 1870 until his death in 1943 at the age of ninety-one, and clung instead to his own version of semen-conservation, diet, and degeneracy theory.

Whereas Kellogg's antisexual doctrine had no guarantee of a permanent following, the antisexual activism of his contemporary Anthony Comstock had its virulence guaranteed in perpetuity by reason of its having been enacted by Congress into the Comstock Laws of 1873. The Comstock Laws are still enforced today by the untrammeled policing power of the U.S. postal inspector. Congress appointed Comstock as the first postal inspector. He used this position to conduct a personal vendetta against all material that he considered sexually offensive or pornographic, the fine arts, literature, and drama not excluded. He classified all contraceptive advertisements and promotions as obscene and exercised unrestrained lunacy in his determination to prevent the dissemination of contraceptive knowledge and of contraceptive devices.

There was a logic of sorts, albeit hidden, to the anticontraceptive campaign in which Comstock so prominently figured. It derived from the irrational fear that legalized contraception would promote nonprocreative copulatory licentiousness whereby men would become victims of semen wastage. Worse still, freed from the constraints of pregnancy, all women would become sexually licentious and, according to the stereotype of the harlot, rob men of their semen.

The stereotype of the ideal woman was that of the madonna. It was set forth by William Acton (1857/1875), a British surgeon, in a passage strongly endorsed by John Harvey Kellogg.

> I have taken pains to obtain and compare abundant evidence on this subject, and the result of my inquiries I may briefly epitomize as follows: I should say that the majority of women, happily for them ["and for society," says the fifth edition] are not very much troubled with sexual feeling of any kind. What men are habitually, women are only exceptionally. I admit, of course, the existence of sexual excite-

ment, terminating even in nymphomania, a form of insanity that those accustomed to visit lunatic asylums must be fully conversant with; but, with these sad exceptions, there can be no doubt that sexual feeling in the female is, in the majority of cases, in abeyance, and that it requires positive and considerable excitement to be roused at all; and even if roused, which in many instances it never can be, is very moderate compared with that of the male. Many men, and particularly young men, form their ideas of women's feelings from what they notice early in life among loose, or at least low and vulgar women. There is always a certain number of females who, though not ostensibly prostitutes, make a kind of trade of a pretty face. They are fond of admiration; they like to attract attention of those immediately around them. Any susceptible boy is easily led to believe, whether he is altogether overcome by the siren or not, that she, and hence all women, must have at least as strong passions as himself. Such women, however, give a very false idea of the condition of sexual feeling in general. Association with the loose women of London streets, in casinos and other immoral haunts, who, if they have not sexual feeling, counterfeit it so well that the novice does not suspect but that it is genuine, all seem to corroborate such an impression. Married men, medical men, or married women themselves, would, if appealed to, tell a different tale, and vindicate female nature from the vile aspersions cast on it by the abandoned conduct and ungoverned lust of a few of its worst examples. There are many females who never feel any excitement whatever. Others, again, immediately after each period, do become, to a limited degree, capable of experiencing it; but this capacity is only temporary, and will cease entirely until the next menstrual period. The best mothers, wives, and managers of households know little or nothing of sexual indulgences. Love of home, of children, of domestic duties, are the only passions they feel. As a general rule, a modest woman seldom desires any sexual gratification for herself. She submits to her husband, but only to please him; and but for the desire of maternity, would far rather be relieved from his attention (pp. 473–74).

Women's Emancipation: Phases 1 and 2

Acton's stereotype of the ideal woman entrapped even the suffragettes, those women of the late nineteenth and early twentieth century who sought women's emancipation in the right to vote. To maintain political credibility in this, the first phase of the women's movement, it was necessary to conform to the anhedonic, neurasthenic stereotype of the unemancipated madonna, and to avoid at all costs the implication that political emancipation might be contaminated by the hedonic, erotic stereotype of the harlot. The price of political emancipation was silence on the issues of procreative emancipation and birth control, and repudiation of women's right to their own sexuality and eroticism.

When the women's movement entered phase two in the 1960s, the era of civil rights, equal rights, gay rights, and the Sexual Revolution, the tide had turned. Now it was men's right to their own sexuality and eroticism that was repudiated. Men's sexuality was denounced by equating it with power, violence, rape, child sexual abuse, pornography, exploitation of women as sex objects, and failure to appreciate women's noncopulatory sexual romanticism. Men have become perpetrators, women and children victims and survivors.

Victimology and Counterreformation

The new specialty of victimology was born, and with it a new child-abuse industry, replete with false accusations of satanism and a lack of industrial safeguards against such false accusations. It became official dogma that children, being sexually innocent and uninformed, never tell lies about sex, as they know only what they've experienced. Another dogma, widely quoted, is that up to 60 percent of women have a childhood history of sexual abuse. The proportion of male adults who do the abusing is not stated, though one is left to assume that it also is as high as 60 percent and not the monopoly of a small minority.

Antisexualism directed specifically against men, or man-bashing, is part of a more generalized counterreformatory reaction to the era of the Sexual Revolution. Man-bashing is not a feminist monopoly, nor even a militant feminist monopoly, for it is also self-righteously endorsed by many men. The payoff for these men is the power that man-bashing gives them over the women whom they protect, either professionally or personally, from the dangers of bad men. Protection predicates dependency and counteracts emancipation. The status quo of male dominance is thus maintained.

In proverbial wisdom, where there's the smoke of man-bashing, there are the fires of some legitimate targets to be bashed. There always have been sex offenders, and not all of them are men. Some sex offenders, women as well as men, offend against children, some against women, and some against men. Whether or not there has been an increase in the frequency as compared with the ascertainment of sex offenses in recent years is open to dispute. There is no dispute, however, that sex offenses do exist, and that the ascertainment of their existence has recently escalated. There is also no dispute that, concomitant with the increase in ascertainment, there has been a major questioning of orthodox psychoanalytic theory and Freud's early theorizing in relation to sex offenses against children.

Freud's Theorizing

From the onset, Freud's theorizing about neurosis showed the influence of semen-conservation theory, specifically with respect to the distinction between actual (*aktuell*) neurosis and psychoneurosis. The German term *aktuell* signifies "present-day in origin," not, as in vernacular English, "involving acts or actions." The *aktuell* neuroses were said to be sexually derived from actively engaging in especially masturbation or perhaps coitus interruptus (or, for good measure, prolonged continence). They were identified nosologically as *neurasthenia* and *anxiety neurosis.*

There are two versions of the history of the term *psychoneurosis.* In one version, it is a synonym for *neurosis, hysteria,* and *hysterical neurosis.* In the other it is the nosological category that comprises hysterical neurosis and obsessional neurosis. In early usage, psychoneurosis in the form of hysteria was said to be sexually derived, as was *aktuell* neurosis, but with a major difference—namely that its origins lay in the past rather than the present. These origins Freud would eventually attribute to the earliest years of childhood.

Breuer, with whom Freud collaborated in publishing *Studies in Hysteria* in 1895, recognized the significance of sex in his patients' neuroses. "I do not think I am exaggerating," he wrote, "when I assert that the great majority of severe neuroses in women have their origin in the marriage bed" (Sulloway, 1979, p. 78). Breuer wrote circumspectly, but he and Freud both knew that the origins of neurosis in some instances long antedated the marriage bed. This was so in Freud's 1883 case of "the daughter of the innkeeper on the Rax" which he contributed to the *Studies in Hysteria* under the name Katharina (Masson, 1985, p. 81). This girl, Katharina, had revealed to Freud at the age of thirteen or fourteen that she had been nocturnally subjected to a sexual violation. In the account published in the 1895 edition of the *Studies,* the attacker was said to be her uncle. In the 1924 edition, however, Freud admitted that the person responsible was not her uncle, but her father.

In his 1896 paper, *The Etiology of Hysteria* (reprinted as Appendix B of Masson's book, 1985), Freud expounded his newly formulated theory of the origin of hysteria, attributing it to "infantile sexual scenes" and "sexual intercourse" in childhood. The words he used to characterize the sexual scenes were "rape," "abuse," "seduction," "attack," "assault," "aggression," and "trauma." From among these terms, in English translation, "seduction" was the one by which Freud's new theory would enter history as the seduction theory of neurosis. Of it Freud wrote:

> All the singular conditions under which the ill-matched pair conduct their love-relations—on the one hand the adult, who cannot escape his share in the mutual dependence necessarily entailed by a sexual relationship, and who is yet armed with complete authority and the right to punish, and can exchange the one role for the other to the uninhibited satisfaction of his moods, and on the other hand the child, who in his helplessness is at the mercy of this arbitrary will, who is prematurely aroused to every kind of sensibility and exposed to every sort of disappointment, and whose performance of the sexual activities assigned to him is often interrupted by his imperfect control of his natural needs—all these grotesque and yet tragic incongruities reveal themselves as stamped upon the later development of the individual and of his neurosis, in countless permanent effects which deserve to be traced in the greatest detail (Masson, 1985, pp. 283–84).

Freud's satisfaction with his seduction theory was short-lived. It was scarcely a year old when, in the fall of 1897, he abandoned it. Possibly he had been insidiously influenced by the skepticism of fellow professionals, of whom he wrote to his friend Wilhelm Fliess as follows:

> A lecture on the etiology of hysteria at the Psychiatric Society [April 26, 1896] met with an icy reception from the asses and from Krafft-Ebing the strange comment: It sounds like a scientific fairy tale. And

> this after one has demonstrated to them a solution to a more than thousand year old problem, a source of the Nile! They can all go to hell (Masson, 1985, p. 9).

Irrespective of insidious influence, it was nonetheless inherent in the very nature of seduction theory itself that Freud would become dissatisfied. The theory was conceptually too constricting. It failed to account for the development of neurosis in the absence of a history of sexual seduction in childhood. It relied too heavily on fortuity in the ontogeny of individual development at the expense of regularity in the phylogeny of species development. Its causality was extrinsic to the organism, not intrinsic to it.

Freud might have resolved his dissatisfaction with seduction theory by keeping it paired with hysterical neurosis in a taxonomical system in which, as in the case of *aktuell* neurosis, each neurosis would have its own etiology. This would have rescued the long-term manifestations of traumatic sexual seduction in childhood from the professional neglect that became their fate for more than half a century.

The route by which Freud resolved his dissatisfaction with seduction theory was not by taxonomy, but by new theorizing. He postulated that, in psychoneurosis, the revelations of seduction pertained not to the history of behavioral acts, but to the history of mental imagery and ideation in fantasies and dreams and in the unconscious. By universalizing this postulate, infantile seduction fantasies became the basis of a comprehensive theory that would be both phylogenetic and endopsychic in origin. In other words, it would be applicable to all members of the human race, and its principles would be consistently of the mind or, in German, of the soul (*Seele*). It would explain mental health as well as pathology. It would become not just the theory of the Oedipus complex, but in its widest scope the entire psychoanalytic theory of all of human nature. Although its constructs would resemble those of the Biblical theory of human nature, it would be, above all, a secular alternative to theological theories of human nature. Being secular, psychoanalytic theory would have immense appeal among the erudite of a scientifically secular twentieth century. It would also invite attack. Its Achilles' heel would prove to be the very seduction theory that it had set aside. Insofar as there was no setting aside of the actualities and the sequelae of seduction and sexual trauma in the lives of some children, seduction theory would eventually be recycled.

Seduction Theory Recycled

Seduction theory was recycled—not under its own name and not even as a theory—under the banner of child abuse and neglect. In the 1960s, after nearly a century of silence (Williams, 1980), there was an awakening of the public conscience regarding cruelty toward children. Child-protection laws and mandatory-reporting laws were enacted to safeguard children against abusive neglect or violence and against sexual molestation or abuse, whether by family members or by outsiders. Within the criminal-justice and health-care systems, victimology became a new specialty.

The lid of Pandora's box had been well and truly lifted and the wasps of incestuous as well as nonincestuous sexual molestation and abuse in childhood and adolescence were indisputably in evidence by the end of the 1970s. In 1973, Schatzmann had published *Soul Murder: Persecution in the Family,* a reassessment of the Schreber case made famous by Freud. Niederland (1974) continued the reassessment in *The Schreber Case: Psychoanalytic Profile of a Paranoid Personality.* By 1984, Jeffrey Masson had let loose his broadside on psychoanalytic orthodoxy for failing to unmask what he considered Freud's error (if not fraudulence) in abandoning the seduction theory. In 1985 he published *The Assault on Truth: Freud's Suppression of the Seduction Theory.*

Masson's exposé gave seduction theory a new lease on life. The name of what the theory explained was no longer hysteria or psychoneurosis, but post-traumatic stress secondary to sexual abuse in childhood. Victimology has no accompanying theory with which to explain the behavior of sexual child abuse itself. In victimology, sex-offending is attributed to criminal intent.

Satanism

Speaking of sex offenders in a recent interview, Judith Herman, a Harvard psychiatrist and specialist in sexual abuse, said: "They are just evil. They do it because they want to and it gives them satisfaction" (Hawkins, 1991, p. 50). In the course of the past decade or so, a new trend has emerged whereby child sexual abusers are classified not only as evil, but also as practitioners of satanism. Attempts to link sexual child abuse to the rituals of satanic cults, although popular in the sexual-abuse industry, have not been authenticated (Waterhouse, 1990). Nonetheless, they wreak sexological havoc with public opinion and intensify the frenzied societal hysteria of contemporary antisexualism.

Professionally, the recycling of seduction theory as victimology has brought in its train a revival of abreaction and catharsis in therapy, a revival of multiple personality in diagnosis, and a revival of the etiological embarrassment of not being able to explain the diversity of pathological sequelae to the same traumatic stress, namely sexual child abuse. As an explanatory principle, the traumatic stress of sexual child abuse is used to explain too many psychiatric symptoms and syndromes and, at the same time, not enough about why one symptom occurs instead of another. Hence the paradox that victimology theory is no theory at all, only a doctrine. This doctrine is adversarial and of the law, not consensual and of science. Victimology criminalizes sexual pathology and removes it from the science of sexology. In victimological doctrine, according to the terminology currently in vogue, the concept of sexological pathology exists epistemologically only as a social construction. It is, therefore, subject to being both deconstructed and reconstructed. In victimology, sexual child abuse has been socially deconstructed as not-pathology and socially reconstructed as crime.

Public Health

Child sexual abuse at its most gruesome includes torture and murder. To classify it only as evil, satanic, or criminal is the adversarial way of the Inquisition and the criminal code that leads, possibly, to the elimination of individual abusers in the gas chambers or the electric chairs of the prison system. But it does not lead to the elimination of sexual child abuse as an epidemiological problem in public health. It is a problem that exists in each new generation and may well increase exponentially as a function of the adverse side effects of society's antisexual attitudes and practices in childhood. Elimination of the problem of sexual child abuse will require a knowledge of the developmental etiology of abuse in those children who grow up to become abusers. Attainment of that knowledge is predicated on medical and scientific sexological research and on the study of abusiveness as pathology, not solely as crime.

One of the unplanned defects of the perpetrator-victim approach to sexual child abuse is that it lacks checks and balances against false accusations of abuse and their disastrous effects on both the accused and the ostensible victim. A second unplanned defect is the paradox that efforts to warn and protect children against exposure to abuse may backfire and themselves be traumatizing (Krivacska, 1990). A third unplanned effect is that sexological research of childhood and adolescence has been effectively halted. There is no pediatric sexology and no developmental science of sexual health. Thus ignorance is virtually guaranteed for the foreseeable future—ignorance of how to ensure normal sexological development in childhood, and ignorance of how to prevent sexological abnormality in adolescence and adulthood.

The theoretical history briefly presented in this article leads from antiquity to the present, and from semen-conservation theory to the recycling of seduction theory as a dogma of victimology. It has included, along the way, the renunciation of women's sexuality in phase one of the women's movement, and the denunciation of men's sexuality in phase two. The sexual abuse of children still lacks a fully satisfactory epidemiological theory. Without one, the problem of sexual child abuse will not be solved. For sexology, herein lies a present and future challenge.

BIBLIOGRAPHY

Acton, W. (1875). *The Functions and Disorders of the Reproductive Organs in Childhood, Youth, Adult Age, and Advanced Life, Considered in Their Physiological, Social, and Moral Relations* (sixth edition). Philadelphia: Presley Blakiston.

Anonymous. (1724). *Onania; or the Heinous Sin of Self-Pollution, and all its Frightful Consequences, in both sexes, Considered. With Spiritual and Physical Advice to Those, who have already injur'd themselves by this Abominable Practice.* Boston: John Phillips. Facsimile reprint edition in *The Secret Vice Exposed! Some Arguments Against Masturbation* (C. Rosenberg and C. Smith-Rosenberg, eds.). New York: Arno Press, 1974.

Breuer, J., and Freud, S. (1895). *Studien über Hysterie.* Leipzig and Vienna: Franz Deuticke.

Graham, S. (1834). *A Lecture to Young Men.* Providence: Weeden and Cory. Facsimile reprint edition, New York: Arno Press, 1974.

Hawkins, J. (1991). "Rowers on the River Styx." *Harvard Magazine* 93(4): 43–52.

Herdt, G. H. (1981). *Guardians of the Flutes: Idioms of Masculinity.* New York: McGraw-Hill.

Herdt, G. H., ed. (1984). *Ritualized Homosexuality in Melanesia.* Berkeley/Los Angeles: University of California Press.

Kellogg, J. H. (1888). *Plain Facts for Old and Young, Embracing the Natural History and Hygiene of Organic Life.* Burlington, IA: I. F. Segner. Facsimile reprint edition, New York: Arno Press, 1974.

Krivacska, J. J. (1990). *Designing Child Sexual Abuse Prevention Programs: Current Approaches and a Proposal for the Prevention, Reduction and Identification of Sexual Misuse.* Springfield, IL: Charles C Thomas.

Masson, J. M. (1985). *The Assault on Truth: Freud's Suppression of the Seduction Theory.* New York: Penguin.

Money, J. (1985). *The Destroying Angel: Sex, Fitness and Food in the Legacy of Degeneracy Theory, Graham Crackers, Kellogg's Corn Flakes and American Health History.* Amherst, NY: Prometheus Books.

Money, J., and Ehrhardt, A. A. (1972). *Man and Woman, Boy and Girl: The Differentiation and Dimorphism of Gender Identity from Conception to Maturity.* Baltimore: Johns Hopkins University Press.

Niederland, W. (1974). *The Schreber Case: Psychoanalytic Profile of a Paranoid Personality.* New York: Quadrangle/New York Times Book Co.

Schatzmann, M. (1973). *Soul Murder: Persecution in the Family.* New York: New American Library, Signet.

Sulloway, F. J. (1979). *Freud, Biologist of the Mind: Beyond the Psychoanalytic Legend.* New York: Basic Books.

Tissot, S. A. (1781). *L'Onanisme, Dissertation sur les Maladies Produites par la Masturbation.* Lausanne: Glasset & Co.

———. (1832). *A Treatise on the Diseases Produced by Onanism. Translated from a New Edition of the French, with Notes and Appendix by an American Physician.* New York: Collins and Hannay. Facsimile reprint edition in *The Secret Vice Exposed! Some Arguments Against Masturbation* (C. Rosenberg and C. Smith-Rosenberg, eds.). New York: Arno Press, 1974.

Van Baal, J. (1966). *Dema: Description and Analysis of Marind-Anam Culture (South New Guinea).* The Hague: Martinus Nijhoff.

Waterhouse, R. (1990). "The making of a satanic myth: Adult 'survivors' tell horrific tales of ritual child abuse but the evidence is missing." *The Independent on Sunday* (U.K.), August 12, p. 8.

Williams, G. J. (1980). "Cruelty and kindness to children: Documentary of a century, 1874–1974." In *Traumatic Abuse and Neglect of Children at Home* (G. J. Williams and J. Money, eds.). Baltimore: Johns Hopkins University Press.

15

Honk If You Masturbate

ONANISM MEDICALIZED

At the time of the Declaration of Independence, our forebears would have only just begun to spell *masturbation* as we spell it today. More likely, they would have used the terms *onanism* or *self-pollution* instead. Later, in the nineteenth century, there would also be the terms *secret vice* and *self-abuse*.

Epistemologically, a word itself is a social construct. So also are the manifold connotations of its meaning. *Masturbation* is no exception. In the two and a half centuries since masturbation (the word) first made its appearance, masturbation (the practice) has been socially constructed as a medicomoral phenomenon. Masturbation is onanism medicalized.

In English, the term was first spelled as *mastupration* and appeared in Burton's *Anatomy of Melancholia* (1621), according to the *Barnhart Dictionary of Etymology.* The *Oxford English Dictionary* (OED) traces the first occurrence of the term in English spelled as *masturbation* to the title of a book translated from the "last Paris edition" by A. Hume

---

Written for the 1993 Milton S. Eisenhower Symposium, The Johns Hopkins University, Baltimore, MD. Originally published in *Trends in Health Care, Law, & Ethics* 10(3): 27–33, 1995.

in 1776. Hume's title is *Onanism, or a Treatise upon the Disorders produced by Masturbation, or the Dangerous Effects of Secret and Excessive Venery.* The original of this work had been published in Latin in 1758 by the Swiss physician, Simon André Tissot. Many reprintings followed in French translation under the title *L'Onanisme, Dissertation sur les Maladies Produites par la Masturbation* (1781). The first American translation, titled *A Treatise on the Diseases Produced by Onanism,* was published in New York in 1832 (reprinted in a facsimile edition, 1974).

The English noun *masturbation* (and its seldom used equivalent, *manustupration*) derives from the Latin *masturbationem* and *masturbari* (ostensibly from *manus,* Latin for "hand," and *stupare,* "to rape or defile"). The historical origin of the Latin verb is obscure, says the OED. The *Oxford Latin Dictionary* attributes it to the Roman poet Martial (43-104 C.E.), known for his books of epigrams.

By its very name, "hand rape" had no chance except to be persecuted by a medical and moral inquisition. In the nineteenth century, masturbation took the place that witchcraft had held in the Inquisition of the era that preceded it. In the twentieth century, masturbation has given away to allegations of satanic sexual abuse in the new inquisition of the current era.

Tissot was not the first to use the word "masturbation" in French writing. He was preceded by Montaigne in 1570, according to the *Barnhart Dictionary of Etymology.* Tissot was, however, the first to assign to the practice of masturbation a causal explanation of disease. His predecessor, whom Tissot named only as Dr. Bekkers of London, had anonymously published, no later than 1717, an undated sermonizing tract under the long-winded title *Onania; or the Heinous Sin of Self-Pollution, and all its Frightful Consequences, in both sexes, Considered. With Spiritual and Physical Advice to Those, who have already injur'd themselves by this Abominable Practice.* The first American printing was of the tenth edition in Boston in 1724 (reprinted in a facsimile edition, 1974).

SEMEN-CONSERVATION THEORY

The extremely ancient philosophical doctrine of the conservation of vital spirits is taken for granted in *Onania* as well as in Tissot's *Trea-*

tise. This doctrine appears in ancient Chinese writings of the balance of yin and yang. It is explicitly spelled out in Indian Ayurvedic medical writings which are traceable to 600 B.C.E. and in oral tradition to an even earlier date. In Ayurveda, the vital spirit, though all-pervasive in the body, is most highly concentrated in the *sukra* of the semen. The concentrate in one drop of semen is equivalent to that of fifty of the most precious drops of blood. Among Indian males today there is still a high incidence of complaints of sickness and loss of well-being attributed to the loss of semen (Dewaraja and Sasaki, 1991). Conversely, pleasure by saving semen and postponing orgasm is the positive version of semen-conservation theory found in Tantric teaching (Joshi and Money, 1995).

In the tradition of Hippocratic as compared with that of Ayurvedic medicine, semen depletion has no prominence as a theory of illness. In the Old Testament, the concept of semen as a vital fluid is absent, whereas the fluid itself is a ritually unclean contaminant (Leviticus 15:16-18). A theological work, dated 1480, is the oldest book in the library of the Institute of the History of Medicine at Johns Hopkins. It addresses the question of whether a priest who has a wet dream is spiritually competent to say mass the next day. Its title is *De Pollutione Nocturna,* its author Jean Gerson, Chancellor of the University of Paris, and its publisher Johann Guldenschaff. The first edition appeared in 1466.

It was the Biblical Onan whose name became, in *onanism,* the Christian eponym for semen wastage (Genesis 38:7-10) before the term *masturbation* came into use. Onan's sin was not masturbation, however, but contraception. He practiced premature withdrawal, spilling his seed on the ground, instead of fathering a child by his brother's widow as required by the Judaic law of the levirate.

Degeneracy Theory

With the knowledge of hindsight, it is possible to recognize that Tissot was searching, in his day, for the cause and prevention of the epidemic of syphilis and gonorrhea—much as we, in our day, are searching for the cause and prevention of the HIV epidemic of AIDS. In Tissot's century, prior to the discovery of germ theory in 1870, two venereal infections, the pox (syphilis) and the clap (gonorrhea), were considered to belong together as manifestations of a single "social disease." Tissot correctly identified many of the mental and physical symptoms, including birth defects, of the social disease. He was correct also in recognizing that promiscuity and prostitution increased the risk of getting the social disease. Then, erroneously, he attributed the cause and the symptoms of the social disease to degeneracy secondary to excessive depletion of semen. It was a momentous error, and it allowed an even more momentous error to follow, namely that semen depletion through solo masturbation would bring about the same degeneracy and the same devastating symptoms as would the social disease. Hence the misbegotten contemporary folklore regarding symptoms brought on by masturbation, from warts and pimples to aches and pains, discharges, memory loss, mental deterioration, blindness, paralysis, seizures, and death.

Tissot kept in step with the medicine of his day and wrote authoritatively. His *Treatise* paved the way for Western civilization's fixation on an antimasturbation industry under the leadership of chiefly its clergy and its medical profession for the entire Victorian era and beyond.

Masturbation and Disease

Before the advent of germ theory and the subsequent development of medical science, the practice of medicine was predominantly holistic, to use today's terminology. There were few therapeutically specific interventions. Remedies were ameliorative. Recovery, when not by spontaneous remission, was attributed to obedient compliancy to prescribed regimens of medication, compresses, diet, drink, exercise, rest, work, sex—almost anything for which the patient could be held personally and morally responsible. Failure to recover could then be blamed not on inadequacy of the treatment, but on noncompliancy.

Tissot's degeneracy theory of disease filled a gap left vacant by the demise of the demon-possession theory of disease, and was ideally suited to medicine as practiced in the eighteenth century and throughout most of the nineteenth century. It gave to the practitioner the prestige of not only having a theory, but also of having a foolproof one that, by attributing causality to the patient's own behavior as a masturbator, placed responsibility for illness and recovery on the patient and absolved the physician from failure.

Tissot's degeneracy theory of masturbation owed its longevity in part to medical economics, for it allowed masturbation itself to be declared a disease for the treatment of which a fee could be charged. In addition, a fee could be charged for the treatment of semen loss under the newly named diagnosis *spermatorrhea,* otherwise known as "nocturnal pollution" and "wet dreams." There was no corresponding diagnosis for females; in fact, degeneracy theory had great difficulty in accommodating itself to females who, lacking the vital spirit in semen, were simply written off in degeneracy theory as inferior to males.

In the nineteenth century, and spilling over into the twentieth, there was a flood of home-doctor's books, hygiene and health manuals, marriage manuals, and sexual-advice books for young and old, as well as of professional texts that extolled the virtues of chastity and abstinence and warned against the hazards, horrors, and catastrophic consequences of masturbation, up to and including insanity and death. Henry Maudsley, renowned founder of the major British psychiatric hospital that bears his name, published an article in 1868, "Illustrations of a Variety of Insanity," in which, beginning with an array of genuine symptoms, he fabricated a spurious insanity of pubescence caused by self-abuse. Its eventual scholarly fate was to become thoroughly discredited.

Antimasturbation Medical Mania

The antimasturbation furor escalated and reached its apogee in the 1870s and 1880s in the writings of John Harvey Kellogg, M.D. (1852–1943), he of corn-flakes fame (Kellogg, 1888, 1906, 1908). Kellogg was an otherwise sane man with a monomaniacal irrationality fixated on masturbation in defiance of medical science. He advised parents that positive signs of the "secret vice" are difficult to detect because "the devotees of Moloch pursue their debasing practice with consummate cunning. . . . If the suspected one becomes very quickly quiet after retiring . . . the bedclothes should be quickly thrown off under pretense. If, in the case of a boy the penis is found in a state of erection, with the hands near the genitals, he may certainly be treated as a masturbator without any error. . . . If the same course is pursued with girls . . . he clitoris will be found congested, with the other genital organs, which will also be moist from increased secretion" (quoted in Money, 1985, p. 88).

In girls, Kellogg wrote, "ulceration about the roots of the nails, especially affecting one or both of the first two fingers of the hand, usually the right hand, is evidence of the habit [of solitary vice] which depends upon [leucorrhea], the irritation of the fingers being occasioned by the acrid vaginal discharge" (Money, 1985, p. 86).

Kellogg listed thirty-nine signs of the secret vice of self-abuse (Money, 1985, Ch. 12). They include general debility and early symptoms of consumption, precocious or defective sexual development, sudden change in disposition, lassitude, sleeplessness, bed-wetting, school failure, bashfulness, unnatural boldness, fearfulness, bad posture, over- or undereating, tobacco smoking, acne, finger-nail biting, sunken eyes, hysteria, epilepsy, and obscenity.

Kellogg died in 1943 at the age of ninety-one without retracting any of his absurd pronouncements. Instead of being of historical interest only, his list of masturbation signs has a ring of present-day familiarity. It has been recycled by the extreme radical wing of contemporary victimology as a grab-bag of diagnostic signs of sexual child abuse.

Masturbation Cures

Kellogg was medically trained in the era of residential health-reform institutes which ostensibly brought about a restoration of health by adherence to prescribed practices related to food, fashion (abandoning tight corsets), fresh air, fitness, and the vital fluid of sex—the five Fs—together with hydrotherapy.

Since boyhood, Kellogg had been a follower of Rev. Sylvester Graham (1794-1851), whose name is remembered in graham crackers. Graham preached vegetarianism and sexual abstinence, both of which Kellogg adhered to, even to the extreme of having an unconsummated marriage. After graduating from Bellevue Medical School in New York City, Kellogg returned to Battle Creek, Michigan, as planned and became the superintendent of the Battle Creek Sanitarium of the newly established Seventh Day Adventist sect. There, in an experimental kitchen laboratory, he devised nut and grain recipes to substitute for carnivorous food, to which he attributed carnal desire. Unless kept in check, the power of carnal desire would triumph over abstinence and bring about its downfall. By 1906, the process of flaking and toasting maize had been perfected. Corn flakes eaten instead of meat for breakfast were no match for carnal desire, however, or even for masturbation. Preventively, or as a cure for masturbation, they were entirely a failure.

An alternative to the dietary method of prevention and cure of masturbation was the method of directly assaulting the genitalia. For intractable cases in which ties and restraints on the hands were of no avail, Kellogg recommended covering the genital organs at bedtime with a cage, or suturing the foreskin of the penis with silver wire so that, unretractable, it would render an erection painful. The corresponding procedure for a girl was to apply pure carbolic acid to the clitoris to allay its abnormal excitement. For boys, Kellogg also recommended a circumcision performed without an anesthetic, so that the pain would have the salutary effect of punishment and the subsequent soreness would interrupt a masturbatory attempt (Money, 1985, pp. 99–100).

Neonatal Circumcision as Prevention

Circumcision of the newborn as a universal prophylaxis against future masturbation became trendy first in British and then in American medicine in the second half of the nineteenth century (Wallerstein, 1980). The practice was based on the fallacy that irritation and itching under the foreskin was a cause of masturbation. It would, of course, have been possible to collect statistics on masturbation among young Jewish males, but the prudery of the Victorian era prohibited such an explicitly sexual survey. Notwithstanding the absence of any confirming data, neonatal circumcision for the prevention of masturbation became a dogma. Today, prophylaxis against masturbation is no longer the defense for neonatal circumcision. Various other defenses have sprung up in its place and are vigorously attacked by anticircumcision organizations. The practice of nonritual neonatal circumcision survives nonetheless, and it does so in large part on the basis of its economic profitability.

EVASION AND HEARSAY

Warnings against the physical, moral, and spiritual hazards of masturbation were watered down in publications of the twentieth century, but they died a lingering death even in some medical texts (Huhner, 1946). They disappeared from the *Boy Scouts' Handbook* only in the post–World War II editions. They still circulate in *Our Youth,* a publication of the Watchtower Bible and Tract Society.

Warnings of the dire consequences of masturbation have never been supported by systematic empirical data, only by anecdote and logical fallacy. Thus the fate of the masturbator has become the subject matter of rumor and hearsay, not of rational discourse. By and large, masturbation is not routinely talked about explicitly and rationally but only evasively and defensively, with the safeguard of teasing, joking, and ribaldry or the cruelty of stigmatization. Beyond the pubertal age (if not earlier) serious curiosity about masturbation with a straightforward request for information is avoided lest it be construed as having self-incriminating reference. To admit doing it is to incriminate oneself as being, if not sinful and immoral, then psychosexually immature. Married or single mature people, it is wrongly said, simply do not masturbate. Ostensibly, they graduate to copulation and leave childish things behind—or at least they make a pretense of having done so. One consequence is that leftover fallacies from the past persist, unchallenged by real-life statistics.

OUTCOME FALLACIES

One of the fallacies left over from the past is a direct descendant of the ancient concept of semen conservation itself. It is the fallacy that masturbation will have the long-term harm of prematurely depleting the genital organs of their vital force so that their subsequent healthy function, and perhaps general health also, will be impaired. One version of this fallacy is that erotic sensation will become numbed as a result of being overstimulated by masturbation, which in turn may have a deleterious effect on genital performance in sexual intercourse and may even impair fertility.

An alternative and equally fallacious version of the outcome of masturbatory overstimulation is that, to ward off the onset of numbness, the frequency of stimulation will escalate until the masturbator becomes a sex addict who must seek ever more varied and sordid varieties of stimulation on the way to rape and child molestation or other sexual crimes. In recent years, there has been a powerful recrudescence of the fallacy of escalation as a dogma of the sex-addiction treatment industry.

A somewhat toned-down version of the fallacy of the long-term harmfulness of masturbation defines the harm as moral and spiritual injury. Neither type of injury is spelled out, except in vague terms like character defect, but the warnings are dire nonetheless. The warnings themselves are able to induce the same long-term psychological harm of obsessional worry and anxiety that warnings of physical harm might also do. Being so intangible and diffusely defined, they are harder to dispel. Masturbation phobia itself, in some cases, escalates to become fixated and psychopathological.

Adults who have themselves discredited the fallacies of the harmfulness of masturbation may, nonetheless, pass them on to children, even despite their own best intentions to the contrary. One of the paradoxes of childrearing is that parents and others who instruct children teach them the principles that they themselves were taught and not the truth of what they did. Teaching the moral and spiritual harms of not abstaining from masturbation establishes the principle of "just say no" without having to lie about the physical harm. Virtually all children absorb the negative societal valence that attaches to masturbation. Some children experience threats of punishment for masturbating as horrendous as threats to cut off the penis with a knife or scissors or to sew up the vagina with a needle. They may also receive abusive punishments, deprivations, and humiliations if caught masturbating. The sexological consequences may be serious and permanent.

Homosexual Fallacy

Somewhere on the periphery of the moral and spiritual, according to contemporary social and political debate, lies the phenomenon of homosexuality. The leftover fallacy that masturbation causes homosexuality, although no longer seriously espoused, has a historical explanation. The term *homosexual* did not come into existence until 1869

(Herzer, 1985) and did not enter into general circulation until early in the twentieth century. Prior to that time, homosexuality was called "sodomy" and referred to anal intercourse only. In the antimasturbation literature, the practice of two males masturbating together was conceptualized not as homosexuality but as the corruption of the younger, inexperienced male by an older and more depraved one. The same applied to females. The fallacy that mutual masturbation is a cause rather than an expression of homosexuality has persisted in folk sexology.

SOCIAL-CONTAGION THEORY

Being taught by bad example was one of the ways in which the nineteenth-century antimasturbation books explained the making of a masturbator. Another way, according to the dogma of the social contagion of evil, was by being led astray by the perception of licentiousness, either at firsthand or by reading or viewing it at secondhand in the erotic imagery of marketplace pornography. That is why some parents still go bonkers today when they find *Playboy* centerfolds under the mattress of their adolescent sons, as they did in an earlier era when they found brassiere and underwear pages from the Sears, Roebuck catalog erotically embellished by hand. Commercial pornography does not cause masturbation; it is the record of manifold masturbation fantasies. Commercial pornography is varied, and unless the masturbation fantasy it depicts matches your own, it will not turn you on.

The dogma that masturbation is an effect of social contagion transmitted by the erotic images of pornography confronts society with an insoluble Catch-22 dilemma. It is the dilemma of being damned if it does and damned if it doesn't inquire about the content of personal masturbation imagery. To inquire about it would be an ostensible stimulus to erotic arousal and thence to masturbation, and not to inquire perpetuates ignorance—which is equivalent to whistling past the graveyard in the era of HIV/AIDS.

Social-contagion theory has had extraordinary longevity and tenacity up to the present. It applies to the exclusion from sex-education curricula, and even from individual school-counseling sessions, of anything related not only to masturbation imagery alone, but also to erotosexual imagery overall. The Catch-22 is so pervasive as to make it impossible to conduct a survey of masturbation imagery in a statistically random probability sample, even under the unlikely circumstances of having obtained funding and of having circumvented the watchdogs of governmental censorship. In any sexological research, the sample will always be skewed by refusals and evasions, some of which are justified. Some people are vulnerable to self-incrimination that might lead to arrest. For example, in a state that has mandatory-reporting laws, disclosure of pedophilic masturbation fantasies, even for the purpose of ensuring treatment, could very well lead to immediate arrest.

Lovemaps

Masturbation fantasies are metaphorically like the Magellan spacecraft's radar depiction of the cloud-wrapped terrain of Venus in that they depict the terrain of one's own personal and idiosyncratic lovemap (Money, 1986, 1993), which may be either conventional and orthodox, or unconventional and unorthodox. One's lovemap depicts, synchronously in the brain and the mind, the ideal partner in the arousal of love and lust, and the ideal activities to engage in to express that love and lust, in attaining the culmination in orgasm. Since masturbation fantasies reveal whether one's lovemap has been warped and vandalized or not, it is in the interest of both the individual and society that the right to disclose one's masturbation fantasies be a legally protected right of privacy and confidentiality. For example, a fifteen-year-old youth whose masturbation fantasies depict serial murdering of prepubertal juveniles should have confidentiality legally guaranteed so that he may seek preventive treatment—not only for his own sake, but for the protection of potential future victims.

Such a preventive approach predicates a new and rational approach to those pubertal and early adolescent masturbation fantasies that are readouts of a lovemap that in prepuberty became developmentally warped and misshapen (in street language "kinky," in legalese "deviant" or "perverted," and in biomedical vocabulary "paraphilic"). Paraphilic lovemaps, like normophilic lovemaps which may be gay or straight, are unfolded in masturbation imagery prior to their being enacted in behavior. The preventive and medical approach to paraphilic masturbation imagery is, however, a tall order for a criminal-justice system still encumbered by archaic concepts of willfulness, crime, punishment, and retribution.

Masturbation Advocated

Of course, not all masturbation imagery is at the criminative, unpropitious, or negative end of the scale. On the contrary, an individual's masturbation imagery may very creatively circumvent the strictures and chastisements of early sexual training. I recall the case of a Catholic youth who at puberty obeyed the injunction against touching his genitals by inventing a no-hands method of masturbating into a "vagina trainer." He formed his trainer by pushing an overstuffed armchair against the mattress of his bed. Then he would thrust his erect penis up and down in the gap between them (Early, 1975). In India, a Brahmin boy invented a similar no-hands method of masturbating by thrusting his penis through the criss-crossed webbing of his cot bed. Boys remanded to a juvenile hall in San Diego invented "Fi-Fi," a girlfriend constructed from rubber gloves purloined from the kitchen and lubricated as a masturbation device. It carried none of the stigmatization of hand practice. Many a boy has used a pillow as a substitute for hands, and many a girl, likewise, the pulsating, high-pressure jet from the shower nozzle.

In the sex-therapy movement initiated by Masters and Johnson (1970), the pendulum swung from masturbation as disease to masturbation as a method of treatment, alone or as a couple, for the cure of sexual inadequacy, especially anorgasmia in women. Masturbation to reinforce a positive response to conventional sexual pictures has also been tried, albeit not convincingly, as a method of treating sex offenders.

More than anything else, however, it is the advent of AIDS that is doing the most, especially among the young and unattached, to dispel masturbation's negative legacy from Tissot's degeneracy theory and to replace it with the seal of strong moral approval.

Masturbation is bona fide safe sex in the era of AIDS, and of merit for the containment, to at least a partial degree, of the HIV epidemic in the pubertal generation. It is a foolish form of criminal neglect to assume that pubertal sexuality does not exist except in orgasmic dreams while asleep. Reversing today's prudery, society might well headline a public-health policy of overtly endorsing and promoting masturbation as a safe-sex practice.

At the outset, masturbation would under such a policy be morally approved and promoted. For the present, and in preparation for the coming era of electronic "virtual reality," explicit erotic videos of the highest cinematic quality and verisimilitude would be broadcast as adjuncts to good masturbation on an exclusive sexological cable channel. The channel's programming would include accurate news and information segments. It would give precise and exact sexual education and answers to personal and youthful sexological concerns—concerns about falling in love and lovesickness, for example, and about growing up gay; or about having bizarre (paraphilic) erotosexual fantasies, thoughts, and dreams (Money, 1986, 1988); or concerns, almost always unjustified, about wasting one's oats by sowing them too wildly and too often and having none left for mid-life and later.

With advancing adolescence, masturbation would progress from being solo to being mutual with a partner, subject to the proviso of a mutual ban on exchange of body fluids. When they reach the age of readiness for first intercourse, a couple might sign a contract of fidelity so as to ensure that neither would introduce the AIDS virus into the relationship for as long as it lasts.

For the implementation of this phantasm of change in the morality of masturbation, the two great agents of moral change—technological innovation and demographic shift—are already in place, or soon will be. Virtual reality is electronically just around the technological corner. AIDS deaths are already creating demographic shifts in population density and age of longevity, the magnitude of which is ever increasing. How rapidly and how effectively virology will be able to stem the HIV tide is unpredictable. My phantasm of the respectability of masturbation as a pleasure in its own right may be no phantasm at all. "Honk if you masturbate" may be on bumper stickers everywhere!

REFERENCES

Anonymous. (1724). *Onania; or the Heinous Sin of Self-Pollution, and all its Frightful Consequences, in both sexes, Considered. With Spiritual and Physical Advice to Those, who have already injur'd themselves by this Abominable Practice.* Boston: John Phillips. Facsimile reprint edition in *The Secret Vice Exposed! Some Arguments Against Masturbation* (C. Rosenberg and C. Smith-Rosenberg, eds.). New York: Arno Press, 1974.

Dewaraja, R. and Sasaki, Y. (1991). "Semen-loss syndrome: A comparison between Sri Lanka and Japan." *American Journal of Psychotherapy* 45:14-20.

Early, J. T. (1975). "How masturbation can improve lovemaking." *Sexology* 41(7):44-46.

Gerson, J. (1480). *De Pollutione Nocturna.* Cologne: Johann Guldenschaff. First edition, 1466.

Herzer, M. (1985). "Kertbeny and the nameless love." *Journal of Homosexuality* 12:1-26.

Huhner, M. (1946). *The Diagnosis and Treatment of Sexual Disorders in the Male and Female Including Sterility and Impotence.* Philadelphia: F.A. Davis.

Joshi, V. N., and Money, J. (1995). "Dhat syndrome and dream in transcultural sexology." *Journal of Psychology and Human Sexuality* 7(3):95–99.

Kellogg, J. H. (1888). *Plain Facts for Old and Young, Embracing the Natural History and Hygiene of Organic Life.* Burlington, Iowa: I. F. Segner. Facsimile reprint edition. New York: Arno Press, 1974.

———. (1906). *Man the Masterpiece, or Plain Truths Plainly Told about Boyhood, Youth, and Manhood.* Warburton, Victoria, Australia: Signs of the Times Publishing Association.

———. (1908). *The Ladies' Guide in Health and Disease: Girlhood, Maidenhood, Wifehood, Motherhood.* Warburton, Victoria, Australia: Signs of the Times Publishing Association.

Masters, W. H. and Johnson, V. E. (1970). *Human Sexual Inadequacy.* Boston: Little, Brown.

Maudsley, H. (1868). "Illustrations of a variety of insanity." *Journal of Mental Science* 14:149-162.

Money, J. (1985). *The Destroying Angel: Sex, Fitness and Food in the Legacy of Degeneracy Theory, Graham Crackers, Kellogg's Corn Flakes and American Health History.* Amherst, NY: Prometheus Books.

———. (1986). *Lovemaps: Clinical Concepts of Sexual/Erotic Health and Pathology, Paraphilia, and Gender Transposition in Childhood, Adolescence, and Maturity.* New York: Irvington. Paperback, Amherst, NY: Prometheus Books, 1993.

———. (1988). *Gay, Straight, and In-Between: The Sexology of Erotic Orientation.* New York, Oxford University Press.

Tissot, S.A. (1781). *L'Onanisme, Dissertation sur les Maladies Produites par la Masturbation.* Lausanne: Glasset & Co.

———. (1832). *A Treatise on the Diseases Produced by Onanism. Translated from a New Edition of the French, with Notes and Appendix by an American Physician.* New York: Collins and Hannay. Facsimile reprint edition in *The Secret Vice Exposed! Some Arguments Against Masturbation* (C. Rosenberg and C. Smith-Rosenberg, eds.). New York: Arno Press, 1974.

Wallerstein, E. (1980). *Circumcision: An American Health Fallacy.* New York: Springer.

PART FOUR

CLINICAL PRINCIPLES

16

Nosological Sexology: A Prolegomenon

PHENOMENOLOGY AND ETIOLOGY

Sexology is one of the many branches of medicine for which today's fund of knowledge is insufficient to permit an etiological classification of all the disorders that come within its purview. There are some syndromes and some individual cases for which an etiology is partly or wholly ascertainable, but these syndromes do not constitute a complete and all-inclusive nosology on the basis of etiology. Hence the basis of nosological sexology is phenomenology. In *Webster's New World Dictionary,* phenomenology is defined as "scientific description of actual phenomena, with avoidance of all interpretation, explanation, and evaluation."

The nosological dilemma of sexology has its counterpart in psychiatry. The psychiatric solution has been, in part, to subdivide psychiatric syndromes into organic and nonorganic. The latter, also named *functional* and *psychogenic,* constitute what might be called a diagnostic trash bin—a receptacle for those syndromes for which the respectability of an organic etiology has not been established. The danger of a diagnostic trash bin is that it becomes littered with too many false diagnoses insofar as, despite differences in etiology in their symptomatic phenomenology, organic and nonorganic syndromes may masquerade as one another.

Originally published in *Journal of Psychology and Human Sexuality* 4(4):111–20, 1991.

The nosological ideal is to begin with a phenomenological classification first and then to address the problems and perplexities of differential etiology. In sexological nosology, the phenomena to be classified are invariably and categorically the phenomena of sexuoerotic functioning—that is, they are both sexual and erotic, simultaneously and synchronously. This is a universal axiom and a principle postulate of sexology, without which sexology has no claim to an independent existence as either a science or a health-care specialty.

Although partially overlapping in meaning, sexual and erotic are not synonymous but complementary. Aphoristically, sexual is between the loins and erotic is between the ears. As compared with erotic, sexual (from the Latin *secare,* "to cut") carries a connotation of the distinction between male and female and of their sex organs and their copulatory function. By contrast, erotic (from the Greek *eros,* "love"), carries a connotation of the reciprocality of male and female and their personal mental representations of copulatory arousal and function.

Sexology may borrow from genetics, cytogenetics, reproductive biology, molecular biology, endocrinology, brain science, ethology, behavioral or psychodynamic psychology, sociology, cultural anthropology, or any other present or future branch of science. There is no one of these, however, that invests sexology with its own unique existence as a science. Sexology's Magna Carta is that it alone, among all the sciences, studies phenomena that qualify explicitly as sexuoerotic —not sexual alone and not erotic alone, but sexuoerotic. Sexology is not the science of sexuality, nor is it the science of eroticality. It is the science that combines both, and its nosology is the nosology of disorders of sexuoerotic functioning.

Phenomenology and Motivation

The impartial way of recording and reporting sexological phenomena is the way of the videorecorder. The raw data are recorded in temporal sequence only and are not contaminated by suppositions or formulations of causal sequence. Formulations of causality are a completely separate operation that may or may not be engaged in later.

By contrast, the nonimpartial and biased way of recording and reporting sexological phenomena is the way of superimposed judgmentalism. In the very act of putting the raw data on record, the reporter contaminates.

Impartiality in the nosology of sexology gives way to the bias of judgmentalism if endopsychic feelings, moods, needs, discomforts, or other mental states expressed by or attributed to patients are used as the criteria of health and well-being, or their lack. There are no objective criteria of endopsychic states. A sexologist's judgment may be arbitrary as well as morally or politically biased, and it may be totally discordant with the patient's own judgment. The dilemma of judgmental bias haunts the nosology of contemporary psychiatry. It should be excluded from the nosology of sexology.

The bias of judgmentalism is insidious. It contaminates raw data while they are being recorded, and it does so through the use of vernacular terms and idioms that surreptitiously imply causal sequence instead of temporal sequence. The ubiquitous conjunction *because* is itself a major offender. Other terminological offenders are *preference, choice, desire, wish, like, want, motive, need,* and so on. They all imply personal responsibility and, if taken at face value, explain everything while explaining nothing. They render the scientific explanations of scientific sexology superfluous. They replace sexological explanations with sexosophical explanations. Sexosophy is the spiritual and moralistic philosophy of sex. Sexosophy is ideology: It posits ideological norms and declares moral judgment—pro or con, approved or disapproved. It is adversarial. Adversarialism is the defining principle of the criminal-justice system. Consensualism is the defining principle of science.

Nosology and Etiology

A nonteleological, nonmotivational sexological nosology formulated according to the foregoing epistemological principles will not be under the constraints imposed by any particular doctrine or dogma of etiology. It will not be vitiated by future additions and revisions, even those necessitated by entirely unforeseen etiological discoveries.

Regardless of the diversity and particularity of syndromes in the sexological nosology, the complete range of etiological possibilities should in each syndrome be differentially considered, both singly and conjunctively. It is not unusual for two or more etiological factors to exert their influence conjunctively. For example, suppose the manifest sexuoerotic phenomenon to be copulatory anhedonia. Then the conjunctive etiological scenario may be as follows: Anhedonia fails to respond to endocrine therapy, which is necessitated by a sex-hormonal deficiency, which in turn is contingent on a congenital gonadal defect, which is contingent on a chromosomal anomaly, which in the ultimate analysis is responsible for sterility and childlessness, from which is derived an unresolved pregnancy envy, of which the outcome is that copulatory pleasure becomes deconnected from the copulatory act.

The general categories of differential etiology that need to be considered and ruled either in or out in each individual case of sexuoerotic disorder are seventeen in number. Each can be multiplicatively subdivided, and necessarily so, for an exhaustively complete nosology. The seventeen are as follows.

- genetic (genomic or chromosomal) anomaly
- birth defect of the reproductive organs
- prenatal brain hormonal anomaly
- postnatal brain hormonal anomaly
- pubertal target-organ hormonal anomaly
- prescribed pharmacologic toxicity
- unprescribed pharmacologic toxicity
- genital microbial infection
- genital neoplastic disease
- debilitating systemic disease
- postoperative surgical impairment
- traumatic accidental impairment
- vascular impairment
- peripheral neural impairment
- spinal-cord lesion or disease
- brain lesion or disease
- endopsychic dysfunction of ideation and imagery

The last is the one that is commonly named *psychogenic*. The attribution of a psychogenic etiology to a sexuoerotic syndrome signifies that it is a sequel to life experiences as subjectively construed. Ideally, such experiences should be authenticated with evidence over and beyond personal recall, insofar as retrieved memories are subject to omission, distortion, and confabulation. In many instances, the etiology of a syndrome, instead of being declared psychogenic, would be more accurately declared simply as unknown or, perhaps, as idiopathic.

Taxonomy

Any taxonomy, by definition, requires major principles or criteria of classification. Membership lists are classified alphabetically, but alphabetization is too arbitrary as a taxonomical principle for the sexological nosology. Another arbitrary principle is the criminological one, according to which syndromes are classified as being or not being criminal offenses. As aforesaid, a third principle classifies sexological syndromes on the putative basis of their being either organic or psychogenic in origin. This distinction should, however, be established pragmatically and empirically, not postulated taxonomically, for the latter leads too often to major nosological errors.

A good and workable taxonomy is one in which the coverage is exhaustively complete and the items are mutually exclusive. These conditions are met in the case of nosological sexology by a taxonomy in which the principles of classification are multivectorial. Altogether, there are five vectors. Each one bears its own component of the totality of sexuoeroticality, and is named as follows.

- The vector of the philias (hypophilia, hyperphilia, and paraphilia).
- The body-image vector (masculine, feminine, or androgynous, and concordant or discordant with natal sex).
- The age-of-onset vector (prenatal, juvenile, adolescent, adult, geriatric).
- The partnership vector.
- The transcultural vector.

In the *vector of the philias,* the syndromes in which sexuoerotic functioning is to some degree insufficient or not up to par are classified as *hypophilias.* The criterion standard is not fixed and absolute, but is reached by consensus and is subject to revision according to time, place, and circumstances. Colloquially, the hypophilic disorders may be called the Masters and Johnson (1970) disorders of sexual inadequacy. Some occur in both men and women, namely sexuoerotic inertia, apathy, or anhedonia, also known popularly as lack of sexual desire; genital anesthesia; anorgasmia; and dyspareunia. In men there are also erectile impotence and premature ejaculation; and in women, vaginal lubrication failure and vaginismus.

The syndromes of the *hyperphilias* are those in which sexuoerotic functioning is to some degree excessive or beyond par. The criterion standard is subject to the same qualifications as in the hypophilic syndromes. Historically, the hyperphilic syndromes have been equated with nymphomania and satyriasis and, perhaps with an envious leer, written off as a joke. There is nothing jocular about epileptiform hyperorgasmia, however, nor about erotomania, as in the Clérambault-Kandinsky syndrome of unrequited love. It was this latter syndrome that, in the case of John Hinckley, nearly cost President Reagan his life. In the era of AIDS, it has become newly fashionable to rename hyperphilia as addiction, or as obsessional compulsivity.

The syndromes of the *paraphilias* are those in which sexuoerotic functioning becomes biased or skewed with respect to, in particular, the ideation and imagery of the proceptive or sexuoerotic arousal phase. According to its Greek derivation, paraphilia means love (*philia*) that is altered (*para*) so as to be beyond the usual. In street vernacular, a paraphilia is kinky sex, and in law, a perversion. There is no absolute criterion standard by which to separate paraphilia as a personal and playful eccentricity from paraphilia as a morbid and, in extreme cases, deadly syndrome. As in the case of hypophilia and hyperphilia, the criterion standard of what is paraphilia is set by consensus and is subject to revision according to time, place, and circumstance. The catalogue of paraphilias is forty-plus, the exact number being contingent on the number of minor subdivisions. There is an extensive coverage of the paraphilias in Money (1986, 1988).

In the taxonomy of the sexological nosology, the second vector is the sexuoerotic *body-image vector,* under which are subsumed three major categories, namely realignment or enhancement; obliteration or relinquishment; and augmentation or amplification (Money, 1991). The body image in all three of these categories may be concordant with the natal sex in which the person was registered and reared, and to which that person belongs societally.

Conversely, the natal sex and the societal sex may be discordant. If so, then the discrepancy signifies that the body image has to some extent assimilated a transposition or crossover of the masculine and feminine stereotypes of G-I/R (gender-identity/role). In its most comprehensive form, *G-I/R transposition* is represented as transexualism, also known as gender dysphoria. Transexualism is the name that applies to both the syndrome and the method of its rehabilitation. The latter entails not only cosmetic, social, and legal sex reassignment, but also hormonal and surgical sex reassignment. The full range of G-I/R transpositions, classified on the dimensions of time (constant vs. episodic), extent (complete vs. partial), and constraints (unlimited vs. limited) is spelled out in Money (1988; see also Chapter 3 above). In transvestism (more accurately termed *transvestophilia*), the transposition, though virtually complete, is episodic, not permanent. In homosexualism and bisexualism, the transposition may be so limited that it applies only to sexuoerotic engagement with a person of the same natal sex and to no other aspects or stereotypes of gender dimorphism. Even though the logic is false, it is commonly declared of a man in such a case that he has an untransposed male identity, but a homosexual orientation and "object choice." For a woman, the counterpart statement is made. The homosexual transposition per se is not classified in the sexological nosology as a syndrome. It is, like left-handedness, say, or color blindness, a minority status. It is not a preference or choice.

The third vector in the sexological nosology is the *age-of-onset vector.* In earliest life, protosexuoeroticality is a more accurate term than sexuoeroticality. The fate of eventual sexuoerotic functioning in adulthood is a major consideration with respect to neonatal surgical intervention in cases of hermaphroditic and related birth defects of the sex organs. A peculiar feature of such cases is that, whereas the baby is the patient, sexuoerotic counseling on its behalf is rendered to the parents for whom no diagnosis (needed for medical-insurance reimbursement) is provided in the current nosology—even though properly-timed counseling prevents the escalation of mental-health fees later (Money, 1987).

All aspects of healthy functioning have their roots in childhood, and healthy sexuoerotic functioning is no exception. Although prospective studies are sadly lacking, retrospective evidence leaves no doubt that many of the sexuoerotic syndromes of later life originate in the thwarting, neglect, and abuse of healthy sexuoerotic phenomena (for example, sexual rehearsal play) in childhood. One of the major societal irrationalities of the present day is the dogma that defines all manifestations of juvenile sexuoeroticality as sexual child abuse, and as the cause of manifold subsequent psychiatric symptoms. In consequence, scientific pediatric sexology is almost universally neglected, and there is no adequate nosology of juvenile sexuoerotic syndromes. Even more bizarre is the absence of ephebiatric (adolescent) sexology and its nosology. Adolescent sexuoeroticality is treated with much moralizing at times, as if it were a disease per se, manifested only in criminal sex offending or in unmarried pregnancy and single parenthood.

It will be from prospective studies that knowledge will finally accrue concerning the natural history and antecedent manifestations of those sexuoerotic syndromes of adulthood that have a history of early onset. Nosologically, it will then be possible to separate them from late-onset syndromes. The same applies to those syndromes that have a still later onset in the geriatric years, some of them a manifestation of geriatric deterioration, as, for example, in association with Alzheimer's disease.

The *partnership vector* derives from the phylogenetic principle that as a species, we human beings are not hermits. Phylogenetically, we are a troopbonding species, and also a pairbonding species. Babies who do not pairbond with their mothers fail to survive. Species survival, despite the technical accomplishments of donor insemination, is contingent on coupling. Even though copulatory coupling may be transient and anonymous, it may also be tied to a long-term continuance of pairbondedness characterized by limerence, the experience of having fallen in love. Copulatory coupling may also become a lackluster practice in a sexuoerotic relationship blighted by adversarialism. The sex organs then become feuding weapons and their sexuoerotic functioning becomes severely compromised. The sexuoerotic malfunction that may ensue in either partner (or both) masks the hidden agenda of power and retaliation. With a different partner, or when alone, the symptoms of sexuoerotic malfunction—impotence, for example, or anorgasmia—may fail to materialize. They are conjured up only within a particular partnership or type of partnership. It is in the relationship between the two partners that they have their being; they exist not as solo phenomena, but as phenomena of reciprocality. One outcome is that the unit of treatment is not the individual, but the couple.

The *transcultural vector* applies, for example, to language as well as to the cultural specificity of sexuoeroticality. The very idea of a transcultural language-free test of linguistic ability is an oxymoron. The ability to use language is measured not in a vacuum, but in tests based on the proficiency of acquiring and using one's language for communication. Sexuoeroticality also must manifest itself in order to be evaluated, and the details of its manifestation will be developmentally shaped by, and assimilated from, the social environment. Like native language, sexuoeroticality is not culture free, but culture bound and regionally diverse. Regional diversity is encoded in the ideology of custom, religion, and law. The standards of what is ideologically accepted and what is forbidden vary according to time and place.

Homosexuality is a classic example. The era of the Inquisition, when homosexuality was equated with sodomy and was punishable by torture and burning, was also, for the inquisitors, the heyday of sadism and masochism. In today's world, homosexuality is variously classified as a criminal offense, an illness, a minority social status, or an institutionalized rite of passage (Herdt, 1981, 1984).

From the vantage point of the taxonomical purist, the transcultural vector introduces an intolerable degree of arbitrary (and in some cases, contradictory) relativism into any classification system and destroys its elegance. There is no way of getting rid of transcultural relativism in sexology, however. It is a feature of the sexological landscape and cannot be removed. Moreover, it is a theoretically significant feature of the landscape, for in demonstrating differences in sexuoerotic ideology, it demonstrates also the individual variability of sexuoerotic expression.

In addition to its theoretical significance, the transcultural vector has practical significance for treatment and case management. For example, it would be absurd to diagnose and report every unmarried youth of the Sambia tribe of New Guinea (Herdt, 1981, 1984) as a pedophile; yet, since time immemorial, it has been dictated by the medical folklore of the tribe that, prior to the marriage age of nineteen, young bachelors must supply prepubertal boys with their "men's milk" in order to ensure the onset of puberty and the rite of passage to heterosexual, head-hunting warriorhood.

Recognizing a transcultural difference is not synonymous with either endorsing or not endorsing it—witness the example of female genital mutilation (Pharaonic circumcision) widespread in central and northeastern Africa (Lightfoot-Klein, 1989).

The challenge of ideological relativity to nosology is not unique to sexology. It affects all branches of medicine and science that deal with human beings and their behavior.

REFERENCES

Herdt, G. H. (1981). *Guardians of the Flutes: Idioms of Masculinity.* New York: McGraw-Hill.

Herdt, G. H., ed. (1984). *Ritualized Homosexuality in Melanesia.* Berkeley/Los Angeles: University of California Press.

Masters, W. H. and Johnson, V. E. (1970). *Human Sexual Inadequacy.* Boston: Little, Brown.

Lightfoot-Klein, H. (1989). *Prisoners of Ritual: An Odyssey into Female Genital Circumcision in Africa.* New York: Haworth Press.

Money, J. (1986). *Lovemaps: Clinical Concepts of Sexual/Erotic Health and Pathology, Paraphilia and Gender Transposition in Childhood, Adolescence, and Maturity.* New York: Irvington Publishers. Paperback edition, Amherst, NY: Prometheus Books, 1988.

———. (1987). "Psychologic considerations in patients with ambisexual development." *Seminars in Reproductive Endocrinology: Sexual Differentiation* 5:307–13.

———. (1988). *Gay, Straight, and In-Between: The Sexology of Erotic Orientation.* New York/London: Oxford University Press.

17

Body-Image Syndromes in Sexology: Phenomenology and Classification

Introduction and Definition

The concepts of the body image and the body schema are attached in the manner of Siamese twins—different, but merged. *Body schema* is the older term. It had its origins early in the twentieth century, in the writings of Henry Head on the phenomena of brain lesions and peripheral neuropathology that would alter the representation or schema of one's body and one's body functions in one's brain. These alterations in the brain would, in turn, alter one's personal recognition of one's own body and of the location and function of its parts and regions.

Whereas in early usage, there was a close connection between the body schema in the brain and the body image in personal recognition (Weinstein and Kahn, 1955; Signer, 1987), in later usage the connection loosened and the terms *body schema* and *body image* became used interchangeably (Schilder, 1950, first edition, 1935).

Eventually, the body image assumed an existence of its own as an intrapsychic construct independent of the body schema. Thenceforth, the representation of the body image in the brain, though it was not denied, was simply taken for granted. Advances in brain technology

---

Originally published in *Journal of Psychology and Human Sexuality* 6(3):31–48, 1994.

might, at some time, allow the body image to be traced to its corresponding representation in the brain schema.

A person's body image may be accurate in the sense of being accepted by other people as being consistent with their conception of that person's bodily appearance and function. By contrast, it may be so inaccurate in the sense of being rejected by other people as being, according to their criteria, a foolish and absurd fixation or delusion. It may also be so obsessively and tenaciously fixated as to be unyielding to rational and critical analysis. It then qualifies as a body-image disorder or syndrome, of which the definition is as follows:

> *body-image syndrome:* a fixation pertaining to one's personal recognition of one's own body, including the location and function of its parts or regions, and characterized by discordancy between what has existed as compared with what presently exists, or between what presently exists as compared with one's projection of how it should be changing or is changing to become.

Body-Image Psychosis, Neurosis, Cosmetics

The intensity of a body-image syndrome ranges across the entire spectrum from lightweight and benign to heavyweight and malignant. It may be as benign as, for example, to become ornamentally tattooed; or as malignant as, for example, to become a eunuch by genital self-amputation, of which the fortuitous outcome may be to bleed to death.

The most virulent manifestations of a body-image syndrome may be characterized as body-image psychosis. That is to say, it may be classified as a psychosis in its own right, and not attributed to some other psychosis, notably schizophrenia or bipolar psychosis. However, a body-image psychosis may share features in common with other psychoses, including psychoses associated with a brain lesion, without being diagnostically identical. Not only is the diagnosis different, but also the treatment and prognosis, insofar as the body-image psychosis is, like a monomania, more likely to be self-contained than psychopathologically diffuse.

This same diagnostic principle applies also to the less virulent manifestations of a body-image syndrome, which may be classified as a body-image neurosis. There is no clear line of demarcation that separates body-image neurosis from body-image psychosis. Demarcation on the criterion of the degree of body-image dysphoria experienced by the patient is contraindicated, insofar as it is impossible to measure subjectively experienced mental states. Moreover, any nosology based on mental states allows diagnosis to rely too much on what may be the wrong or capricious judgment of the diagnostician. The alternative and more reliable criterion is the degree to which the body-image syndrome incapacitates the patient for the daily routines and responsibilities of living.

The least virulent of the body-image syndromes need no pathological classification at all, for they belong in the realm of cosmetology. A body-image cosmetic syndrome may be simply a matter of adherence to the ideals of contemporary fashion—for example, changing the shape of the nose by surgery. It may also be a credential of membership in a minority group or cult—for example, having the nipples pierced for the display of gold rings. Or it may be a tribally imposed ritual which is, in effect, an enforced mutilation—for example, neonatal circumcision of American males (Wallerstein, 1980), and Pharaonic circumcision of juvenile females in the geographical region northeast of Nilotic Africa. The female ritual entails surgical removal of the entire vulva (clitoris, labia minora, labia majora) and sewing up of the wound so that only one small hole remains open (Lightfoot-Klein, 1989).

The body-image syndromes do not have a place of their own in today's official nosology. The body-image cosmetology syndromes are accorded legitimacy in plastic surgery and named according to the organ or region on which surgery is performed. The body-image neuroses and psychoses are diversely assigned a psychiatric diagnosis (which may or may not be in the category of somatoform disorder) as a body-dysmorphic disorder or dysmorphophobia. It may also be diagnosed as a delusional disorder of the somatic subtype.

Three Principles of Body-Image Syndromes Converge in Transexualism

The three principles listed in Table 1, namely realignment and enhancement, obliteration and relinquishment, and augmentation and amplifica-

Table 1. Body-Image Syndromes: Three Principles of Body Alteration

Realignment and Enhancement
Obliteration and Relinquishment
Augmentation and Amplification

tion, are the principles of body alteration that apply to all the body-image syndromes, including the sexological ones. All three principles of alteration are exemplified in the procedures of sex reassignment.

The procedures of sex reassignment were originally developed for the rehabilitation of patients whose natal sex was ambiguous or hermaphroditic and whose body image developed to be discordant with that of the sex in which they had been officially named and registered, and in which they were socially assigned and reared.

In the 1960s, sex reassignment (Benjamin, 1966; Green and Money, 1969) became recognized as an acceptable procedure for people whose natal sex was not ambiguous or hermaphroditic but whose body image nonetheless developed to be discordant with their natal sex. The same term, *transexualism,* names not only the syndrome but also the method of rehabilitation: changing the body to be concordant with the body image.

In the case of the male-to-female transexual, the body image of the face is feminine and is discordant with that of the actual physiognomy, which in the majority of cases is bearded and has masculine features. The principle of alteration according to which congruence between the femininity of the facial body-image and the actual physiognomy is effected is realignment and enhancement. The method is electrolysis for facial-hair removal, administration of female hormones for feminized skin texture, and plastic surgery for changes of the physiognomy (though these are not invariably necessary).

The corresponding alterations for the female-to-male transexual are also of the realignment and enhancement type, but the method is more simple. Treatment with male sex hormone suffices. It produces facial hair, masculine skin texture and, ultimately, thinning or balding head hair. By enlarging the larynx, it also realigns the voice to conform to the body image—an effortless process unmatched in male-to-female reassignment, which requires vocal retraining.

The principle of obliteration and relinquishment is of paramount importance in the male-to-female transexual with respect to the external genitals, which are a reproach and an offense to the feminine body image. In a majority of cases, being rid of the offensive male genitals takes precedence over the augmenting and amplifying procedure of vaginoplasty.

In the female-to-male transexual, the offensive organs are those responsible for menstruation. Their extirpation takes precedence over the augmenting and amplifying procedure of phalloplasty, for which, despite its importance to the patient, there is no completely successful surgical technology.

In female-to-male transexuals, the obliteration and relinquishment principle applies also to surgical extirpation of the breasts. By contrast, in male-to-female transexuals it is the principle of augmentation and amplification that applies to the breasts. Hormonally induced breast enlargement (gynecomastia) may fail to match the body image of mammary hyperplasia in some patients, who may then resort to augmentation mammoplasty either by surgery or by the very dangerous procedure of silicone injections. The latter may also be resorted to for hip enlargement.

The transexual body image is individually variable with respect to the hierarchical position of the three principles of body alteration on the agenda of sex reassignment. Thus, in a case of male-to-female transexualism in which the principle of realignment and enhancement is hierarchically above relinquishment and obliteration, even an appointment with the hairdresser may take precedence over an admissions appointment for genital-reassignment surgery.

In another case, by contrast, in which the obliteration and relinquishment principle is uppermost, the patient may embark on a frantic round of clinic-shopping for a surgeon who will extirpate the offending external genital organs on the basis of personal request alone, with no waiting period and without the delay of a psychologic, psychiatric, or sexologic consultation.

In yet another case in which the augmentation and amplification principle is uppermost, large breasts may be so high on the agenda that a patient will find a way of meeting the cost of obtaining them, despite failing to meet other medical expenses.

Body-Image Syndromes: Organs and Regions

Sex reassignment involves a plurality of alterations involving different regions and organs of the body so that they match the body image. The number of alterations is individually variable. In some sexological body-image syndromes, by contrast, alteration of only one part of the body may be involved—for example, gonadectomy, so as to be able to live as a eunuch. Table 2 presents a list of body parts, organs, or regions and the types of alteration required so that the specified part, organ, or region is made concordant with the body image.

Alteration of the Entire Physique

The most comprehensive alteration of the body is that entailed in sex reassignment from female to male or male to female. The outcome is more satisfactory overall if sex reassignment is accomplished before the hormones of puberty have induced the irreversible sexually dimorphic characteristics of the body typical of the adult male or female. Prepubertal sex reassignment is feasible in some cases of hermaphroditism or related birth defect of the sex organs (agenesis of the penis and micropenis, for example), whereas in cases in which the natal sex is anatomically normal, legal obstacles intervene.

There are some cases of sex reassignment in which the body image does not include alteration of the genitalia. These are cases of gynemimesis (woman-miming) in males, sometimes called the lady-with-a-penis syndrome (Money and Lamacz, 1984). The counterpart in females is andromimesis (man-miming)—the male-with-a-vulva syndrome. Sex reassignment in gynemimesis and andromimesis is achieved socially, hormonally, and maybe with some reconstructive surgery. Both syndromes exist cross-culturally.

A body image discordant with the entire physique may entail not sex reassignment but a closer approximation to the idealized body type of members of one's own natal sex who are renowned as erotic icons and sexual magnets. The fixation on achieving the ideal cannot be relinquished despite its being technically unattainable. Thus the patient

Table 2. Sexological Body-Image Syndromes: Body Part and Type of Alteration

Body Part	*Alteration*
Entire physique	Reconstruction
Face	Reconstruction
Hair	Removal
	Generate anew
	Restoration
Breasts	Removal
	Construction
	Enlargement
External genitalia	Sex reassignment
	Reconstruction
Gonads	Removal
	Prosthetic replacement
Penis	Enlargement
	Refunctionalization
Foreskin	Restoration
Internal genitalia	Removal
	Organ transplantation
Limbs	Amputation
Skin	Decoration

is self-condemned to a life of loveless celibacy relieved only, perhaps, by masturbation fantasies of the unattainable.

There are some examples of a body-image syndrome pertaining to the entire physique in which the development of the actual physique has been pathological. An example in the male (Money, unpublished data) is the syndrome of adiposogenital dystrophy, characterized by adiposity of the feminine type, genital hypoplasia, insufficient secondary sexual virilization, metabolic disturbances, and possible lesions of the hypothalamus. In the female, a corresponding example is a complex syndrome of endocrine and metabolic disturbances, unnamed as yet. It partly resembles Cushing's syndrome, Stein-Leventhal syndrome, and a late-onset variant of the adrenogenital syndrome of congenital virilizing adrenal hyperplasia (CVAH). In a particular case (unpublished), the limbs and torso had become hirsute and the muscles flabby. Though lacking substantiation, there was a primary complaint of progressive body shrinkage. To be concordant with the ideal body image, the body itself should be restored to its full size and strength, and should also be that of a man rather than a woman. Since childhood, the possibility of being a male had had an appeal, but not to the extent of a fixation on sex reassignment. The therapeutic and prognostic prospects in such a case are pessimistic.

Alteration of the Face

Altering the face to be concordant with the facial-body image may be a component of altering the entire physique, or it may be limited to the face alone. Altering the face may be temporary, with makeup, or permanent, with tattoo, scarification, or plastic-surgical remodeling. The alteration may be imposed as a stigma, for example of disease or criminality. More commonly it has something to do with customary standards of being sexually attractive. As a full-fledged sexological body-image syndrome, alteration of only the face either does not exist or has not yet been reported.

Alteration of Hair

Removal of excess hair, or inducing growth or regrowth of missing hair, is usually a matter of expediency. Only very rarely does it assume the proportions of a body-image syndrome. One extraordinarily rare example is that of total pubic baldness, which occurs in some cases of the androgen-insensitivity syndrome (AIS) in women who have the 46,XY chromosomal pattern typical of the normal male but are morphologically female. It has been known that some AIS women will become exaggeratedly fixated on lack of pubic hair. It becomes a symbol for the other concomitants of their condition, in particular sterility, that deleteriously controls their lives. As a body-image syndrome, it does not yield to the patient's own rational considerations, which make it even more devastating for her to deal with.

Baldness of the scalp may also become the fixation of a sexological body-image syndrome in a 46,XY male. In one case, the fixation took the form of a phobia of the social stigmatization of familial baldness before age thirty. The patient earnestly pleaded not to have to suffer what his father had suffered. His explicit agenda was to be castrated. His covert agenda was to be relieved of the sin of masturbation accompanied by homosexual fantasies. Denied castration, he went off in search of another surgeon.

Alteration of Breasts

Matching the chest to the mammary body image may require mastectomy, augmentation mammoplasty, or the hormonal induction of breast growth de novo. Surgical or hormonal intervention is most often required to correct a developmental defect or deficiency or, less frequently, to implement sex reassignment. Fixation exclusively on breast removal has recently been reported as a specifically sexological body-image syndrome without sex reassignment.

Alteration of the External Genitalia

There is no need to further belabor the point, aforementioned, that alteration of the external genitalia may be one of the procedures of sex reassignment. In infants and juveniles, male and female, it may be also in obedience to extremely ancient cultural customs, the origins of which are now completely lost. In adult males, genital alteration was a religious custom of recent vintage in the Christian Skoptic sect. The sect existed in Russia and the Balkans from the eighteenth to the early twentieth century. Membership in the sect required renunciation of the flesh which, for males, entailed amputation of the testicles and scrotum and, for full piety, the penis. For females, it entailed that nipples be burned off so that a baby could not be fed.

Skoptic has become the eponym for the Skoptic syndrome, a sexological body-image syndrome in males characterized by a fixation on becoming a eunuch so as to be relieved of the demands of the flesh.

There are some clinical examples of the Skoptic syndrome characterized by self-amputation of the penis. More usually, however, the Skoptic syndrome is manifested as removal of only the testicles.

Alteration of the Testicles

The Skoptic syndrome may be manifested as a fixation on becoming a eunuch by either professional surgical castration (gonadectomy) or self-castration. Self-castration may be associated with a fantasy of becoming more feminine, but not of sex reassignment (Money, unpublished data). It would appear likely, however, that self-castration is more often associated with escaping from all expressions of carnal desire. In one published case (Money, 1988), self-castration failed to obliterate carnal desire and was followed by self-attempted denervation of the penis. In another case, partly published (Kalin, 1979) and partly not (Money, unpublished data), a college student of very high IQ manufactured a hypothalamic-inhibiting substance designed to block the release of pituitary gonadotropins. Its impurities when self-injected produced life-threatening ulcerations. Prevented by maternal intervention from undergoing a trial treatment with the antiandrogen Depo-Provera, he returned home and castrated himself. Still not relieved of carnal desire, he studied adrenal surgery alone in the library in preparation for self-adrenalectomy to remove the last vestiges of androgen from the adrenal cortices. After seven hours of self-surgery, the pain of lifting the liver to reveal the adrenals proved so excruciatingly painful that he telephoned for an emergency ambulance and was admitted to the emergency room of the local hospital.

The converse of getting rid of the testicles is their replacement by prosthetic testicles after they have been lost or are congenitally absent. There is no recorded instance of a sexological body-image syndrome characterized by a specific fixation on obtaining testicular prosthesis. By contrast, in cases of testicular agenesis, there are instances of resistance to acceptance of the artificiality of prosthetic testicular implants. In one noteworthy case, the body image incorporated the implanted testicles only after a dream of having swallowed them (Money and Sollod, 1978).

Alteration of the Penis

There is a multimillion-dollar market awaiting whoever might discover a foolproof method of penis enlargement. Among those who would pay for an enlarged penis, however, there are few who qualify as having a body-image syndrome with a fixation on penis size.

One such fixation is known by its Malaysian name, Koro, the shrinking-penis syndrome. Once considered to be culturally limited to southeast Asia, Koro is now known to occur more widely (Money and Annecillo, 1987). In the body-imagery of this syndrome, the penis shrinks and retracts until, when it has completely disappeared, death may ensue. In actuality, there is no substantiating evidence of penile alteration. The symptoms do not respond to rational appeal, but with supportive understanding, the body image returns to its earlier state.

In some penile body-image syndromes, there is a prior history of traumatic injury of the penis, for example, ablatio penis; or of disease of the penis, for example, Peyronie's disease; or of a birth defect of the penis, for example, micropenis (Money, 1984). The common denominator in such cases is that the penis is unable to effect penetration in either a heterosexual or homosexual relationship. Not all of those so affected, however, develop a full-fledged body-image syndrome. Some find an unpathological means of coping.

Alteration of the penis in a body-image syndrome applies also, in some cases, to its function. Thus there may be a frenetic search, in vain, for restoration of erection from the permanent impotence that is frequently a sequel to priapism (Money and Hirsch, 1965). Impotence as a sexological body-image syndrome is, however, more likely to be manifest as a fixation on failure prior to even trying—in fact, it is obsessional fixation on failure that prohibits the attempt to copulate, despite the evidence of full erection in masturbation (Money, unpublished data). In an undetermined proportion of cases of impotence, erectile failure is a body-image syndrome. The same applies to premature ejaculation, in which the fixation is on one's penis as an intrusive and offensive organ from which the partner should be protected.

Fixation on the penis as an offensive organ that preordains the absolute impossibility of an erotosexual partnership may pertain to its size or shape. Even though there is no substantiating evidence of penile hypertrophy, a patient may have a penis represented in his body image as being so large that it would tear up any vagina it might penetrate, or as being so crooked that it would wreak similar havoc (Money, unpublished data). In such a case, medical photography poses a threat to exposure of the error of the body image, as does a physical examination. Thus, appointments for both are plausibly evaded.

Female counterparts of penile body-image syndromes have not yet been recorded. It is theoretically possible, however, that in girlhood development, an absence of positive endorsement of achieving orgasm leaves a void in the body image where orgasm should be. Subsequently, the longer this void persists unfilled, the longer does the woman remain unknowing of what an orgasm is.

An analogous situation exists in cases of sex reassignment. Thus, there is no guarantee whatsoever that the male-to-female's body image of a female orgasm corresponds to orgasms as experienced by women. Correspondingly, the same applies to the female-to-male transexual and the male orgasm.

Alteration of the Foreskin

To lose the foreskin after its constancy in the body image has become well established is more traumatic than to have lost it neonatally, or never to have had it. Even so, the body-image syndrome of foreskin restoration occurs not only in men who were circumcised as juveniles, but also in those whose circumcision was neonatal. The morbidity of the syndrome ranges from mild to severe (Money, 1991). If surgery is resorted to (Greer et al., 1982; Mohl et al., 1981) the outcome may be cosmetically disfiguring. In some cases, self surgery has been resorted to (Walter and Streimer, 1990; Money, 1991). As in other body-image syndromes, an appeal to rationality is counterproductive. However, with caring support, even severe cases are likely to go into remission. There is a national network and newsletter for men with a shared interest in foreskin restoration (Berkeley and Tiffenbach, 1983).

Whether or not there is a body-image syndrome as a sequel to female circumcision, so-called, has not yet been ascertained. Variations in tribal custom range from removal of the clitoral hood to removal of the entire vulva and closure of the wound. As immigrant Africans transplant their custom of female circumcision to Europe and America, it is possible that some of their daughters will develop a sexological body-image syndrome of vulval restoration.

Pseudocyesis, or false pregnancy, is a body-image syndrome remarkable for physiological changes that, in conformity with the body image, mimic the early stages of pregnancy. When the absence of a fetus is discovered, grieving occurs as if a miscarriage had taken place. The origin of the physiological changes in pseudocyesis has not been ascertained, but there are animal models that indicate a role for the sense of smell.

Alteration of the Internal Genitalia

A fixation on hysterectomy as a sexological body-image syndrome has been known to occur at least once, but its prevalence is unknown. It eradicates the menses and permanently ensures relief from a phobia of pregnancy.

The converse—a fixation on obtaining a uterine transplant as a sexological body-image syndrome—is probably equally rare. It has been known to exist in association with male internal and external genitalia in unoperated male-to-female transexualism, accompanied by a cyclical, overwhelming "hunger" to be pregnant. Cyclically recurring symptoms—for instance, severe testicular cramps—may be early signs of impending development of the full syndrome of male-to-female transexualism in a man who is already an episodic cross-dresser.

Alteration of the Limbs

The body-image syndromes and the syndromes of paraphilia (Money, 1986, 1988) overlap notably, though not exclusively, in the amputation paraphilia (Money et al., 1977) named *apotemnophilia* (from the Greek *apo,* "from" + *temnein,* "to cut" + *philia,* "love"). For the apotemnophile, erotic arousal and the facilitation of orgasm are responsive to and contingent on being an amputee. An apotemnophile becomes fixated on carrying out a self-contrived amputation or on obtaining one in a hospital. The location of the amputation is highly specific. Though apotemnophilia occurs in women (Money, 1990) as well as men, it is probably less prevalent in women. It is predominantly heterosexually oriented, but occurs homosexually also. Many apotemnophiles can trace the onset of their fixation to childhood, especially around the age of eight. There is a nationwide network and newsletter for those with an amputee body-image and for interested amputees (Riddle, 1989).

Alteration of the Skin

Adornment of the body by stretching, binding, tattooing, scarifying, and piercing the skin in many societies signifies sexual attractiveness and erotic eligibility. It pertains sexologically to the body image, but in the vast majority of instances does not qualify as a body-image syndrome, sexologically or otherwise.

Alteration of the skin by piercing may, however, qualify as a sexological body-image syndrome when there is a fixation on having one's genitalia pierced. There are men and women who undergo multiple genital piercings so as to decorate their genitalia with gold rings and bars or other forms of jewelry. There are still others whose piercing fixation is an unrelenting, repetitive ritual, as in the case of a man whose sexual ecstasy was contingent on passing the needle of an injection syringe through the skin of his penis or scrotum and into the tissue beneath. In this way his genitalia became concordant with their depiction in his body image as the genitalia of a sacrificial martyr. There was a transcendental element of expiation and penance in this sexological body-image syndrome.

DISCUSSION

The principle idea of this paper is a new one, here applied for the first time, namely to give conceptual kinship to otherwise scattered sexological syndromes by giving them a classification of their own as sexological body-image syndromes. The term *body image* has a slippery epistemological history, its meaning half-merged with that of *body schema* (Gallagher, 1986) and its definition undecided by whether, or by how much, it belongs to both the mind or the body. There are those who might argue that, until it is established that body image is either mental or physical, it is too soon to propose an entire nosological category of body-image syndromes. The answer to this argument is that the very challenge of recognizing the relatedness of the various body-image syndromes will lead to a greater understanding of where body image belongs, how it gets there, where it comes from, how to define it, and how to prevent its pathologies. Without a nosology of their own, the sexological body-image syndromes are scattered amongst various other diagnoses and thus are misdiagnosed.

A sexological body-image syndrome may coexist with and be secondary to a primary syndrome—for example, a primary endocrine or a genetic disorder. It may then be wrongly attributed to the primary disorder exclusively, or equally wrongly detached from the primary disorder and given an independent diagnosis (typically a psychiatric one).

Unlike their nosological counterparts, the sexological body-image syndromes are only rarely diagnosed as being contingent on a brain lesion that disrupts the sexual body schema, even when such is the case. Thus, erotic parasthesias and other sexological manifestations of, for example, multiple sclerosis are likely to be misdiagnosed, probably as psychogenic reactions. So also are epileptiform orgasmic attacks which cannot be relieved, except with anticonvulsant medication. Persistent noncoital genital pain and orgasmically triggered migraine attacks may similarly be misdiagnosed, commonly as being of psychogenic origin.

Among the psychiatric diagnoses listed in the Diagnostic and Statistical Manual III-R of the American Psychiatric Association (1987), somatoform disorder, either body-dysmorphic disorder (#300.70 in DSM-III-R) or conversion disorder (#300.11 in DSM-III-R), might be diagnostically assigned to a sexological body-image syndrome. Neither, however, is sufficiently precise. The same applies to the diagnosis of delusional (paranoid) disorder (#297.10 in DSM-III-R), somatic type, insofar as a sexological body-image syndrome is characterized by a fixated idea which is not a genuine delusion. The fixated idea is insistent, tenacious, and unyielding. Thus, it may in vernacular speech be characterized as "obsessive" or "compulsive," but it does not meet the DSM-III-R #300.30 requirements for a diagnosis of obsessive-compulsive disorder (neurosis).

There are no fixed criterion or tests for the diagnosis of a sexological body-image syndrome. However, an informal list of indicators, compiled over a period of years, is useful as a preliminary guide. One indicator is usually insufficient to suggest a sexological body-image syndrome, but not all indicators need be present. These indicators are as follows:

- the complaint pertains to a sexual part, organ, or function of the body or to erotosexual functioning
- a history of multiple prior evaluations
- self-referral by telephone or letter

- expansive or fancy handwriting on the envelope
- envelope marked "private," "personal," or "confidential" (or all three)
- letter sent by special delivery, express mail, or courier
- on the telephone, a peremptory insistence on bypassing intermediaries and speaking only to the person named
- the prerogative of interrupting, irrespective of time (even long after office hours) or day of the week, is taken for granted
- a presumption that it will be an honor or privilege to have such a rare case for either treatment or research
- money is said to be no object, even though none is available to pay bills
- conversation is loquacious and circumstantial, an answer to a question is not to the question actually asked, and details are not pinned down
- the patient is well acquainted with professional information pertaining to the symptom
- the patient assigns to the doctor the role of technical assistant to himself or herself, who is the expert on the case.

In some cases of sexological body-image syndrome, it is possible to retrieve biographical information sufficient to formulate a psychodynamic connection between the symbolism of the syndrome and the biographical experiences that antedated its onset. For example, in the biography of a girl with the androgen-insensitivity syndrome of male hermaphroditism, the unspeakable stigma of having male chromosomes and testicles may be sealed off behind a fixation on the stigma of pubic baldness.

To understand the history of a fixation, however, is to understand a temporal, not a causal, contingency. A temporal relationship is not synonymous with a causal relationship and it does not guarantee either an accurate prognosis or a valid form of treatment. Long-term chronological follow-up may, however, show that the natural history of a body-image syndrome is that it resolves and goes into remission. That has proved to the case in at least some sexological body-image syndromes. Hence the value of therapeutic support.

Accurate description and phenomenological definition are the precursors of causal understanding. Phenomenologically, body-image syndromes—including those that are sexological—are disorders of recognition. It is under the criterion of recognition that, in the brain and in the mind, the causality of all body-image disorders will eventually be comprehended.

References

American Psychiatric Association. (1987). *Diagnostic and Statistical Manual of Mental Disorders,* Third Edition (Revised). Washington, DC: American Psychiatric Association.

Benjamin, H. (1966). *The Transsexual Phenomenon: A Scientific Report on Transsexualism and Sex Conversion in the Human Male and Female.* New York: Julian Press.

Berkeley, B., and Tiffenbach, J. *Foreskin: Its Past, Its Present and . . . Its Future?* San Francisco: Bud Berkeley, P.O. Box 26011, San Francisco, CA 94126.

Gallagher, S. (1986). "Body image and body schema: A conceptual clarification." *Journal of Mind and Behavior* 7:541–54.

Green, R., and Money, J., eds. (1969). *Transsexualism and Sex Reassignment.* Baltimore: Johns Hopkins University Press.

Greer, D. M., Jr., Mohl, P. C., and Sheley, A. A. (1982). "A technique for foreskin reconstruction and some preliminary results." *Journal of Sex Research* 18:324–30.

Kalin, N. H. (1979). "Genital and abdominal self-surgery: A case report." *Journal of the American Medical Association* 241:2188–89.

Lightfoot-Klein, H. (1989). *Prisoners of Ritual: An Odyssey into Female Genital Circumcision in Africa.* New York: Haworth Press.

Mohl, P. C., Adams, R., Greer, D. M., and Sheley, K. A. (1981). "Prepuce restoration seekers: Psychiatric aspects." *Archives of Sexual Behavior* 10:383–93.

Money, J. (1984). "Family and gender-identity/role. Part II: Transexual versus homosexual coping in micropenis syndrome with male sex assignment." *International Journal of Family Psychiatry* 5:341–73.

———. (1986). *Lovemaps: Clinical Concepts of Sexual/Erotic Health and Pathology, Paraphilia, and Gender Transposition in Childhood, Adolescence, and Maturity.* New York: Irvington. Paperback edition, Amherst, NY: Prometheus Books, 1988.

———. (1988). "The Skoptic syndrome: Castration and genital self-mutilation as an example of sexual body-image pathology." *Journal of Psychology and Human Sexuality* 1(1):113–28.

———. (1991). "Sexology, body image, foreskin restoration, and bisexual status." *Journal of Sex Research* 28:145–56.

———. (1994). "Paraphilia in females: Fixation on amputation and lameness; two personal accounts." *Journal of Psychology and Human Sexuality* 3(2):165–72.

Money, J., and Annecillo, C. (1987). "Body-image pathology: Koro, the shrinking-penis syndrome in transcultural sexology." *Journal of Sex and Marital Therapy* 2:91–100.

Money, J., and Hirsch, S. R. (1965). "After priapism: Orgasm retained, erection lost." *Journal of Urology* 94:152–57.

Money, J., Jobaris, R., and Furth, G. (1977). "Apotemnophilia: Two cases of self-demand amputation as a paraphilia." *Journal of Sex Research* 13:115–25.

Money, J., and Lamacz, M. (1984). "Gynemimesis and gynemimetophilia: Individual and cross-cultural manifestations of a gender coping strategy hitherto unnamed." *Comprehensive Psychiatry* 25:392–403.

Money, J., and Sollod, R. N. (1978). "Body image, plastic surgery (prosthetic testes) and Kallmann's syndrome." *British Journal of Medical Psychology* 93:432–34.

Riddle, G. C. (1989). *Amputees and Devotees.* New York: Irvington.

Schilder, P. (1950). *The Image and Appearance of the Human Body: Studies in the Constructive Energies of the Psyche.* Psyche Monographs, No. 4. London: Kegan, Paul, Trench, Trubner & Co. Ltd., 1935. New York: International Universities Press.

Signer, S. F. (1987). "Capgras' syndrome: The delusion of substitution." *Journal of Clinical Psychiatry* 48(4):147–50.

Wallerstein, E. (1980). *Circumcision: An American Health Fallacy.* New York: Springer.

Walter, G., and Streimer, J. (1990). "Genital self-mutilation: Attempted foreskin reconstruction." *British Journal of Psychiatry* 156:125–27.

Weinstein, E. A., and Kahn, R. L. (1955). *Denial of Illness.* Springfield, IL: Charles C Thomas.

18

Orgasmology, the Science of Orgasm: Brain, Genitals, Phantom Orgasm, Clinical Syndromes

Try to compare orgasms and you are immediately confronted by a conundrum, a question that is unanswerable and purely speculative, rooted in the constraints of solipsism. Is your orgasm better than mine, or mine better than yours? Is the man's orgasm better than the woman's or the woman's better than the man's? Is the post-prepubertal orgasm better than the prepubertal one? The only orgasm you can ever know and talk about in its entirety is your own. Its self-generated sensations and feelings are yours alone. The proprioceptions and interoceptions of orgasm are personal and private.

We all work on the assumption that the experience of orgasm in others (if they have it) is similar to our own. We use the "rule of thumb" to test that, no matter how they name it, those who are not sure if they've had an orgasm almost certainly have not. We generally assume that, sooner or later, they will share our capacity to have one. Nonetheless, we do not know whether there may be degrees of "orgasm blindness" (orgasm agnosia) analogous to degrees of color-blindness.

One strategy for circumventing the dilemma of solipsism is to rely on information transmitted not as spoken or written language, but as

---

Originally published in Prakash Kothari and Rafi Patel, eds., *Proceedings of the First International Conference on Orgasm,* February 3–6, 1991, New Delhi, India. Bombay: VRP Publishers, 1992.

instrumentally recorded physiological changes in the person having an orgasm. It is a little known fact of history that John B. Watson, the Johns Hopkins professor world famous as the originator, in 1913, of the theory of behaviorism in psychology was also, in 1919, the originator of the instrumental method of recording the physiology of orgasm (Pauly, 1979; Magoun, 1981). His data have been forever lost. After a divorce trial in 1921, they mysteriously disappeared along with all the court records. Only a box containing the apparatus survived to bear mute witness.

Watson's experimental subject, Rosalie Rayner, was one of his two graduate students. The other was Curl Richter (1894-1989), Watson's successor at Johns Hopkins. Rayner was also Watson's lover. She became his second wife. The media featured Watson's divorce as a sensational scandal and published love letters from him to Rosalie purloined from her apartment in New York. The university required Watson's immediate resignation, not on account of the scandal of divorce, but because of the unspeakable "moral delinquency" of the unmentionable, namely orgasm research. Adolph Meyer, head of the Department of Psychiatry (where Watson's laboratory was located) wrote to Frank Goodnow, President of the University, as follows: "Without clear-cut and outspoken principles on these matters, we could not run a co-educational institution, nor could we deserve a position of honor and respect before any kind of public, not even before ourselves."

Watson's orgasm research soon became no more than unverified rumor. It was probably unknown to Alfred Kinsey when he began his career in sex research, in the late 1930s. Thus, Kinsey began anew the accumulation of data on the bodily accompaniments of orgasm. Kinsey's data were derived from either the analysis of explicit films or the direct observation of volunteer couples. Information on the anatomy and physiology of sexual response and orgasm is presented in *Sexual Behavior in the Human Female* (Kinsey et al., 1953, Ch. 14, 15).

Kinsey died in 1956 before being able to confront the political and funding hazards of equipping a laboratory for orgasm research. That task fell to Masters and Johnson. The first major report of their work is well known—*Human Sexual Response* (1966). This book is important not only for its contents, but also because it was not censored. It reports the direct observation and recording of human sexual response and orgasm not only in individuals alone, but also in copulating couples. The authors did not suffer the fate of Wilhelm Reich (1897–1957) who, as a refugee from Hitler's persecution of sexologists in Germany, was persecuted in the United States for his unorthodox ideas on orgasm and died in prison.

Animal Model

There are vogues in sex research. Victimology is presently in vogue, and the words heard everywhere are *exploitation, perpetrator, sexual abuse,* and *victim.* Being a sex therapist, educator, or researcher is no guarantee of invulnerability to false charges of abuse. The present, therefore, is a time when an animal model is not an option but a necessity for explicit orgasm research. The obstacle is, of course, that animals cannot talk to us and tell us whether they have an orgasm or not. We must rely on trying to decipher body language in synchrony with physiological changes, instrumentally recorded. Then we must make an inference as to whether something happened that may legitimately be called "orgasm."

This dual method has, to the best of my knowledge, allowed the existence of orgasm to be attributed unequivocally to only one subhuman species, namely the stump-tailed macaque monkey (Goldfoot et al., 1980). The study was done at Erasmus University in Rotterdam. The two animals in the photographic record are females: One is in the receptive role typical of the female, the other in the rear-entry mounting role typical of the male. In each one, the body language of orgasm corresponds, respectively, to that observed in a female/male pairing. Thus one may infer that both females are having an orgasm. The animal in the male role has no penis and no ejaculate, but exhibits the body language of orgasm as if a male. Thus it is obvious that, as in human beings, orgasm in stump-tailed monkeys is not contingent on ejaculation of semen.

One of the bonuses of the study of orgasm in subhuman primates is the possibility of scheduling statistically controlled experiments of an invasive type that, in human beings, are ethically forbidden. For example, surgical deconnection of the brain from the innervation of the pelvic genitalia may be experimentally scheduled in animals, whereas the human alternative is the unscheduled clinical experiment of spinal-cord deconnection by disease, wound, or accident.

DECONNECTION OF THE BRAIN AND PELVIC GENITALIA

The 33 vertebrae of the spinal cord are numbered from the neck down in five levels: cervical, 1-7; thoracic, 8–19; lumbar, 20-24; sacral, 25–29; and coccygeal, 30–33. In the case of broken neck, severance of the spinal cord is at the cervical level. Insofar as innervation of all four limbs is completely deconnected from the brain, the condition is named *quadriplegia.* If severance is below the cervical level so that innervation of the arms and hands is spared but that of the lower torso is deconnected from the brain, then the condition is named *paraplegia.*

If the deconnection of the brain from the spinal cord is not below the thoracic level T-11, then all of the neural-reflex feedback loops between the genitalia and the spinal cord prerequisite to the release of ejaculate in the male remain intact (Szasz and Carpenter, 1989). In such cases, ejaculation may be induced by applying a vibrator to the penis. In this way, it is possible to collect semen if noncoital insemination of the spouse is needed to ensure pregnancy.

Under these circumstances, ejaculation is not referred to as orgasm, for the man has not had the cognitional experience of orgasm. Nor has he had the cognitional experience of ejaculation, unless he was able to look and see what was happening or to palpate his genitalia with his fingers and know what was happening through the sense of touch. If the spinal-cord deconnection is below T-11, erection may be retained in response to vibration, but not ejaculation. Here again, cognition of the erection is only by seeing or touching it.

The experience of the paraplegic woman is similar to that of the paraplegic man, except that there is less visual evidence to be seen and less tactual evidence to be touched. Pregnancy is possible for the paraplegic woman without any experience that corresponds to ejaculation or orgasm. One articulate young black paraplegic woman characterized her genital region in its entirely as being numb. She couldn't be bothered with going through the motions of sexual intercourse, she said, even for the sake of her lover. Her word for coital reciprocity was "corresponding." Being numb, she had lost the capacity to correspond. She was sure, therefore, that no matter what her boyfriend said to the contrary, there would be nothing in it for him (Money, 1960b).

Not all paraplegic men and women lose interest in sex. With practice and experience, some achieve an intensification of erotic sensuousness in the nipples and the upper part of the body, the neural innervation of which is not deconnected from the brain. They do not, however, have the experience of orgasm as they did when the spinal cord was intact. If they do experience an orgasm-like building up of voluptuous rapture, it is not cognized as happening in the genital region.

PHANTOM ORGASM

In paraplegia, it is only while dreaming during sleep that the experience of orgasm, as it was prior to the spinal-cord injury, may again be experienced (Money, 1960). This dream orgasm is properly characterized as a "phantom orgasm," for it occurs only in the imagery and ideation of the dream, deconnected from the pelvic genitalia.

The phantom orgasm of the dream is not reported by all paraplegics. Among those who have reported having experienced it, its occurrence is infrequent until, progressively, it disappears within a maximum of two years after the spinal-cord injury. Sexologically, one must conclude that as a mental representation, orgasm may exist retroactively in a brain that has been deconnected from orgasm in the pelvic genitalia. However, the continuity of its existence in the brain is contingent on the continuity of its existence, synchronously, in the pelvic genitalia. Synchrony itself is contingent on uninterrupted connectedness between the brain and the neural innervation of the pelvic genitalia by way of the spinal cord. The orgasm is not exclusively a physiological phenomenon, nor is it exclusively a disembodied psychological or transcendental phenomenon. It is, par excellence, a phenomenon of mind/body unity.

For the paraplegic, the orgasm becomes a memory and a penumbra of its former self. Like pain, the orgasm cannot be evoked and relived exactly as it was. It can be longed for, and its loss is a bitter loss, but one which the paraplegic appears to bear not frantically, but stoically. Lacking reciprocal communication between orgasm in the brain and orgasm in the genitalia, the paraplegic lacks also the post-traumatic desperation of the man who, though otherwise intact, is the victim of irreversible penile trauma (Money, 1961b).

Genital Trauma

The desperation of the man with a permanently flaccid, post-priapism penis is not the desperation of being anorgasmic. It is the desperation of being orgasmic and, at the same time, of being irreversibly impotent. His penis is incapacitated for penetration of the vagina. He is mortified by the failure of his penis to match his penile body-image. As a sexual partner, he is desperate to fulfill his personal expectation of his own manhood (Money and Hirsch, 1965). Paradoxically, the failure of his penis began with a prolonged erection. It was unable to detumescence; its corpora became filled with stagnated and congealed blood. Then, progressively, the corpora became irreversibly fibrotic and permanently nonerective.

The desperation of being orgasmic although no longer able to copulate as formerly also affects the man with accidental or surgical ablation of the penis, or with partial ablation that leaves only a penile stump. For most people, it comes as a surprise to learn from such cases that orgasm in the male is not absolutely contingent on the intactness of the penis. Nor in women, according to evidence from two sources, is orgasm absolutely contingent on the intactness of the clitoris. One source is the testimony of female hermaphrodites with congenital virilizing adrenal hyperplasia (CVAH) who had undergone surgical feminization which entailed excision of the grossly hypertrophied clitoris. Typically, the surgery had been done early in infancy, so that there were no pre- and post-surgery comparisons. Though clitoridectomy in adulthood was infrequent, the "before" and "after" comparison of orgasm was, however, positive.

The other source of evidence regarding clitoridectomy comes from women in Egypt (Krieger, 1990) and in Sudan (Lightfoot-Klein, 1989). As girls, their informants had been subjected to the ritual mutilation of Pharaonic circumcision—that is, complete removal of the clitoris, its hood, the labia minora, and the labia majora, bilaterally. Many of these women gave evidence of orgasm, though a minority did not.

The evidence that orgasm is not absolutely contingent on the intactness of the penis or clitoris comes as no surprise to those who have had the experience of orgasm induced, simultaneously in the brain and in the genitals, from nongenital parts of the body. Many lovers have discovered a uniquely personal "lover's spot" in some unlikely place on the torso. Adolescent lovers, not undressed but already primed with excitement, may have an orgasm (with ejaculation also, in the male) triggered by passionate tongue-kissing, by being squeezed on the thigh, or by breast fondling.

Some men, as well as some women, may have an orgasm induced by having the nipples sucked, either without genital contact or as an adjunct to it. Some nursing mothers have an orgasm induced by the suckling of the baby at the breast. Many women are able to testify as experts regarding orgasm induced by penile penetration of the vagina without direct clitoral stimulation—as in the quadrupedal ("doggie-style") coital position, for example.

HORMONES AND ORGASM

The majority of people find it incredible that there exists a minority among them who repudiate orgasm as a threat to their well being. Origen (185-284 C.E.), a founding father of Christian philosophy, struggled against the sins of the flesh and castrated himself to become abstinent. Castration, plus or minus amputation of the penis, was a secret rite of the Skoptics, members of a Christian sect that originated in Russia early in the eighteenth century. The sect existed for 200 years. *Skoptsy* is the plural of *skopets,* the Russian term for a castrated ram. The name of the sect became the eponym for the Skoptic syndrome of elective castration and genital self-mutilation (Money, 1988b).

In men, as in mammalian males in general, loss of the testicles is fairly rapidly followed by loss of the secretion and expulsion of the ejaculatory fluid. In probably a majority of castrates, the loss of ejaculation signifies the loss of orgasm. What may remain is the peak of sensation resembling that of some prepubertal boys. The full orgasm with ejaculation can be restored by endocrine-replacement therapy with the hormone testosterone.

It is possible for a prepubertal male to have a build-up of orgasm-like sensation towards a nonejaculatory peak. Before and after accounts from hypogonadal patients requiring testosterone-replacement therapy in order to enter puberty and to become mature indicate that the peak attained with ejaculation after hormone therapy is not the same as the pretreatment peak without ejaculation. The peak of ejaculatory orgasm is reported as better and stronger (Money and Alexander, 1967)

Loss of ejaculation without the loss of orgasmic peak, the so-called dry orgasm, is a pharmacologically induced side effect associated chiefly with antihypertensive drugs and with some antipsychotic drugs (see review by Sitsen, 1988). The sexological effects of these drugs are unpredictable and individually variable in men: They may suppress orgasm as well as ejaculation, and they may induce impotence. In women, they may also suppress orgasm, and in both sexes they may induce sexual anergia.

The estrogenic and progestinic female hormones have an antiandrogenic effect in males. This effect includes suppression of ejaculation (though orgasm may be retained). Surgical castration is permanently antiandrogenic, since it removes the testicles, the source of the androgen testosterone. The effects of hormonal antiandrogenic treatment resemble those of surgical deandrogenization, but with the extremely great advantage of being temporary and reversible—which is the rationale for the use of the progestinic antiandrogen, medroxyprogesterone acetate (Depo-Provera), in the treatment of male sex offenders (Money 1970, 1987).

Male-to-female transexuals undergoing hormonal sex reassignment are prescribed estrogen, or a combination of estrogen and progestin, during the two-year real-life test prior to undergoing sex-reassignment genital surgery. The effect of these hormones on orgasm is to weaken or suppress the orgasmic peak, along with abolishing ejaculation and possibly abolishing erection also. These changes are appreciated by male-to-female transexuals as being more "ladylike." After they undergo feminizing genital surgery, there are no complaints about loss of the orgasm as formerly known, but rather a new-found satisfaction in having relinquished the former spasmodic and paroxysmal orgasmic peak for a slow-spreading, all-body orgasmic glow. For many (if not all) male-to-female transexuals, there is more satisfaction in giving the male partner his orgasm than in receiving one's own.

When female-to-male transexuals undergo hormonal sex reassignment, they take the androgenizing male hormone testosterone. Its effect on their orgasm is to intensify it without changing either the speed or the frequency of reaching the orgasmic peak. If formerly multiorgasmic, then the female-to-male transexual continues to be multiorgasmic as a male. In surgical masculinization of the genitalia, it is standard policy to preserve the clitoris. This organ then serves as the primary focus for the induction of orgasm by pressing and rubbing against the pudenda of the partner. An artificial penis constructed from grafted skin has no sensory feeling.

The intensification effect of the androgen testosterone on orgasm in female-to-male transexuals is observed also in nontransexual women who have received androgen for various other therapeutic reasons. The hypothesis that androgen is the "libido hormone" for both sexes was first promulgated thirty years ago (Money, 1961a) Since then, this hypothesis has found confirmation in animal experimental studies (reviewed in Money and Ehrhardt, 1972, Ch. 11) and in clinical studies of ovariectomized women receiving hormonal-replacement therapy (Sherwin and Gelfand, 1987).

In the normal mature female, the hormones secreted from the ovaries include a low level of testosterone. There is also a low level of androgenic steroids secreted by the adrenocortical glands. The relationship of ovarian and adrenocortical androgens to orgasm in females remains still to be elucidated.

Preorgasmic Arousal and Paraphilia

In the sequential analysis of human sexuality and procreation, orgasm is at the peak of the middle or acceptive phase. It is preceded by the preorgasmic, proceptive phase of courtship, and it may or may not be followed by the postorgasmic, conceptive phase. Apart from solo masturbation, when a partner may be represented in mental imagery, orgasm usually entails contiguity of the genitalia with some part of the body of the partner. Orgasm is a phenomenon of reciprocality.

The vernacular English word for reciprocal genital acceptivity, "fuck," derives from the gerund *phuktos* of the Greek verb *phuteuein,* which means "to sow or plant in the ground," hence "to beget or to impregnate." (The Latin verb is *futuere.*) The lack of a respectable vernacular English word for *copulation* has its counterpart in the lack of a respectable vernacular term for *orgasm.* In consequence, scientific and professional attention to issues related to orgasm and anorgasmia is also stigmatized. Attention to issues related to the explicit imagery and ideation of preorgasmic arousal in the proceptive phase is subject to an even greater degree of stigmatization.

Preorgasmic arousal manifests itself in the cognitional sexuoerotic rehearsals of dreams, daydreams, and fantasies, as well as in actual engagements (Money, 1960a). Preorgasmic arousal in the pelvic genitalia and in the brain/mind are in reciprocal synchrony. Even when the arousal is normophilically heterosexual and ideologically acceptable, its explicit depiction in the print, film, or electronic media, as well as in the spoken word, is likely to be condemned as obscenely or pornographically offensive. Condemnation is even more intense, even to the point of societal mania, if the content of preorgasmic arousal is not normophilic, but paraphilic.

In the language of the street, a paraphilia is "bizarre" and "kinky" sex. In legal terminology, it is a "perversion" or "sexual deviancy." The same terminology was formerly used medically and scientifically, but is now officially replaced by the term *paraphilia.* The formal definition of paraphilia is as follows (Money, 1988a):

> *Paraphilia:* A condition occurring in men and women of being compulsively responsive to and obligatively dependent on an unusual and personally or socially unacceptable stimulus, perceived or in the ideation and imagery of fantasy, for optimal initiation and maintenance of erotosexual arousal and the facilitation or attainment of orgasm (from the Greek *para,* "altered," + *philia,* "love").

On the criterion of content, there are at least forty different paraphilias. They may be at times enacted as an erotic ritual, and at other times replayed in fantasy, as if on a mental videotape. They vary from playful (ludic) to deadly, and in the extent to which they are compulsory to the attainment of orgasm.

Among people who never or rarely have had an orgasm (anorgasmia and hypoorgasmia, respectively), there are some for whom the orgasmic deficit masks the covert existence of a paraphilia too personally embarrassing to admit to the partner. Devoid of paraphilic ritual, the sexuoerotic relationship with the partner fails to induce preorgasmic arousal and orgasm.

By contrast, at the other extreme among those whose paraphilia is overtly expressed is hyperorgasmia, that is, orgasms occurring so often that they become an unrelenting nuisance. In men the number may be upwards of ten or more orgasms with ejaculation per twenty-four hours; in women, the number may be even higher.

In an unidentified but rare proportion of cases of hyperorgasmia, there is no preorgasmic preparatory imagery, thought, or perceived stimulus. Instead, the onset of orgasm begins of its own accord and may endure, unrelieved, for half an hour or more, producing great distress. It is a distress made worse by a misdiagnosis of (in the case of women) nymphomania, and a recommendation to go out and pick up a man. The correct diagnosis is orgasmic epilepsy, and the attacks are suppressed by antiepileptic medication. Stimulation of the genitalia, either manually or coitally, fails to bring the relief that ensues from the attainment of orgasm. Only when the seizure ceases does relief ensue. Orgasmic epilepsy is a rare manifestation of autonomous orgasmic functioning of the sexual brain.

In addition to orgasmic epilepsy, there is another orgasm-related, exclusively intracranial phenomenon, namely orgasmic cephalgia. It is experienced as an intense, migraine-like headache (Niedermeyer, 1974), the onset of which is acute and contingent on the occurrence of orgasm. Symptomatically, orgasmic cephalgia is analogous to cephalgia epileptica or epileptic headache. It may be secondary to cerebral vasospasm.

Orgasm and Ethology

From the viewpoint of ethology, orgasm is a phylism. For our own species, a phylism is defined as follows (Money, 1990):

> *Phylism:* A unit or building block of human existence that belongs to human beings, as individuals, through their heritage as members of the species.

Orgasm is phylogenetically designed so that it is a uniform response to stimuli from multiple induction sites. Metaphorically, orgasm is the Rome to which all roads lead, irrespective of the induction site at which they begin. Each road must, however, feed into the two-lane highway of the spinal cord that connects the sexual neural networks of the brain with the peripheral neural networks of the pelvic genitalia, and vice versa. Orgasm occurs synchronously in the brain and in the genitalia. When there are no breaks in the highway, orgasm can survive various insults and injuries at either end. When the brain and the innervation of the pelvic genitalia are deconnected, however, orgasm does not occur. Endowment of the organism with multiple stimulus locations for the induction of orgasm may be interpreted as a phylogenetic contingency plan—nature's overkill, so to speak, to guarantee the experience of orgasmic ecstasy. In the diecious species, it is one way of guaranteeing that male and female meet and mate. It is also a way of guaranteeing the continuity of the species.

Definition

The definition of orgasm that follows is formulated on the basis of the foregoing sources of evidence.

> *Orgasm:* The zenith of sexuoerotic experience that men and women characterize subjectively as voluptuous rapture or ecstasy. It occurs simultaneously in the brain/mind and the pelvic genitalia. Irrespective of its locus of onset, the occurrence of orgasm is contingent upon reciprocal intercommunication between neural networks in the brain above and the pelvic genitalia below, and it does not survive their deconnection by the severance of the spinal cord. However, it is able to survive even extensive trauma at either end.

Orgasmology

Andre Bejin (1985) wrote of "the decline of the psychoanalyst and the rise of the sexologist." In a footnote (p. 183), he attributes to Wilhelm Reich the term *orgasmography* He himself coins the terms *orgasmotherapy* and *orgasmology.*

Orgasmology is a name for the science of orgasm that sounds respectable and user-friendly. It promises to destigmatize the scientific study of human coition and give it legitimacy as a phenomenon of research. Scientifically, it gives center stage to the zenith of personal sexuoerotic experience instead of relegating it to an inconspicuous niche in the science of reproductive behavior. It has many tangents and many avenues for expansion in experimental and clinical research. Happy birthday to orgasmology, and happy birthday to orgasmologists as well.

References

Bejin, A. (1985). "The decline of the psychoanalyst and the rise of the sexologist." In *Western Sexuality: Practice and Precept in Past and Present Time* (P. Aries and A. Bejin, eds.). Oxford: Blackwell.

Goldfoot, D. A., and Westerborg van Loon, H., Groeneveld, W., and Slob, A. K. (1980). "Behavioral and physiological evidence of sexual climax in the female stump-tailed macaque (*Macaca arctoides*)." *Science* 208:1477–79.

Kinsey, A. C., Pomeroy, W. A., Martin, C. E., and Gebhard, P. H. (1953). *Sexual Behavior in the Human Female.* Philadelphia: Saunders.

Krieger, L. (1990). Personal communication.

Lightfoot-Klein, H. (1989). *Prisoners of Ritual: An Odyssey into Female Genital Circumcision in Africa.* New York: Haworth Press.

Magoun, H. W., and Watson, J. B. (1981). "The study of human sexual behavior." *Journal of Sex Research* 17:368–78.

Masters, W. H., and Johnson, V. E. (1966). *Human Sexual Response.* Boston: Little, Brown.

Money, J. (1960a). "Components of eroticism in man. III: Cognitional rehearsals." In *Recent Advances in Biological Psychiatry* (J. Wortis, ed.). New York: Grune and Stratton.

———. (1960b). "Phantom orgasm in the dreams of paraplegic men and women." *Archives of General Psychiatry* 3:373–82.

———. (1961a). "Components of eroticism in man. 1: The hormones in relation to sexual morphology and sexual desire." *Journal of Nervous and Mental Disease* 132:239–48.

———. (1961b). "Components of eroticism in man. II: The orgasm and genital somesthesia." *Journal of Nervous and Mental Disease* 132:289–97.

———. (1970). "Use of an androgen-depleting hormone in the treatment of male sex offenders." *Journal of Sex Research* 6:165–72.

———. (1987). "Treatment guidelines: Antiandrogen and counseling of paraphilic sex offenders." *Journal of Sex and Marital Therapy* 13:219–23.

———. (1988a). *Gay, Straight and In-Between: The Sexology of Erotic Orientation.* New York: Oxford University Press.

———. (1988b). "The Skoptic syndrome: Castration and genital self-mutilation as an example of sexual body-image pathology." *Journal of Psychology and Human Sexuality* 1(1):113–26.

———. (1990). "Pedophilia : A specific instance of new phylism theory as applied to paraphilic lovemaps." In *Pedophilia: Biosocial Dimensions* (J. R. Feierman, ed.). New York: Springer-Verlag.

Money, J., and Alexander, D. (1967). "Eroticism and sexual function in developmental anorchia and hyporchia with pubertal failure." *Journal of Sex Research* 3: 31–47.

Money, J., and Erhardt, A. A. (1972). *Man and Woman, Boy and Girl: The Development of Gender Identity from Conception to Maturity.* Baltimore: Johns Hopkins University Press. Facsimile reprint edition, New York: Jason Aronson, 1996.

Money, J., and Hirsch, S. R. (1965) "After priapism: Orgasm retained, erection lost." *Journal of Urology* 94:152–57.

Niedermeyer, E. (1974). *Compendium of the Epilepsies.* Springfield, IL: Charles C Thomas.

Pauly, P. J. (1979) "Psychology at Hopkins: Its rise and fall and rise and fall and. . . ." *The Johns Hopkins Magazine* 30(6):36–41.

Sherwin, B., and Gelfand, M. M. "The role of androgen in the maintenance of sexual functioning in oophorectomized women." *Psychosomatic Medicine* 49:397–409.

Sitsen, J. M. A. (1968). "Prescription drugs and sexual function." In *Handbook of Sexology, Volume 6: The Pharmacology and Endocrinology of Sexual Function* (J. Money, H. Musaph, and J. M. A. Sitsen, eds.). Amsterdam: Elsevier.

Szasz, G., and Carpenter, C. (1989). "Clinical observation in vibratory stimulation of the penis of men with spinal cord injury." *Archives of Sexual Behavior* 18:461–74.

19

Homosexology vs. Homosexosophy

NOMENCLATURE

If there is to be a science of homosexuality, it could be suitably named *homosexology.* Then the name of its reciprocal would be *heterosexology.* The two coexist complementary to one another as subsections of the science of sexology. What scholarship finds out about either one of them is equally informative regarding the other.

Whereas sexology is the science of sex, by contrast the ideology of sex is sexosophy, a set of principles and propositions that constitute a moral, religious, and legal philosophy of sex. Sexology's history is barely more than a century in age, whereas the history of sexosophy reaches back beyond the written record and is also transculturally divergent.

In the homosexual community, there is one faction that is extremely antagonistic toward homosexology. This faction is phobic about the genesis of new homosexological knowledge, and reciprocally of new heterosexological knowledge as well, lest it be surreptitiously misused in a biomedical crusade to pathologize and stigmatize homosexuality. New scientific knowledge of any sort, however, is not in and of itself responsible for the use or misuse to which it is applied.

Previously unpublished.

The application of new knowledge is under the control of doctrinal ideology which typically antedates the appearance of new scientific knowledge. Thus, it is homosexosophy, not homosexology, that controls religious, political, and legal policy toward homosexuals. Societally, the prevailing homosexosophical ideology is a function of economic, police, and voting power, irrespective of what homosexological science has to say.

Like all sciences, homosexology has its own ideology, and it is manifested as the principles and practices of the scientific method. Homosexological knowledge, unlike homosexosophical knowledge, is not enshrined as fixed dogma, but is forever subject to empirical testing and to being updated whenever new data displace the old. Thus, instead of being doctrinally fixated, homosexological explanations are constantly exposed to being reviewed, revised, and updated if they fail to be empirically confirmed.

In being committed to the repudiation of dogma, homosexology is the polar opposite of homosexosophy. In its very essence, homosexosophy is opinionated and doctrinaire. Those who accept homosexosophical dogma do so on faith, without empirical testing. Homophobic sexosophy is an example.

Sexosophy of Semen Depletion

The negation of homosexuality that is widespread in contemporary sexosophy has its roots in the extremely ancient folk-medical theory of semen depletion and conservation. This theory appears in the earliest written records of Indian Ayurvedic medicine dating from an estimated 2,500 years ago and stemming from a much earlier oral tradition (see Money et al., 1992).

It was postulated in semen-conservation theory that semen was the most concentrated source of *sukra,* the vital fluid or essence that nourished and sustained life itself. One drop of semen was equivalent to fifty or more most precious drops of the blood. Semen should not, therefore, be squandered wantonly, but conserved as a source of health and longevity.

Semen depletion was not a prominent feature of ancient Chinese sexosophy. The basic Chinese premise was not loss of the male principle, but balance between the female and male principles, the yin and the yang, respectively. They were said to be reciprocally exchanged during sexual intercourse.

Semen depletion seems also not to have been a prominent feature of the sexosophy of ancient Egypt, nor of the sexosophy of Hippocratic medicine. Likewise, it did not get incorporated into Hebraic sexosophy, even though Jehovah smote Onan, son of Judah, dead for spilling his seed upon the ground (Genesis 38:7-10). Onan's sin was his defiance of the law of the Levirate, by which he was required to marry the widow of his brother Er and "to raise up seed to thy brother." Instead, he practiced premature withdrawal.

European Onanistic Sexosophy

It was not by way of either Hippocratic or Biblical tradition that the Ayurvedic premise of semen depletion entered European medicine, but by way of an eighteenth-century Swiss physician, Simon André Tissot, who in 1755 published in Latin a treatise titled *Onanism: Dissertation on Maladies Produced by Masturbation* (Tissot, 1974/1832). Tissot borrowed heavily from an undated sermon, anonymously published in London perhaps as early as the end of the seventeenth century under the title: *Onania, or the Heinous Sin of Self-Pollution, and all its Frightful Consequences, in Both Sexes, Considered* (Anonymous, 1974).

With the knowledge of hindsight, one recognizes that Tissot was engaged in combat against the epidemic of syphilis, which had spread all over Europe after Columbus discovered the New World at the end of the fifteenth century. In Tissot's day, syphilis (the pox) and gonorrhea (the clap) were lumped together as the "social disease." Tissot attributed the combined symptoms to degeneracy caused by semen wastage, itself attributable to the social vice of promiscuity and venery. Then he made the momentous leap from the social vice to the secret vice of self-abuse. He attributed syphilitic degeneracy to semen depletion by way of masturbation and nocturnal pollution (wet dreams) as well as by way of promiscuous excess with prostitutes.

Victorian Masturbation Sexosophy

There was no effective way to demolish Tissot's theory of degeneracy through semen loss until germ theory was formulated by Pasteur and Koch around 1870 (Woodward, 1989) and applied to syphilitic and gonococcal bacterial infection. In the interim, degeneracy theory spawned the epidemic of antimasturbation mania that climaxed in the Victorian era.

In Victorian sexosophy, masturbation was considered socially contagious. Older boys were blamed for initiating younger boys into the vice. Their vice was not defined as homosexuality, as might be expected today, for the term did not come into existence until 1869 (Kennedy, 1988; Money, 1990) and did not become part of the vernacular language until the early part of the twentieth century. By that time, masturbation was becoming progressively less threatening through lack of evidence that it induced degeneracy. The harmfulness of masturbation became attributed not to the act per se, but to doing it with a same-sexed partner, for which the new term *homosexual* was ready made. With an erroneous twist of logic, it was said that homosexuality is caused by masturbation, an error that still persists among those who are sexologically poorly informed. Thus, in the legacy of contemporary Western sexosophy, there is a direct line of descent from the ancient doctrine of semen conservation and depletion to the still widespread negation of homosexuality.

Sambia Sexosophy

The virtual antithesis of semen-conservation theory is found in the reinvestment theory of semen recycling, extant until recently among the stone-aged Sambia people of the Eastern Highlands of New Guinea. They were studied by the anthropological sexologist, Gilbert Herdt (1981; 1984; 1987).

A prime principle of Sambia sexology is that a boy cannot make the transition from juvenile to fierce warrior manhood without, by analogy with imbibing women's milk to grow in infancy, imbibing men's milk to undergo the growth changes of puberty. It is axiomatic in Sambia sexosophy that statural growth and sexual maturation of the body at puberty are contingent on receiving a sufficient supply of men's milk.

Initiation into the rites of puberty and warriorhood begins as early as age seven or eight. Boys are then removed from the softening influences of females and infants by leaving the family dwelling to live in the men's clubhouse, a large structure in the center of the village from which all females are excluded. The first stage of the boys' initiation into warriorhood is a week-long sequence of sometimes brutally abusive hazing which, like military hazing in our own culture, requires total subservience and obedience. One of the ceremonies is named "sucking the flute," which is a metaphor for fellatio. On that same ceremonial night, the initiates are fed men's milk by sucking the penises of the older adolescent boys who are still underage for marriage. The initiates continue ingesting men's milk until they have matured enough to be able to ejaculate their own and recycle it to the next generation of young initiates. After the tribal marriage age of nineteen, they recycle their semen to their wives, for a brief period orally, and then for the rest of their lives vaginally.

It is considered very wrong and abnormal for a postpubertal male to give his semen to anyone except a prepubertal boy who needs it. There is a severe injunction against giving semen to any female before marriage, and when married to anyone other than the designated wife.

Properly speaking, homosexuality in the Sambia culture should be called serial bisexuality. For some of the younger boys, ingesting semen was a perfunctory activity. So also, when they were adolescent, was the giving of semen. In these cases, it could be said that males engaged in homosexual acts, but not that they developed a homosexual identity. In other cases, by contrast, a boy developed a particular fondness for a particular partner, possibly with reciprocated pairbondedness. Nonetheless, their bond did not override the possibility of an affectionate male-female pairbond with the tribally assigned wife. In only one case could it be said that a village boy grew up to have what, in Western culture, would be called a homosexual identity (Herdt, 1981; Stoller, 1985). His mother had a history of having been repudiated by his father of conception, who should have taken her as a second wife. Therefore, the boy had no relative to sponsor his initiation into warriorhood. As an adult, he was pedophilically fixated on sucking young males who should themselves have been sucking to receive semen. In village life, he was marginalized as an outcast. He was married four times but never able to consummate his marriage. He was abandoned by each wife.

The Sambia example demonstrates not only that a single homosexual act does not engender a homosexual identity, but also that multiple homosexual acts do not, even though they occur on a regular basis from the juvenile years until young adulthood, at first as the acceptor and then as the donor of semen, orogenitally. The early sexological history of Sambia boys may be of significance here: before the onset of segregation and initiation, although juvenile heterosexual rehearsal play was punishable, it was possible and, in at least some cases, had occurred (Herdt, personal communication, Sept. 1995).

Homosexual Act versus Identity

In a completely different context, the difference between act and identity, homosexually, is exemplified in a Catch-22 dilemma of whether to go over the parapet of a skyscraper or to perform a homosexual act at the behest of a sex-crazed terrorist with a handgun aimed at your head. Most people elect to save their lives. They know that a single event will not begin a chain of events culminating in a homosexual identity.

The defining criterion of a homosexual identity, whether gay or lesbian, is that only a person with the same sexual body morphology as one's own is able to be erotogenically and limerently (i.e., love-smittenly) attractive to oneself.

A second defining criterion of a homosexual identity is that the sexual dimorphism of the homosexual person's own natal body morphology and the sexual dimorphism of his/her own body image are mutually compatible.

Within the confines of these two defining criteria, there are various homosexual subtypes. In males, for example, there is a long history of differentiating the virilistic subtype from the feminoid subtype (Money, 1991a). The virilistic male homosexual (or bisexual) may be indistinguishable from the heterosexual in all of life's activities except for orogenital, anogenital, or digitogenital erotogenic encounters with one male partner, or a series of partners. Correspondingly, among lesbians and female bisexuals who are not of the masculinoid subtype, there are those who are indistinguishable from heterosexual women except for their erotogenic activities with a female partner.

The feminoid extreme in the natal male is the syndrome of gynemimesis, or the "lady with a penis." The complete gynemimetic lives and dresses full time as a woman and may undergo cosmetic alteration and feminizing hormonal treatment, but not genital surgery, to agree with the feminoid gender identity.

In the natal female, the syndrome that corresponds to gynemimesis in the natal male is andromimesis, or the "man with a vulva and breasts." Masculine intonation, hirsutism, and amenorrhea can be and are in some cases achieved by means of testosterone hormonal treatment, and the chest flattened by surgery, to agree with the masculinoid gender identity.

There is no logical challenge in classifying the erotogenic activities of gynemimetic natal males as homosexual if they are engaged in with a partner who is also a natal male (albeit not gynemimetic) with a penis. There is a logical challenge, however, in the case of the transexual before and after sex reassignment. The erotogenic encounters of a preoperative male-to-female transexual are classified as homosexual if the partner has a penis, and as heterosexual if the partner (possibly a wife) has a vulva and vagina. Postoperatively, the same male-to-female transexual becomes socially classifiable as heterosexual if the partner is a natal male with a penis. The partner also becomes socially classifiable as heterosexual, even though self-classified as gay. Correspondingly, the preoperative wife of a male-to-female transexual who continues to have erotogenic encounters with her sex-reassigned spouse becomes classifiable as a lesbian, even though she remains self-classified as heterosexual.

To complicate the logic of classification still further, there are some known cases of female-to-male sex reassignment in which self-defined erotogenic attraction is toward a lesbian, whose response to a male is anerotic. Correspondingly, in some cases of male-to-female reassignment, attraction is self-defined as being toward gay men, whose response to a female is anerotic.

Hermaphroditic Heuristic

Over and beyond the syndrome of transexualism, the syndromes of hermaphroditic and related birth defects of the sex organs demonstrate that body morphology and body image are the criteria by which *homosexual* and *heterosexual* are defined. Two syndromes that are particularly informative (Kappy et al., 1994, Chs. 12, 13, 19; Money, 1994; see also Part 5 below) are the androgen-insensitivity syndrome (AIS) in its complete degree (Money, 1991b) and the congenital adrenocortical-hyperplasia (CAH) syndrome in its complete degree (Money, 1993, Chs. 5, 6). Both syndromes have their onset in embryogenesis, AIS in an embryo that is chromosomally male (46,XY), and CAH in an embryo that is chromosomally female (46,XX).

As a sequel to complete cellular resistance to masculinizing hormone, the embryo with the complete form of AIS develops into a baby who is born with a completely female external body morphology, despite having two undescended testes in the abdominal cavity. By contrast, as a sequel to an excess of masculinizing hormone of fetal adrenocortical origin, the embryo with the most complete form of CAH develops into a baby who is born with a completely male external body, although the scrotum contains no testes. Instead, in the abdominal cavity, there are two ovaries. In both syndromes, the hormonal error is transmitted genetically and may occur more than once in the family pedigree.

For the AIS baby there is no treatment, and none is needed, for the rearing is as a girl. At the age of puberty, the body continues to be androgen-resistant and develops a female morphology under the influence of the female hormone estrogen, normally produced in the male by the testes. Internally, there is no uterus, so there is no menstruation. If necessary, the vagina can be lengthened by dilation (more rarely by surgery) so as to be fully adequate for sexual intercourse. Sexual attraction and falling in love is as a female, and so also is pairbonding to a male. If the two should marry, no one in his/her right mind would say that either the husband or wife is homosexual, even though they both have the chromosomal status of a male. It is the male/female difference in their genital and overall body morphology that defines their relationship as heterosexual. So also does the male/female difference in their body image.

The converse of the AIS heuristic is found in the baby with the complete CAH syndrome who is assigned to grow up as a boy with hormonal and surgical management. Even if left untreated, he will undergo full pubertal virilization, with the function of the ovaries and uterus suppressed by masculinizing adrenocortical hormones. He will be able to have penovaginal intercourse as a male with orgasm and at least a small quantity of sterile sexual fluid. His sexual attraction will be with statistical predictability toward females, as will his falling in love (limerence). Reciprocally, to females he will be an attractively virile man. His marriage to a woman will be that of two individuals born with 46,XX (female) chromosomal sex, ovarian sex, and internal female reproductive organs. Nonetheless, neither of them will be considered homosexual. Their external genital anatomy and their dimorphism in body morphology will declare them heterosexual. In addition, each partner will have a different body image, namely one consistent with the natal sex of the genitalia.

Prospective Homosexological Research

Two new prospects for homosexological and, pari passu, heterosexological research emerge from the foregoing. One is the prospect of discovering the multiple and sequential steps whereby either the male or the female body morphology of another person becomes recognized as one's own erotogenic stimulus. The other is the parallel prospect of discovering the multiple and sequential steps whereby one's own sexual body image becomes either consistent or inconsistent with the natal sexual morphology of one's own body.

In each prospect, the search for determinants will address both the prenatal and the postnatal period of development. Eventually the prenatal search will look for sexological instructions coded on the genome and for instructions coded in the brain prenatally by hormones or other sex-related neurochemistries. The postnatal search will be directed toward brain coding under the influence of sensory and cognitional input, especially in early life via the social environment.

A likely hypothesis is that erotogenic response to the sexual body morphology of either male or female (or, in bisexuality, both) is imprinted into the brain either prenatally or in very early postnatal life by a neurochemical agent still to be ascertained. Whereas most males are erotogenically responsive to images of female morphology, even during the prepubertal years, other boys who will later become practicing homosexuals respond to images of male morphology. The primary response may be subject to secondary overlay, as in the case of male amputeeism, in which a male is erotogenically responsive specifically to the live image or visual representation, in erotic dreams and fantasies, of adolescent boys with a leg amputated above the knee.

A parallel hypothesis may apply to lesbian erotogenic responsiveness to images of female morphology. However, in females it is likely that contrectative imagery is more erotogenic than visual imagery, whereas males are erotogenically more dependent on visual erotosexual arousal than are females.

The male-to-female and female-to-male transposition of one's own body image (as in transexualism) so that it mismatches the natal body morphology requires an explanatory hypothesis of its own. A clue can be discerned in those cases, typically of male-to-female transposition, characterized under the rubric of "two names, two wardrobes, and two personalities" (Money, 1974). Some of these individuals undergo episodes of crossed-dressed transposition throughout life. Others sooner or later stabilize in the gender-transposed role, some in youth, some much older. Some become sex reassigned as transexuals.

The two names, two wardrobes, and two personalities phenomenon represents a persistence of the sexual developmental principle of ambisexuality beyond the time when it has usually yielded to monosexuality as either male or female. Dimorphic sexual differentiation from embryonic life onward begins in a primal state of bipotentiality which resolves into monopotentiality. This is a fundamental principle of two-sexed (diecious) species. It applies to differentiation of the body and the mind.

Gendermap Polarity

In the human mind there are many cognitive maps or templates, one example of which is the gendermap. Foodmaps and speechmaps are other examples. All the maps are polarized into positive and negative. The polarity of the gendermap represents masculine and feminine or, more specifically, masculine/nonmasculine versus feminine/nonfeminine. One polarity represents "me" and the other "thee," male or female, respectively. Each reciprocates and monitors the other. In most people, the two become stabilized as separate and dissociated, and they do not change places. Cultural differences notwithstanding, fewer people are likely to rate themselves as bisexual than monosexual, and in the majority of cases, self-rated monosexuals are likely to rate themselves as heterosexual rather than homosexual.

Nonetheless, monosexual maps, whether homosexual or heterosexual, are bipotentially coded. Under special circumstances, their two poles may interchange. One possible outcome might best be called an extremely morbid type of episodic, or phasic, bisexuality. Although rare, it may happen in such a case that either the homosexual or heterosexual phase is expressed only in combination with sadistic brutality and even the murder of a homosexual partner, as in homosexual serial lust killings. The dynamic of such brutality is that it permits the simultaneous exercising and exorcising of one's hidden sexual demons. It is a dynamic which crosses the border that separates sexual variation from sexual pathology, namely the pathology of paraphilias. Paraphilic pathology occurs in males and females, and is not specifically associated with homosexuality any more than with heterosexuality or bisexuality. There is, as yet, no fully satisfactory scientific explanation of the origin of the forty-odd named paraphilias. They are not subject to voluntary control.

CONCLUSION

The heuristic of the science of homosexology applies pari passu to the science of heterosexology, and hence to bisexology as well. Understand the one, and you understand all three. They constitute a single tripartite science of sexology. To the extent that sexology is genuinely scientific, it is nondiscriminatory, nonjudgmental, and nonstigmatizing. Discrimination and judgmentalism, like stigmatization, belong to sexosophy, not sexology. Sexosophy is cocksure about sexual causality and attributes it to personal voluntary choice and perversity. Sexology more cautiously searches for recurrent temporal sequences and does not jump to conclusions about cause and effect. As a science, sexology is too youthful to have discovered its rules of causality on which to make accurate predictions. Prophecy it leaves to the augurs of sexosophy.

REFERENCES

Anonymous. (1974). *Onania, or the Heinous Sin of Self-Pollution and All its Frightful Consequences, in Both Sexes, Considered with Spiritual and Physical Advice to Those Who Have Already Injur'd Themselves by this Abominable Practice.* Boston: John Phillips, 1724. Facsimile reprint edition in *The Secret Vice Exposed! Some Arguments Against Masturbation* (C. Rosenberg and C. Smith-Rosenberg, eds.). New York: Arno Press.

Herdt, G. H. (1981). *Guardians of the Flutes: Idioms of Masculinity.* New York: McGraw-Hill.

———, ed. (1984). *Ritualized Homosexuality in Melanesia.* Berkeley: University of California Press.

———. (1987). *The Sambia: Ritual and Gender in New Guinea.* New York: Holt, Rinehart and Winston.

Kappy, M. S., Blizzard, R.M., and Migeon, C.J., eds. (1994). *Wilkins the Diagnosis and Treatment of Endocrine Disorders in Childhood and Adolescence,* Fourth edition. Springfield, IL: Charles C Thomas.

Kennedy, H. (1988). *Ulrichs: The Life and Works of Karl Heinrich Ulrichs, Pioneer of the Modern Gay Movement.* Boston: Alyson Publications.

Money, J. (1974). "Two names, two wardrobes, two personalities." *Journal of Homosexuality* 1:65–70.

———. (1990). "Androgyne becomes bisexual in sexological theory: Plato to Freud and neuroscience." *Journal of the American Academy of Psychoanalysis* 18:392–413.

———. (1991a). "The transformation of sexual terminology: Homosexuality in sexological history." *SIECUS Report* 19, no. 5 (June/July): 10–13.

———. (1991b). *Biographies of Gender and Hermaphroditism in Paired Comparisons: Clinical Supplement to the Handbook of Sexology.* Amsterdam: Elsevier.

———. (1993). *The Adam Principle: Genes, Genitals, Hormones, and Gender —Selected Readings in Sexology.* Amherst, NY: Prometheus Books.

———. (1994). *Sex Errors of the Body and Related Syndromes: A Guide to Counseling Children, Adolescents, and Their Families.* Baltimore: Paul H. Brookes.

Money, J., Joshi, V. K., and Prakasam, K. S. (1992). "*Kama Sutra*: Woman's sexology versus semen conservation theory in Sanskrit teachings." In *The Present and Future of Preventive Research: In Honor of George W. Albee, Ph.D.* (M. Kessler, S. E. Goldston, and J. M. Joffe, eds.). Newbury Park, CA: Sage.

Stoller, R. J. (1985). *Observing the Erotic Imagination.* New Haven: Yale University Press.

Tissot, S. A. (1974). *A Treatise on the Diseases Produced by Onanism. Translated from a New Edition of the French, with Notes and Appendix by an American Physician.* New York: Collins and Hannay, 1832. Facsimile reprint edition in *The Secret Vice Exposed! Some Arguments Against Masturbation* (C. Rosenberg and C. Smith-Rosenberg, eds.). New York: Arno Press.

Woodward, T. E. (1989). "The golden era of microbiology: People and events of the 1880s." *Maryland Medical Journal* 38:323–28.

20

Medicine and Law: Case Consultation, Ablatio Penis

1. INTRODUCTION

In the summer of 1996, the following case consultation by mail was requested by a representative of the office of the Attorney General for the Protection of Minors in a foreign jurisdiction. The case is that of a nine-month-old male infant with a history of ablatio penis. The infant's genitalia had been mutilated at the age of four months, ostensibly by a small dog, although confirmatory evidence of canine intervention was absent. The testicles were missing, along with an estimated 80 percent of the scrotal tissue and penis. Whereas the surgeon who tended to the wound on an emergency basis advised sex-reassignment surgery, the civil authorities authorized and sought additional expert advice, for which they also authorized the release of the medical records for professional discussion and instruction.

There are, in the clinical pediatric sexological literature, no standardized guidelines regarding case management of infantile ablatio penis, and no consensus regarding the full complement of multiple and sequential variables that need to be considered as determinants of the outcome with or without sex reassignment in infancy. In response to

Written for and submitted to *Medicine and Law,* August 1996. Published as "Case Consultation: Ablatio Penis," *Medicine and Law* 17:113–23, 1998.

the request for a written consultation, I wrote that I would not be in a position to make a specific recommendation, but that I would be able to list the pros and cons of sex reassignment that need to be weighed by an advisory board in charge of any case of infantile ablatio penis.

At the outset, let it be said that the dilemma in this case is of the type that in U.S. idiom is known as a Catch-22. That is, it is a case in which you're damned if you do undertake sex reassignment, and damned if you don't. Neither procedure is wholly satisfactory on all counts.

2. Societal Ideology

Even among experts, there is no unanimity regarding the criteria for sex assignment in cases of intersexed birth-defective genitalia, nor in cases of severe infantile genital mutilation, such as ablatio penis, with or without loss of the testicles. On the contrary, the lack of unanimity may become adversarial and strident. In case of litigation to settle a malpractice claim, it is easy for the defense and the prosecution to find expert witnesses whose testimony is mutually oppositional. Thus it is all too easy for a child to be a victim twice over: first of genital mutilation, and second of legal wrangling as to how much the mutilation and its resultant disability are worth if there is a malpractice claim, and who controls the spending of what may be a very large compensation award.

3. Sex Reassignment Surgery, Male to Female

Postpubertally, as in the case of male to female transexualism, it is technologically possible to achieve a functional genital appearance that does not arouse suspicion of the genital surgical history, even under a gynecological examination. Prepubertally, it is not possible to achieve the same convincing appearance, insofar as feminizing surgery is done in two stages. In the first stage, the urethral meatus is relocated into the feminine position, possibly with a simulated clitoris. Construction of the vulval cleft is delayed until the second stage, after toilet training is complete, and is dependent on the simultaneous construction of the vaginal cavity. This is typically delayed until mid-teenage so that, with the larger size and hormonalization of the body, the neovagina will more easily be kept open and free from contracture. The second surgical stage may require two admissions, the final one for cosmetic adjustment.

4. Reconstructive Male Surgery

With or without sex-reassignment surgery, the natal male with a history of genital mutilation is destined to have an anomalous genital appearance during some of the juvenile years, for which the explanation is that tissue transplants and grafts in infancy and childhood may have a growth rate out of synchrony with tissue in the new location. At an older age, it has proved possible in plastic surgery to use a microsurgical free flap from the forearm to replace an amputated penis. With microsurgical technique, the blood vessels and nerves of the graft are joined to those of the stump of the amputated penis (Gilbert, Jordan et al., 1993). The neopenis eventually is able to respond to temperature and pain stimuli. Data on penile erotic feeling are few, but it is known that the ability to masturbate to climax has been reported postpubertally (Gilbert, personal communication, 1996). Although the graft is nonerectile, as it lacks the erectile spongy tissue of the corpora cavernosa, it is not as flabby as a penis constructed from a split-thickness skin graft, which requires a penile prosthetic implant to permit intravaginal coitus.

5. Timing of Hospital Admissions

Not infrequently, surgical admissions are subjectively experienced by infants and juveniles as the nosocomial equivalent of injurious child abuse. Thus, the fewer early surgical admissions, the better. As a sequel to male genital mutilation, male-to-female sex reassignment entails surgery, for the sake of urinary function and genital cosmetics, at a very young age. The outcome, being less than perfect, does not have a guaranteed cosmetic advantage, however, over the imperfect cosmetics of a boy waiting to grow old enough for penile plastic surgical reconstruction. Either alternative presents a major morphological and body-image hurdle for the child, as well as for those responsible for child-care, rearing, and for sex and health education.

6. Body Image

The body image of a boy with a history of genital mutilation is built up in part through the eyes and in part through the cutaneous senses. It is not yet known whether there is, in the brain, a residual phantom representation or schema of a penis that has been amputated. It is possible, however, that an imprinted male genital body image survives the loss of the penis and, in a diffuse way, in the mental experience of the sex-reassigned child, is inconsistent with being reared as a girl.

A masculinized level of skeleto-muscular kinetic-energy expenditure is a feature of the body image that survives sex reassignment following early loss of the penis and/or the testicles. In the juvenile years, the outcome is known colloquially as "tomboyism," and is manifested as competitive interest in vigorous sports that are popularly stereotyped as suitable for boys more than for girls. Concomitantly, there is a lack of interest in maternal rehearsal play with dolls.

In the ideology of equal rights and women's emancipation, there is no contraindication to being a tomboyish girl and woman. In an unemancipated family or community, however, it meets with societal disapprobation, which adds an additional burden to a sex-reassigned child's life.

7. Health Education

One of the defining sexological characteristics of Christendom is the age-discrepancy taboo which restricts intergenerational exchange of explicit sexual information. This taboo affects not only the parents of children with a history of genital mutilation, but also their professional health-care workers. Thus, it can be taken for granted that the children themselves are deprived of information about their genital history. They obey the rule of silence. They receive evasive answers if they do ask questions, and they are mortified by the explicitness of those who are sexologically trained and prepared to talk openly. All too often, the exigencies of time, place, medical economics, and antisexual ideology allow them to become lost to sexological follow-up, so that their personal health concerns are not addressed developmentally as they arise.

8. Pubertal Hormonalization

There is no ancient taboo against the ideology of endocrine treatment, which is new, as there is of sex education, which is not new. Thus, children with a history of genital mutilation are more likely than not to return for follow-up when they reach the age of puberty. For those living as boys without testicles, hormonal treatment is with testosterone, the major androgenic or masculinizing hormone. For those living as girls, also without testicles, hormonal treatment is with estrogen, the feminizing hormone, supplemented with a progestogen, since the two hormones are secreted cyclically in the normal female. In bringing about complete masculinization and feminization of the body morphology and secondary sexual characteristics, the respective male and female hormonal treatments are efficacious. Patients living as females, however, do not menstruate, since the uterus is lacking, and no technique has yet been developed for the surgical transplantation of a uterus without immunological rejection of the transplant.

9. Sterility/Fertility

Likewise, no surgical procedure has yet been developed for the transplantation of ovaries or testicles. Artificial prosthetic testes may be implanted in a boy's empty scrotum, for the sake of visual and cutaneous cosmetics. In the case of genital mutilation in which a boy's testicles are spared, male hormonal function will be unimpaired, and so will production of spermatozoa. If there is no impediment to ejaculation, then fertility can be anticipated, even if sexological expert intervention is needed to transfer the semen from the damaged male organ into the female vagina.

In the case of a history of male-to-female sex reassignment, it is not yet an actuality, although it is a technological feasibility for an in vitro fertilized donor egg to be transplanted ectopically into the abdominal cavity and to grow into a baby, delivered by caesarean section (Jackson, Barrowclough, et al., 1980; Frydman, Testart, et al., 1988; Sauer, Lobo, and Paulson, 1989). Though still in the realm of science fiction, knowledge of this possibility diminishes the trauma of growing up as a girl with the stigma of sterility.

10. Postpubertal Surgical Admissions

Provided there are no unexpected postoperative complications, the completion of male-to-female sex-reassignment surgery in teenage or young adulthood usually requires two admissions. The first is to invaginate a canal in the tissue between the urethra and the rectum and line it with a split-thickness skin graft from the buttock. The second is to sculpt the exterior tissues to resemble labia majora and, if possible, a clitoral hood and clitoridean body.

More than two surgical admissions are needed for the construction of a simulated penis, the exact number being contingent on how much of the shaft of the penis and penile urethra have been preserved; on the preparation of the tubular skin graft at the donor site so that it has its own blood supply before being transferred to the genital site; on joining the grafted section of the penis with the urethra; on cosmetic sculpting of a glans penis; and on the implantation of an erectile prosthesis to compensate for the lack of spongy erectile tissue. In the worst-case scenario, there may be up to fifteen surgical admissions with less than a successful urinary and coital outcome.

11. Coitus and Orgasm

In female-to-male sex-reassignment surgery, postsurgical constriction and closure of the neovagina is known to occur despite compliancy in the application of vaginal dilation. It may be resistant to treatment. The neovagina that stays open is coitally functional. The prevalence of orgasmic climax remains unknown. Its subjective experience is idiosyncratically described and there is no uniform criterion by which it has been rated.

In adult males, traumatic penile injury or mutilation—provided the internal genital anatomy and nerve supply are intact—does not abolish orgasm, which can be triggered by erotic stimulation of what remains of the original penile shaft and surrounding tissue. Similarly, in cases of birth defect of the genitalia, orgasm survives surgical repair. One presumes that orgasm also survives surgical repair of the penis traumatized by infantile mutilation, even in those cases in which the postsurgical penis is not conducive to penovaginal intromission. However, there is no available data bank from which to calculate follow-up statistics.

12. Lesbian Identity

The lovemap is a mental representation or schema of, among other things, the body morphology of the erotically idealized sexual partner. It is a question still without answer in sexology as to whether this schema of the body morphology of the idealized partner is to a variable degree preordained, from prenatal life onward, to be masculine, feminine, or bisexual. One possibility is that it could, like other male/female differences in the brain, be hormonally imprinted, prenatally or neonatally. If so, then a normal boy with a future history of sex reassignment would at birth carry a brain imprint to be erotically attracted later in life toward the female body morphology. That brain imprint might survive the sex-reassigned juvenile years of living as a girl. Should that be so, then in adolescence, the girl would discover herself to be erotically attracted toward females. Thereupon, she might experience the incompatibility between living as a female and being erotically aroused by female morphology as a sign pointing toward changing to live as a boy.

Living as a female, she would be societally stigmatized as a lesbian and quite possibly be self-stigmatized as well. Politically and legally, homosexuals do not yet have full human rights in most parts of the world. Thus, although both a homosexual and a heterosexual erotic attraction should be equally acceptable in cases of a childhood history of sex reassignment, in point of fact that is not the case.

There is presently no way of predicting heterosexual versus homosexual erotic attraction as a sequel to early sex reassignment. There is also no available pool of data from which to calculate outcome statistics, including the proportion of cases in which, in adolescence or later, sex reassignment is attempted for the second time.

13. Cost Accounting

In planning for or against sex reassignment as a sequel to male genital mutilation in infancy, it is obligatory to plan also for not only present but also future procedures, and to ensure that funding for follow-up procedures will be guaranteed. Surgical, endocrine, and psychosexological counseling all must be provided for. In the case of either male-to-female sex reassignment, or assignment as a castrated male, the cost of hormonal-replacement therapy will be lifelong, whereas surgical costs may terminate (though not invariably) in young adulthood. It is imperative that funding be available for psychosexological and health counseling at spaced intervals, as needed, throughout childhood, adolescence, and young adulthood, if not longer.

This counseling service is, of necessity, rendered in collaboration with parents, siblings, and school officials. Otherwise, these significant people, if left to improvise without the guidance of an experienced expert, fail to anticipate and respond to the various exigencies that invariably arise in the life of a child with a history of genital mutilation, with or without sex reassignment.

14. Discussion

Ablation of the penis (ablatio penis) in infancy has been known to occur as a sequel to erroneous use of an electrical cautery for circumcision, to mutilatory use of a sharp tool by a psychiatrically disordered adult, and to accidental trauma. In cases of mutilation or accident, the testicles may be ablated also. The prevalence of each of the three types of trauma has not been ascertained.

In an earlier era, little could be done for traumatic loss of the external male genitalia other than to dress the wound surgically and antiseptically, and to preserve urinary function. In the second half of the twentieth century, by contrast, progress in sexological surgery and rehabilitation for infants with intersexual and related birth defects of the sex organs illustrated the technical and clinical feasibility of masculine repair in some cases of ablatio penis, and female sex reassignment in others, dependent on the nature and severity of the wound.

As of the present time, there are no universally agreed upon criteria of when to pursue either of these two alternatives. The issue is sexosophical as well as sexological. That is to say, it is debated on religious, ethical, legal, and economic grounds, as well as on biomedical and scientific grounds. Scientifically, outcome data are too few to provide a statistically sufficient data base. In part, this may be attributed to the rarity of infantile ablatio penis, so that too few cases are concentrated in any one treatment center for a statistical, matched pair study of the variables that affect the outcome of treatment with and without sex reassignment. Ideally, therefore, there should be a centralized depository for pooling and cataloguing prevalence and outcome data.

Whether or not such a depository will come into existence in the twenty-first century cannot be foreseen. Clinical pediatric research is not currently a funding priority in the United States, and clinical pediatric sexological research least of all. In addition, the rules for obtaining sexologically informed consent, as presently construed, put a virtual legal and ethical blackout on the publication of any biographical sexological data at which a patient might take offense, even though the data are unrecognizable except to the self. Whatever the outcome, data that presently exist on the outcome of ablatio penis in infancy seem doomed to be lost to science.

Later than infancy, surgical sex reassignment is not an optional sequel to traumatic loss of the penis, nor to peotomy for cancer, as the masculine gender-identity/role becomes too firmly differentiated to be feminized (except when spontaneously feminized in cases of male-to-female transexualism).

Transculturally, in India, those known as transexuals in Western sexology have long been known as members of a part-caste/part-cult of *hijras* who worship their own goddess, Bahuchara Mata. Since ancient times, experienced surgical gurus among the *hijras* have trained their successors in the technique of castration, removing not only the testicles but the penis also (Money and Lamacz, 1984; Nanda, 1990).

In the West, self-castration has been attempted by some male-to-female transexuals in lieu of professional sex-reassignment surgery (Money and DePriest, 1976). Self-castration is also known in males with a fixation not on sex reassignment but on becoming a eunuch to be relieved of what is personally construed as the distress of having an unwanted sexual urge (Martin and Gattaz, 1991). This condition has been named the *Skoptic syndrome* (Money, 1988). The Skoptics were an ascetic religious sect active in Russian and Romania from the eighteenth to the early twentieth century. Taking the New Testament literally, they "made themselves eunuchs for the kingdom of heaven's sake" (Matthew 19:12). In the lesser operation, the testicles and scrotum were amputated, and in the greater, the penis as well. In Skoptic women, the nipples were cauterized.

Eunuchs have been accorded powerful bureaucratic roles in the imperial courts of China for centuries, and likewise in the courts and harems of Islamic potentates and rulers.

Prepubertal castration to preserve the high pitch of the voices of boy virtuosos for soprano performances in the opera houses of Europe, and in the choirs of cathedrals and basilicas, was fashionable into the eighteenth century. In this earlier era, these boys grew up as *castrati,* not as girls and women.

The idea of sex reassignment as a sequel to infantile genital trauma or mutilation is, in history, a phenomenon of twentieth-century medicine. Its historical recency no doubt accounts for a good part of the unresolved controversy which it still engenders and which perpetuates the absence of the very data upon which the scientific resolution of that controversy is contingent.

In the absence of scientific outcome data, professional consensus on a set of guidelines for the treatment of infantile ablatio penis with and without loss of the testicles is unlikely. Should dispute arise, its resolution might then become a matter of litigation. If so, then the court decision, established according to the adversarial system of the law, would establish a legal precedent. A legal precedent is, in fact, the equivalent of a legal guideline. It would prescribe in part what medicine may or may not do in cases of infantile ablatio penis. It would require that medicine forfeit the use of its own judgment and decision-making to that of the judiciary. In the long run, it would be better if medicine, and sexological medicine particularly, not forfeit its responsibility. Instead, it might take the steps necessary to achieve consensus and produce a set of its own guidelines which the law might then use.

References

Frydman, R., Testart, J., Parneix, I., Raymond, J.-P., Fries, N., and Bouchard, P. (1988). "Pregnancy in a 46,XY patient." *Fertility and Sterility* 50: 813–14.

Gilbert, D. A., Jordan, G. H., Devine, C. J., Jr., Winslow, B. H., and Schlossberg, S. M. (1993). "Phallic construction in prepubertal and adolescent boys." *Journal of Urology* 149:1521–26.

Jackson, P., Barrowclough, I. W., France, J. T., and Phillips, L. I. (1980). "A successful pregnancy following total hysterectomy." *British Journal of Obstetrics and Gynaecology* 87:353–55.

Martin, T., and Gattaz, W. F. (1991). "Psychiatric aspects of male genital self-mutilation." *Psychopathology* 24(3):170–78.

Money, J. (1988). "The Skoptic syndrome: Castration and genital self-mutilation as an example of sexual body-image pathology." *Journal of Psychology and Human Sexuality* 1(1):113–28.

Money, J., and DePriest, M. (1976). "Genital self-surgery: Relationship to transexualism in three cases." *Journal of Sex Research* 12:283–94.

Money, J., and Lamacz, M. (1984). "Gynemimesis and gynemimetophilia: Individual and cross-cultural manifestations of a gender coping strategy hitherto unnamed." *Journal of Sex and Marital Therapy* 10:105–16.

Nanda, S. (1990). *Neither Man Nor Woman: The Hijras of India.* Belworth, CA: Wadsworth.

Sauer, M. V., Lobo, R. A., and Paulson, R. J. (1989). "Successful twin pregnancy after embryo donation to a patient with XY gonadal dysgenesis." *American Journal of Obstetrics and Gynecology* 161:380–81.

21

Ablatio Penis: Nature/Nurture Redux

Horoscopy and Causality

Proximity and causality are separate and distinct from one another when human beings are thinking logically. Two or more phenomena may with regularity occur in close proximity in time or space and yet be without cause and effect. Correlation does not prove causality, yet it has been falsely assumed as causal, apparently since time immemorial. Without the principle of causality, the human intellect is unable to make genuine predictions. Without the power of prediction, the human intellect is rendered powerless in the cosmos. Thus, the mind grasps at predictory straws even though their predictive promise proves to be hollow. The English language is littered with the residue of predictory failures in the form of proverbs, rhymes, and sayings, many of them perhaps of prehistoric origin. The casting of horoscopy, a still popular pastime, is a residual of the ancient system of astrology, forerunner of astronomy. In astrological doctrine, celestial alignments at the time of birth have causal power over our individual destinies.

Horoscopy exemplifies the human quest for a system of causality beyond the self with which to explain the self and its affairs and experiences. Reincarnation and spiritism exemplify another and even more

Previously unpublished.

primordial quest for a system of causal explanation external to the self: Whether for good or for ill, spirits may possess the self and control its destiny. Unlike the causal power of celestial bodies, however, the causal power of spirits may be challenged, even though in vain, by exorcism, whether coerced or consensual.

The very idea of spirits that possess the power of causality spawns two ideas of personal responsibility. One is to placate the spirits and the other is to take revenge against them. Placation is by means of personal sacrificial appeasement and penance. Revenge is by attacking whomever is held responsible for using spirits in sorcery. Both placation and revenge incorporate causality within the self. The self, in other words, becomes responsible for its own destiny.

There is no historically retrievable record of when self-responsibility for one's own destiny entered into human thinking. In the intellectual history of Western civilization, the record begins with the philosophy of ancient Greece, most likely by way of Persia from Hindu India. Self-responsibility for one's own sin and redemption, as compared with being saved by God's grace, became a major issue for the philosophers and theologians of the early Christian centuries in their effort to reconcile the writings of their Greek and Judaic predecessors with the teachings of the new Christian religion.

Two of the great intellects of the church at the end of the fourth century failed to find agreement. One was Augustine, Bishop of Hippo in North Africa. The other was Pelagius, a British monk who taught mostly in Asia Minor. Augustine's theology incorporated the principle of original sin, from which an omnipotent God external to the self granted redemption through divine grace. By contrast, the rival theology of Pelagius taught that grace alone did not suffice. Pelagianism incorporated the principle, internal to the self of responsibility to seek and earn redemption. According to Augustine, Pelagius deprived God of absolute omnipotence by making human beings responsible for the acceptance or rejection of redemptive grace.

Centuries later, Augustine's position would become gelled into the doctrine of predestinarianism, especially in the teachings of John Calvin and his follower, John Knox, founder of Presbyterianism. This Augustinian doctrine is incompatible with the nonconformist and fundamentalist doctrine of salvation by a confession of faith and being born again, which has Pelagian origins. Pelagius is also consistent with orthodox Roman Catholic teaching on the necessity of repentance and penance, despite the ecclesiastical authority accorded to Augustine by the Church.

Biology and Social Constructionism

The Augustinian/Pelagian antithesis is by no means a dead letter of history. In contemporary behavioral and social science, it is reincarnated as the antithesis between, respectively, biology as destiny and social construction as voluntary consent or dissent. Biology is popularized as nature, and social constructionism as nurture; biology preordains that which lies ahead, whereas social construction is historical and, it is said, subject to deconstruction by the individual.

In its stripped down and simplistic form, biological determinism in sexology is construed as being inborn and under the control predominantly of either the genes or the fetal sex hormones. This reductionistic view of biology allows no place for the brain's biology of learning and remembering, and it neglects the extensive neuroscience literature on that subject.

Social-constructionist determinism in sexology, in its stripped-down, simplistic form, is construed as originating in society and history exclusively. This reductionist view allows no place for biology. The biological model and the medical model are anathema to the proponents of social constructionism, maliciously contrived to rob individuals of autonomy, power, and responsibility.

At each polar extreme, biological determinism and social constructionism run to monomaniacal fanaticism. The majority of sexologists, however, are not extremist. Although they may gravitate toward one pole rather than the other, mostly they hedge their bets by acknowledging the existence of the other. The intellectually more sophisticated among them no longer pit biological nature against social nurture. For them, the new maxim is that nature needs nurture, and the new paradigm of development is nature/critical period/nurture. Without nurture, nature fails to thrive, and without nature, nurture has nothing that either thrives or fails to thrive.

Nature/Nurture: History of Homosexuality

The polarity of nature versus nurture in sexology is as old as the history of sexology itself, dating from the second half of the nineteenth century. Nowhere is this polarity more evident than in the history of homosexuality.

Strictly speaking, homosexuality had no history prior to 1869, the year in which the term was coined by Karl M. Benkert, alias Kertbeny (Kennedy, 1988, p. 153), an activist for German sexual-law reform. Another sexual-law reform ideologist, the German jurist Karl H. Ulrichs, had in an 1864 publication coined the noun *urning*. He derived this term from Uranus, the Greek male deity who, according to Plato, gave birth to the motherless, heavenly Aphrodite. Ulrichs explicitly linked his new term to the idea of "a woman's soul enclosed in a man's body" (*anima muliebris virili corpore inclusa*)—an idea borrowed from a lamentation in the diary of Jakob Stutz, a Swiss writer and contemporary of Ulrichs (Kennedy, 1988, p. 103).

The two new terms, *homosexual* and *urning,* had no immediate impact on either the professional or the vernacular vocabulary. In 1905, Magnus Hirschfeld promoted Kertbeny's term by republishing his 1869 article in Volume 5 of the *Jahrbuch für Sexuelle Zwissenstufen* (*Yearbook for Sexual Intermediate Stages*). Thereafter, the word "homosexual," and with it "heterosexual," became rapidly assimilated into international usage.

Unlike his terminology, Ulrichs' theory of *anima muliebris virili corpore inclusa* to explain male/male sexual attraction met with no competition from Kertbeny. Thus, although Ulrichs's vocabulary fell into disuse, his theory did not. It was fated, however, not to promote tolerance and homosexual-law reform, as Ulrichs advocated, but paradoxically to promote prejudice. In advocating the decriminalization of homosexuality, Ulrichs did not foresee that the alternative would be to pathologize it as a psychiatric syndrome. Tolerance and prejudice are not based on natural law, nor on rational science as Ulrichs had hoped, but on historical precedent and social power.

Ulrichs anchored his theory of the origin of homosexuality in natural science, namely the newest embryological discoveries concerning sexual differentiation of the embryo and fetus. Under the pseudonym of Numa Numantius, in 1864 he published "Inclusa," the first of a series of tracts. "In each embryo," he wrote,

> until approximately the 12th week of its existence, there is a double generative principle, one male and, at the same time, one female. Until that time, the generative principle is capable of developing male sexual parts, testicles, etc., and at the same time is capable of developing female sexual parts, ovaries, etc. . . . We as Urnings have been equipped as embryos with the feminine generative principle that could have developed into ovaries, labia majora (womb), etc.; and partially with the generative principle of the lactative glands and the nipples. . . . The feminine generative principle with which we were equipped as embryos in the bodily substratum corresponds to our development of a womanly sense of sexual love. . . .
>
> It is erroneous to assume that testicles naturally and innately always coexist with male sexual love . . . or that female sexual love is a natural occurrence only when there are ovaries. Perhaps the place where sexual love might be found is entirely elsewhere than in testicles, ovaries, or any other sexual parts, namely in the brain.

Those who accepted Ulrichs's theory, but not his nomenclature, were obliged to coin their own terms. Westphal's (1869) term in German was *conträre sexual Empfindung* (contrary sexual feeling). Krafft-Ebing's highly influential 1886 textbook, *Psychopathia Sexualis,* in its twelfth and final edition (1901; 1931) carried the term *antipathic sexual instinct* in its subtitle, although *homosexual* appeared in the text.

The term *sexual inversion* was already in the professional literature when Havelock Ellis used it in 1896 as the title of Volume I (later Volume II) of his six volume *Studies in the Psychology of Sex.* He used *homosexual* as the generic term to refer to the behavior, whether it be determined opportunistically or by reason of a congenital inversion of the sexual instinct (Ellis, 1920, pp. 2–3).

As a causal explanation of homosexuality, a contrary or inverted sexual instinct needs its own causal explanation. In the era before the discovery of germ theory in 1870, the theory of degeneracy was in vogue in nineteenth-century medicine. Degeneracy itself was widely attributed to hereditary taint. Being tainted might lead to an evolutionary throwback to a more primitive, more atavistic state (Lombroso, 1876).

The origins of hereditary taint could have been acquired by one's forebears and passed on according to the Lamarckian premise of the inheritance of acquired characteristics. In the nineteenth century, Lamarckianism had not yet been supplanted by the Mendelian theory of genetics. Thus, the manifold causes of hereditary tainting in one's genealogy were as widely varied as mental retardation, epilepsy, crime, insanity, tuberculosis, drunkenness, prostitution, promiscuity, masturbation, and more (Money and Lamacz, 1989).

SEMEN-CONSERVATION THEORY

Masturbation as a cause of degeneracy has extremely ancient roots in semen-conservation theory, according to which semen is regarded as the most precious of the vital fluids (Money, 1985). Its depletion was anciently believed to cause death in addition to the diseases of degeneracy. Reversing cause and effect, nineteenth-century degeneracy theory led to the still popular belief that homosexuality is caused by boys teaching boys to masturbate, not that homosexual attraction leads to mutual masturbation.

The doctrine that hereditary taintedness causes degeneracy is cast partly in the Augustinian mold of biological fatalism, and partly in the Pelagian mold of personal moral responsibility to control degeneracy caused by semen depletion. Control of masturbation as a cause of semen depletion became a major medical quackery in the nineteenth century (and well into the twentieth).

From its inception in the mid-1890s onwards, psychoanalytic theory circumvented the principle of hereditary taintedness and degeneracy by replacing it with the principle of developmental arrest or of regression to a more primitive stage of development. From its primordial bipotential state, the embryo could develop to be psychically heterosexual, bisexual, or homosexual. In this principle of development, there was no criterion by which to judge homosexual differentiation as a pathology, and Freud himself did not do so. Not so his followers, however. In their ideology, homosexuals constituted not only a statistical minority but a psychopathological one. Their causal explanation of homosexuality was no longer biological but social, with special attention to the family dynamics of the Oedipus complex. The pendulum of causation in matters of human sexuality had swung away from nature toward nurture, where it remained for half a century and more.

ANIMAL HORMONAL BIPOTENTIALITY

The germ of the idea of a sexually bipotential brain capable of being influenced by "vital spirits" or "sympathies" (i.e., hormones) can, with the knowledge of hindsight, be traced to the eighteenth-century experiments of John Hunter in London (see Money, 1993, pp. 23–34). His actual anatomical specimens have survived, together with a brief note to the effect that, in young chicks, he had "transplanted the testicles of a cock into the abdomen of a hen, and that they had sometimes taken root there, but not frequently, and then had never come to perfection." The hens had, however, manifested some of the appearance of a rooster, and also the brain-mediated behavior of crowing. Hunter's findings were replicated in 1849 by Arnold Berthold in Germany. The full significance of hormonal sex reversal went on hold, however, until 1912–1913, when Eugen Steinach in Vienna published his "feminization of males and masculinization of females" by transplanting heterotypic gonadal tissue into castrated newborn guinea pigs, thus achieving an "intentional reversal of sexual characteristics of both the body and behavior."

The Berlin sexologist Magnus Hirschfeld immediately recognized the significance of Steinach's animal model for an explanation of homosexuality in human beings, but his voice was not widely heard, and would not be until synthetic sex hormones became synthesized and marketed in the 1930s. Then a French biologist, Vera Dantchakoff, working in Chicago in 1938, updated Steinach's findings. She reported that "female guinea pigs born to mothers given intrauterine injections of testosterone propionate contained a normal internal female genital tract with ovaries together with a more or less well-developed epididymis, ductuli efferentes, prostate, Cowper's gland, and penis. In their behavior, when they were given male hormone, they performed completely as males" (quoted from Young, 1961, p. 1199).

Dantchakoff returned to France. The intervention of World War II may have been a factor in the neglect of her findings, or she may have been too far ahead of her time with her data on the biology of sexual behavior in intersexed guinea pigs. Whatever the explanation, it remained for William C. Young and his associates at the University of Kansas to take up where Dantchakoff left off and to confirm her findings in a renowned article in *Endocrinology* (Phoenix et al., 1959). In 1961, Young's summary of his own guinea pig data was as follows:

> Pregnant females were injected intramuscularly with 5 mg. of testosterone propionate on day 10 of the pregnancy and with 1 mg. daily from day 11 to day 68 of the gestation period. At birth the external genitalia of the female offspring were indistinguishable macroscopically from those of the sibling males and examination of the genital tracts by laparotomy was necessary for identification of the sex. Internally there were hypertrophied Wolffian ducts (detectable microscopically), failure of Mullerian duct-urogenital sinus fusion, and, by the time of sexual maturation, abundant evidence of ovarian dysfunction. Tests given after these female hermaphrodites had been gonadectomized and injected with estrogen and progesterone, or with an androgen, revealed that striking modification of the behavior pattern had been produced.
>
> Much less of the feminine measures of behavior was displayed; there was a decrease in the percentage of tests positive for estrus, in the duration of estrus, and in the duration of maximal lordosis. An effect on the tissues mediating the masculine component of the pattern was revealed by the greater amount of male-like mounting. The hermaphroditic females had become more responsive to the androgen than ovariectomized but otherwise normal females. The effects on the females receiving the androgen prenatally were permanent. (Young, 1961, pp. 1199–1200).

One of Young's graduate students was Milton C. Diamond. He was profoundly impressed by the power of prenatal exposure to male hormone to transform otherwise female guinea pigs to hermaphrodites (intersexes) masculinized in both body and behavior. For him it was the ultimate triumph of biology over rearing—a triumph with which he identified and for the ensuing forty years could not let go.

HUMAN HERMAPHRODITE HISTORY

The following brief overview of the medical and social history of hermaphroditism is taken from *Hermaphroditism: An Inquiry into the Nature of a Human Paradox* (Money, 1952).

"Partisan feeling waxed high in the week preceding the Town Meeting of 1843 in Salisbury, Connecticut. Both parties anticipated a close contest, and 'almost everything bearing the semblance of the human form, of the male sex, was brought to the ballot box' (Barry,

1847). The Whigs presented one Levi Suydam for registration as an enfranchised freeman. Persistently and heatedly the Republicans disputed Suydam's status on the technicality of gender. It had been rumored in the town that he was half woman. A local physician, Dr. Barry, had examined Suydam and pronounced him male, but the Republicans raised a last-minute protest at the commencement of the Meeting, and were satisfied only when Suydam consented to an examination by a doctor of their choice. Suydam and Dr. Ticknor retired into a side room; and Dr. Ticknor eventually reported to the meeting that he was convinced that Suydam was a male. Suydam was accordingly admitted a qualified freeman. The Whigs triumphed by a one vote majority, and the subtle question of the civil rights of hermaphrodites was carried no further. It was perhaps as well, for Levi Suydam was probably one of the rare examples of true hermaphroditism. The doctors had palpated one testicle and Suydam later reluctantly admitted menstruating, scantily but regularly.

"The common sense of the citizens of Salisbury in accepting the independent verdict of two physicians is not unique. The layman has seldom been concerned with discriminating against hermaphrodites. He has a folklore about 'morphodites' and a salacious interest in tales of ambisexual prowess. But the 'half-man, half-woman' figure is a legend of sorts in his thinking. Even when he sees what purports to be the real thing in a side-show, he retains a healthy skepticism. He is satisfied that it is a freak, but at the back of his mind is the feeling that, however freakish, it must be essentially either a man or a woman. The dichotomy of the sexes is too deeply imbedded to be disposed of lightly. Outside the circus, 'morphodites' scarcely exist for the average person.

"In present day societies in the Western tradition, hermaphrodites are not the subject of special legislation. Nor are they subject to harsh legal discrimination or imposition. In fact, expositions of jurisprudence have singularly little to say about hermaphroditism. It is mentioned in common law only in very specific contexts. Thus, according to Lord Coke in the sixteenth century, an hermaphrodite may by the common law of England 'be either male or female, and it shall succeed according to the kind of sex which doth prevail.' Succession to an hereditary title is today the only occasion on which litigation as to the prevailing sex is likely to arise. In English common law, hermaphroditism is recognized as sufficient cause for annulment of a marriage contract.

"Old French legal precedent permitted an ambiguous hermaphrodite to choose one sex and thereafter adhere strictly to it. In 1602 the

Parisian Parliament condemned an hermaphrodite to death because he had made use of the sex which he had abjured. French law recognized a marriage as void, if a man's spouse turned out to be an hermaphrodite incapable of intercourse. It was not so specific when the tables were turned and a wife found her husband to be an hermaphrodite.

"In the United States, a contemporary hermaphrodite may make a formal change of sex and may, with medical evidence, have his birth certificate changed as a matter of routine. An hermaphroditic marriage may be annulled on grounds of sterility, if the spouse was not previously informed. The legality of withholding information about incongruity between the gonadal and the civil status has not been tested.

"Ancient custom devolved with the implicit assumption that hermaphrodites are either predominantly male or female. It could not have been otherwise for common-sense experience reinforced the assumption. And common sense was the only source of knowledge. For centuries the medical profession knew no more than the educated layman. In the sixteenth century, after Leonardo da Vinci and Vesalius had initiated great advances in anatomy, writings on hermaphroditism began to appear. The famous French exponent of the art of surgery, Ambroise Paré, summarized the medical knowledge of this period as follows: 'And here also we must speak of hermaphrodites, because they draw the cause of their generation and conformation from the abundance of seed, and are called so, because they are of both Sexes, the Woman yielding as much seed as the Man. For hereupon it cometh to pass that the forming faculty (which always endeavors to produce something like itself) doth labour both the matters with equal force, and is the cause that one body is of both sexes. Yet some make four differences of Hermaphrodites; the first of which is the male Hermaphrodite, who is a perfect and absolute male, and hath only a slit in the *Perineum* not perforated, and from which neither Urin nor Seed doth flow. The second is the female, which besides her natural Privity, hath a fleshy and skinny similitude of a mans Yard, but unapt for erection and ejaculation of seed, and wanteth the Cod and Stones. The third difference is of those, which albeit they bear the express figures of members belonging to both sexes, commonly set the one against the other, yet are found unapt for generation, the one of them only serving for making of water. The fourth difference is of those who are able in both sexes, and thoroughly perform the part of both man and woman, because they have the genitals of both sexes complete and perfect, and also the right brest like a man, and the left like a woman: the Laws command those to chuse the sex which they will use, and in which they will remain and live, judging them to death if they be found to have departed from the sex they made choice of, for some are thought to have abused both and promiscuously to have had their pleasure with men and women. There are signs by which the Physicians may discern whether the Hermaphrodites are able in the male or female sex, or whether they are impotent in both: these signs are most apparent in the Privities and Face; for if the matrix be exact in all its dimensions, and so perforated that it may admit a mans Yard, if the Courses flow that way, if the hair of the head be long, slender and soft, and to conclude, if to this tender habit of the body a timid and weak condition of the mind be added, the Female sex is predominant, and they are plainly to be judged Women. But if they have the *Perineum* and fundament full of hairs, (the which in Women are commonly without any) if they have a yard of convenient largeness, if it stand well and readily, and yield seed, the Male sex hath the preheminence, and they are to be judged men. But if the conformation of both the genitals, be alike in figure, quantity and efficacy, it is thought to be equally able in both sexes: although by the opinion of Aristotle, those who have double genitals, the one of the male, the other of the female, the one of them is always perfect, the other imperfect' (Johnson, 1678).

"In the century after Paré, several treatises on hermaphroditism appeared. By the end of the next century, the eighteenth, an extensive bibliography existed. In England, James Parsons (1741) had published his painstaking inquiry. In the cellar of his London property—a combined home, anatomy school and research menagerie—the great anatomist, John Hunter (1779), had dissected a hermaphroditic cow. Throughout the eighteenth and in the first part of the nineteenth century there was much controversy among anatomists as to the analogous male and female organs of generation, and the possibility of their coexistence. Spectacular cases of hermaphrodites naturally attracted attention. Some of them became famous in the medical schools of Europe where students paid to examine them and the great masters disputed their true sex until an autopsy settled the matter. But even autopsy did not always remove every vestige of doubt. The gonads themselves were often malformed and ambiguous, and it was not until the nineteenth century was well advanced that the microscope was widely used to identify their structures.

"With the 1846 advent of surgical anaesthesia, it became feasible to use the histologic structure of a gonadal biopsy as the ultimate criterion in determining the sexual status of a hermaphrodite. In some quarters the microscope became a sort of tyrant controlling the destiny of ambiguously sexed patients. It was known that the gonads did not always permit an accurate prediction of pubertal and secondary sexual development, but in keeping with the prevailing biological outlook of the time, it was taken for granted that they would determine the erotic inclinations. Lurking in the background there seemed also to be a moralistic horror at the possibility of an error of sex leading to marriage between persons of the same sex. Franz Neugebauer (1908), a gynecologist from Warsaw, who made a comprehensive catalogue in German of references to cases of hermaphroditism within historical times, warned ominously against rearing a hermaphrodite with testes as a girl and sending her to a girls' school to become a veritable 'wolf in a sheepfold.' In doubtful cases, Neugebauer advised postponing a declaration of true sex until adolescence, or even the age of thirty, rather than make an error of sex. By that time either menstruation or ejaculation should have indicated nature's intentions.

"The wisdom crystallized in common law was not entirely forgotten, however. There had always been physicians who made their decisions after evaluating the case in its totality, paying heed to the psychological disposition of the patient and the general bodily appearances as well as the gonadal structure. Yet it has been only in the most recent decades that some physicians have advocated giving primary weight to the emotional disposition of the patient, despite patently contradictory gonadal evidence, in making a decision for or against a change of sex. Still more recently, a few physicians have advocated resolving doubts about the rearing of an infant or newly born hermaphrodite by disregarding the gonads if discordant virile or feminine development can confidently be predicted.

"The declaration of an hermaphroditic baby's sex at birth has been, and still is, a very vexed question. Most opinions have erred in the direction of being too general, for the fact is that different types of hermaphrodite develop differently. With the advance of medical knowledge it has been possible to predict and control that development more accurately, and so to make wiser decisions. But there are still some decisions which must be made with the future taken on faith.

"The only hermaphrodites who have been medically followed and treated from birth are today young adolescents or adults. Many who are still living, as well as others who have been reported during the last half century, were not treated as youngsters. In some cases their gonads belied their rearing; in others their bodily development and mature appearance contradicted their social sex. All, even those who have been under medical care, are living a paradox. They provide invaluable material for the comparative study of bodily form and physiology, rearing, and psychosexual orientation" (Money, 1952, pp. 2–10).

In 1951, Money moved from Harvard to Johns Hopkins where he has been, for the best part of half a century, a research psychoendocrinologist documenting, inter alia, the long-term outcome of the clinical treatment of hermaphrodites relative to diagnosis, prognosis, rearing, surgery, and hormonal therapy. He has published major follow-up studies in the periodical literature, for example: Money (1970); Money and Ogunro (1974); Money and Daléry (1976); Money et al. (1984); Money et al. (1985); Money et al. (1986); Money and Norman (1987). He has published also a book of long-term outcome histories under the title *Biographies of Gender and Hermaphroditism in Paired Comparisons: Clinical Supplement to the Handbook of Sexology* (1991).

In the course of the history of hermaphroditism, as briefly reviewed in the foregoing, nature was looked to as the ultimate arbiter of whether a hermaphrodite should be declared a male or a female. Over time, the criterion of what constituted nature changed. The earliest criterion was 'the kind of sex that doth prevail,' with no formula with which to evaluate prevalence in ambiguous cases. If testicles could be seen or palpated, they became the criterion, and even more so after the discovery of anesthesia in 1846 made surgical exploration feasible. In cases of uncertainty, specialists like Neugebauer advocated waiting until, at puberty or later, nature declared itself. After the sex hormones were discovered and manufactured in the early twentieth century, they also became criteria. Chromosomal sex could not be a criterion until, in mid-century, a method was discovered for counting and photographing human chromosomes. People simply assumed that the behavioral sex of hermaphrodites would fall in line with nature without attempting to find out whether it did or not. The stumbling block was that there is no single criterion of what constitutes nature that applies to every variety of hermaphroditism.

Albert Ellis (1945) tried to find out whether the behavioral sex of hermaphrodites agreed with their somatic nature or nurture (i.e., rearing). He followed the nineteenth-century three-way system (Klebs, 1876) of separating true hermaphrodites, who have both ovarian and testicular tissue, from pseudohermaphrodites, male and female, i.e., hermaphrodites with, respectively, testicular or ovarian tissue only.

This classification does not distinguish between female hermaphrodites who virilize at puberty from those who feminize; nor male hermaphrodites who feminize at puberty from those who masculinize. Although Ellis's findings were not conclusive, they did open the door to the possibility that the behavioral sex of hermaphrodites may be discordant with their biological sex and concordant with the sex in which they were reared.

In concluding, Ellis wrote: "The linkage between physical convenience and heterosexuality is relatively slight, and may easily be upset by environmental or psychological factors. . . . This is shown in the present study in the case of hermaphrodites who are psychologically reared as members of one sex though their somatic characteristics are predominantly those of the other sex." In the precomputer era of indexing services, Ellis's findings on behavioral hermaphroditism did not become widely known.

In 1950 Money began his dissertation research (quoted above), namely a review of the English language literature on hermaphroditism from 1895 to 1950, and a detailed study in person of ten cases. In 1951, after he moved from Harvard to Johns Hopkins with his colleague, Joan Hampson (later joined by her husband, John Hampson), he was able to follow dozens more hermaphroditic patients in person in the pediatric endocrine clinic. The first of its kind in the world, Lawson Wilkins' pediatric endocrine clinic was already a world-renowned center for pediatric hermaphroditism.

In January 1950, Wilkins became a codiscoverer, simultaneously with Bartter and Albright at Harvard, of the efficacy of the hormone cortisone, newly synthesized, in preventing the postnatal virilization of female hermaphrodites with CAH (congenital adrenal hyperplasia). The prenatal hormonal explanation of the etiology of this syndrome of hermaphroditism made it the first to be classifiable by etiology.

In the CAH syndrome of hermaphroditism, the gonadal sex (ovarian) is female, whereas the hormonal sex is male and masculinizing both in utero and subsequently if left untreated. This and other discordancies of sex found in the study of hermaphroditism led Money (1955) early in his career to formulate a theory of multiple variables of sex, all of which are typically concordant, though not invariably so. He wrote (1955, p. 258): "Chromosomal, gonadal, hormonal, and assigned sex, each of them interlinked, have all come under review as indices which may be used to predict an hermaphroditic person's gender—*his* or *her* outlook, demeanor, and orientation. Of the four, assigned sex stands up as the best indicator. Apparently, a person's gender role as boy or girl, man or woman, is built up cumulatively through the life experiences he encounters and through the life experiences he transacts. Gender role may be likened to a native language. Once ingrained, a person's native language may fall into disuse and be supplanted by another, but it is never entirely eradicated. So also a gender role may be changed or, resembling native bilingualism, may be ambiguous, but it may also become so deeply ingrained that not even flagrant contradictions of body functioning and morphology may displace it."

This was the first public appearance in print of the term *gender role* to refer to an individual's "outlook, demeanor, and orientation" as his or hers. Gender role was used "to signify all those things that a person says or does to disclose himself or herself as having the status of boy or man, girl or woman respectively. It includes, but is not restricted to, sexuality in the sense of eroticism" (p. 254).

It is possible for a hermaphrodite to grow up with a male gender role, even though lacking a properly formed penis for a penogenital sex role and, conversely, with a female gender role though lacking a properly formed vulva and vagina for a vaginogenital sex role. The gender role may (and usually does) incorporate the genital sex role, but in hermaphroditism and related birth defects, the two do not necessarily overlap.

Although the manifestations of gender role are behavioral and social, the dogma—namely that the development of gender role is exclusively a function of the behavioral and social history—does not logically follow. Genetic, hormonal, or morphological determinants are not excluded. "Our studies of hermaphroditism," Money wrote on behalf of his coauthors in 1955, "have pointed very strongly to the significance of life experiences encountered and transacted in the establishment of gender role and orientation. This statement is not an endorsement of a simple-minded theory of social and environmental determinism. Experiences are transacted as well as encountered—conjunction of the two terms is imperative—and encounters do not automatically dictate predictable transactions. There is ample place for novelty and the unexpected in cerebral and cognitional processes in human beings" (Money et al., 1955b, p. 309; reprinted in Money, 1986, Ch. 12).

In this same article (pp. 309–10), Money went on to say: "The evidence from examples of change or reassignment of sex in hermaphroditism, not to be presented here in detail, indicates that gender role becomes not only established but also indelibly imprinted. Though gender imprinting begins by the first birthday, the critical period is reached by about the age of eighteen months. By the age of two and one-half years, gender role is already well established."

The reassignment data were discussed in more detail in a companion paper (Money et al., 1955a, pp. 289–90; reprinted in Money, 1986, Ch. 11), as follows: "Difficult though it be for parents and others to negotiate a child's change of sex, it is even more difficult for the child, once he or she has established a conviction of gender. It is not possible to state a fixed age at which gender awareness becomes established: as in other matters pertaining to development and maturation, it is not the same age for all infants. As a general guide, it may be said that the crucial age is somewhere around eighteen months. This claim is based on a study of 11 cases of change of sex; 4 of them were changed before nine months of age and subsequently assimilated their new gender role without identifiable signs of psychologic maladaptiveness. The other 7 were changed at or after fifteen months, the latest at sixteen years, voluntarily, and the other 6 before school age. All of these 7 had assimilated their new gender role in varying degrees of pervasiveness, but all except one, who was changed at two years and three months, subsequently evidenced at least one indisputable, chronic symptom of psychopathology. Severity of the symptom varied, though in no instance reached psychotic proportions. The incidence of psychologic maladaptiveness was conspicuously less frequent among cases with no history of change of sex.

"Gender role is so well established in most children by the age of two and one-half years that it is then too late to make a change of sex with impunity. One must calculate the risk of ensuing psychologic disturbance. This risk may very occasionally seem worth taking, especially in cases of complete incongruity between assigned sex and external genital equipment, but psychiatric supervision and follow-up should never be omitted.

"After the transition from infancy to childhood—which is another of those unfixed points in the developmental sequence, occurring some time between the ages of three and one-half years and four and one-half years—it is too late to impose a change of sex. In the exceptional instance of an hermaphroditic child who has privately construed that an error of sex assignment has been made, and who has secretly half-resolved on a change of sex, successful negotiation of a change may prove possible. But our experience has led us to believe that voluntary requests for a change of sex in hermaphrodites belong to the teenage.

Though such requests are rare, they deserve serious evaluation, for they are usually a culminating attempt to resolve years of well founded perplexity and doubt."

The foregoing data on hermaphroditic sex reassignment were misconstrued by Lawrence Kohlberg in his "A Cognitive Developmental Analysis of Children's Sex Role Concepts and Attitudes" in Maccoby (1966, p. 87). He wrote that Money et al. (1957; see also 1955a) "suggest that the development of normal adult sexual behavior is contingent on having been socially assigned to a given sex before the age of three or four." In fact, Money et al. had written that "the crucial age is somewhere around eighteen months" (1955a, p. 289).

In 1980 (p. 231), Maccoby also perpetuated Kohlberg's type of error by writing: "Before the age of two-and-a-half years a child's sex identity can be changed without creating any great psychological trauma." What Money et al. (1955a, p. 289) had written was that in only one of seven cases of sex reassignment at or after age fifteen months was there no follow-up evidence of chronic psychopathology, whereas in all four cases of reassignment before age nine months psychopathology was not in evidence at follow-up. It was too late to close the barn door; the horses had fled with Kohlberg's news that the criterion age for sex assignment was three or four. For Maccoby it was age three: "After age three," she wrote, "a child's sex identity is quite fully established" (1980, p. 231).

The term *gender role* diffused slowly at first into the professional and vernacular vocabulary. A psychoanalytic working group at UCLA split *role* from *identity,* gender identity being intrapsychic and gender role being behavioral and socially prescribed, as well as socially and historically stereotyped. From this same group came the split between *Sex and Gender,* the title of Robert Stoller's 1968 book, whereupon the nature/nurture wheel had turned a full 360 degrees. It is still a popular dictum that sex is what you're born with, gender is what you become. According to this dictum, sex is nature, gender is nurture; sex is biology, gender is sociology or social construction.

Throughout its history, the doctrine of the multivariate and sequential bipotentiality of the development of gender role (or gender-identity/role, G-I/R, to be more accurate) has been anathema to the proponents of both extreme biological determinism and extreme social-constructionist determinism. Social constructionism, which deconstructs Money's hermaphroditic data as being too biological, is now firmly established in the academic departments of English and history, as well as in feminist, gay, and transgender studies.

The extremists of biological determinism also reject Money's hermaphroditic data and attack his gender theory, but on the grounds that it is not biological enough, and too inclusive of postnatal sociocultural determinants. Imperato-McGinley, for example, (Imperato-McGinley et al., 1974) attributed female-to-male change of "identity" in a Dominican Republic pedigree of male hermaphrodites with 5α-reductase deficiency exclusively to the pubertal activation of testicular testosterone (see also Money, 1976, 1981). Imperato-McGinley claimed that testosterone gave the hermaphrodites a normal "penis at twelve," whereas the medical photographs show a phallus that is small, hermaphroditically ambiguous, and abnormal (Imperato-McGinley and Peterson, 1976).

Another academic who found Money's work not biological enough was Steven Goldberg, a sociologist, who sought a prenatal hormonal underpinning in support of his theory on *The Inevitability of Patriarchy: Why the Biological Difference between Men and Women Always Produces Male Domination* (1973).

A third academic who found Money's work not biological enough was Milton Diamond, already mentioned as William C. Young's student. He published a lengthy polemic, "A Critical Review of the Ontogeny of Human Sexual Behavior," in *The Quarterly Review of Biology* (1965, pp. 147–75). In this review, he wrongly attributed to Money the independent views of Hampson and Hampson (1961) after their collaboration with Money had been completed. Diamond's specific target was the explanation of "psychosexual maturation as developing from a neutral rather than a sexual base" (p. 147). For the ensuing thirty-odd years, sexual identity and partner choice in relation to biology (nature) versus rearing (nurture) have played, in a metaphor drawn from Herman Melville's *Moby Dick,* the role of the great white whale to Dr. Diamond's Captain Ahab.

Ablatio Penis

In 1982, Diamond published a Brief Communication in the *Archives of Sexual Behavior,* titled "Sexual Identity, Monozygotic Twins Reared in Discordant Sex Roles and a BBC Follow-up."

He wrote: "It is in regard to my work in the field of sexual development and my strong belief in the force of an inherent male or female nervous system bias for the development of sexual identity and partner choice, that I was called to consult for a BBC television production on the 'twin case' " (1982, pp. 183–84).

The "twin" was one of two identical twin boys who in 1966 had been scheduled for an unnecessary circumcision at the age of seven months. For reasons undisclosed, it had been decided to use a surgical cauterizing apparatus instead of a blade. The cautery failed to remove the foreskin, so the operator stepped up the electrical current until the penis became overheated to the point of being overcooked. Over the next few days, the entire organ dried up and, like an umbilical cord, sloughed off, a case of total ablation of the penis. There was no surgical hope of reconstructing a penis. It was a no-win situation with only two possibilities. One was to rear the child as a boy without a penis together with an identical twin brother who had one. The other was to reassign the child to be reared as a girl, with feminizing genital surgery in two stages, the first in infancy, the second after puberty, following female hormonal-replacement therapy beginning at the age of puberty. The parents had been initially advised at a major medical center that nothing could be done for the child and were sent home in despair, whereas consultants in the home city were in favor of the option of sex reassignment. By coincidence the parents saw a male-to-female transexual on a network television program. Her appearance and demeanor helped them to opt for sex reassignment. The social reassignment was delayed until the late age of seventeen months. The first visit to Johns Hopkins was five months later, in 1967, for surgery, namely gonadectomy and the first (external) stage of feminizing genital reconstruction. The child was already twenty-two months of age. Since the child was not toilet-trained, surgery to create a vaginal cavity was postponed so as to avoid postsurgical fecal infection.

It was already known from the follow-up studies of hermaphroditic infants that sex reassignment delayed until as late as age eighteen months is very difficult for the parents and family, and ultimately for the child as well, to cope with. At such a late age, sex reassignment should be undertaken only as a last resort, and with provision for long-term counseling and support. If, for whatever reason, a hermaphroditic baby's sex of assignment should require reassignment, ideally it should not be delayed beyond the age of twelve months, and the earlier the better. Despite various claims to the contrary, by age two years the gender identity and role are so well on the way to being differentiated as boy or girl that it is too late to impose a sex reassignment with impunity, so that it should be done only under exceptional circumstances. This has been Money's position consistently since 1955.

The sex announced in the delivery room may need to be reannounced; but that is not the same as undergoing a sex reassignment subsequent to a neonatal sex assignment. Diamond and his coauthor, Sigmundson, confuse the two in the title of their paper, "Sex Reassignment at Birth" (1997a), when the title should be "Sex Assignment at Birth," or more properly, "Sex Reassignment at Age 22 Months."

After surgery for sex reassignment in 1967, the twin was followed at Johns Hopkins for the next seven years until the family moved to the west coast and resided there until fire destroyed their mobile home. The child was twelve. The family returned to Johns Hopkins for the last time a year later, in May 1978, when the child was thirteen. She was afflicted with a morbidly intense phobia for anything pertaining to sex education or to her sexual self-knowledge and future prospects, including the possibility of vaginoplasty. If an interview had anything to do with the topic of sex, she was unable to participate and became stricken with elective mutism. On one occasion, after finding that her mother had left the suite, she ran outside, distraught, looking for her, but without losing sight of the nurse who accompanied her and calmed her.

The twins saw Money only once more, in March 1979. That was six months later when, after lecturing at the university in their home city, he made a house call by appointment. The twins, at their parents' bidding, greeted him, talked about school, and then withdrew to their own quarters. According to the ethics of patient's rights, they could not be interrogated coercively nor forced to engage in follow-up. The case became managed exclusively and without publicity by professionals in the home city.

Another six months passed by, whereupon the family's privacy was invaded for a second time by an investigative television journalist from the BBC (British Broadcasting Corporation). Milton Diamond was the consultant. "I was asked," Diamond wrote, "to give my opposing position as a foil against which the main thesis could be argued. My argument was that an individual's biological heritage sets limits to the degree of sexual variation any person can comfortably display" (1982, p. 183).

The behavior of the BBC people was clandestine. From England, they had scheduled an appointment with Money, with the proviso that, to protect the family's privacy and confidentiality, they would not interview the twin or discuss her case on camera. Instead, they would interview another, similar male-to-female patient and her mother, both of whom had already been on national television without having been traumatized. Both had given informed consent to be interviewed on camera again.

It transpired that an investigative journalist from the BBC, having tracked down the family name and address of the twins, had gone to their home city. Failing to obtain filmed interviews, he had shadowed the twins, observing them. Although the BBC failed to obtain interviews from doctors who treated the patient, it had picked up by hearsay information that was later published, without evidence of informed consent, by Diamond (1982, pp. 183–84).

In Baltimore, one of the BBC investigators appeared in advance to interview Money in preparation for the scheduled filming. When it became evident that the twin's privacy had in fact been invaded, and that Money had been wrongly typecast as the advocate of social rearing to the exclusion of biology, he canceled his appearance on camera. Thereupon, one of the BBC film crew phoned the mother and daughter, who were to have flown into Baltimore early the next morning for their interview on camera. He fabricated a cock-and-bull story to the effect that Dr. Money was unavailable and had asked him to act on his behalf. The next morning, he and his partner met the mother and daughter at the airport and took them to a hotel where their TV camera gear was set up. They did a filmed interview and then returned the bewildered mother and daughter to the airport. The upshot of this bizarre conduct was that Money disengaged from all further contact with the BBC. The date of this incident was September 1979. The title of the program, aired in 1980, was "Open Secret."

In 1981, Money received from the *Archives of Sexual Behavior* a review copy of the manuscript in which Diamond (1982) reported what he had learned from the BBC. Money wrote a "Response to Milton Diamond" which the *Archives* did not publish. Part of this response was written so as to set the record straight: "I was interviewed by a representative of the BBC," Money wrote. "He had typecast me as the theorist of Nurture, a position alien to me. I have consistently maintained an Interactionist theory, i.e., interaction between the Genetic Code, Critical Period, and Environment. Thus I was unsuitable for the proposed role of exponent of Nurture. . . . I continue to be very strongly of the opinion that Diamond's manuscript should not be published at this time, and indeed that it contravenes the ethics of informed consent to do so, without the written informed consent of the twins. Publicity, which might be generated from the *Archives of Sexual Behavior,* about their lives could be traumatic to the twins and their parents, even to the point of suicide. They should not be exposed to the risk of becoming the victims of the Nature-Nurture argument which is, in any case, already a conceptual anachronism. The complete contribution of their lives to science will be lost."

Thereafter, the twins did not return to Johns Hopkins, and the case was regarded as being lost to follow-up, at least until such time as the twins elected otherwise.

According to Colapinto (1997, p. 94), early in 1991 Diamond "decided to redouble his efforts to locate and learn the fate of the famous twins." Eventually he made contact with Keith Sigmundson, of whom Colapinto (1997, p. 92) wrote that he "had been seeing [Diamond's] advertisements. They appeared like clockwork every year in the *American Psychiatric Society Journal* and they always said the same thing: 'Will whoever is treating the twins please report' . . ." Sigmundson is quoted by Colapinto as saying "I couldn't bring myself to answer," and that his reservations were in part "derived from colleagues who had warned him that Diamond was a 'fanatic' with an ax to grind regarding Dr. Money" (Colapinto, 1997, pp. 92, 94). Eventually, however, Sigmundson did join with Diamond in contacting the twins and their family.

The Diamond and Sigmundson (1997) follow-up report revealed that the twin whose media name would become John/Joan had undergone a second sex reassignment, socially, hormonally, and surgically. The case hit the print and television media, as well as the Internet. It was featured on page one of the *New York Times* (March 14, 1997) under the heading, "Sexual Identity Not Pliable After All, Report Says." In the media, the case became politicized as the triumph of nature over nurture and as final proof, on the basis of N=1 with no control case, of the primacy of biology over rearing.

By focusing too narrowly on the triumph of biology, the media—following in the footsteps of Diamond and Sigmundson—failed to consider other possible contributing variables related to a second sex reassignment. One needs to evaluate, for example, the possible influence of the following, particularly in the juvenile years:

- The post-traumatic effect of the pain of having a penis burned off incrementally by electrocautery, without an anesthetic, at the age of seven months.
- The effect of delay in hospitalization for gonadectomy and first

stage of feminizing genitourinary reconstruction until the advanced age of 22 months.

- The effect of having an identical twin brother with whom to compare oneself, in the sexual play of childhood, and thus to recognize the abnormal appearance, neither male nor female, of the genital self.
- The effect of knowledge of oneself as an identical twin, and of learning that identical twins are always both boys or both girls.
- The effect of hearing about one's infantile medical history from the children of adult members of the community grapevine.
- The effect of existence of a trust fund for only one twin, not both.
- The effect on the child of post-traumatic pathology in the mental health of parents, grandparents, or other relatives.
- The shock effect on the parents of misinformation about the surgical outcome of phalloplasty in sex reassignment.
- The effect of not presenting a lesbian lifestyle as a viable alternative to a second sex reassignment.
- The effect on the family of the investigative mission of intrusive outsiders, and their explanation of the purpose of their mission.

As important as is the twin's case and that of other cases like it (Bradley et al., 1998) for sexological science, it wasn't scientific impartiality that the media was after so much as the politicization of the John/Joan story. Covertly, the case was used to support the "biology is destiny" explanation of male/female differences, and to undercut the philosophy of feminism and, in the humanities and social sciences, the philosophy of social constructionism. Whether by design or coincidence, the John/Joan case was used also to schismatize the sexology community, to the detriment of both sides and their still immature science. The schism is not only unnecessary but also absurd, insofar as Diamond declares himself not to be an opponent of nature/nurture interactionism, and Money has long been known as interactionist—witness his well-known and frequently reproduced diagram of the multivariate and sequential determinants of gender-identity/role, from conception to maturity. The earliest version of this diagram dates from a 1970 teaching slide. In 1972 it was published in Money and Ehrhardt's *Man and Woman, Boy and Girl: The Differentiation and Dimorphism of Gender Identity from Conception to Maturity* (Facsimile edition, 1996). Since then, it has required periodic updating to keep abreast of the latest in genomic findings (see Figure 1, Chapter 8, p. 126). For further explication, see Money's *Principles of Developmental Sexology* (1997) and *Reinterpreting the Unspeakable* (1994).

Intersex Constituency

In the year before the publication of the John/Joan case, Diamond (1996; see also Zucker, 1996) found a constituency in the recently formed "Intersex Society of North America" (ISNA), whose newsletter is titled "Hermaphrodites with Attitude." A major premise in the ISNA credo is that surgery performed on intersexed babies constitutes genital mutilation and should be postponed until after they are old enough to give informed consent. Then they can consent to surgery and to the sex in which they should belong. ISNA adopted John Money as a primary scapegoat, in view of the policies for neonatal treatment of hermaphroditism he had enunciated in his *Sex Errors of the Body and Related Syndromes: A Guide to Counseling Children, Adolescents, and Their Families* (1994, second edition). ISNA's policy is to be militantly activist, to create media attention, and coincidentally to take hermaphroditism out of the closet of taboo into public discourse.

The etiological causes and varieties of hermaphroditism are manifold. So also are the possible discordancies among the several variables of sex. These possible discordancies are such as to defy Diamond's attempt to reconcile his position of biological determinism with ISNA's position on surgical nonintervention irrespective of the biological determinants of sex. There is no single criterion of the biological sex of hermaphrodites; their biological sex is mixed. In their second 1997 publication, the "Management of Intersexuality: Guidelines for Dealing with Intersexuality," Diamond and Sigmundson tangled with this issue, while adhering to ISNA's policy of surgical nonintervention in infancy. "Underlying our guidelines," they wrote, "is the key belief that the patients themselves must be involved in any decision as to something so crucial to their lives. We accept that not everyone will welcome this opportunity or these suggestions" (p. 1046). This "key belief" implies raising a newborn hermaphrodite as an "it," until it is old enough to give informed consent to intervention to be a he or she—which the idiom of the English language simply will not permit. Everyone in America is addressed as either "he" or "she," never as "it."

There is no point in rewinding the calendar to the era when no intervention was available, and families kept hermaphroditic offspring in seclusion, provided they had not died in infancy. Diamond and Sigmundson published their guidelines too precipitously, without sufficient pediatric hands-on experience of intersexuality in the clinic.

In the aftermath of Diamond and Sigmundson's (1997) report on the twin case, the media concatenated the John/Joan case and the ISNA stories into a modern-day biomedical version of David and Goliath. Plucky little David from faraway Hawaii confronted the big Goliath of the medical establishment, The Johns Hopkins Hospital, in Baltimore. The most offensive media article was an unsigned editorial in the tabloid *New York Post,* dated December 8, 1997. It begins with an inflammatory assertion: "Nearly 15,000 American children have had their genitalia mutilated in the last quarter century, not by perverts, but by trained surgeons. The practice is known as 'sex reassignment.'" This false assertion is based on Diamond and Sigmundson's linguistic trickery of using "sex reassignment" instead of "sex assignment." In cases of hermaphroditic, ambiguously deformed sex organs at birth that are neither male nor female, it is necessary to determine the sex of assignment, not reassignment. The *New York Post* editorial as a whole is defamatory, slanderous, and legally actionable for libel.

An eighteen-page feature story by John Colapinto in *Rolling Stone* magazine (December 11, 1997) is also offensive, as well as factually inaccurate in many places. It follows the example set by Diamond and Sigmundson by not referencing or quoting any of Money's scores of publications on hermaphroditism since 1972, including the volume of *Biographies of Gender and Hermaphroditism in Paired Comparisons* (1991), already mentioned, and the book *Gendermaps: Social Constructionism, Feminism, and Sexosophical History* (1995).

The magazine *New York,* in its issue of December 14th, 1997, reported (p. 78) that "*Rolling Stone*'s story on John/Joan, the boy who became a girl who became a man, won't hit the stands until next week, but it's already attracting attention on Publisher's Row. Although famous in the medical literature, John/Joan had never spoken to a writer before opening up to author John Colapinto. ICM agent Lisa Bankoff sold Colapinto's book proposal to HarperCollins last Thursday for around $450,000, industry insiders say. Continuing the 'which came first' marketing plan, Colapinto's handlers plan to send the magazine around Hollywood next week, in the hopes of lining up a director for the movie version of the yet-to-be-written book." In the market place, it is said that money talks—but it does not always guarantee the truth.

Despite the rapprochement between Diamond and ISNA, there is an Augustinian/Pelagian incompatibility between the two. Diamond is Augustinian, with biological sex as the predestinarian principle of redemption. ISNA is Pelagian, with moral choice as the contingent principle of redemption. Diamond's predestinarian biology excludes social constructionism. It presumes that, in hermaphroditism, biological sex can routinely be neonatally divined, and that the outcome of both mental and bodily development can be prophesied. This position is acceptable to Reiner (1997a,b) in commentaries on Diamond and Sigmundson. However, in hermaphroditism, there is no single unified biological criterion of sex (for example, genetic sex) upon which to make and guarantee such a prophesy in all cases.

In ISNA's noninterventionist policy, there is no doctrine of biological determinism, only the doctrine that a hermaphroditic baby can exist as an it, neither male nor female, until old enough to sign its own informed consent to remain unchanged or to be socially constructed with surgery and/or hormones to become a he or she. However, a hermaphroditic baby does not grow up in a gender vacuum as a genderless it, but more likely as a self-defined freak. The very process of growing up swings the gender pendulum one way or the other, and not always predictably.

The point of commonality between Diamond and ISNA is the doctrine that hermaphroditic juveniles and adolescents should not be coerced into living as either one sex or the other. Maybe they both agree with Lord Coke's sixteenth-century dictum that hermaphrodites "be either male or female according to the kind of sex which doth prevail." This same dictum applies also to cases, like that of John/Joan, of traumatic loss of the penis. The "sex which doth prevail" is variable, as the case of Bradley et al. (1998) shows. In some instances, female has prevailed.

Sexology is still not able to tell Lord Coke how to define the sex that doth prevail, nor to predict it in babyhood. An adventitious outcome of the publicity accorded the John/Joan case may be greater public awareness of hermaphroditism and greater funding for sexological research. Alternatively, it may have a chilling effect in preventing the publication of other cases with quite different outcomes. That certainly is the case at Johns Hopkins, where the rules of confidentiality and informed consent, strictly applied, forbid the publication of detailed sexological biographies, including that of the voluminously documented John/Joan case, as well as other cases of ablatio penis and of congenital 46,XY micropenis reared female. Yet another adventitiously negative outcome might be that managed-care companies, echoing ISNA, declare treatment of hermaphroditic birth defects to be unnecessary cosmetic surgery, elective and not covered by insurance. Diamond may have opened a Pandora's box that he knows not of.

REFERENCES

Angier, N. (1997). "Sexual identity not pliable after all, report says." *New York Times* (March 14), pp. A1, A18.

Barry, W. J. (1847). *New York Journal of Medicine.* Reprinted in S. H. Harris, "Case of doubtful sex." *American Journal of Medical Sciences* 14:121–24.

Bradley, S. J., Oliver, G. D., Chernick, A. B., and Zucker, K. J. (1998). "Experiment of nurture: Ablatio penis at 2 months, sex reassignment at 7 months, and a psychosexual follow-up in young adulthood." *Pediatrics* 102(1):323–67.

Colapinto, J. (1997). "The true story of John/Joan." *Rolling Stone* (December 11), pp. 55ff.

Diamond, M. (1965). "A critical evaluation of the ontogeny of human sexual behavior." *Quarterly Review of Biology* 40:147–75.

———. (1982). "Sexual identity, monozygotic twins reared in discordant sex roles and a BBC follow-up." *Archives of Sexual Behavior* 11:181–86.

———. (1996). "Prenatal predispositions and the clinical management of some pediatric conditions." *Journal of Sex and Marital Therapy* 22:139–47.

Diamond, M., and Sigmundson, H. K. (1997a). "Sex reassignment at birth: Long-term review and clinical implications." *Archives of Pediatrics and Adolescent Medicine,* 151:298–304.

———. (1997b). "Management of intersexuality: Guidelines for dealing with persons with ambiguous genitalia." *Archives of Pediatrics and Adolescent Medicine* 151:1046–50.

Ellis, A. (1945). "The sexual psychology of human hermaphrodites." *Psychosomatic Medicine* 7:108–25.

Ellis, H. (1920). *Sexual Inversion.* Vol. II of *Studies in the Psychology of Sex.* Philadelphia: F. A. Davis.

Goldberg, S. (1973). *The Inevitability of Patriarchy.* New York: Morrow.

Hampson, J. L., and Hampson, J. G. (1961). "The ontogenesis of sexual behavior in man." In *Sex and Internal Secretions* (W. C. Young, ed.). Baltimore: Williams and Wilkins.

Hunter, J. (1779). "Account of a free martin." *Philosophical Transactions.* Reproduced in *Observations of Certain Parts of the Animal Oeconomy,* London, 1792 and 1838 (2nd ed.).

Imperato-McGinley, J., Guerrero, L., Gautier, T., and Peterson, R. E. (1974). "Steroid 5α-reductase deficiency in man: An inherited form of male pseudohermaphroditism." *Science* 186:1213–15.

Imperato-McGinley, J., and Peterson, R. E. (1976). "Male hermaphroditism: The complexities of male phenotypic development." *American Journal of Medicine* 61:251–72.

Johnson, T., trans. (1678). *The Works of that Famous Chirurgeon Ambrose Parey.* Book 25, Chapter 4, "Of Hermaphrodties or Scrats." London.

Kennedy, H. (1988). *Ulrichs: The Life and Works of Karl Heinrich Ulrichs, Pioneer of the Modern Gay Movement.* Boston: Alyson Publications.

Klebs, E. (1876). *Handbuch der pathologischen Anatomie.* 1.Band, Zweite Abtheilung, 718. Berlin: August Hirschwald.

Kohlberg, L. A. (1966). "A cognitive-developmental analysis of children's sex-role concepts and attitudes." In *The Development of Sex Differences* (E. E. Maccoby, ed.). Stanford, CA: Stanford University Press.

Krafft-Ebing, R. von. (1931). *Psychopathia Sexualis* (trans. F. J. Rebman, revised twelfth German edition, 1901). Chicago: Logan Brothers.

Lombroso, C. (1972). *Criminal Man* (trans. of *L'uomo delinquente,* 1876). Montclair, NJ: Patterson Smith.

Maccoby, E. E. (1980). *Social Development: Psychological Growth and the Parent-Child Relationship.* New York: Harcourt Brace Jovanovich.

Money, J. (1952). *Hermaphroditism: An Inquiry into the Nature of a Human Paradox.* Doctoral dissertation, Harvard University Library. University Microfilms Library Services, Ann Arbor, MI 48106 (1967).

———. (1955). "Hermaphroditism, gender and precocity in hyperadrenocorticism: Psychologic findings." *Bulletin of The Johns Hopkins Hospital* 96:253–64.

———. (1970). "Matched pairs of hermaphrodites: Behavioral biology of sexual differentiation from chromosomes to gender identity." *Engineering and Science* 33:34–39.

———. (1976). "Gender identity and hermaphroditism." *Science* 191:872.

———. (1981). "The development of sexuality and eroticism in humankind." *Quarterly Review of Biology* 56:379–404.

———. (1985). *The Destroying Angel: Sex, Fitness and Food in the Legacy of Degeneracy Theory, Graham Crackers, Kellogg's Corn Flakes and American Health History.* Amherst, NY: Prometheus Books.

———. (1986). *Venuses Penuses: Sexology, Sexosophy, and Exigency Theory.* Amherst, NY: Prometheus Books.

———. (1991). *Biographies of Gender and Hermaphroditism in Paired*

Comparisons: Clinical Supplement to the Handbook of Sexology. Amsterdam: Elsevier.

———. (1993). *The Adam Principle: Genes, Genitals, Hormones, and Gender—Selected Readings in Sexology.* Amherst, NY: Prometheus Books.

———. (1994a). *Sex Errors of the Body and Related Syndromes: A Guide to Counseling Children, Adolescents, and Their Families,* 2nd ed. Baltimore: Paul H. Brookes.

———. (1994b). *Reinterpreting the Unspeakable: Human Sexuality 2000.* New York: Continuum.

———. (1995). *Gendermaps: Social Constructionism, Feminism, and Sexosophical History.* New York: Continuum.

———. (1997). *Principles of Developmental Sexology.* New York: Continuum.

Money, J., and Daléry, J. (1976). "Iatrogenic homosexuality: Gender identity in seven 46,XX chromosomal females with hyperadrenocortical hermaphroditism born with a penis, three reared as boys, four reared as girls." *Journal of Homosexuality* 1:357–71.

Money, J., Devore, H., and Norman, B. F. (1986). "Gender identity and gender transposition: Longitudinal outcome study of 32 male hermaphrodites assigned as girls." *Journal of Sex and Marital Therapy* 12: 165–81.

Money, J., and Ehrhardt, A. A. (1972). *Man and Woman, Boy and Girl: The Differentiation and Dimorphism of Gender Identity from Conception to Maturity.* Baltimore, Johns Hopkins University Press. Facsimile reprint edition, New York: Jason Aronson, 1996.

Money, J., Hampson, J. G., and Hampson, J. L. (1955a). "Hermaphroditism: Recommendations concerning assignment of sex, change of sex, and psychologic management." *Bulletin of The Johns Hopkins Hospital* 97:284–300.

———. (1955b). "An examination of some basic sexual concepts: The evidence of human hermaphroditism." *Bulletin of The Johns Hopkins Hospital* 97:301–19.

———. (1957). "Imprinting and the establishment of gender role." *Archives of Neurology and Psychiatry* 77:333–36.

Money, J., and Lamacz, M. (1989). *Vandalized Lovemaps: Paraphilic Outcome of Seven Cases in Pediatric Sexology.* Amherst, NY: Prometheus Books.

Money, J., Lehne, G., and Pierre-Jerome, F. (1985). "Micropenis: Gender, erotosexual coping strategy, and behavioral health in nine pediatric cases followed to adulthood." *Comprehensive Psychiatry* 26:29–42.

Money, J., and Norman, B. F. (1987). "Gender identity and gender transposition: Longitudinal outcome study of 24 male hermaphrodites assigned as boys." *Journal of Sex and Marital Therapy* 13:75–92.

Money, J., and Ogunro, C. (1974). "Behavioral sexology: Ten cases of genetic male intersexuality with impaired prenatal and pubertal androgenization." *Archives of Sexual Behavior* 3:181–205.

Money, J., Schwartz, M., and Lewis, V. G. (1984). "Adult erotosexual status and fetal hormonal masculinization and demasculinization: 46,XX congenital virilizing adrenal hyperplasia and 46,XY androgen-insensitivity syndrome compared." *Psychoneuroendocrinology* 9:405–14.

Neugebauer, F. L. von. (1908). *Hermaphroditismus beim Menschen.* Leipzig: Werner Klinkhardt.

Parsons, J. (1741). *A Mechanical and Critical Inquiry into the Nature of Hermaphrodites*; Philosophical Transactions, Number 41; and 8vo, London.

Phoenix, C. H., Goy, R. W., Gerall, A. A. and Young, W. C. (1959). "Organizing action of prenatally administered testosterone propionate on the tissues mediating mating behavior in the female guinea pig." *Endocrinology* 65:369–82.

Reiner, W. (1997a). "To be male or female—That is the question." *Archives of Pediatrics and Adolescent Medicine* 151:224–25.

———. (1997b). "Assignment in the neonate with intersex inadequate genitalia." *Archives of Pediatrics and Adolescent Medicine,* 151: 1044–45.

Stoller, R. J. (1968). *Sex and Gender.* New York: Science House.

Ulrichs, K. H. (Numa Numantius). (1864). *Forschungen über das Räthsel der mannmännlichen Liebe* (*Inquiry into the Enigma of Man-to-Man Love*). Vol. 2, *"Inclusa": Anthropologische Studien über Mannmännliche Geschlechtsliebe, Naturwissenschaftlicher Theil: Nachweis das einer Classe von Männlich gebauten Individuen Geschlechtsliebe zu Männern geschlechtlich angeboren ist* (*"Inclusa": Anthropological Studies of Man-to-Man Sexual Love, Natural Science Section; Proof of a Class of Male-Bodied Individuals for Whom Sexual Love for Men Is Sexually Inborn*). Leipzig, Selbstverlag der Verfassers, in Commission bei Heinrich Matthes.

Westphal, K. F. O. (1869). "Die Conträre Sexualempfindung." *Archiv für Psychiatrie und Nervenkrankheiten* 2:73–108.

Young, W. C., ed. (1961). *Sex and Internal Secretions.* Baltimore: Williams and Wilkins.

Zucker, K. J. (1996). "Commentary on Diamond's 'Prenatal disposition and the clinical management of some pediatric conditions.' " *Journal of Sex and Marital Therapy* 22:148–60.

Part Five

Pediatric Psychoendocrinology

PART FIVE

PEDIATRIC PSYCHOENDOCRINOLOGY

I. INTRODUCTION: PEDIATRIC PSYCHOENDOCRINOLOGY

Psychoendocrinology is the study of the relationship between, on the one hand, the hormones of the endocrine system and, on the other hand, the manifest performance and communication of the system designated as the mind/brain when it is regarded not as dualistic, but as unitary and synchronous. The influence of hormones on mind/brain is, in the present state of the art, more accessible to investigation than is the influence of mind/brain on hormones. A classic example of the latter is the syndrome of psychosocial growth retardation induced by child abuse, and treated by rescue from abuse.

Originally published as "Hormones, Hormonal Anomalies and Psychological Health Care," Chapter 19 in M. S. Kappy, R. M. Blizzard, and C. J. Migeon, eds., *Wilkins The Diagnosis and Treatment of Endocrine Disorders in Childhood and Adolescence, Fourth Edition* (Springfield, IL: Charles C Thomas, 1994).

Psychoendocrinology is both experimental and clinical. Experimental psychoendocrinology cannot, for ethical reasons, be imposed on human beings. Clinical syndromes, the so-called experiments of nature, are the source of data in classical psychoendocrinology. Pediatric clinical psychoendocrinology had its beginnings as a subspecialty in 1951, under the aegis of Lawson Wilkins, the first pediatric endocrinologist.

Methodologically, the data of clinical psychoendocrinology are obtained in a manner analogous to those of the pediatric endocrine work-up (Money, 1986a). That is to say, there is a systematic protocol, a formal Schedule of Inquiry. It covers all the required items and topics. For each topic, inquiry begins open-endedly and not with a true-false or multiple-choice type of interrogation (which might come later).

For example, an open-ended question about composition of the household is preferable to a question about number of siblings, for it permits inclusion of cognate as well as agnate offspring, those born of parent-child incest, and those who are adopted, fostered, or invited members of the household. Interrogatory questioning, oral or written, forces the omission of qualifying provisos and personal idiosyncrasies, some of which may be highly relevant.

The open-ended inquiry, with or without an interrogatory, is audiotaped—if not in full, then in summary, topic by topic, with the participation of the patient. It is transcribed and indexed so as to be readily available for evaluation whenever numerical ratings or scores need to be assigned.

Testing, as for IQ, is done if the test is constructed so that the score is earned directly from the response itself, and not at second hand from personal ratings or estimates of degree of intensity or magnitude on a scale that has no absolute zero.

Evaluations that require ratings of oneself or others are of doubtful value. They are misconstrued as being "objective tests." They are, in fact, subjective, insofar as the criterion standard is individually subjective and not the same for each respondent. Greater consistency is obtained if the raw data are evaluated by professionals trained to apply the same criterion standard to each member of a group of patients or subjects.

II. COUNSELING: THE AGENDA

A. Know Your Syndrome

The injunction "know your syndrome" applies to the counselor. Each syndrome has its own psychology as well as its own genetics, endocrinology, symptoms, prognosis, and so forth. Knowing the syndrome expedites counseling, for it anticipates the agenda that should eventually be covered. Some items on the agenda are more syndrome-specific than others; they are dealt with in separate sections in what follows. Other items apply across syndromes, and they are dealt with here.

B. Explaining the Syndrome

In the age of the Freedom of Information Act, the ancient tradition of medical secrecy and evasiveness has fallen by the wayside. Patients, even those who are minors, have the right to know as much as they can comprehend of the details of their diagnosis and prognosis, as well as the rationale and expected outcome of treatment. So also, of course, do their parents.

Withholding information from minors has been justified as being ostensibly for their own good and to spare them the trauma of knowing. In actuality, it is to spare not them but their elders the trauma of communication. Minors are left with the trauma of ignorance and the possibility to expand it into phantasmagorias of apprehension. Even at a young age, children despise being excluded from what is being told to their parents and not shared with them. It renders them dependent on surreptitious sources of information, as in eavesdropping or finding and reading their unguarded medical charts. In today's world, medical information is diffused on television talk shows and science programs and in the print media, as well as in high school and college texts. Many patients learn something about their own syndrome from these sources. Others do active library research as they become more academically sophisticated, and some do specialty medical or biomedical training.

Like their parents, children need counseling in the rehearsal of words and phrases that explain their condition without stigmatization and loss of self-respect. The rehearsal may be as simple as having an answer for siblings or schoolmates asking about the reason for a hospital admission, or an excuse from participation in school sports. Or it may be as complex as giving a correct diagnosis to a school nurse or a physician attending to a medical emergency. Under some circumstances, being able to give accurate information may be life-saving. In the case of congenital adrenal hyperplasia (CAH), for example, a child in a salt-losing adrenocortical crisis may literally save his/her own life by being able to insist on increased salt intake and increased cortisol dosage.

Vocabulary used routinely in the medical clinic may be extremely traumatizing to patients and their parents—nosological terms like *mongolism* (now respectabilized as Down syndrome), *gargoylism, leprechaunism,* and *bird-headed dwarfism,* for example. Even the term *dwarfism* is anathema to many "Little People." So also is *hermaphroditism* to those who can with greater dignity refer to themselves as having a birth defect of the sex organs.

When counseling, therefore, one searches for and systematizes ways of saying and explaining things so that the effect is more likely to be detraumatizing, in order to avoid the genesis of secondary psychopathology. This principle applies even when the outlook is not propitious as, for example, in cases of multiple congenital defects, including the prospect of severe pedagogical handicap (Money and Norman, 1988). For most people, it is easier to negotiate the known than to grope in the darkness of the unknown. For parents and patients alike, to be able to join forces with the counselor and physician in the attack on the syndrome, or on one of its undesirable side effects, is to avoid the intolerable burden of feeling implicitly accused and blameworthy for having it. To illustrate: a girl with CAH who discovers at adolescence that she is romantically and erotically attracted only to other girls finds relief in discovering that to have a history of that syndrome, with or without treatment, is to have an increased chance of a bisexual or homosexual orientation (Money et al., 1984).

C. Compliancy

In counseling, explanations of a syndrome and of the timing and rationale of its treatment will be reiterated in follow-up. For children, reiterations are absolutely necessary. Even as adults, patients will, like their parents before them, need continuing-education courses. Recall fades according to not only the principle of disuse, but also the principle of inexistence, namely that which is no longer recalled no longer exists. This is the principle at the basis of the high prevalence of noncompliancy.

Noncompliancy affects parents responsible for the medications and appointments of young patients, and later it affects the patients themselves. Its commonest form is irregularity in following instructions—in taking medications, for example—without complete discontinuance. The consequences of this type of noncompliancy may be insidious in onset, or else so rapid and so severe, even life-threatening, that they induce an immediate resumption of compliancy. Noncompliancy with hormonal-replacement therapy in Addison's disease and other cases of total adrenocortical insufficiency is one example, and another is noncompliancy in insulin administration producing a diabetic crisis, notorious in adolescents with diabetes mellitus.

Prolonged noncompliancy occurs amongst those who are on hormonal-substitution therapy indefinitely and who experience no immediate dire consequence when medication is discontinued. Agonadal and hypogonadal males completely dependent on testosterone replacement are at risk for this type of noncompliancy. So also are adolescents, both boys and girls, with CAH. For girls, two long-term consequences are irreversible virilization of the voice and growth of facial and body hair, whereas a short-term reversible consequence is amenorrhea.

Among CAH patients in whom noncompliancy cannot be unequivocally established, the challenge in counseling is that some are probably compliant, whereas others almost certainly are not. Among the latter are those whose noncompliancy is contingent on a masculinized gender-identity/role of which the erotic component is that of a lesbian. In such a case, noncompliancy is discordant with the physician's plan of treatment, but concordant with the patient's personal schema and lifestyle.

In the extreme instance, noncompliancy changes its name and becomes discontinuance of treatment. A woman with Turner syndrome, for example, may find no further value in estrogen-replacement therapy. A hypogonadal male with extreme physical deformity may discontinue testosterone-replacement therapy and return to a state of sexual inertia rather than be tormented by love unrequited. A woman with hypogonadotropic hypopituitarism may find sex-hormone therapy incompatible with her dedication to a religious way of life.

In some cases, discontinuance or avoidance of treatment masks a genuine phobia, derived possibly from earlier medical experience. Phobic avoidance of injection needles, of anesthesia, of hospital elevators, of genital examinations, of medical photography, of being displayed to an audience, of being asked about taboo sexual topics—all may be of such extreme intensity, especially in childhood, as to result in depriving the patient of essential and life-saving procedures, unless the taboo is breached first.

Noncompliancy may be related to Munchausen syndrome, a condition of dissociation or dual personality. One personality is that of obedient compliancy, the other that of noncompliant disobedience. The latter furtively engenders the symptoms for which the former pleads for assistance.

In pediatric Munchausen syndrome by proxy (Money, 1986b), it is a parent, most commonly the mother, who has a dual personality. One is the personality of self-sacrificing motherhood, the other the personality of the sacrificial priestess, sacrificing her own child as an atonement for her own sins. In one case, that of a child intensively worked up for hypothalamic-pituitary disease, it was finally discovered that the mother had been force-feeding the girl since early infancy and had authored an entirely fictitious medical history for her. She dreamed repetitively of seeing the child dead in a pink-lined coffin, surrounded by the scent of death lilies. She herself had grown up with a schizophrenic mother. Despite the semblance of impostoring, Munchausen syndrome alone and by proxy both are masquerades of psychosis.

D. Hereditary Transmission

For some parents, the ultimate question of causal responsibility is genetic, which, in popular genetics, means: "Was it on his side of the family, or mine—my side or hers?"

Genetic counseling goes beyond the provision of mathematical probability and epidemiological statistics to include what may be termed the psychological cost-effectiveness of another pregnancy. For the parents, the issue is the effect of another affected baby on themselves and their other children and, of course, on the baby, should it have the syndrome.

For some couples, genetic counseling translates into moral decisions about prenatal diagnosis and abortion of an affected conceptus.

For others, it translates into religious injunctions regarding the morality of using birth control versus the morality of abstaining from sexual intercourse altogether, or of having unprotected intercourse and counting on the power of prayer to decide the outcome.

Some parents become linguistically paralyzed and are unable to talk not only to relatives and siblings, but also to the patients themselves, regarding matters of heredity. Provided transmission is not fortuitous, but is predictable, as, e.g., a Mendelian recessive, then the physician or counselor must take over the responsibility for appropriate explanation.

Many patients and their siblings grasp the concept of a heterozygous carrier more readily if the term is changed to "hidden" carrier. Correspondingly, homozygous carrier is changed to "open" carrier. With these terms, siblings of patients with a history of treated CAH are able to understand how the matching of two members of a kinship increases the chance that each will be a hidden carrier and that some of their progeny will be open carriers of the syndrome. Correspondingly, it increases the chance that a patient with the syndrome will marry a hidden carrier and produce affected progeny.

Matching with a stranger from outside the kinship does not exclude the possibility that the stranger will be a hidden carrier. Most people do not, however, expect to subject their boyfriends or girlfriends to genetic screening. The pairbonding of lovers is contingent on far more than Mendelian genetics, especially when a syndrome is relatively benign, as is CAH.

In weighing the pros and cons of genetic transmission, young couples at risk must be counseled to avoid compounding their risk by not preparing, before pregnancy, for the potential medical costs of having an affected offspring. In the United States, which lacks national health insurance, being prepared means having private health-insurance coverage before pregnancy. Otherwise, medical expenses may spell financial ruin for those who are not already indigent.

It is the siblings who benefit from genetic counseling in families affected with 46,XY androgen-insensitivity. In this syndrome, genetic transmission is in the maternal line as an X-linked recessive trait. If a patient's fertile sister carries the mutation on one of her X chromosomes, and if this X matches with a Y-bearing sperm, then the XY progeny will not be a morphologic male, but an androgen-insensitive morphologic female.

E. Confidentiality

In some families, genetic probabilities of transmission may translate into questions about the morality of breaking the code of the patient's privacy in order to advise siblings or other relatives of the details of a syndrome and its heritability within the kinship. Yet, advanced information may be of inestimable value in the delivery room if another baby is born with the same syndrome—as has proved to be the case with respect to birth defects of the sex organs. The ideal, therefore, is to have privacy shared only with designated persons within the family. Such privacy is understood by many children as family medical secrets. For the patient, the great advantage of shared privacy is the sharing of confidentiality and trust. There is someone to talk to, not the silence and solitude of being excommunicated.

For the patient's siblings, there is also an advantage of shared privacy. It gives them an understanding of why they are treated differently—neglected, as they may perceive it—whereas the affected child gets too much attention and is taken away to the city and the hospital while they are left at home.

In the case of a newborn baby with ambiguous genitalia, it is virtually inconceivable that the older siblings can be kept ignorant of a sex reannouncement, if such occurs. It is obligatory to take them into confidence as guardians of the family medical secret. They need counseling in how to deal with it among their peers and in the community, and they need counseling on sex reannouncement, with proof that it is not arbitrary and that it will not happen to them.

For those infants whose diagnosis becomes publicly known, there is always the possibility that future gossip will prevail over privacy. It is not possible to obliterate one's proverbial footprints in the snow. This is especially so in cases of birth defects of the sex organs, if parents live with the illusion that news of the defect in the community will be self-obliterating. Often it is better for them to take members of the community into confidence, to give an adequate medical explanation, and then to request respect for the child's future privacy (Money et al., 1969). Gossip ceases when nothing remains to be gossiped about. There is no guarantee against an information leakage in the future, however. It is wise, therefore, not to play an evasive game of secrets, but to give a child conceptually age-graded knowledge of his/her condition. The child who already knows is better prepared against subsequent information leakages.

In the juvenile years, children are especially vulnerable to invasion of privacy if the evidence of their endocrine anomaly is not on view when they are clothed. Bodily exposure in association with the sexual rehearsal play of normal infancy and early childhood, or in the shower room of the school gymnasium or sports field in the later juvenile years, may draw attention to the self and bring ridicule. So also may the conspicuous avoidance of nude exposure.

Information shared in confidence, even with a best friend, may backfire and become publicly disseminated. This problem becomes particularly acute in teenage or later, if the best friend is also a lover and potential spouse. Then it is wise to share information from the medical history too late rather than too soon, for the strength of the bond of being in love overcomes obstacles. Even if a relationship is short-lived, developmentally it is in accordance with the poetic wisdom of "better to have loved and lost, than never to have loved at all." In a society in which some syndromes are engulfed by secrecy and shame, as in the case of syndromes related to sex and the genitalia, there are no support groups for those affected, and no philanthropies to support research and provide public education and enlightenment. Each newly affected baby or child is metaphorically closeted in an isolation chamber. A few have escaped by going public on television and have earned respect and admiration, not repudiation and avoidance. Subjectively, they have gained the inner freedom of having nothing to hide and nothing by which to be betrayed.

F. Infertility

In those syndromes in which reproduction is impaired or in which there is, or will be, corrective gonadectomy, infertility counseling must be provided.

It is traumatizing to tell a child that he or she will not be able to have children. The precise statement should be about the prospects of procreation or pregnancy. Information should be given about alternate means of forming a family, including strategies other than pregnancy. Having children will be possible by adoption; by "instant" parenthood (i.e., by marrying a partner who is a single parent); by donor sperm from the sperm bank; by donor egg and in vitro fertilization—whichever may apply.

The image of being able to achieve normalcy shares the power of its actual achievement. It is normalizing for a girl with no uterus to know that there is an authentic case on record from New Zealand of a woman who delivered a normal daughter by Caesarean section nine months after she had had a total hysterectomy (Jackson et al., 1980). Her own fertilized egg had survived the operation and attached itself to the wall of the small intestine.

The feasibility and reality of pregnancy in cases of pure gonadal dysgenesis will also provide a normalizing image to 46,XY girls and women. A patient with pure gonadal dysgenesis is a 46,XY woman with a hypoplastic uterus and streak gonads. Using in vitro fertilization, with a donated ovum and sperm from the husband, delivery of healthy babies has been possible (Frydman et al., 1988; Sauer et al., 1989).

G. Sex Education

Age-graded knowledge of procreation and sex is conceptually a prerequisite to counseling about fertility, treatment for birth defects of the sex organs, or pubertal precocity or delay. For these children, as well as for others, assistance with sex education is often needed, as even the best-intentioned parents have difficulty in breaking the taboo that forbids explicit exchange of information on intercourse and orgasm across the generation gap. This may be achieved if parents and child each have a private session simultaneously, followed by a session shared with one another and with participating counselors.

In early childhood, the sex-education story is told with self-defining terms and illustrations: the baby egg, baby nest, and baby canal; the penis that fits into the canal, and the sperms that it pumps out; the swimming race of sperms, two or three hundred million of them; only one sperm wins the race; it joins with the egg; the drama of gestation; and delivery through the baby canal.

Especially in cases of birth defect of the sex organs, it is a concern of parents that their child will grow up to have a normal sex life. The closer they come to sharing the child's own sexual concerns, explicitly and in a relationship of trust and confidence, the more they will facilitate the realization of normalcy. Explicitness pertains not only to "eggs, sperms, and menstrual periods," but also to falling in love and going steady; to erotic imagery in dreams and fantasies; to being gay, straight, or in-between; to masturbation, foreplay, and coition; to contraception and abortion; to protection against sexually transmitted diseases; and to the terrible contemporary dilemma of how to share sexual activity with a partner without exposure to and premature death from AIDS.

III. Sex Assignment and Sex-Organ Birth Defect

A. Multivariate Conceptualization

Rather than submit an insurance-reimbursement claim bearing the term "hermaphroditism" or "intersex," some parents will forfeit benefits to lessen the risk of an information leakage through the claims department at their workplace. The nomenclature of hermaphroditism in the medical record of a genetic male assigned and being reared as a girl creates a semantic trauma for parents and patient alike, as do all male-related terms in the description of the genitalia. The same applies to words denoting genetic female in a hermaphroditic child being raised as a boy. In both instances, the trauma emanates from the conceptualization of sex difference as a dichotomous absolute—an all-or-none antithesis of either male or female. In contrast to some ethnic cultures (Herdt and Davidson, 1988), our Western culture does not recognize sexual indeterminacy, except as a stigma.

Abnormal sex differentiation in utero demonstrates that the accurate conceptualization of sex is not dichotomous but multivariate (Money, 1952, 1985; Money et al., 1955), which is the way it was redefined in the 1965 edition of *Dorland's Medical Dictionary.* Parents and older patients are reassured by actually reading the definition. In normal development, all the variables are concordantly either male or female. In hermaphroditic development, by contrast, one or more of the variables is discordant with the other. Thus, the external appearance may be male and the internal reproductive anatomy female, or vice versa, and either or both may be discordant with the chromosomal sex.

B. Chromosomal Sex

In counseling the parents of a newborn hermaphroditic baby, and the older patient also, one may say that, chromosomally, there are some girls and women who are 47,XXX or 45,XO, not to mention mosaics, and some who are 46,XY. Correspondingly, some boys and men are 47,XXY, and a few are 46,XX. In other words, females cannot without exception count on being chromosomally 46,XX, nor can males count on being 46,XY. To be able to refer to oneself or one's child as a 46,XY girl or a 46,XX boy will confer self-respect and dignity. It detraumatizes the otherwise brutal discovery of being, according to the unguarded secrets of the medical chart, ostensibly a daughter who is really a male, or ostensibly a son who is really a female. In the new era of mapping and sequencing the genome, medical records are less likely to contain such an unguarded secret, insofar as an error of the genomic sequence responsible for hermaphroditism is not classified as being either a male or a female error.

C. Gonadal Sex

Initially, one talks about gonads or sex glands, the embryological history of their differentiation from the early bipotential phase, and how they may differentiate as tissue that is neither testis nor ovary, but so-called gonadal streaks. One talks also of mixed ovotestis, and of gonads that develop discordantly, so that their appearance is ovarian instead of testicular in a boy or man, and testicular instead of ovarian in a girl or woman. In medical histories, one should explain, the gonads are called ovaries or testes, respectively, even though they fail to do their proper work. For self-reference, as when giving a medical history, an older patient is best advised to insist on the term *gonads,* or *sex glands,* and to circumvent the conventional medical vocabulary as a matter of personal dignity.

D. Bipotentiality of the Genitalia

Patients' rights and, in pediatrics, the rights of parents do not permit the health-care professional to lie or be evasive. Hence an appropriate explanation of discordancy between the genital sex, on the one hand, and the chromosomal and/or gonadal sex, on the other, must be given. The explanation is the same for the older juvenile or adult patient as for the parents of the newborn, and is based on the physiologic bipotentiality of embryonic and fetal differentiation. In the case of the internal genitalia, it is the principle of the heterologous bipotentiality of the Mullerian and the Wolffian ducts, whereas for the external genitalia, it is the principle of homologous bipotentiality of the genital anlagen. Comprehension of both principles is greatly expedited if explanatory diagrams are used or, better still, three-dimensional models (Figures 1, 2). The value of these diagrams is multiplied if copies of them, along with a simplified printed explanation, are furnished to parents who need to explain the child's birth defect of the sex organs to members of the family or friends.

Discordancy between the natal appearance of the external genitalia and the sex of assignment can be explained rationally by using the term *clitoridean penis* (or *phallus*) if the child is to be announced (or reannounced) and reared as a boy. Correspondingly, the term *penile* (or *phallic*) *clitoris* is used if the child is to be announced (or reannounced) and reared as a girl.

E. Sex Announcement

Ideally, no child with a birth defect of the sex organs should ever need a reannouncement of sex. The fulfillment of this ideal requires that the first announcement be that the sex of the baby cannot be declared without further investigation; that, after having waited nine months, it will be necessary to wait at least a few more days before making a definitive announcement.

A pragmatically straightforward and common-sense principle is that no newborn baby with a birth defect of the sex organs should be assigned to the sex in which, after surgical correction and hormonal intervention, the genitals will be inadequate for a romantic, erotic, and coital sex life in maturity.

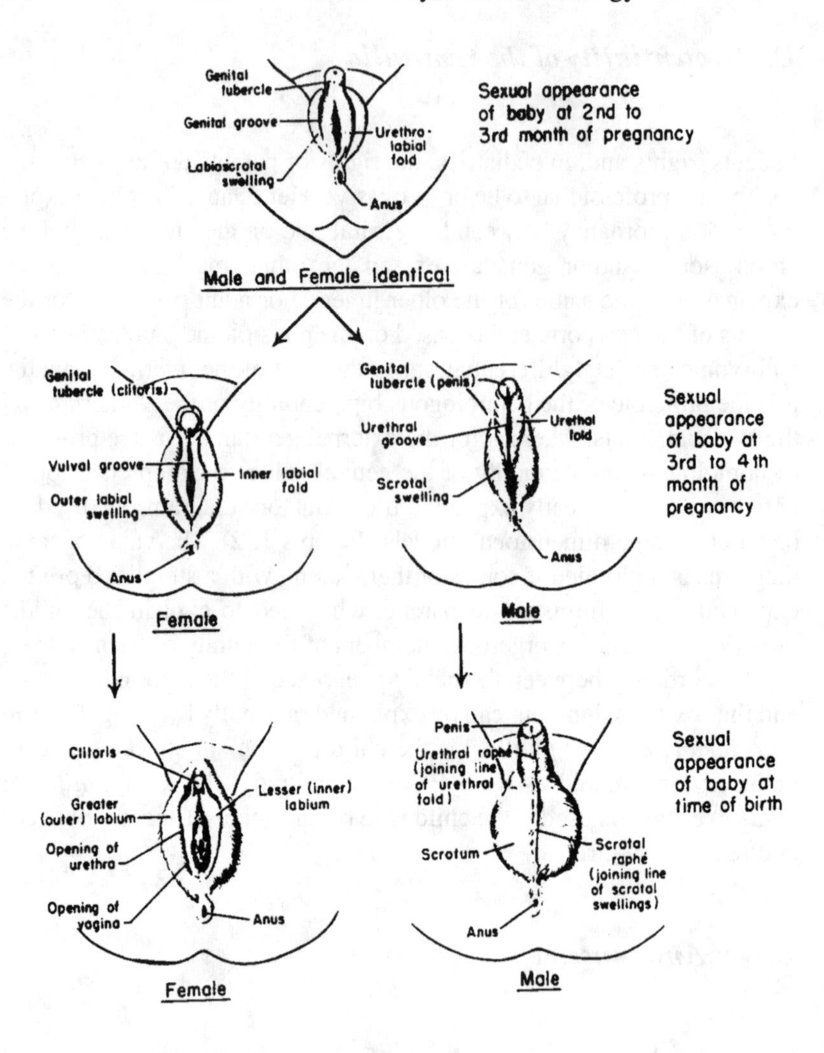

Figure 1.

Diagrammatic representation of external genital differentiation in the human fetus

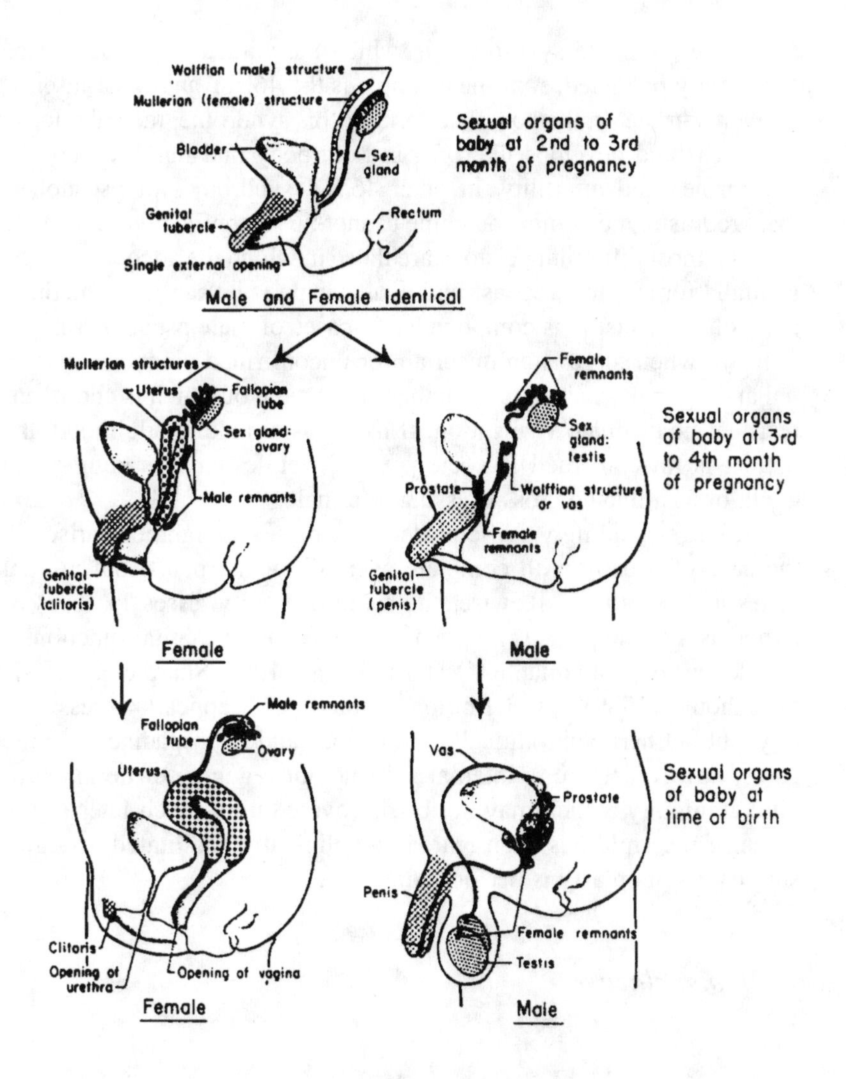

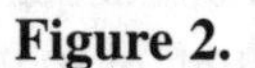

Figure 2.

Diagrammatic representation of internal genital differentiation in the human fetus.

There are some syndromes in which the clinical outcome can be confidently predicted. A prime example is the 46,XY androgen-insensitivity syndrome. In the complete form of this syndrome, the baby looks like a girl and develops like one, in both body and mind, except for amenorrhea and infertility. In other 46,XY syndromes of pseudohermaphroditism, the clinical outcome cannot be so confidently predicted.

The most difficult decisions are those in which the adequacy of the genitalia for surgical reconstruction as a male is borderline. The difficulty of the decision is compounded in cases of male pseudohermaphroditism when there is an uncertain or unconfirmed diagnosis of partial androgen insensitivity, the pubertal outcome of which is androgen-resistant, inadequate virilization. If living as a male in adulthood, the patient is misconstrued in society as a juvenile masquerading as an adult, or as a female cross-dressing as a male.

A correspondingly difficult decision of sex assignment arises in the case of a baby with complete agenesis of the penis, but normal testes and scrotum. Likewise, the same difficulty arises in cases of hypoplasia of the penis (micropenis) so extreme that coital function as a male will be unattainable (Oesterling et al., 1987; Sharp et al., 1987; Woodhouse, 1989). By definition, a micropenis appears excessively tiny, but not hermaphroditically ambiguous and hypospadiac. In some cases, however, there is internal evidence of a degree of hermaphroditic ambiguity, which may not be discovered until much later in life when, if the child has been reared and clinically habilitated as a girl, surgical vaginoplasty is performed.

F. Nomenclature

The principle of providing for an adequate sex life in maturity is sometimes overridden by a conviction, in some instances religious in origin, that testes are synonymous with masculinity, and ovaries with femininity, irrespective of fertility and irrespective of their future vulnerability to malignancy. Among some health-care providers, this point of view is expressed as the principle that the chromosomal and the gonadal sex should take precedence over the external anatomy in deciding the sex of assignment. The 1876 Klebs nomenclature of hermaphroditism reinforces this view, insofar as hermaphroditic males and females are classified as pseudohermaphrodites, as distinct from true hermaphrodites (Klebs, 1876) who possess both ovarian and testicular tissue. All three types of hermaphrodite are genuine.

G. Surgical Intervention

Patients with testes are traditionally the province of urology, where their male status is nosologically guaranteed by such terminology as *pseudovaginal perineal hypospadias.* Urological surgeons have a tradition of surgical optimism with respect to corrective masculinization of the genitalia. It is an optimism that often turns into multiple surgical admissions which the child may experience subjectively as nosocomial abuse (see below).

Correspondingly, patients with ovaries are traditionally the province of gynecology. For gynecological surgeons, it goes against tradition to remove the ovaries, uterus, and fallopian tubes in order to preserve normally formed male external genitalia in those rare 46,XX patients with CAH who, during fetal life, masculinized their external genitalia completely into a penis with penile urethra and an empty scrotum. Psychoendocrinologically, however, preservation of the penis and scrotum (later to be filled with prosthetic testes) and assignment, rearing, and hormonal management as a boy would be feasible (Money and Daléry, 1977), and compatible with masculinization of both body and mind. By contrast, feminization of the mind cannot be guaranteed if the rearing and clinical correction are as a girl.

The dilemma of being able to predict feminization of the body with less certainty than of the mind is one that applies to CAH babies born with ambiguous genitalia. In a longitudinal outcome study of 46,XX CAH individuals (Money et al., 1984), eleven of thirty (37 percent) identified themselves as bisexual or lesbian in erotic orientation; seven (23 percent) were noncommittal; and twelve (40 percent) disclosed themselves to have been heterosexual on the criterion of either erotic imagery or activity, or both. This finding has been replicated by Dittmann et al. (1992).

The dilemma of assigning a 46,XX CAH baby as a girl who might grow up to be bisexual or lesbian could be acute for some parents. The alternative would be to assign, rear, and clinically habilitate the baby as a boy who would grow up to have a male sexual orientation. This alternative, viable for 46,XX CAH babies with a fully formed penis and penile urethra, would be contraindicated in those with a clitoridean hypospadiac phallus too small for masculinizing surgical reconstruction and coital function in adulthood. The same applies to 46,XY babies with a clitoridean hypospadiac phallus.

IV. Differentiation of Gender-Identity/Role

A. Criteria of Sex

The syndromes of abnormal sex differentiation are experiments of nature in which one or more of the variables of sex is discordant with the others. In the CAH syndrome, for example, the prenatal hormonal sex (masculinizing) and the phallic clitoris (which may be a fully formed penis) are discordant with the chromosomal sex (46,XX), the gonadal sex (ovaries), and the female internal sexual anatomy (uterus and fallopian tubes).

In everyday speech, "male" and "female" are polar opposites, distinguished by the external sex organs which, it is tacitly agreed, are the criterion of sex differences, and all the other variables of sex in male and female are concordant with the anatomy of the external genitalia. When the natal anatomy of the sex organs is ambiguous, however, the principle of concordance assumed in everyday speech no longer holds.

There is no in-between position for the sex of assignment on the birth certificate. For better or worse, it is a cultural as well as a linguistic imperative that every newborn must be assigned as a he or a she. The assigned sex in which a baby with ambiguous genitalia is reared is not necessarily concordant with the chromosomal sex, the gonadal sex, the prenatal hormonal sex, the hormonal sex of puberty, or any other variable of sex, including the sex of the external genitalia. Thus, the sex of the child must be specified according to which variable is used as the criterion.

In sexological science, the relationship between each of the variables of sex to the ultimate outcome of the sex of assignment and rearing is of major theoretical significance. To attribute this outcome, a priori, to sex-role learning is to ignore the input from, for example, prenatal hormonal programming of sexual dimorphism in the brain.

In 1955 I coined the term *gender role* (Money, 1955, 1985). It is defined as *everything* that one says and does to indicate that one is either male or female, or androgyne. The other side of the same coin is *gender identity.* It is defined as the persistence of one's individuality as male, female, or ambivalent as it is experienced in self-awareness and behavior. Gender identity is the private experience of gender role, and gender role is the public manifestation of gender identity. Both together are *gender-identity/role.*

Since 1955, *gender role* and *gender identity* have entered the vernacular and the scientific language. The word *gender* itself has become an all-purpose synonym for "sex" in some biological as well as social-science writings, but generally *sex* and *gender* are dichotomized. In popular usage, sex is what you're born with, and gender is what you acquire. Gender identity is commonly defined as "I am a male" or "I am a female." Gender role is often hybridized as "gender-role behavior." "Gender-identity behavior" has also been used. Sexual orientation (or preference) and gender identity are frequently regarded as independent of one another, so that dirty sex doesn't contaminate wholesome gender. In the literature that specifically addresses issues of gender, including the literature on hermaphroditism, there has been little or no attempt to achieve a terminological consensus, so that published research findings tend to resist comparison.

B. Reductionism: The 5α-Reductase Hypothesis

Failure to share a common language in the study of gender is contingent in part on differences in methodology, which are themselves contingent on different principles and criteria regarding the philosophy of science. To illustrate: on the overall issue of sexual orientation, in social science there are two divergent schools of thought, the social constructionists and the essentialists. Constructionists are fervently in favor of the view that homosexuality and heterosexuality are no more than social labels which individuals either adhere to or reject on the basis of preference. In addition, constructionists do not recognize the existence of biological determinants that would be independent of preference and moral choice.

Constructionists are also reductionists, for they reduce the determinants of sexual orientation, and in fact of all variations in erotic orientation, to a single determinant, namely social pressure, very loosely defined.

Reductionism of another variety is biological reductionism. It is espoused by proponents of the medical model in its simplest version, namely "one cause, one effect." Its antithesis is the developmental model of multivariate, sequential determinism, which is the one exemplified herein.

The most common example of biological reductionism as applied to the gender identity of hermaphrodites is that of the 5α-reductase hypothesis (Imperato-McGinley et al., 1974, 1979). In brief, according to this hypothesis, a 46,XY fetus that is genetically homozygous for this enzymatic defect is unable to convert testosterone to dihydrotestosterone. Testosterone secreted by the fetal testes is alone sufficient to ensure the masculine development of the prostate and other reproductive structures, but not of the external genitalia. Their development requires that testosterone be converted to dihydrotestosterone, which does not occur in the absence of the enzyme 5α-reductase. In consequence, the anlagen of the external genitalia remain female (in nature's scheme of things, Eve takes precedence over Adam). Hence, the baby is born with the external genital appearance closely resembling that of a female, but with undescended testes and normal male internal ducts.

At the age of puberty, there is a paradox: 5α-reductase is no longer important, insofar as testosterone from the patient's own testes, which may descend into the labioscrotal folds, is sufficient to ensure enlargement of the clitoridean penis, a male pattern of pubic hair, and lack of breast growth. Pubertal masculinization overall is either virile or eunuchoidal, but it is definitely not feminizing. There is no uterus, no ovarian cycle, and no menstruation.

According to the hormonally reductionist 5α-reductase hypothesis of Imperato-McGinley, the testosterone of puberty also causes a "male sex drive" to emerge. In a patient with 5α-reductase deficiency brought up as a girl during childhood, pubertal testosterone ostensibly reverses the gender identity from female to male, and the erstwhile girl takes up life as a man.

The change in gender identity presupposes that, in the juvenile years, it was that of a girl. Perhaps that was so when, several generations ago, an inbred pedigree in Salinas in the mountains of the Dominican Republic produced its first patients. Eventually, the village people learned how to recognize babies who, despite appearing to be girls, would masculinize at puberty. However, they had no effective solution to the question of whether to declare them boys or girls. As boys they would, according to village tradition, run naked until age seven or eight, with the pelvic region on display for all to see that they had no penis. As girls, they would wear panties that hid their anomaly until it became publicly apparent at puberty that they had no breasts and had not developed as females. Either way, neither the families nor the children themselves could be spared public humiliation and stigmatization. In village talk, they were stigmatized as *guevodoces* and *machihembras,* of which the respective English equivalents are "balls at twelve" and "half-boy, half-girl."

Stigmatized in this way, 5α-reductase patients grew up in a society that characterized everyone as either male or female, but lacked the medical facilities to correct hermaphroditic anomalies. Their status while growing up as either girl or boy was a social concession: They were as-if female or as-if male, respectively. Therefore, it would be misconstruing the evidence to say that they were consistently reared as either normal females or normal males. Under the circumstances, it would not be possible for either the gender identity or the gender role to differentiate as exclusively feminine or masculine, uncontaminated to some degree by the ambiguity of being hermaphroditic. Thus, those who grew up officially declared as girls, and who changed after puberty to live as men, did not have their gender identity reversed by testosterone, for it was already, in part, androgynous. Moreover, testosterone masculinized the body and so signaled society that this person did not qualify for marriage and motherhood. The pressure of society to change to live as a man then impinged upon the inner promptings of gender identity, whatever they may have been. Another important consideration would be the advantage of being considered as a man, rather than as a woman, in most social groups. Many individuals yielded, some recently under the aegis of modern surgical treatment in the United States. A few held out and remained ambiguous, but they were not offered the option of hormonal and surgical feminization.

The hormonal-reductionist hypothesis has been espoused and applied to another large pedigree of 46,XY patients with genital ambiguity of Arabic lineage in Israel and elsewhere in the Middle East (Roesler and Kohn, 1983; Kohn et al., 1985; Gross et al., 1986). The enzyme deficiency in this pedigree is 17ß-hydroxysteroid dehydrogenase. As in the case of 5α-reductase deficiency, affected babies are born looking female and masculinize at puberty. Postpubertally, some change from having been reared as a girl to having a life of greater autonomy and economic independence, as well as religious advantage, as a man.

One of them migrated to the U.S. and was treated at The Johns Hopkins Hospital (Money, unpublished data). As a man, his clitoridean micropenis was much too small for vaginal intromission. Overall, his gender-identity/role remained equivocal, even though he was adamant in maintaining a male civic role because of its perceived social advantages.

C. Multivariate Sequential Determinism: "Turnim Man"

Reductionism has been challenged and rejected in favor of multivariate sequential determinism on the basis of a meticulously detailed body of sexological data gathered by the anthropologist, Gilbert Herdt (Herdt, 1990; Herdt and Davidson, 1988; Herdt and Stoller, 1985). In the Eastern Highlands of Papua New Guinea, there exists among the Sambia people another pedigree of 5α-reductase deficiency. For an unrecorded number of generations, 46,XY individuals with this condition have been known in the Sambian language as *kwolu-aatmwol* ("male-like thing, adult person masculine") or, in a recently introduced Pidgin term, as *turnim man* ("he turns into a man"). Experienced midwives can differentiate an affected baby from a normal girl. If an inexperienced midwife declares the baby as a girl, she grows up as one until the failure of menses and copulatory activity declares otherwise.

The baby whom the midwife recognizes as a *kwolu-aatmwol* is assigned to live as a boy. Together with other boys his age, as a seven-year-old he is permitted to commence the rituals of initiation into the role of warrior head-hunter, but not to continue them to their completion in young adulthood. The fulfillment of his male gender-identity/role remains forever incomplete. In their different ways, the histories of Sambia 5α-reductase-deficient individuals demonstrate that their gender-identity/role cannot be reduced to a single hormonal determinant independent of the cultural impact of rearing.

D. Brain Dimorphism: Prenatal and Postnatal Programming

The tribal Sambia people had what might be called a Stone Age method of dealing with male pseudohermaphroditism. They had no endocrine treatments and no corrective surgery, for their contact with the world beyond their mountains did not commence until the 1950s. Until recently, the rural village people of the Dominican Republic and the Arabic people of the Middle East were in a somewhat similar position.

In all three instances, affected babies who were assigned as girls were destined to go through puberty not feminizing but masculinizing. The same thing can happen in our own culture. It is, however, avoidable. With foresight and a plan of surgical and hormonal intervention, it is possible to ensure that the affected infant who is assigned as a girl will grow up without the stigma of masculine-looking genitalia and a masculinizing puberty. Concordance between clinical care and unstigmatized rearing as a girl is itself concordant with living all of one's life as a woman, male pseudohermaphroditism notwithstanding (Cantu et al., 1980).

In a longitudinal outcome study of 46,XY individuals with ambiguous genitalia reared as girls (Money et al., 1986), those who in adolescence or adulthood underwent elective male sex reassignment included some who had, at puberty, spontaneously feminized, as well as some who had masculinized. In their histories, there was a shared common factor of having grown up stigmatized. Stigmatization characterized also the histories of those who had been reared as boys (Money and Norman, 1987), and who were either bisexual, homosexual, or sex-reassigned.

In a comprehensive review of the experimental animal literature edited by Sitsen (1988), the principle of prenatal and/or neonatal programming of sexual dimorphism in the brain has been established. According to the principle of "Eve first, then Adam," male sex hormones do the programming by being the additive factor that masculinizes the otherwise feminizing brain. At puberty, the sex steroids activate whichever program for sexual mating that is already in place in the animal's brain.

It is highly likely that, in an attenuated form, this same principle applies to the human species. A comprehensive review of pediatric endocrine syndromes and their outcome (Money, 1988a) lends support to this likelihood. However, prenatal and neonatal hormonal programming establish only a precursor, not a finality, of sexual dimorphism in the human brain. Male/female differentiation continues postnatally, under the influence of sensory and cognitional input from participation in the social environment. One type of preparatory participation is juvenile sexual rehearsal play, which is widespread (if not universal) among primate species. In the human species, the adverse sequelae of its suppression have not yet been fully investigated.

The concept of two phases in the sexually dimorphic differentiation of the human brain, the first prenatal and hormonal, the other postnatal and sensory-cognitional, lends logical orderliness to the phenomena of erotic orientation, not only in hermaphroditism, but in the genitally normal as well. It provides a rational explanation for the powerful influence of the sequelae of sex of assignment and rearing on erotic orientation, and also for those instances in which it is overpowered.

V. From Behavior to Hormones to Developmental Arrest: Psychosocial Growth Retardation

A. The Behavior-Hormone Paradigm

In theoretical psychoendocrinology, there are three paradigms applicable to the correlation of hormones and behavior. One gives primacy to hormones with behavior as a sequel, one gives primacy to behavior with hormones as a sequel, and one gives primacy to neither but to a third variable shared in common. In each paradigm, the relationship is in temporal sequence. It may or may not be causal.

In substantiation of the second paradigm, there is the example of elevation of the level of adrenocortical output as a sequel to competition, rivalry, offense, and defense. There is also the example of the release of prolactin and oxytocin in nursing mothers as a sequel to the suckling of the infant, which may, in turn, in some women trigger a maternal orgasmic reaction.

Another example of the behavior-hormone sequence is the loss of cyclicity in the release of hypothalamic-pituitary-gonadal hormones, with consequent cessation of the menstrual cycle, as a sequel to the depletion of subcutaneous body fat—which may itself be a sequel to fasting. In the psychiatric syndrome of anorexia nervosa, fasting is pathological in degree. The syndrome is more prevalent in females than males, and occurs predominantly during adolescence and young adulthood. The fasting is characteristically synonymous with penitential self-purification and the renunciation of lust. The irrational logic of fasting to death is often resistant to rational counseling regarding adequate nutrition.

Irrationality is less likely when loss of menstrual cyclicity is a sequel to severe depletion of body fat in athletes undergoing intensive training, or in fashion models undergoing weight reduction on a restrictive diet, or in ballet dancers undergoing both.

In juveniles, recent studies have shown that the self-initiated behavioral change of adhering overzealously to a nutritionally insufficient diet may induce severe inhibition of prepubertal statural growth and delayed onset of puberty. In one comprehensive study among affluent families, affected boys and girls were found to have restricted their nutritional intake through dissatisfaction with their body proportions, concern with becoming overweight, or intent to escape a family history of hypercholesterolemia and coronary heart disease (Pugliese et al., 1983; Lifshitz et al., 1987). Taking cues from their mothers, even the very young daughters of fashion models and ballet dancers became growth-retarded on the basis of self-imposed dietary restriction (M.I. New, unpublished communication).

In infants between the ages of seven and twelve months, severe impairment of statural growth ensued as a sequel to nutritional restriction initiated by mothers intent on the beauty of a slender child (Pugliese et al., 1987).

In some (if not all) cases of the foregoing types of nutritional deficiency, parents and patients are compliant when given rational nutritional instructions for a change of diet. Catch-up growth ensues and, in older children, pubertal delay yields to the onset of puberty.

There is no corresponding compliancy in the syndrome known as psychosocial growth retardation, psychosocial dwarfism, or child-abuse dwarfism. This syndrome is contingent on parental neglect, deprivation, and abuse. In infancy and childhood, it is characterized by retarded statural, intellectual, and social growth, and in teenage by retarded onset of puberty.

B. Neglect, Deprivation, and Abuse

Historically, the syndrome of growth retardation or dwarfism as a sequel to child neglect, deprivation, and abuse was misclassified nosologically under the all-inclusive diagnosis of failure to thrive. When

Talbot et al. (1947) first recognized it as a distinct syndrome, they related it to emotional and nutritional disturbances, and to hypopituitarism. In Patton and Gardner (1962, 1963), the role of surreptitious abuse, over and beyond maternal deprivation, was mentioned as a possible etiological factor. It has since been independently confirmed (Evans et al., 1972; Money, 1977; Silverton, 1982; Taitz and King, 1988). Insofar as abuse is surreptitious, however, and may not be unmasked, its significance has been underestimated; and the etiology of the syndrome has been attributed to psychosocial, emotional, or maternal deprivation instead.

Emotional and maternal deprivation recently has become mislabeled as "nonorganic," and the diagnosis of "nonorganic failure to thrive" has become popularized, especially in referring to children below age two, as a respectable substitute for psychogenic failure to thrive. However, since everything psychogenic has no existence except in the brain and its extended communication network, the very notion that thriving or its failure might be nonorganic is scientifically implausible. The logic of attributing failure to thrive to a nonorganic origin leads to the etiological conclusion that it is of spiritual, astrological, or occult origin.

In growth retardation secondary to abuse, there is a collusional relationship between the parents in the manner of folie à deux. Typically, it is the mother in whom the psychopathology of abuse is primary. Her untrustworthy version of the child's developmental and medical history is not contradicted by her husband, even though it is circumstantially incomplete and factitious, in the manner of Munchausen syndrome (see above). Hence the psychiatric formulation of her diagnosis as Munchausen syndrome by proxy (Money and Werlwas, 1976; Money, 1986b). The mother's psychopathological role as primary abuser eventually is sometimes a quasi-religious ritual of atonement. Metaphorically, she sacrifices her child as an atonement for her own unspeakable sin, such as the sin of having herself been born as the offspring of father-daughter incest (Money et al., 1985; Money, 1989).

The prime significance of growth retardation due to abuse lies not, however, in the masked psychosis of the mother and the collusion of the father. It lies rather in opening a new window onto the psychosomatics of growth and maturation (Green, 1986). Parental neglect, deprivation, and abuse inexorably alter not only the behavioral and intellectual but also the hormonal functioning and growth of the child.

In 1967, a two-part report was published (Powell et al., 1967a,b) that differentiated the origin of growth-hormone deficiency in the syndrome of psychosocial growth retardation from that in other growth-hormone deficient hypopituitary syndromes. This report set the guidelines for differential diagnosis and treatment. It demonstrated that, in this syndrome, growth-hormone deficiency was reversible upon change of domicile, whereupon catch-up growth would commence. Growth failure and growth-hormone deficiency would return if the child returned to the original domicile.

There are on record extreme cases in which a child at four to five years of age, has the bodily size and development of an eighteen-month-old; or at age nine years has the size and development of a three-and-a-half-year-old. Injections of growth hormone are relatively ineffective in restoring normal growth compared to their effect in truly growth-hormone-deficient patients.

It can be shown that, at least in some cases, growth failure correlates with abuse-induced impoverishment of sleep and, presumably, with loss of growth-hormone secretion during sleep (Wolff and Money, 1973; Guilhaume et al., 1982; Taylor and Brook, 1986).

There is experimental evidence from neonatal rats that growth-hormone secretion is activated in response to the tactual stimulation of being groomed, and suppressed in response to grooming deprivation (Schanberg and Kuhn, 1985). In clinical human investigation of grooming and grooming deprivation, the subjects were preterm babies. Those who received grooming grew and gained weight almost twice as fast as those who did not. They were also more active and alert, and more rapid in developmental advance (Schanberg and Field, 1987).

The neurochemistries through which the sensory receptors of the skin are linked to the brain, and thence to the pituitary and the release of growth hormone, remain to be discovered. Brain opioids may play a part, as is to be inferred from the evidence of pain agnosia in abused children prior to rescue (Money et al., 1972). Vasointestinal polypeptide (VIP) and somatostatin may also play a part. So also may other hormones of the gut, liver, and pancreas that mediate growth (Uvnaas-Moberg, 1989), insofar as nutritional and fluid deprivation may exist prior to rescue.

According to the evidence of growth velocity in one longitudinally studied case of psychosocial dwarfism, the synchronous monitoring of nutritional intake and hormone levels indicated that there must have been at least one other etiological variable, as yet unidentified (Saenger et al., 1977). There were periods of retardation and acceleration of growth velocity that occurred without changes in either nutritional or hormonal levels. Their only ascertainable correlation was with, respectively, absences or return of one particular nurse, the patient's favorite, who had become his mother surrogate.

For as long as the abused child is not rescued, the discrepancy between physical developmental age and chronological age progressively increases in magnitude. The hormonal onset of puberty may be delayed (Money and Wolff, 1974). The social-behavioral age lags, and so does the mental age (Money et al., 1983 a,b). There is a high likelihood of behavior that is not only immature for age, but also so warped by abuse as to appear peculiar or bizarre (for extreme cases, see Ferholt et al., 1985).

Relocation to a benign living environment prevents further retardation and allows catch-up growth to begin (Sarr et al., 1987). The briefer the period of abuse, the greater the potential for catch-up growth. The longer the period of abuse, the greater the degree of permanent residual deficit in height, in IQ, and in social-behavioral autonomy.

The duration of abuse may continue after ostensible rescue, for foster placements do not always measure up to the ideal of parent-child bonding. In addition, there is some evidence that children become addicted to abuse (the so-called Stockholm syndrome). They provoke their would-be rescuers who, unless specifically trained, respond abusively.

The conditions that produced psychosocial growth retardation may persist into the time of the expected onset of puberty. In that case, the hypothalamic-pituitary mechanism of the biological clock of puberty fails to release gonadotropins. Thus the onset of gonadal puberty will join the overall retardation of growth typical of the syndrome. It, too, is correctable by relocation to a benign living environment.

A hypothesis in need of further investigation is that some cases of retarded puberty are actually late-onset cases of psychosocial growth retardation without a history of excessively short stature in the early years (Lewis et al., 1977; Magner et al., 1984). In such cases, puberty may eventually begin spontaneously, or be hastened by a "rest cure" in a new environment, or be set in motion in boys by a brief trial period of testosterone treatment.

Hypothetically, it is possible that there is a vulnerability factor without which children exposed to neglect, deprivation, and abuse will fail to manifest psychosocial dwarfing and developmental delay. Rather than being either nature or nurture exclusively, vulnerability is likely to be a permanent residual of a nature-nurture encounter at a critical period of development.

VI. Age-Discordant Rate of Growth and Maturation: Growth Retardation, Precocity, Delay

A. Chronological Age, Behavioral Age, Physique Age

It is axiomatic that the tyranny of the eyes governs one's initial response to those whose developmental age deviates from the norm for chronological age. Irrespective of their behavioral age, those who are very small for their chronological age are infantilized when young. When older they are juvenilized, the more so if prepubertal in appearance. Those who are taller but delayed in puberty are also juvenilized (Sonis et al., 1987). By contrast, those who are prematurely tall and precociously pubertal for age are "adolescentized": it is expected that they will behave as teenagers.

Behavioral age is an all-inclusive entity that includes academic, social, recreational, vocational, sartorial, psychosexual, and mental age. Mental age, from which the IQ is calculated, is measured on standardized tests of intelligence. Academic age is gauged on the basis of school grade level attained on a standardized achievement test. There are rating scales with age norms for social maturity, but they are more applicable to the young or retarded than the more socially sophisticated. The fashion industry has age-graded clothing styles, but has no standardized norms. Other components of behavioral age similarly lack standardized norms.

Physique (physical developmental) age is a complex entity based on developmental norms for height (height age), weight for height, and bone age, to which is added the developmental stage of puberty, ranging from prepuberty to complete postpuberty, according to the five-stage scale of Tanner.

The simple expediency of making a distinction between chronological age and physique age has helped many young people with growth and maturation anomalies. It defines for them the dilemma of a behavioral age adrift between physique age and chronologic age. For those with delayed physique age, behavioral age needs to become anchored as closely as feasible to chronologic age. For those who are too large and precociously mature, behavioral age needs to be anchored as closely as feasible to physique age.

For those with discordant chronological and physique ages, the tyranny of other peoples' eyes spawns daily indignities. Well-meaning strangers often address short, nonpubertal teenagers condescendingly, as child prodigies, whereas their age-peers exclude them from age-concordant adolescent social activities (Holmes et al., 1985). At the other extreme, tall and precociously pubertal children are benignly pitied by adults as mentally handicapped adolescents and ridiculed by those whose physique they match.

The tyranny of the eyes is so insidious that it dictates relationships even within the intimacy of the family, as well as within the clinic, the school, the neighborhood, and the community at large. Parents may protest otherwise, but they may not escape the tyranny completely. If they expect the same from their atypical child as from the siblings, their demands may be extreme and inconsiderate of his/her limitations. The alternative extreme is to make allowances, falsely equating proscriptive constraints and restrictions with protectiveness. Either way, the toll on family mental health is prohibitive, and so also are the costs of therapeutic intervention. Fortunately, some families of good mental health steer clear of extremes.

The antidote for the tyranny of the eyes is the power of language. Initially, parents may speak up on behalf of the child who is either too small or too large relative to chronological age, as for example in telling a waitress to disregard size and address the child according to either birthday age or social age whichever is greater. Parents who succeed in adopting this strategy pass it on to the child in what constitutes a de facto program of social-skills training. Children of normal size assimilate social skills in synchrony with their peer group. The child who is too little or too big for age has no true peer group. That is why personal tutoring at home, in the clinic, at school, or wherever it may be found in the community is needed to augment not only social skills in general, but also specific recreational and educational skills and, at a later age, vocational skills.

At home and at school, portable furniture of the wrong size is adjusted or replaced. Methods are devised for coping with or circumventing immovable fixtures and appliances. Responses are rehearsed in advance of comments and questions about age, size, or appearance of pubertal maturation. Role-playing helps, as in learning how to demolish teasing with wounding repartee and teasing back. Training is provided in how to play with children of different size and to become a team participant by having a special role. Later in childhood, social skill applies to clothing style and adornment. Those who are too small and immature dress up to their age. Those who are too large and mature make a compromise between dressing down to their age and up to their physique; a very young precociously pubertal girl gets adjusted to wearing a bra, for example. For a few, cosmetic dentistry or surgery—all too often overlooked—will be essential to the advancement of social acceptance.

The tyranny of the eyes encroaches upon schooling by conspiring with educators to delay entry for those who are too small for their age, and to refuse entry for those who, although too big for their age, are not behaviorally mature enough for their size. The error, in both instances a form of pedagogical malpractice, stems from a faulty pedagogical doctrine of school readiness, namely that behavioral maturation takes place at a preordained rate, independently of social exposure and experience.

The logistics of special pedagogical planning requires input from the physician, either in writing or in person, regarding the nature and prognosis of each particular child's syndrome. Adapted for presentation in a classroom "seminar," a medical explanation of a child's unusual condition serves to bring an end to teasing and stigmatization and to replace it with rehabilitative cooperation. Older patients may themselves participate, with good effect, in such a classroom seminar.

Beyond the classroom, growth-retarded or growth-accelerated children may, as they grow older, find rehabilitative support by joining a nosological special-interest group such as exists in Little People of America, Human Growth Inc., and the Turner Syndrome Society. Some, however, resist joining with their own nosological kin. Membership is for them an open admission of defect, deformity, or stigma, and their parents may agree.

B. Statural Delay and Pubertal Insufficiency

There are three policies for the psychoendocrine case management of growth retardation and short stature during childhood and, after age fifteen, the management of delayed puberty. Each policy is contingent on the prognosis and prospect of treatment for the different syndromes, with respect to both growth in size and pubertal maturation (Money, 1970).

Policy I applies to syndromes of short stature in which catch-up growth and spontaneous puberty are projected. Growth retardation induced by long-term glucocorticoid treatment of a specific illness is an example, insofar as resumption of growth and onset of puberty can be expected following the termination of glucocorticoid treatment.

Psychosocial growth retardation with pubertal delay is also a syndrome to which Policy I applies. In such cases, psychoendocrine intervention is directed toward the logistics of relocating the patient in a benign living environment conducive to catch-up growth in stature and/or the onset of puberty. Relocation is defined initially as a "rest cure" to confirm the diagnosis by demonstrating the beginnings of catch-up growth and development. Relocation may need to be continued indefinitely. Upgrading the original living environment from malignant to benign is usually difficult as it requires costly and prolonged family monitoring and counseling and a coordinated team effort. Authority to enforce compliancy is invested not in the pediatric endocrine clinic, but in the law. Parents and sometimes social-service officials who view compliancy as an unjustifiably imposed penance are likely to become litigious and adversarial. The adversarial system of the law and the consensual system of therapeutics meet at an impasse.

Policy II applies to syndromes of short stature in which puberty of spontaneous onset is projected, but catch-up growth is not. The deficiency in height may be diagnostically attributed to familial short stature, or it may be diagnostically recognized as an attribute of a genetic error. Examples are, in males, Noonan syndrome, and in both sexes, Prader-Willi syndrome and the chondrodystrophic syndromes. There may be accompanying congenital anomalies and defects, some of them unsightly and some amenable to plastic-surgical reconstruction. Psychological intervention is palliative and takes the form of situational and supportive counseling.

Policy III applies to those syndromes of short stature, notably hypopituitarism (and to a lesser extent, Turner syndrome), in which a gain in height, contingent on hormonal intervention, is predicted, as also is pubertal maturation—if not spontaneously, then with hormone replacement therapy. Often, there is a planned delay in the hormonal-induction of puberty, with a view to gaining an unknown increment of extra height (eg., with growth-hormone therapy or with a growth-promoting anabolic steroid like oxandrolone) before pubertal closure of the epiphyses and the termination of growth.

Psychohormonal intervention is directed towards weighing the pros and cons of a still uncertain degree of gain in height age against an uncertain degree of loss in behavioral age and social maturation while awaiting the social benefits of looking postpubertal and mature. Psychoendocrine intervention is directed also toward monitoring, in the child and the parents, concordance between expectancy and actuality of gain in height. There is also the hurdle of readjusting from being uniquely the smallest to being ordinary or, worse still, not tall enough. During the prolonged years of receiving growth-hormone injections, there is also the hurdle of adjusting versus maladjusting to the role of patient. Longitudinal psychoendocrine follow-up allows some of these adjustment problems to be recognized early and dealt with. Some, however, may prove to be therapeutically recalcitrant. They may possibly be linked to hypothalamic-pituitary dysfunction by way of a coexistent hypothalamic-behavior dysfunction. In Turner syndrome, although hormonal feminization favors romantic yearnings, it does not necessarily augment erotosexual initiative. It remains to be ascertained whether hormonal-substitution treatment with estrogen and progestin is all that is needed to overcome the sluggish sexuoerotic energy and low marriage rate that is prevalent in the Turner population.

Sexological follow-up is the same as for hypopituitarism without short stature as in what follows.

C. Delayed or Failed Puberty without Short Stature

In psychoendocrine case management of the onset of puberty, the upper limit of normal for the manifestation of the first visible signs of puberty is age fourteen for boys and thirteen for girls. When, with no prior history of short stature, the onset of puberty is delayed beyond these ages, there are three different psychoendocrine policies of case management, each contingent on the prognosis and prospect of treatment for the different syndromes.

Policy I applies to syndromes in which puberty would predictably not occur except for hormonal intervention, insofar as the gonads are missing. Congenital anorchia is one example. Gonadectomy, either accidental or therapeutic, is another. Therapeutic gonadectomy may have been performed as part of a comprehensive plan of sex assignment or reassignment in cases of severe birth defect of the genitalia (as in aplasia of the penis or micropenis) or in cases of traumatic ablatio penis. Sex-hormone replacement therapy will bring about an excellent degree of pubertal feminization or virilization, as the case may be. Exceptions are cases of androgen insensitivity where virilization in response to testosterone therapy is deficient, partially or totally. If living as a male, the patient has the appearance of a eunuch. Treatment with an antiestrogen may reverse sterility (Gooren, 1989) but has not yet been tested for its possible virilizing effect. For a boy who fails to virilize with androgen therapy, psychoendocrine intervention is palliative at best. The outcome is individually variable. In sexological counseling, the agenda includes sex reassignment which, even though logical, is virtually certain to be personally not feasible. The issue of congruence between gender-identity/role as male or female and the sex of induced puberty as hormonally male or female is an important item on the sexological agenda for all cases.

A variant of Policy I applies to hypergonadotropic hypogonadism, specifically Klinefelter (47,XXY) syndrome, in which the outcome of what at first may appear to be slow progress of puberty is permanently weak virilization and, in some cases, gynecomastia (breast enlargement). With respect to puberty in this syndrome, psychoendocrine intervention pertains not to its timing, but to the inadequacy of its outcome. It pertains also to evaluation of the patient as a candidate for a trial period of treatment with exogenous testosterone, with a view to increasing virilization of appearance and reducing erotosexual indifference. These changes do not occur until the pretreatment level of testosterone in the bloodstream shows a significant increase.

Prepubertally in Policy I, psychoendocrine intervention is directed toward ensuring compliance in returning on time for follow-up evaluation. Hormonal replacement therapy to induce the development of pubertal physique can then be timed so as to be in synchrony with the development of chronological agemates and with their advances in social and behavioral age. In sexological counseling, attention is given, as needed, to cosmetic prosthetic testes for boys, the timing of vaginoplasty for girls, and coping with infertility for both sexes.

Policy II applies to syndromes of hypogonadotropic hypogonadism in which, without hormonal-replacement therapy, puberty would be delayed indefinitely. Gonadal failure is consequent upon failure of the pituitary to secrete luteinizing hormone (LH) and follicle-stimulating hormone (FSH), which, in turn, may be consequent upon failure of the hypothalamus to secrete gonadotropin-releasing hormone (GnRH) after surgical ablation or irradiation of a brain tumor. In Kallmann syndrome, hypothalamic hypopituitarism is congenital and coexists with anosmia. Counseling with respect to anosmia may, in some life situations, be beneficial.

Psychoendocrine intervention is along the same lines as in Policy I, except that hormonal replacement may have been deferred until later in teenage, in deference to a presumptive diagnosis of constitutional delay of puberty, thus allowing behavioral maturation to lag.

In all of the hypogonadotropic syndromes, the outcome of replacement gonadal-steroid therapy is often inadequate on the criterion of maturity of appearance. In hypopituitary males, virilization in response to testosterone is notoriously inadequate. A dramatically better response has been achieved in a pilot study by substituting or adding human chorionic gonadotropin (hCG) therapy for testosterone replacement for a year or more (Clopper et al., 1983).

Policy III applies to those cases in which the prepubertal state persists beyond the age of fifteen, until eventually puberty begins of its own accord. The late onset of puberty may prove to be either an isolated phenomenon or one manifestation, among others, of a subsequently identifiable anomaly, defect, or dysfunction, possibly a lesser genetic disorder. A rare example would be the so-called fertile-eunuch syndrome (LH deficiency).

Psychoendocrine intervention is directed toward the indications, in each case, for or against the induction of puberty with a brief (four- to six-month) period of testosterone treatment. The hormone is given with a view to facilitating concordance of behavioral age with physique age and hence chronological age. The rule-of-thumb criterion regarding the timing of hormonal-replacement treatment is against the prolongation of prepuberty beyond the age of fifteen. Boys constitute the major population of Policy III.

D. Accelerated Growth with Precocious Onset of Puberty

Psychoendocrine policy when growth is too rapid and puberty too early follows the basic principle of concordance between chronological age, physique age, and behavioral age. In the era before the inexorable advance of precociously pubertal physique could be slowed, behavioral age was the target for effecting concordance, and psychoendocrine intervention was directed towards strategies for advancing behavioral age and thus reducing the duration of the discordance between physique age and behavioral age.

In the 1950s, it became possible to slow the premature advance of puberty in virilizing CAH by cortisol-replacement therapy. In the 1980s, it became possible not only to slow, but to arrest the premature advance of development in other syndromes of precocious puberty, thanks to the discovery of synthetic analogues of the gonadotropic-releasing hormones of the hypothalamus, as well as other pharmacologic suppressors of pituitary gonadotropic function (Grumbach and Kaplan, 1988).

The demand for supportive psychoendocrine counseling will not become totally obsolete, however. There remains the issue of stress which affects all children who require prolonged or chronic treatment, especially by injection. For some pubertally precocious children—girls more often than boys—undergoing a genital examination under the gaze of medical bystanders is experienced subjectively as being the equivalent of sexual abuse. Such is the weight of the sexual taboo in our society.

The psychoendocrine service of evaluation will no doubt continue to be in demand if the cosmetic endocrine practice of inducing, not suppressing, early puberty continues to be in demand. Applied to very tall girls, this treatment has reduced their adult height by an average of 5 cm (2 inches) in conformity with their ideal body image, reportedly without ill effect.

VII. Sex Hormones: Genital and Erotic Function

A. Prepubertal Lovemap Development

According to the Utopian canon of sentimentalized childhood, the age of innocence prevails until puberty; and according to the Freudian canon of psychoanalytic childhood, the latency period blankets the juvenile years. Neither canon is correct. In nonhuman primates, it has been shown experimentally that juvenile sexual rehearsal play among agemates is prerequisite to sexual normalcy and to procreation in adulthood (reviewed in Money, 1988a, pp. 62–66). In the human species, sexual rehearsal begins before birth. Ultrasound studies have demonstrated that the fetal penis becomes erect and may be grasped by the fetal hand (Meizner, 1987). Spontaneous erections continue episodically from birth onward. They are the infantile precursors of episodes of nocturnal penile tumescence that persist throughout life and are associated with REM (rapid-eye-movement) sleep and on some occasions with erotic dreaming. In female infants and girls, the complex developmental history and phenomena of tumescence, being concealed, have not yet been reported. In adult women, tumescence has proved rather intransigent to measuring devices.

In deference to society's moral veto on normal childhood sexual rehearsal play, the stages of its development in health and pathology and throughout infancy and childhood have lacked systematic study. The earliest stage is contrectative (tactual). It includes genital self-fondling during the first year of life. By the time the native language is being imprinted, so also is the brain/mind template to which has been given the name *lovemap* (Money, 1988b). Insofar as the lovemap typically differentiates from bipotential to either male or female, it is a component of the more extensive dipolar differentiation known as *gender-identity/role* (G-I/R). The lovemap, in fact, is the sexuoerotic component of the G-I/R.

Male/female polarization of the brain and its mental representation as a lovemap is both prenatal and postnatal in origin, according to the evidence of both human clinical and animal experimental hermaphroditism (summarized in Sitsen, 1988). Prenatally, it is dependent on steroidal sex hormones, the primary principle being that androgen masculinizes and the absence of androgen feminizes (which is not precisely synonymous with demasculinizes). Postnatally, it is dependent on the input of information channeled through the senses from sources in the social environment.

One source of postnatal lovemap polarity that appears to be of major developmental importance is the "show me" play which commonly occurs in the preschool years. It is followed in the early school years by pelvic-thrusting play, and then by sexual-positioning play. This type of play, according to ethnographic evidence, occupies an essential but not an obtrusive place in normal lovemap development, if untrammeled by wrong timing or by neglect, deprivation, restriction, coercion, or punishment. When its normal development is interfered with, prevented, or mismanaged, the lovemap becomes defective.

Defective lovemaps are classified as hypophilic, hyperphilic, or paraphilic (the biomedical synonym for the legal term "perverted"). The defect may be well established, though not obvious, by as early as age eight. As if in a state of dormancy, it may pass unnoticed until the hormones of puberty expose it and enforce its recognition.

B. The Hormones of Puberty

It has long been medically axiomatic to attribute sexuality and eroticism to a sexual drive or libido. For many years, gonadal hormones have been assumed to be the source of the sexual drive or libido and of its difference in the male and female, respectively. Animal experiments have provided substantiating evidence: Testosterone given to castrated male animals reactivates mounting, intromission, and ejaculation. Administration of progesterone and estrogen to spayed females reactivates the positioning of lordosis and mating with the male.

The simplicity of these experiments is, however, misleading. Sexually, the hormones-and-behavior story is more complicated (Young, 1961, Chs. 19, 22; Sitsen, 1988), and not the same in all species. In mammals, mating behavior is not rigidly either male or female, but to some degree interchangeable. Gonadal hormones are not sex-dichotomous as they are present in the bloodstream, although in different ratios, in both sexes. Studies with gonadal hormones in experimental animals have shown interchangeable mating behavior.

In human females, the erotic function of both estrogen and progesterone, as compared with their procreative function, remains enigmatic. It may, in fact, be negligible, and testosterone may be the libido hormone, so-called, for both sexes (Money, 1961; Sherwin et al., 1985). This proposition is challenged, however, by the erotic phenomenology of the 46,XY androgen-insensitivity syndrome. Individuals with this syndrome raised as women are not sexuoerotically deficient. They also are not sexuoerotically distinguishable from their clinical counterparts, namely 46,XX women with the Mayer-Rokitansky-Kuester syndrome (Lewis and Money, 1983). By contrast, subjects with partial androgen insensitivity raised as males tend to be somewhat sexuoerotically deficient.

It is possible that neither testosterone nor any other gonadal steroid deserves the sobriquet of "libido hormone." Rather, it may be that gonadal steroids are catalysts to an as yet unidentified network of neurochemical events that, in concert with sensory stimuli, including appropriate stimuli from the genitalia, increase the magnitude and prevalence of what is subjectively experienced as the feeling of sexual drive or libido.

With respect not only to libido but also to sexuoeroticism overall, the hormones of puberty are responsible for remarkedly little that is entirely new other than the ejaculatory fluid of the penis and the lubricatory fluid of the vagina. Their predominant responsibility is to augment, enhance, or intensify that which is already present in precursor form. However, there is a threshold above which an increase in hormonal level does not increase sexuoerotic response. Rape, for example, is not contingent on an elevated level of testosterone. The influence of hormones is contingent on the intactness of the connection between brain and external genitalia. The person with a severed spinal cord has no response of the external genitalia to erotic ideation and imagery originating within the brain.

C. Precocious Hormonal Puberty

The augmentational as compared with the inaugurational function of the hormones of puberty shows up clearly in extreme cases of pubertal precocity (Money and Alexander, 1969; Money and Walker, 1971). A boy of six (Money and Hampson, 1955) whose body is as well virilized as that of an adolescent boy of fourteen has a penis that becomes erect recurrently, whether he is awake or asleep. Erection is usually synchronous with explicitly erotic ideation and imagery, the content of which is contingent upon age-related cognition and learning. Hence, copulation is absent from imagery and ideation until information and knowledge pertaining to it have been assimilated. Signs of lustful longing may be in evidence from time to time, but they do not lead to a sexual advance. An actual love affair does not materialize, possibly through lack of a partner who is both chronologically young enough and pubertally mature enough.

The girl as well as the boy who has by age six the body development of a postpubertal teenager (Hampson and Money, 1955) is constantly reminded by her appearance alone that she is exceptional. Unlike the boy, she has also the recurrent reminder of her menstrual periods, but no exact counterpart of his recurrent erections and ejaculation. The explicitly erotic imagery and ideation that accompanies the boy's erections and ejaculations may be entirely lacking in the girl, as may also the experience of orgasm, either awake or asleep, even if she knows about the act of copulation. By contrast, her dreams and fantasies are of kissing, hugging, dating, honeymooning, being a bride, and, maybe, expecting a baby. The girl may have a crush on a boy from her own social group, but a reciprocated love affair comes much later.

In those cases of sexual precocity in which the pubertal hormones are therapeutically suppressed, as for example by the use of GnRH analogs, the aforesaid phenomena may be correspondingly subdued, but no studies have yet been published.

D. Late Hormonal Puberty

In boys who have not begun hormonal puberty by age fifteen, the extent to which erotosexual development remains juvenile varies widely and appears to be contingent not only on the lack of pubertal hormones, but also on the etiology of the delay. A man with congenital anorchia and still prepubertal at age twenty-one represented one extreme (Money and Alexander, 1967). His wife's testimony, and his own, was that for the two years of their marriage, they had had intercourse approximately three times a week. His erection lasted until she reached orgasm, whereupon his penis would get a "burning feeling" or "thrill," although without throbbing or ejaculation. After one month of treatment with testosterone, the feeling of orgasm began to change, step by step, as the fluid of ejaculation progressively increased. The frequency of intercourse doubled, and he was more enthusiastic about it. He became more "hot-natured" and began chasing other women, which led to many new partners, divorce, and eventually remarriage.

At the opposite extreme is the virtual sexuoerotic anergia which is common to teenagers with untreated hypogonadotropic hypogonadism secondary to hypopituitarism, with or without dwarfing, and of either idiopathic or postsurgical origin. Delayed puberty that originates in hypogonadotropinism is of the type in which the prepubertal body virilizes more effectively if, instead of testosterone-replacement therapy alone, there is also a period of treatment with human chorionic gonadotropin (hCG) (Clopper et al., 1983). The greater virilization that ensues allows for more sociobehavioral maturity on the basis of a social-feedback effect. In addition, there appears to be a primary erotosexual behavioral sequel to the treatment. Erotosexual energy and arousal replace the erotosexual inertia and apathy which is otherwise typical and widespread in hypopituitarism. So also is a low marriage rate (Mazur and Clopper, 1987), as well as a low incidence of limerence—that is, the experience of being love-smitten.

Erotosexual maturation is additionally complicated, especially in Kallmann syndrome (hypogonadotropic hypogonadism with anosmia), by an unnamed and variable degree of peculiar social ineptitude that is strange and disquieting to other people. It may be related to impairments of pairbonding. Such impairments are prevalent in hypogonadotropic hypogonadal syndromes of all types, regardless of stature.

There is a dearth of systematic information on erotosexual function in females with hypogonadotropic pubertal failure. This is a reflection, no doubt, of the disproportionate underrepresentation of females in the sex ratio for late puberty of hypopituitary origin. One's overall impression, however, is that erotosexual anergia is as typical of females as of males with hypopituitarism, even under hormonal-replacement therapy.

Women with Turner syndrome also have a relative lack of erotosexual energy. It shows up in a low rate of dating and marriage, both of which might be attributed to the social stigma of shortness, or to a history of having had pubertal hormonal treatment withheld too long in the hope of gaining extra height. However, social stigma per se does not explain lack of experience with genital stimulation, lack of orgasm, and a low intensity of imagery and ideation of an erotosexual nature (McCauley et al., 1986). Another possibility is that hormonal-substitution therapy with only estrogen and progestin is insufficient. It would be worthwhile, on a research basis, to investigate the addition of a minimal amount of androgen or of some other pharmacologic agent related to sexual function, maybe a peptide hormone, for example vasointestinal polypeptide (VIP).

E. Hormones: Homosexual/Heterosexual

If the hormones of puberty caused homosexuality, then it could be predicted that lesbians would be girls who virilize at puberty and vice versa, and gay males would be boys who feminize at puberty and vice versa. No such prediction is possible. In the prepubertal years, there are no hormonal measures that can be used as predictors of postpubertal homosexuality. There is also no technique for retrieving, retrospectively, the prenatal history of the hormonalization of the brain as masculine, feminine, or mixed. Even in girls with CAH in which the prenatal hormonal history is known to have been excessively androgenic, it is possible to make only an actuarial prediction of an increased manifestation of juvenile tomboyism (Berenbaum and Hines, 1989) and an increased (up to 50 percent) likelihood of a bisexual or lesbian postpubertal outcome, but not to make an individual prognostication with confidence (Dittmann et al., 1992; Money et al., 1984). Actuarially, the likelihood of a lesbian orientation is—like juvenile tomboyism, lack of pregnancy, and low marriage rate—more prevalent in the salt-wasting than the simple virilizing form of CAH in girls (Dittmann et al., 1990a,b; Mulaikal et al., 1987).

A similar masculinizing effect is manifested also in young women with a history of having been exposed in utero to DES (diethylstilbestrol) administered to the mother during pregnancy. Between 20 to 25 percent of thirty women studied reported a history of some degree of bisexualism manifested in romantic and erotic fantasy (Ehrhardt et al., 1985).

By contrast, somewhat more confidence may be justified in making a prepubertal prediction of a postpubertal homosexual orientation on the basis of a behavioral criterion, namely in those cases of gender transposition so extreme that a boy insists on being a girl and a girl insists on being a boy. This so-called gender-identity disorder of childhood may be fully manifest by age five, or even younger. The failure of gender-identity/role to differentiate concordantly with the genital sex may require a predisposition, as yet unidentified. It may also require to be catalysed by malignant, even though surreptitious, sexual and social feuding between the parents, accompanied by the threat of losing one of them (Money, 1984). Typically, the outcome in postpuberty is not a demand for sex reassignment, but the development of an ordinary homosexual gender identity.

The preponderance of children who pass through puberty with a homosexual orientation do not have abnormal hormone levels. The sum total that has emerged from all the studies of postpubertal hormonal determinations is that homosexuals and heterosexuals, male or female, are not hormonally distinguishable (reviewed in Money, 1988a).

Children whose hormonal sex at puberty is discordant with the sex of their genitalia typically are mortified by what they consider to be something wrong with their bodies. Boys with adolescent gynecomastia are in this predicament. They may ask themselves if breast enlargement is a first sign of changing sex, but dismiss the idea as incompatible with the mental certainty of knowing that they are male. There are exceptions, however, and in these cases the growth of the breasts confirms their erstwhile stigmatization as "sissy boys." In adolescence these boys must come to terms with being gay, which is not easy for them. Boys with CAH (postnatally treated with cortisol) who never develop breasts at puberty do not develop either a bisexual or a homosexual erotic orientation (Money and Lewis, 1982).

In a child with a history of birth defect of the sex organs, the sex of erotic orientation may develop to be discordant with the sex in which the child has been reared (Money, 1968). In addition, the sex of rearing may be either discordant or concordant with the pubertal gonadal hormones. Thus, among the various possible permutations and combinations, one may find a teenaged boy with a surgically-repaired, birth-defective penis, hormonally masculinized at puberty with androgen from his own testes and erotically oriented homosexually toward a male partner exclusively.

Instead of settling into a homosexual life style, another such boy might have found himself confronted with the dilemma of whether to undergo hormonal and surgical sex reassignment and to live in adulthood as a heterosexual woman. Even if he had grown breasts and virilized very poorly, his gonadal status as male may have led to his being denied the right of sex reassignment.

If, however, in a similar type of case, another child had been confronted by the dilemma of sex reassignment to live as a man after having been reared as a girl, and if as a girl she had undergone a masculinizing puberty and had been exclusively oriented toward a female partner erotically, then the testicular status of her gonads would almost certainly have led to approval of sex reassignment.

As they have done for centuries, the gonads exercise almost mystical power as the ultimate arbiters of sex. This power is today shared with the chromosomes, though not always to the ultimate advantage of the newborn with ambiguous external genitalia.

There are, of course, some very difficult no-win cases in which the decision either for or against sex reassignment is unsatisfactory. In these cases the two-year, real-life test (Money and Ambinder, 1978) is strongly recommended so that the irreversible step of genital surgery is not embarked on too soon. The ultimate aim is to rehabilitate a human life as well as can be done, not to give obedience to a dogma.

Biographies of children born with congenital defects of their external genitalia are of extraordinary scientific importance in determining the criteria of what constitutes heterosexuality and homosexuality. By way of illustration, consider the case of the 46,XX gonadally female hermaphrodite, born with a uterus and a penis with an empty scrotum, who has lived always as a boy and a man, who has virilized hormonally at puberty, and who falls in love with and becomes the sexual partner of a normal, 46,XX woman. The reciprocal of this case is that of the 46,XY gonadally male hermaphrodite born with a normal vulva but lacking a uterus, who has lived always as a girl and a woman, who has feminized at puberty, and who falls in love with and becomes the sexual partner of a normal, 46,XY man. In each pair, who is homosexual—each partner, only one, or neither? For actual case biographies, see Money (1991).

From these examples, it is apparent that the criterion by which heterosexuality should be defined is not the chromosomal sex nor the gonadal sex, but the heterology of the external genitalia and of the body morphology of the two partners. If two people with a penis and a virilized body morphology are together erotically, they are classified as homosexual males, irrespective of the heterology of chromosomal or gonadal sex. Similarly, if two people with a vulva and a feminized body morphology are together erotically, they are classified as lesbian.

As an intellectual exercise, assign a man with 46,XX chromosomes, two ovaries with a uterus, but a virilized body morphology with a penis and empty scrotum to a normal woman who also has 46,XX chromosomes and two ovaries and a uterus, but a feminized body morphology and a vulva. Any one in possession of common sense will classify the pair as heterosexual. Similarly, assign a woman with 46,XY chromosomes, two testicles, a feminized body, and a vulva and a normal man who also has 46,XY chromosomes, a penis, two testicles, with a masculinized body morphology. Again, any one with common sense will classify the pair as heterosexual.

Being together genitally engaged in a sexual act, either a homosexual or a heterosexual act, is not the same as being a person with either a homosexual or a heterosexual orientation. The ultimate criterion of being a homosexual or heterosexual person is the criterion of falling in love, and whether, respectively, the person is able to fall in love only with someone with the same external genitalia and body morphology as the self, or only with someone whose external genitalia and body morphology are the antithesis of those belonging to the self.

VIII. Hormones, IQ, and Learning

A. Hormone-Brain-IQ Paradigm

In any of the pediatric endocrine syndromes, insofar as the growth of intelligence and learning might be hormonally affected, the two possibilities are either impairment or enhancement of intellectual growth. Of these two, enhancement has not been proved, whereas impairment has. In fact, impairment of intellectual growth and learning in untreated congenital thyroid deficiency is the example par excellence of a direct, primary influence of hormones on mental functioning and the brain.

1. Congenital Hypothyroidism

Historically, the 1930s saw the beginning of pediatric studies that combined diagnosis and treatment of congenital hypothyroidism early in childhood with the application of intelligence tests to measure the effect of treatment on intellectual growth. By the mid-1950s, it had become apparent, notably in two papers from the Wilkins clinic (Money, 1956; Smith et al., 1957), that there was a relationship between the age at onset of treatment with attainment of euthyroidism, on the one hand, and the amount of catch-up intellectual growth and ultimate level of IQ, on the other. In brief, the sooner the treatment, the higher the IQ. But there were exceptions. The most grossly defective IQs (below 50) were widely distributed so as to include some of the early treated; and an IQ above 110 was compatible with delay of treatment until age two (but not beyond).

The exceptions raised questions about differential etiology and about neurological damage, not all of which are resolved even today, despite the expansion of knowledge regarding the etiology of sporadic congenital hypothyroidism (in developed countries) and endemic cretinism (in Third World countries). How thyroid deprivation translates into mental deficiency is still poorly understood. It has become clear, however, that timing is a significant variable. Experimental animal studies have shown that there is a critical period in brain development when thyroid deprivation has a permanently damaging effect, especially on dendritic proliferation.

In human beings, the critical period for thyroid deprivation is in the first postnatal days and weeks up to around age three months. The data come from the outcome studies of neonatal diagnosis and treatment made possible since the introduction in the latter part of the 1970s of programs for mass screening of the newborn for thyroid deficiency. Data from a number of programs in Europe (Illig et al., 1986, 1987; Kalverboer and Bleeker, 1988; Murphy et al., 1986), Australia (Thompson et al., 1986), Canada (Glorieux et al., 1985; Rovet et al., 1987) and the U.S. (NECHC, 1985) are quite remarkable for their consistency. They demonstrate the virtual abolition of mental retardation in children with congenital hypothyroidism, provided thyroid replacement is begun within days—preferably no longer than a week to ten days—after birth. The beneficial effect of treatment applies to thyroid deficiency per se rather than to its etiological subtype. Discontinuance of treatment, even briefly for confirmatory diagnostic testing, is contraindicated during the first two years of life.

The data are also consistent in showing that, whereas the IQs of children with a history of treated congenital hypothyroidism fall within the limits of normal, the range of IQs is constricted so that there are too few at the above-average levels. Thus it would appear that, even at the earliest age of intervention, the maximum amount of catch-up intellectual growth may fall short of a full 100 percent. In other words, the IQ of each individual child may be some points lower than it would otherwise have been. This minor deficit is more obvious in the performance of movements and visual-motor coordination than in verbal development, and it persists up to age seven and presumably beyond.

Whether this relative degree of psychomotor delay will be subject to eventual catch-up or not remains to be seen. The annual rate of the growth of intelligence is not necessarily constant, any more than is the annual rate of growth in height. Thus it is possible for the rate of the growth of intelligence, verbal as well as nonverbal, to pick up speed after a period of being in the doldrums. The test/retest interval in one study was five to eleven years, and the change in IQ (Mean ±SD) for forty-three erstwhile hypothyroid children was from 75.0±17.8 to 84.5±16.8 (Money and Lewis, 1964). In a twenty-five-year follow-up of ten of the children, it was found that remarkable leaps of IQ had been sustained in two cases. They were, respectively, from 55 to 80, and from 84 to 127 (Money et al., 1978).

Hypothyroidism that is first manifested during the juvenile years (so-called acquired hypothyroidism) has a slowing effect on learning until it is corrected, but it does not arrest intellectual growth in such a way as to prohibit catch-up growth under the influence of thyroid-replacement therapy.

B. Common-Denominator, Multiple-Defect Paradigm

Some pediatric endocrine syndromes are characterized by multiple anomalies, among which one is hormonal and another is a neurocognitional impairment that affects IQ and learning. Both stem from the same source, which may be a brain lesion from accidental trauma, tumor, or infection, or the source may be genetic. In the pediatric endocrine clinic, two anomalies of the sex-chromosome constitution are particularly frequent: the 45,XO (Turner) syndrome and the 47,XXY (Klinefelter) syndrome.

1. 45,XO (Turner) Syndrome

In this syndrome, in all of its chromosomal variations, the neurocognitional impairment that affects intelligence and learning is in evidence throughout childhood. Thus, there is no doubt that its existence is not dependent on, but coexistent with, the lack of secretion of gonadal hormones at puberty by the inert gonadal streaks.

The error of embryogenesis responsible for the differentiation of gonadal streaks is responsible also for other deformities that occur not universally but sporadically in Turner embryos. One of these additional sporadically occurring errors will ultimately impair intelligence and learning. One infers, therefore, that it must be an error of brain differentiation. If there are regional or hemispheric localizations, they have not yet been demonstrated.

For a quarter century after Turner first described the syndrome, impairment of intellect and learning, if present, was mislabeled as "mental retardation." The correct label, "specific cognitional deficit," was discovered in the course of psychohormonal testing (Shaffer,

1962) in the Wilkins clinic and has since been confirmed in many studies. It is widely agreed that, whereas the deficit does not affect verbal intelligence, it may severely affect nonverbal intelligence. The disparity between the verbal and nonverbal (performance) IQs may be as great as thirty points, with the verbal IQ being above 130.

By pooling and comparing the data drawn from various studies based either on standardized psychological tests (e.g., Money, 1964; Bekker and Van Gemund, 1968; Garron, 1977; Nielsen et al., 1977) or on special tests (e.g., Alexander and Money, 1966; Silbert et al., 1977; Waber, 1979; Rovet and Netley, 1982; McCauley et al., 1987), it may be construed that the basic deficiency pertains to the mental processing and sequencing of rotational transformations of shapes in the spatial dimensions of left/right, up/down, and back/front. The latter is also the push/pull rotation which rotates the self-image, as in a mirror. In the activities of everyday life, the rotational-transformation deficit translates into a handicap in map-reading, following travel directions, drawing a floor plan of a familiar room, deciphering sounds stereophonically, and recognizing changes in facial expression.

In psychological testing, rotational transformation wreaks havoc on the drawing of a person. This test necessitates rotational transformation of the self-image onto a flat page on which the left and right of the figure depicted before one's very eyes is a mirror rotation of one's own left and right.

The mirror-rotational effect interferes also with copying either a human figure or a geometric shape (Alexander et al., 1966). The rotation of angles and points has the effect of turning the shape that they define inside out, and creates more evidence of distortion than does the rotation of curves.

The link between rotational disability and shapes apparently extends from geometry to calculation in general. Mathematics is a great academic stumbling block for Turner girls. It frequently necessitates intervention from the physician in order to obtain from the school a special dispensation so that a verbally superior Turner student will not be penalized for a genetically derived specific nonverbal disability.

Vocationally, as well as academically, rotational-transformation disability is a handicap in all assignments that involve arrangements and rotations of designs and configurations. With accumulated experience, a Turner girl's degree of handicap may be lessened by the device of transliterating from shapes and directions into silently spoken language.

Rotational-transformation disability is not a handicap to learning to read. It may even be an advantage, insofar as the shapes of letters and words retain their meanings by remaining stable and not rotated. Rotate *b* and it becomes *d,* or *p,* or *q.* Rotate *was* and it becomes *saw.* The psychological law of object constancy dictates that the meaning of a shape or object perceived remains constant, even if it is turned around or upside down, or added to, or subtracted from, or broken. The ordinary child, in learning to read, has to resist the law of object constancy. Turner girls are spared this resistance.

2. 47,XXY (Klinefelter) Syndrome

In this syndrome, intelligence may or may not be impaired. Impairment, if present, is evident prepubertally, prior to the manifestation of hypergonadotropic hypogonadism that characterizes the syndrome from puberty onward.

Epidemiologically, the incidence of intellectual impairment among 47,XXY males is a function of the type of population cytogenetically screened. When large-scale screening began in the 1960s, the focus was on males segregated in penal, psychiatric, and mental-retardation institutions. In each type of institution, the proportion of 47,XXY males was in excess of the 1:500 ratio that would be found among newborn males. So also was the proportion of 47,XXY males with a below-average or defective IQ. It required cytogenetic screening of males in infertility clinics, and subsequently in newborn nurseries, to show that the majority of 47,XXY males are of average and sometimes superior IQ. Even though average, however, the IQ may have been several points higher without the supernumerary X chromosome—and this does appear to be the case when 47,XXY males as a group are compared with, say, their 46,XY siblings or a matched 46,XY control group (Thielgaard et al., 1971).

It became evident, from early in the 1970s onwards, that the missing IQ points are more often missing from the verbal IQ than the nonverbal or performance IQ. The disparity is more explicitly manifested on tests specific for verbal reasoning as compared with those specific for praxic (nonverbal) reasoning.

Specific linguistic disability is more pronounced in some 47,XXY males than others. In the case (unpublished) of one XXY youth, whereas expressive language was totally lacking, the understanding of requests and instructions was clearly evident. In some 47,XXY boys, the disability is manifested early in infancy as a developmental delay in the use of speech. It may be severe enough to require speech therapy. Later in childhood, it may be manifested pedagogically as a learning disability specific for reading (dyslexia) and spelling.

Oral and written language development was followed prospectively (Graham et al., 1988) in fourteen boys who had been identified as 47,XXY in a New England neonatal screening program. They were compared with fifteen 46,XY control boys when they were between the ages of nine and ten, at which age they were academically at the transition between third and fourth grade. On the basis of a broad spectrum of tests, it was concluded that linguistic disability in 47,XXY boys is characterized by deficits in processing the rate and order of auditory stimuli, and in word finding, narrative sequencing, and arranging meanings syntactically.

The hypothesis that linguistic disability might be lateralized in one hemisphere of the brain was experimentally investigated (Netley, 1988) in a cohort of twenty-three prepubertal boys (average age, ten to eleven years) who had been identified as 47,XXY in a Canadian neonatal screening program. The scores, compared with those of a normative sample of seventy-nine children, indicated that the ratio of left/right lateralization deviated from the norm and could be interpreted to indicate an inadequate degree of linguistic lateralization in the left versus the right hemisphere of the brain.

The foregoing data are compatible with those from an earlier sentence-verification experiment (Netley and Rovet, 1982) in which 47,XXY boys (and also 47,XXX girls) matched sentences and pictures for agreement on meaning (e.g., the boy is kicking the girl; the girl is kicking the boy; the boy is not kicking the girl; the girl is not kicking the boy). The boys and girls with the extra X chromosome did not do as well as the chromosomally normal controls.

From all the foregoing findings considered together, it may be construed that the basic deficiency pertains to the mental processing of sequence and synchrony in time. Language is a temporal sequence: It takes time to speak a sentence, or to read it, just as it takes time to tell or read a story. By contrast, it does not take time to perceive a landscape, a picture, or a vehicle—only to inspect it, or to watch its rotational transformation in space.

Whereas 47,XXY males in general do not have difficulty with rotational transformation, they do so with temporal sequencing. It is possible that one extension may be to the sequencing and synchrony of logical meaning as manifested in the sporadic occurrence of pseudologia fantastica in 47,XXY boys and adolescents. The same may apply to paranoid ideation, which is more prevalent than bipolar disorder in those 47,XXY men who develop a severe psychopathological disorder.

The relationship of anomalies of sequencing and synchrony to anomalies of hemispheric lateralization in the brain is conjectural only, and will undoubtedly remain so until technological advances allow data to be obtained directly from the brain itself. In the meantime, ascertainment of such anomalies in those 47,XXY boys and men who have them is by means of behavioral and psychological tests. It is clinically important that they be ascertained. The design of pedagogical and vocational planning can then be more effective.

3. Pseudohypoparathyroidism

This syndrome serves as an example of multiple congenital defects of genetic origin with chromosomal euploidy. It is also an example of a syndrome which has both hormonal and cognitional manifestations, each apparently independent of the other although sharing a common genetic origin. Although the secretion of parathyroid hormone is not deficient, its effects on target cells are impaired. The additive effect of patchy cognitional impairments is to lower the IQ reversibly when the symptoms are of late onset (Money and Ehrhardt, 1968) and irreversibly when they are congenital. The cognitional impairments are not directly attributable to parathormone deprivation, insofar as in simple hypoparathyroidism of infancy and childhood intellectual catch-up can be expected with hormonal-replacement therapy (Money and Ehrhardt, 1966). By contrast, in the syndrome of idiopathic hypercalcemia of infancy which is genetic in origin, if the excess of calcium is not corrected at birth, its effect on intellectual and linguistic growth is destructive and irreversible (Ehrhardt and Money, 1967; Udwin et al., 1987).

4. Psychosocial (Abuse) Growth Retardation

The multiple anomalies observed in this syndrome (see above) do not appear to be genetic in origin, but behavioral and social, though perhaps not exclusively so. It has endocrine and cognitional manifestations that, according to present evidence, are parallel but separate, namely retardation of statural growth and retardation of intellectual development and social-behavioral maturation. On all three counts, catch-up growth is contingent on early intervention. The longer the period prior to intervention, the greater the reduction in intellectual catch-up and hence the larger the amount of permanent IQ impairment.

C. Hormone-Learning Derivative Paradigm

Some endocrine disorders of childhood and adolescence induce symptoms which interfere with cognitional functioning and learning.

1. Hyperthyroidism

A notorious example of hormone-induced distractibility and attention deficit is that of hyperthyroidism (Money et al., 1966). In fact, insidious decline in academic achievement, misattributed to laziness and disobedience, may precede other symptoms of the condition (Money and Drash, 1968). This effect is reversible when the elevated thyroid hormone level is brought under control.

2. Addison Disease

Pervasive fatigue, hypersomnia, anorexia, dehydration, and aching accompany adrenocortical insufficiency. So also do apathy, inertia, and irritability. They are incompatible with achievement at school or work. These impairments are reversible under the influence of glucocorticoid hormonal-replacement therapy, the sooner the better. The growth of intelligence is not permanently impaired (Money and Jobaris, 1977). Adrenocortical glucocorticoid secretion is elevated in Cushing's syndrome, which is pituitary in origin. In children who are successfully treated, there are no known residual effects on intellect and learning.

D. Hormone-Neutral Influence Paradigm

The psychoendocrine significance of some pediatric endocrine syndromes is that the hormonal changes of the syndrome and the growth of intelligence and learning are independent of one another.

1. Precocious Puberty

Irrespective of the etiology and age of onset of precocious puberty, the rate of intellectual development does not parallel the rate of statural growth and maturation. The level of IQ ranges from retarded to very superior. There is no consistent trend toward fluctuation in the rate of intellectual growth, measured as fluctuation in the level of IQ over time. Nor is there any consistent discrepancy between verbal as compared with nonverbal IQ and specific abilities, although large discrepancies may occur sporadically (Money and Meredith, 1967; Rovet, 1983; Bruder et al., 1987).

2. Congenital Adrenal Hyperplasia (CAH)
Due to 21-Hydroxylase Deficiency

Among the population of both boys and girls with this condition, it is extremely rare to find a case of mental retardation. Learning disability is, in effect, zero, even under circumstances of extreme social disacculturation, bilingualism, and personal stigmatization, a few claims to the contrary notwithstanding (Nass and Baker, 1989).

The prevalence of above-average to very-superior IQ is greater than expected on the basis of test norms. In other words, the IQ distribution curve is shifted toward the higher levels (Money, 1955, 1971; Money and Lewis, 1966; Perlman, 1973; Mattheis and Foster, 1980). This increase is not related to the age of onset of glucocorticoid treatment. It is not an artifact of socioeconomic sampling. It is, however, family related (McGuire and Omen, 1975) insofar as the IQs of parents and siblings of CAH boys and girls fall on a distribution curve that also is shifted to the right (Baker and Ehrhardt, 1974). It is possible that the genetic code for CAH confers an IQ advantage on heterozygous carriers (parents and siblings) as well as homozygous carriers (patients). This possibility remains to be investigated.

Even in individual cases, it is rare to find a noteworthy disparity between verbal and nonverbal IQ (Lewis et al., 1968; Resnick et al., 1986). The theoretical significance of this lack of disparity is that it occurs in a clinical population of girls with a prenatal and perinatal history of hormonal masculinization. In the normal population at around the time of puberty and thereafter, male/female disparity becomes evident in scores on verbal versus nonverbal tests. More boys than girls have high nonverbal scores, for example, in mathematics, whereas more girls than boys have high verbal scores. CAH test data do not support the attribution of male superiority in nonverbal reasoning to male hormonalization either prenatally or later. Conversely, CAH data do not support the attribution of female superiority in verbal reasoning to the lack of male hormonalization. It is probably no coincidence that CAH data also do not support the attribution of male aggressiveness to male hormonalization per se.

3. Androgen-Insensitivity (46,XY) Syndrome

According to the scanty amount of published data, the distribution of the full IQ of girls and women with this 46,XY syndrome follows the normal curve. When there is a discrepancy between the verbal and the nonverbal performance IQ, however, it is in favor of the verbal IQ. Thus the verbal IQ distribution is skewed toward an overrepresentation at the higher levels. When the verbal IQ is above 120, the discrepancy with performance IQ may be as great as from twenty to thirty-five points (Masica et al., 1969).

The significance of these findings is that they do not lend support to the idea that female superiority in verbal ability has its origin in 46,XX and not 46,XY chromosomes.

4. 46,XY Hermaphroditism

Congenital anomalies of the sex organs with 46,XY karyotype (other than the androgen-insensitivity syndrome) in their various etiological and hormonal subtypes do not bear any systematic relationship to the growth of intelligence and learning, and thus to the distribution of IQ from high to low. However, in this group of patients, there are sporadic occurrences of retarded mental growth and learning disability, commonly in association with one or more other birth defects. Diagnostic advances may show that some of them can be segregated into as yet unrecognized syndromes.

In one family (unpublished data), an aunt was born with a tiny micropenis. Minor internal sexual ambiguity was not discovered until the time of vaginoplasty in teenage. Her niece had the same genetic (46,XY) condition, but was born with external ambiguity also, namely a hypospadiac micropenis with no urethral closure. Technically, this baby was a male hermaphrodite.

5. Micropenis: CHARGE Syndrome

Hypoplasia of the penis is not a syndrome, but an anomaly that may exist alone or in conjunction with other congenital anomalies. One set of anomalies is acronymed CHARGE (Coloboma; Heart disease; Atresia choanae; Retarded growth and development and/or CNS anomalies; Genital hypoplasia; Ear or auditory anomalies). A subset of children with this condition require special pedagogical planning to circumvent visual and/or auditory handicaps, variable in degree, and the additional handicap of anomalies of linguistic and social development (Money and Norman, 1988). These handicaps are not hormone-dependent.

6. Other Genital Anomalies

For the sake of keeping the record complete, it may be noted that there is no known regularity or consistency of relationship between intelligence and learning, on the one hand, and congenital anatomical deformities or anomalies of hormonal functioning, on the other, in the following varieties of birth defect of the sex organs: true hermaphroditism; non-CAH female pseudohermaphroditism; Swyer syndrome (46,XY pure gonadal dysgenesis); the 45,XO/46,XY syndrome; and the Mayer-Rokitansky-Kuester (46,XX) syndrome of vaginal atresia and vestigial uterus.

7. Short Stature and Delayed Puberty

When retardation of growth in height and intelligence coexist, the differential diagnosis should routinely include the syndrome of psychosocial (abuse) growth retardation. In most syndromes of short stature, with or without late onset of puberty, there is no correlation between rate of statural growth and intellectual growth. The same applies to syndromes in which the rate of statural growth is within normal limits but the onset of puberty is either delayed or, without hormonal-replacement therapy, impossible. In brief, in the vast majority of males and females with statural or pubertal delay, there is no relationship between the timing or amount of the hormones of puberty, on the one hand, and the level of IQ (either verbal IQ or nonverbal IQ) on the other (Pollitt and Money, 1964; Money et al., 1967; Drash et al., 1968; Steinhausen and Stahnke, 1976; Abbott et al., 1982).

IX. Pediatric Endocrine Syndromes and Mental Health

A. Primary Sequelae

1. Major Disorders

None of the major psychiatric disorders of childhood listed in DSM3-R (the revised third edition of the *Diagnostic and Statistical Manual* of the American Psychiatric Association) is specific to, or invariably related to, an endocrine disorder of childhood. On what appears to be a sporadic basis, a child with a major psychiatric diagnosis may also have a hormonal disorder.

In the Klinefelter (47,XXY) syndrome, there is a sporadic association with a wide variety of psychiatric disorders ranging from epilepsy and extreme mental deficiency to phobia, gender disorder, and schizophrenia on an apparently arbitrary basis. In prepubertal boys with Klinefelter syndrome, the hormonal anomalies typical of postpubertal boys with the syndrome—namely elevated gonadotropins and testosterone deficit—cannot be implicated as a source of psychiatric disorder. Whether and how the supernumerary X chromosome which is present in every cell of the body (including cells of the brain and peripheral nervous system) is involved, is not clear.

In some childhood endocrine syndromes, there are mental manifestations that are characteristically, though not inevitably, present. These mental manifestations pertain to cognitional and intellectual functioning that may be either transiently or permanently impaired. They have been reviewed in the preceding section. In this present section, other mental impairments or dysfunctions are reviewed.

2. Hypokinesis

The hypokinetic condition comprises fatigue, tiredness, weakness, slowness, apathy, anergy, and anorexia. In juveniles and adolescents with Addison disease, hypokinesis is one of the early and primary signs of adrenocortical failure, and its reversal is one of the early signs of the efficacy of glucocorticoid-replacement therapy.

In the present era of neonatal screening, the hypokinesis of hypothyroidism is not encountered as much as formerly except, perhaps, as one of the early signs of acquired hypothyroidism. In fact, one of the earliest indications of this disorder may be seen at school as progressive sluggishness, tardiness, plodding, and not being able to finish assignments on time.

Hyperthyroidism has a rare and paradoxical form, apathetic hyperthyroidism, seldom seen in childhood. It is accompanied by hypokinesis instead of the usual hyperkinesis.

3. Hyperkinesis

The hyperkinetic condition comprises being distractable, inattentive, restless, undertaking but not completing things, overtalkative, overactive, agitated, and sleepless.

When acquired hypothyroidism is corrected with thyroid treatment, the return to behavioral normalcy is preceded by a period of hyperkinesis which may last several months. A similar phenomenon of "behavioral overshoot" is observed also in the syndrome of abuse dwarfism on the way to normalcy following rescue from the domicile of abuse.

Hyperkinesis is a phenomenon typical of hyperthyroidism. It may be one of the earliest signs of the onset of the disease. In school children, it is likely to be punished as a sign of naughtiness, laziness, and of "you could do better if you'd try." If hyperthyroidism remains undiagnosed and untreated, the manifestations of hyperkinesis may intensify so as to qualify as a manic episode, and possibly to be misdiagnosed as bipolar manic-depressive disorder. Hyperkinesis may also be manifested in delinquent and reckless escapades.

4. Anxiety/Panic

Anxiety, in the sense of apprehension, is not specific to any of the endocrine syndromes of childhood. In its other sense, namely panic (as in a panic attack) anxiety is specific to pheochromocytoma. It accompanies the overall rush of physiological symptoms that characterize a panic attack and that, in the case of pheochromocytoma, are contingent on an excess of adrenalin for which the tumor is responsible.

5. Depression

In adult endocrinology, severe depression has long been recognized as one of the phenomena of myxedematous (hypothyroid) psychosis, especially in the elderly. In childhood, however, hypothyroid depressive psychosis either has never been seen or never reported in the literature, or both.

In psychopathological terminology, the one word *depression* is used for different degrees of melancholy. In its lesser degree, depression has been claimed to be a frequent accompaniment of Cushing syndrome in adults, although with uncertainty as to whether it has primary or derivative status. In pediatric endocrinology, Cushing syndrome is a rare diagnosis, and data on mental health in the syndrome are deficient. In a series of six juvenile or early adolescent cases at Johns Hopkins (unpublished data), none qualified as being depressed.

6. Aggression/Rebellion

Males have a Y chromosome, two testes, and a higher level of male hormone than do females (or eunuchs). Therefore, according to popular-science dogma, they are more aggressive. The sex-hormonal syndromes of pediatric endocrinology do not lend support to this dogma. Testosterone given to a boy with late puberty does not change him from being agreeable and cooperative to being antagonistic, belligerent, and violent. The exceptions are so rare as to be almost unheard of.

In former years, before treatment was available, boys with either precocious puberty or CAH virilized while very young, under a flood of their own male hormone. They were noteworthy for being gentle, not aggressive or bad-tempered, even though in size and strength they could have defeated all of their agemates. Although sexual aggressiveness has been seen in athletes taking pharmacologic amounts of anabolic steroids, testosterone does not make males into killers or rapists. Nor does hypertestosteronism. The testosterone level is not a mediating factor in the behavior (criminal behavior included) of 47,XYY males (Schiavi et al., 1984).

7. Premenstrual Moodiness

In the era before very early puberty in girls could be treated, there were some who, according to their mothers, were premenstrually emotionally labile and moody. Others were not. The girls themselves did not verbalize it. In no instance did this moodiness have any resemblance to the periodic psychosis of puberty (Berlin et al., 1982), a major, albeit rare, psychotic disorder. All too often misdiagnosed, this psychosis can be treated with an estrogen-suppressant progestinic hormone (e.g., medroxyprogesterone acetate).

8. Erratic Behavior

There is no handy term for behavior that is erratic, eccentric, or bizarre without being schizophrenic. There is also no pediatric endocrine syndrome with which such behavior is routinely associated. In Kallmann's syndrome, however, when more data are collected, it may transpire that erratic behavior is more prevalent than expected in cases of hypogonadotropic hypogonadism overall. The same may well apply also to the Prader-Willi syndrome which has, in addition, the complication of impairment of IQ and of hypothalamic appetite-control among its many symptoms.

9. Paraphilias

Formerly the paraphilias were known biomedically as "the perversions," which is still the legal term for sex-offending paraphilias. Typically originating in childhood, paraphilias are developmental disorders of erotosexual imagery, ideation, and behavior. Children with a history of birth defect of the sex organs may be more at risk than most children (Money and Lamacz, 1989), secondary to sexological stigmatization, neglect, and abuse. Paraphilias become fully manifest postpubertally. They may be associated with a supernumerary X or Y chromosome (Money et al., 1974; Schiavi et al., 1988), but they are not hormonal disorders. Rape is not a correlate of elevated androgen level, for example. Nonetheless, all the paraphilias, raptophilia included, may ameliorate in response to treatment with an androgen-depleting agent. Treatment of paraphilic sex-offending adolescents and adults with the progestinic hormone, medroxyprogesterone acetate (Depo-Provera), an antiandrogen, originated in the Wilkins clinic at Johns Hopkins in 1966 (Money, 1987).

B. Secondary Sequelae: Stigmatization-Stress Reaction

Parents who produce an abnormal child, or one who has a chronic disability or illness, stigmatize themselves for having done so. They are also sensitive to even subtle signs from other people that might signify stigmatization. They may react to their child's condition by becoming fiercely protective and self-martyring. In addition, they may insidiously develop an antipathy not only to the child's condition, but also, unavowedly, to the child in person as an uninvited intruder who disrupts the harmony of family life. Either way, the child is singled out for special treatment which, in its own way, is a covert form of stigmatization.

Stigmatization may be so completely covert that the stigma may become literally unmentionable by name. It becomes the unspeakable monster in one's life. A birth defect of the sex organs is a prototypic example. Health practitioners as well as parents may go to remarkable extremes of euphemism and evasion so as to not mention the names of the defective organs, the chromosomal sex, or gonadal sex.

In addition to the disguised stigmatization of the unspeakably shameful, there is also the undisguised stigmatization of humiliation, ridicule, insult, name-calling, teasing, harassment, and molestation.

Harassment and molestation may be of such magnitude as to qualify as tyranny and abuse. Children tyrannize and abuse other children. Adults also inflict injury, both mental and physical, on children. The adults may be teachers, guardians, parents, or relatives. There is a maudlin sentimentality about parenthood and the family that may easily allow those whose duty is to provide social and health-care service not to recognize parental tyranny and abuse. This is particularly so in that furtive form of tyranny and abuse known as Munchausen syndrome by proxy, already mentioned earlier in this chapter.

It is difficult for most health-care practitioners to concede that, from a child's viewpoint, their own practices and procedures, no matter how well intentioned, may inadvertently constitute nosocomial abuse. In the experience of some children, for example, the negative effects of long-term treatment with growth hormone have outweighed the positive (Money and Pollitt, 1966; Kusalic, 1975; Saenger et al., 1977; Rotnem et al., 1980; Mitchell et al., 1986). Routine clinical practices and procedures may, indeed, be subjectively the equivalent of abuse, professional good intentions notwithstanding (Money and Lamacz, 1986, 1987). Thus, genital examinations may be subjectively equated with rape, medical photography with exposure, surgery with violence, and hospitalization itself with abduction.

Just as stigmatization is variable in form and severity, so also is the stress and trauma of stigmatization variable in the form and magnitude of the toll it exacts on health and well-being.

There is no single syndrome which is the outcome of traumatic stigmatization. Instead, there is a diversity of syndromes. They represent not only mental dysfunction but bodily dysfunction as well, or both together. They include such divergent manifestations as academic dropout, learning disability, dyslexia, anxiety attack, phobia, multiple personality, addiction, chronic pain, diarrhea, enuresis, encopresis, nausea, vomiting, gender transposition, paraphilia, and suicidal ideation.

If stigmatization-stress reaction is not included in the differential diagnosis, it is possible to consume an inordinate amount of time in pursuit of a wrong diagnosis, with consequent prognostic and treatment failure. With a correct diagnosis, although a remission of symptoms may ensue, the greater likelihood is amelioration only. In some cases, however, all symptoms prove intractable to present methods of treatment.

C. Diagnostic Testing

The mental-health sequelae of pediatric endocrine syndromes are classified as either primary or secondary on a clinical basis. Those that appear regularly in association with the syndrome are classified as primary, especially if they fit coherently with the overall hormonal pathology and if they are arrested or reversed under hormonal therapy. Those that appear only sporadically and differ among patients with the same endocrine diagnosis are classified as secondary, especially if they occur in association with a history of major stigmatization stress.

There are no psychological tests with which to diagnose and distinguish primary from secondary mental-health sequelae in pediatric endocrine syndromes. Nonetheless, psychological tests in the form of check lists and rating scales have been used as if they had diagnostic capability with respect to mental health. Each one purports to measure a diffusely defined disorder of personality, behavior, or social maturity. They are used to make comparisons between a group of people with a particular syndrome and a control or contrast group. Among pediatric endocrine syndromes, one that has fallen prey to this type of testing is Turner syndrome.

Tests designed to uncover disorder yield data and scores that are presented in the terminology of disorder. Thus, girls and young women who, in increasing numbers, have ready access to the Turner literature (as do members of the Turner Syndrome Society) read of themselves as specimens of pathology. From various sources, they are cruelly told that they have an increased incidence of behavior problems reflecting immaturity and poor attention skills, as well as poor peer relationships; that that they have fewer friends, need more structure to socialize and to complete tasks, and have more difficulty understanding social clues; or that they are immature in terms of social and sexual development and exhibit social withdrawal and depressed/anxious behavior.

Those whose professional career is in a hospital or clinic have a vested interest, whether they know it or not, in identifying and treating pathology. Their tests are designed to find pathology, not the absence of it. They are tests not of mental health, but of its lack. These tests fail to reveal the enormity of the challenges that, as direct effects of a missing chromosome, confront girls and women with Turner syndrome. They fail to reveal that these girls and women are remarkable not for their difficulties, but for their success in coping with adversity.

As pediatric endocrinology and psychoendocrinology enter the third millennium, it will be wise to remember that everything we write will be available by computer to those about whom we write. It should be written for them, not against them.

REFERENCES

Abbott, D., Rotnem, D., Genel, M., et al. (1982). "Cognitive and emotional functioning in hypopituitary short-statured children." *Schizophrenia Bulletin* 8:310.

Alexander, D., Ehrhardt, A. A., and Money, J. (1966). "Defective figure drawing, geometric and human, in Turner's syndrome." *Journal of Nervous and Mental Disease* 142:161.

Alexander, D., and Money, J. (1966). "Turner syndrome and Gerstmann syndrome." *Neuropsychologia* 4:265.

Baker, S. W., and Ehrhardt, A. A. (1974). "Prenatal androgen, intelligence, and cognitive sex differences." In *Sex Differences in Behavior* (R. C. Friedman, R. M. Richart, and R. C. Vande Wiele, eds.). New York: Wiley.

Bekker, F. J., and Van Gemund, J. J. (1968). "Mental retardation and cognitive deficits in XO Turner syndrome." *Maandschrift Kindergeneeskunde* 36:148.

Berenbaum, S. A., and Hines, M. (1989). "Hormonal influences on toy preferences." *Society for Research in Child Development Abstracts* 6:193, Biennial Meeting, Kansas City, MO, April 27-30.

Berlin, F. S., Bergey, G. K., and Money, J. (1982). "Periodic psychosis of puberty: A case report." *American Journal of Psychiatry* 139:119.

Bruder, G. E., Meyer-Bahlburg, H. F., Squire, J. M., et al. (1987). "Dichotic listening following idiopathic precocious puberty: Speech processing capacity and temporal efficiency." *Brain and Language* 31:267.

Cantú, J. M., Corona-Rivera, E., Diaz, M., et al. (1980). "Post-pubertal female psychosexual orientation in incomplete male pseudohermaphroditism type 2 (5α-reductase deficiency)." *Acta Endocrinologica* 94:273.

Clopper, R. R., Mazur, T., McGillivray, M. H., et al. (1983). "Data on virilization and erotosexual behavior in male hypogonadotropic hypopituitarism during gonadotropin and androgen treatment." *Journal of Andrology* 4:303.

Dittmann, R. W., Kappes, M. H., and Kappes, M. E. (1990a). "Congenital adrenal hyperplasia I: Gender-related behavior and attitudes in female patients and sisters." *Psychoneuroendocrinology* 15:401.

———. (1990b). "Congenital adrenal hyperplasia II: Gender-related behavior and attitudes in female salt-wasting and simple virilizing patients." *Psychoneuroendocrinology* 15:421.

———. (1992). "Sexual behavior in adolescent and adult females with congenital adrenal hyperplasia." *Psychoneuroendocrinology* 17:153.

Drash, P. W., Greenberg, N., and Money, J. (1968). "Intelligence and personality in four syndromes of dwarfism." In *Human Growth: Body Composition, Cell Growth, Energy and Intelligence* (D. B. Cheek, ed.). Philadelphia: Lee and Febiger.

Ehrhardt, A. A., Meyer-Bahlburg, H. F. L., Rosen, L. R., et al. (1985). "Sexual orientation after prenatal exposure to exogenous estrogen." *Archives of Sexual Behavior* 14:57.

Ehrhardt, A. A., and Money, J. (1967). "Hypercalcemia: A family study of psychologic functioning." *The Johns Hopkins Medical Journal* 121:14.

Evans, S. L., Reinhart, J. B., and Succop, R. A. (1972). "Failure to thrive: A study of 45 children and their families." *Journal of the American Academy of Child Psychology* 11:440.

Ferholt, J. B., Rotnem, D. L., Genel, M., et al. (1985). "A psychodynamic study of psychosomatic dwarfism: A syndrome of depression, personality disorder, and impaired growth." *Journal of the American Academy of Child Psychology* 24:49.

Frydman, R., Parneix, I., Fries, N., et al. (1988). "Pregnancy in a 46,XY patient." *Fertility and Sterility* 50:813.

Garron, D. C. (1977). "Intelligence among persons with Turner syndrome." *Behavioral Genetics* 7:105.

Glorieux, J., Dussault, J. H., Morissette, J., et al. (1985). "Follow-up at ages 5 and 7 years on mental development in children with hypothyroidism detected by Quebec Screening Program." *Journal of Pediatrics* 107:913.

Gooren L. (1989). "Improvement of spermatogenesis after treatment with the antiestrogen Tamoxifen in a man with the incomplete androgen insensitivity syndrome." *Journal of Clinical Endocrinology and Metabolism* 68:1207.

Graham, J. M., Bashir, A. S., Stark, R. E., et al. (1988). "Oral and written language abilities of XXY boys: Implications for anticipatory guidance." *Pediatrics* 81:795.

Green, W. H. (1986). "Psychosocial dwarfism: Psychological and etiological considerations." *Advances in Clinical Child Psychology* 9:245.

Gross, D. J., Landau, H., Kohn, G., et al. (1986). "Male pseudohermaphroditism due to 17ß-hydroxysteroid dehydrogenase deficiency: Gender reassignment in early infancy." *Acta Endocrinologica* 112:238.

Grumbach, M. M., and Kaplan, S. L. (1988). "Recent advances in the diagnosis and management of sexual precocity." *Acta Paediatrica Japonica* 30:155.

Guilhaue, A., Benoit, O., Gourmelen, M., et al. (1982). "Relationship between sleep stage IV deficit and reversible HGH deficiency in psychosocial dwarfism." *Pediatric Research* 16:299.

Hampson, J. G., and Money, J. (1955). "Idiopathic sexual precocity in the female." *Psychosomatic Medicine* 17:16.

Herdt, G. (1990). "Mistaken gender: 5α-reductase hermaphroditism and biological reductionism in sexual identity reconsidered." *American Anthropology* 92:433.

Herdt, G., and Davidson, J. (1988). "The Sambia 'turnim-man': Sociocultural and clinical aspects of gender formation in male pseudohermaphrodites with 5α-reductase deficiency in Papua-New Guinea." *Archives of Sexual Behavior* 17:33.

Herdt, G. H., and Stoller, R. J. (1985). "Sakulambei—a hermaphrodite's secret: An example of clinical ethnography." *Psychoanalytic Study of Society* 11:115.

Holmes, S., Karlsson, J. A., and Thompson, R. G. (1985). "Social and school competencies in children with short stature: Longitudinal patterns." *Journal of Developmental and Behavioral Pediatrics* 6:263.

Illig, R., Largo, R. H., Qin, Q., et al. (1987). "Mental development in congenital hypothyroidism after neonatal screening." *Archives of Disease in Childhood* 62:1050.

Illig R., Largo, R. H., Weber, M., et al. (1986). "Sixty children with congenital hypothyroidism detected by neonatal thyroid: Mental development at

1, 4, and 7 years: A longitudinal study." *Acta Endocrinologica* (Suppl.) 279:346.

Imperato-McGinley, J., Guerrero, L., Gautier, T., et al. (1974). "Steroid 5α-reductase deficiency in man: An inherited form of male pseudohermaphroditism." *Science* 186:1213.

Imperato-McGinley, J., Peterson, R. E., Gautier, T. et al. (1979). "Androgens and the evolution of male-gender identity among male pseudohermaphrodites with 5α-reductase deficiency." *New England Journal of Medicine* 300:1233.

Jackson, P., Barrowclough, I. W., France, J. T., et al. (1980). "A successful pregnancy following total hysterectomy." *British Journal of Obstetrics and Gynaecology* 87:353.

Kalverboer, A. F., and Bleeker, J. K. (1988). "Mental and psychomotor development of young patients with congenital hypothyroidism detected in early screening." *Nederlands Tijdschrift voor Geneeskunde* 132:539.

Klebs, E. (1876). *Handbuch der pathologisher Anatomie.* Berlin: August Hirschvald.

Kohn, G., Lasch, E. E., El Shawwa, R., et al. (1985). "Male pseudohermaphroditism due to 17ß-hydroxysteroid dehydrogenase deficiency (17ß HSD) in a large Arab kinship. Studies on the natural history of the defect." *Journal of Pediatric Endocrinology* 1:29.

Kusalic, M., and Fortin, C. (1975). "Growth hormone treatment in hypopituitary dwarfs: Longitudinal psychological effects." *Canadian Psychiatric Association Journal* 20:325.

Lewis, V. G., and Money, J. (1983). "Gender-identity/role: G-I/R Part A: XY androgen-insensitivity syndrome and XX Rokitansky syndrome of vaginal atresia compared." In *Handbook of Psychosomatic Obstetrics and Gynaecology* (L. Dennerstein and G. Burrows, eds.). Amsterdam: Elsevier.

Lewis, V. G., Money, J., and Bobrow, N. A. (1977). "Idiopathic pubertal delay beyond age fifteen: Psychologic study of twelve boys." *Adolescence* 12:1.

Lewis, V. G., Money, J., and Epstein, R. (1968). "Concordance of verbal and nonverbal ability in the adrenogenital syndrome." *The Johns Hopkins Medical Journal* 122:192.

Lifshitz, F., Moses, N., Cervantes, C., et al. (1987). "Nutritional dwarfing in adolescents." *Seminars in Adolescent Medicine* 3:255.

Magner, J. A., Rogol, A. D., and Gorden, P. (1984). "Reversible growth hormone deficiency and delayed puberty triggered by a stressful experience in a young adult." *American Journal of Medicine* 76:737.

Masica, D. N., Money, J., Ehrhardt, A. A., et al. (1969). "IQ, fetal sex hormones and cognitive patterns: Studies in the testicular feminizing syndrome of androgen insensitivity." *The Johns Hopkins Medical Journal* 124:34.

Mattheis, M., and Forster, C. (1980). "Psychosexual development of girls with the adrenogenital syndrome." *Zeitschrift für Kinder und Jugendpsychiatrie* 8:5.

Mazur, T., and Clopper, R. R. (1987). "Hypopituitarism: Review of behavioral data." In *Current Concepts in Pediatric Endocrinology* (D. M. Styne and C. G. D. Brook, eds.). New York: Elsevier.

McCauley, E., Kay, T., Ito, J., et al. (1987). "The Turner syndrome: Cognitive deficits, affective discrimination, and behavior problems." *Child Development* 58:464.

McCauley, E., Sybert, V. P., and Ehrhardt, A. A. (1986). "Adult women with Turner's syndrome: A re-evaluation of psychosocial functioning." *Clinical Genetics* 29:284.

McGuire, L. S., and Omen, G. S. (1975). "Congenital adrenal hyperplasia: 1. Family studies of IQ." *Behavioral Genetics* 5:165.

Meizner, I. (1987). "Sonographic observation of in utero fetal 'masturbation.' " *Ultrasound Medicine* 6:111.

Mitchell, C. M., Joyce, S., Johanson, A. J., et al. (1986). "A retrospective evaluation of psychosocial impact of long-term growth hormone therapy." *Clinical Pediatrics* 25:17.

Money J. (1952). *Hermaphroditism: An Inquiry into the Nature of a Human Paradox.* Doctoral Dissertation, Harvard University Library. University Microfilms, Ann Arbor, MI 48106 (1967).

———. (1955). "Hermaphroditism, gender and precocity in hyperadrenocorticism: Psychologic findings." *Bulletin of The Johns Hopkins Hospital* 96:253.

———. (1956). "Psychologic studies in hypothyroidism, and recommendations for case management." *Archives of Neurology and Psychiatry* 76:296.

———. (1961). "The sex hormones and other variables in human eroticism." In *Sex and Internal Secretions, Third Edition* (W. C. Young, ed.). Baltimore: Williams and Wilkins.

———. (1964). "Two cytogenetic syndromes: Psychologic comparisons. 1. Intelligence and specific-factor quotients." *Journal of Psychiatric Research* 2:223.

———. (1968). "Psychologic approach to psychosexual misidentity with elective mutism: Sex reassignment in two cases of hyperadrenocortical hermaphroditism." *Clinical Pediatrics* 7:331.

———. (1970). "Hormonal and genetic extremes at puberty." In *The Psychopathology of Adolescence* (J. Zubin and A. M. Freedman, eds.). New York: Grune and Stratton.

———. (1971). "Prenatal hormones and intelligence: A possible relationship." *Impact of Science on Society* 21:285.

———. (1977). "The syndrome of abuse dwarfism (psychosocial dwarfism or reversible hyposomatotropinism): Behavioral data and case report." *American Journal of Diseases of Children* 131:508.

———. (1984). "Gender transposition theory and homosexual genesis." *Journal of Sex and Marital Therapy* 10:75.

———. (1985). "Gender: History, theory and usage of the term in sexology and its relationship to nature/nurture." *Journal of Sex and Marital Therapy* 11:71.

———. (1986a). "Longitudinal studies in clinical psychoendocrinology: Methodology." *Journal of Developmental and Behavioral Pediatrics* 7:31.

———. (1986b). "Munchausen syndrome by proxy: Update." *Journal of Pediatric Psychology* 11:538.

———. (1987). "Treatment guidelines: Antiandrogen and counseling of paraphilic sex offenders." *Journal of Sex and Marital Therapy* 13:219.

———. (1988a). *Gay, Straight, and In-Between: The Sexology of Erotic Orientation.* New York: Oxford University Press.

———. (1988b). *Lovemaps: Clinical Concepts of Sexual/Erotic Health and Pathology, Paraphilia, and Gender Transposition in Childhood, Adolescence, and Maturity.* Paperback edition, Amherst, NY: Prometheus Books. First edition, New York: Irvington, 1986.

———. (1989). "Paleodigms and paleodigmatics: A new theoretical construct applicable to Munchausen syndrome by proxy, child-abuse dwarfism, paraphilias, anorexia, and other syndromes." *American Journal of Psychotherapy* 43:15.

———. (1991). *Biographies of Gender and Hermaphroditism in Paired Comparisons: Clinical Supplement to the Handbook of Sexology.* Amsterdam: Elsevier.

Money, J., and Alexander, D. (1967). "Eroticism and sexual function in developmental anorchia and hyporchia with pubertal failure." *Journal of Sex Research* 3:31.

———. (1969). "Psychosexual development and absence of homosexuality in males with precocious puberty: Review of 18 cases." *Journal of Nervous and Mental Disease* 148:111.

Money, J., and Ambinder, R. (1978). "Two-year, real-life diagnostic test: Rehabilitation versus cure." In *Controversy in Psychiatry* (J. P. Brady and H. K. H. Brodie, eds.). Philadelphia: Saunders.

Money, J., Annecillo, C., and Hutchison, J. W. (1985). "Forensic and family psychiatry in abuse dwarfism: Munchausen syndrome by proxy, atonement, and addiction to abuse." *Journal of Sex and Marital Therapy* 11:30.

Money, J., Annecillo, C., and Kelley, J. F. (1983a). "Growth of intelligence: Failure and catchup associated respectively with abuse and rescue in the syndrome of abuse dwarfism." *Psychoneuroendocrinology* 8:309.

———. (1983b). "Abuse-dwarfism syndrome: After rescue, statural and intellectual catchup growth correlate." *Journal of Clinical Child Psychiatry* 12:279.

Money, J., Annecillo, C., Van Orman, B., et al. (1974). "Cytogenetics, hormones and behavior disability: Comparison of XYY and XXY syndromes." *Clinical Genetics* 6:370.

Money, J., Clarke, F. C., and Beck, J. (1978). "Congenital hypothyroidism and IQ increase: A quarter century followup." *Journal of Pediatrics* 93:432.

Money, J., and Daléry, J. (1977). "Hyperadrenocortical 46,XX hermaphroditism with penile urethra. Psychological studies in seven cases, three reared as boys, four as girls." In *Congenital Adrenal Hyperplasia* (P. A. Lee, L. P. Plotnick, A. A. Kowarski, and C. J. Migeon, eds.). Baltimore: University Park Press.

Money, J., Devore, H., and Norman, B. F. (1986). "Gender identity and gender transposition: Longitudinal outcome study of 32 male hermaphrodites assigned as girls." *Journal of Sex and Marital Therapy* 12:165.

Money, J., and Drash, P. W. (1968). "Juvenile thyrotoxicosis: Behavioral and somatic symptoms and antecedents leading to referral and diagnosis." *Journal of Special Education* 2:83.

Money, J, Drash, P. W., and Lewis, V. (1967). "Dwarfism and hypopituitarism: Statural retardation without mental retardation." *American Journal of Mental Deficiency* 72:122.

Money, J., and Ehrhardt, A. A. (1966). "Preservation of IQ in hypoparathyroidism of childhood." *American Journal of Mental Deficiency* 71:237.

———. (1968). "Correlation of mental functioning and calcium regulation in a rare case of pseudohypoparathyroidism." *The Johns Hopkins Medical Journal* 123:276.

———. (1972). *Man and Woman, Boy and Girl.* Baltimore: Johns Hopkins University Press. Facsimile reprint edition, New York: Jason Aronson, 1996.

Money, J., and Hampson, J.G. (1955). "Idiopathic sexual precocity in the male." *Psychosomatic Medicine* 17:1.

Money, J., Hampson, J. G., and Hampson, J. L. (1955). "An examination of some basic sexual concepts: The evidence of human hermaphroditism." *Bulletin of The Johns Hopkins Hospital* 97:301.

Money, J., and Jobaris, R. (1977). "Juvenile Addison's disease: Followup behavioral studies in seven cases." *Psychoneuroendocrinology* 2:149.

Money, J., and Lamacz, M. (1986). "Nosocomial stress and abuse exemplified in a case of male hermaphroditism from infancy through adulthood: Coping strategies and prevention." *International Journal of Family Psychology* 7:71.

———. (1987). "Genital examination and exposure experienced as nosocomial sexual abuse in childhood." *Journal of Nervous and Mental Disease* 175:713.

———. (1989). *Vandalized Lovemaps: Paraphilic Outcome of Seven Cases in Pediatric Sexology.* Amherst, NY: Prometheus Books.

Money, J., and Lewis, V. (1964). "Longitudinal study of IQ in treated congenital hypothyroidism." In the Ciba Foundation Study Group No. 18, *Brain-Thyroid Relationships* (M. P. Cameron and M. O'Connor, eds.). London: J. and A. Churchill.

———. (1966). "IQ, genetics and accelerated growth: Adrenogenital syndrome." *Bulletin of The Johns Hopkins Hospital* 118:365.

———. (1982). "Homosexual/heterosexual status in boys at puberty: Idiopathic adolescent gynecomastia and congenital virilizing adrenocorticism compared." *Psychoneuroendocrinology* 7:339.

Money, J., and Meredith, T. (1967). "Elevated verbal IQ and idiopathic precocious sexual maturation." *Pediatric Research* 1:59.

Money, J., and Norman, B. F. (1987). "Gender identity and gender transposition: Longitudinal outcome study of 24 male hermaphrodites assigned as boys." *Journal of Sex and Marital Therapy* 13:75.

———. (1988). "Pedagogical handicap associated with micropenis and other CHARGE syndrome anomalies of embryogenesis: Four 46,XY cases reared as girls." *American Journal of Psychotherapy* 42:354.

Money, J., and Pollitt, E. (1966). "Studies in the psychology of dwarfism: II. Personality maturation and response to growth hormone treatment." *Journal of Pediatrics* 68:381.

Money, J., Potter, R., and Stoll, C. S. (1969). "Sex reannouncement in hereditary sex deformity: Psychology and sociology of habilitation." *Social Science and Medicine* 3:207.

Money, J., Schwartz, M., and Lewis, V. G. (1984). "Adult erotosexual status and fetal hormonal masculinization and demasculinization: 46,XX congenital virilizing adrenal hyperplasia and 46,XY androgen-insensitivity syndrome compared." *Psychoneuroendocrinology* 9:405.

Money, J., and Walker, P. (1971). "Psychosexual development, maternalism, nonpromiscuity and body image in 15 females with precocious puberty." *Archives of Sexual Behavior* 1:45.

Money, J., Weinberg, R. S., and Lewis, V. (1966). "Intelligence quotient and school performance in twenty-two children with a history of thyrotoxicosis." *Bulletin of The Johns Hopkins Hospital* 118:275.

Money, J., and Werlwas, J. (1976). "*Folie à deux* in the parents of psychosocial dwarfs: Two cases." *Bulletin of the American Academy of Psychiatry and the Law* 4:351.

Money, J., and Wolff, G. (1974). "Late puberty, retarded growth and reversible hyposomatotropinism (psychosocial dwarfism)." *Adolescence* 9:121.

Money, J., Wolff, G., and Annecillo, C. (1972). "Pain agnosia and self-injury in the syndrome of reversible somatotropin deficiency (psychosocial dwarfism)." *Journal of Autism and Childhood Schizophrenia* 2:127.

Mulaikal, R. M., Migeon, C. J., and Rock, J. A. (1987). "Fertility rates in female patients with congenital adrenal hyperplasia due to 21-hydroxylase deficiency." *New England Journal of Medicine* 316:178.

Murphy, G., Hulse, J. A, Jackson, D., et al. (1986). "Early treated hypothyroidism: Development at 3 years." *Archives of Disease in Childhood* 61:761.

Nass, R. D., and Baker, S. W. (1989). "Hormones and learning disabilities: Incidence in congenital adrenal hyperplasia." Poster, Child Neurology Society, Oct. 12-14.

Netley, C. (1988). "Relationships between hemispheric lateralization, sex hormones, quality of parenting and adjustment in 47,XXY males prior to puberty." *Journal of Childhood Psychology and Psychiatry and Allied Disciplines* 29:281.

Netley, C., and Rovet, J. (1982). "Verbal deficits in children with 47,XXY and 47,XXX karyotypes: A descriptive and experimental study." *Brain and Language* 17:58.

NECHC (New England Congenital Hypothyroidism Collaborative). (1985). "Neonatal hypothyroidism screening: Status of patients at 6 years of age." *Journal of Pediatrics* 107:915.

Nielsen, J., Nyborg, H., and Dahl, G. (1977). "Turner's syndrome. A psychiatric-psychological study of 45 women with Turner's syndrome, compared with their sisters and women with normal karyotypes, growth retardation and primary amenorrhoea." *Acta Jutlandica XLV,* Medicine Series 21, Aarhus, Denmark.

Oesterling, J., Gearhart, J., and Jeffs, R. (1987). "A unified approach to early reconstructive surgery of the child with ambiguous genitalia." *Journal of Urology* 138:1079.

Patton, R. G., and Gardner, L. I. (1962). "Influence of family environment on growth: Syndrome of 'maternal deprivation.' " *Pediatrics* 30:957.

———. (1963). *Growth Failure in Maternal Deprivation.* Springfield, IL: Charles C Thomas.

Perlman, S. M. (1973). "Cognitive abilities of children with hormone abnormalities: Screening by psychoeducational tests." *Journal of Learning Disorders* 6:21.

Pollitt, E., and Money, J. (1964). "Studies in the psychology of dwarfism. I. Intelligence quotient and school achievement." *Journal of Pediatrics* 64:415.

Powell, G. F., Brasel, J. A., and Blizzard, R. M. (1967a). "Emotional deprivation and growth retardation simulating idiopathic hypopituitarism. I. Clinical evaluation of the syndrome." *New England Journal of Medicine* 276:1271.

Powell, G. F., Brasel, J. A., Raiti S., et al. (1967b). "Emotional deprivation and growth retardation simulating idiopathic hypopituitarism. II. Endocrinologic evaluation of the syndrome." *New England Journal of Medicine* 276:1279.

Pugliese, M. T., Lifshitz, F., Grad, G., et al. (1983). "Fear of obesity: A cause of short stature and delayed puberty." *New England Journal of Medicine* 309:513.

Pugliese, M. T., Weyman-Daum, M., Moses, N., et al. (1987). "Parental health beliefs as a cause of nonorganic failure to thrive." *Pediatrics* 80:175.

Resnick, S. M., Berenbaum, S. A., Gottesman, I. I., et al. (1986). "Early hormonal influences on cognitive functioning in congenital adrenal hyperplasia." *Developmental Psychology* 22:191.

Roesler, A., and Kohn, G. (1983). "Male pseudohermaphroditism due to 17ß-hydroxysteroid dehydrogenase deficiency: Studies on the natural history of the defect and effect of androgens on gender role." *Journal of Steroid Biochemistry* 19:663.

Rotnem, D., Cohen, D. J., Hintz, R., et al. (1979). "Psychological sequelae of relative 'treatment failure' for children receiving human growth hormone replacement." *Journal of the American Academy of Child Psychiatry* 18:505.

Rovet, J. (1983). "Cognitive and neuropsychological test performance of persons with abnormalities of adolescent development: A test of Waber's hypothesis." *Childhood Development* 54:941.

Rovet, J., Ehrlich, R., and Sorbara, D. (1987). "Intellectual outcome in children with fetal hypothyroidism." *Journal of Pediatrics* 110:700.

Rovet, J., and Netley, C. (1982). "Processing deficits in Turner's syndrome." *Developmental Psychology* 18:77.

Saenger, P., Levine, L. S., Wiedemann, E., et al. (1977). "Somatomedin and growth hormone in psychosocial dwarfism." *Pädiatrie und Pädologie* Suppl. 5, 1.

Sarr, M., Job, J. C., Chaussain, J. L., et al. (1987). "Psychogenic growth retardation. Critical study of diagnostic data." *Archives Française Pediatrie* 44:331–38.

Sauer, M. V., Lobo, R. A., and Paulson, R. J. (1989). "Successful twin pregnancy after donation to a patient with XY gonadal dysgenesis." *American Journal of Obstetrics and Gynecology* 161:380.

Schanberg, S. M., and Field, T. M. (1987). "Sensory deprivation stress and supplemental stimulation in the rat pup and preterm human neonate." *Child Development* 58:1431.

Schanberg, S. M., and Kuhn, C. M. (1985). "The biochemical effects of tactile deprivation in neonatal rats." In *Perspectives on Behavioral Medicine, Volume 2* (R.B. Williams Jr., ed.). New York: Academic Press.

Schiavi, R. C., Theilgaard, A., Owen, D. R., et al. (1984). "Sex Chromosome Anomalies, Hormones, and Aggressivity." *Archives of General Psychology* 41:93.

———. (1988). "Sex chromosome anomalies, hormones, and sexuality." *Archives of General Psychology* 45:19.

Shaffer, J. W. (1962). "A specific cognitive deficit observed in gonadal aplasia (Turner syndrome)." *Journal of Clinical Psychology* 18:403.

Sharp, R., Holder, T., Howard, C., et al. (1987). "Neonatal genital reconstruction." *Journal of Pediatric Surgery* 22:168.

Sherwin, B. B., Gelfand, M. M., and Brender, W. (1985). "Androgen enhances sexual motivation in females: A prospective, crossover study of sex steroid administration in the surgical menopause." *Psychosomatic Medicine* 47:339.

Silbert, A., Wolff, P. H., and Lilienthal, J. (1977). "Spacial and temporal processing in patients with Turner's syndrome." *Behavioral Genetics* 7:11.

Silverton, R. (1982). "Social work perspective on psychosocial dwarfism." *Social Work in Health Care* 7:1.

Sitsen, J. M. A., ed. (1988). *Handbook of Sexology, Volume 6: The Pharmacology and Endocrinology of Sexual Function.* Amsterdam–New York–London: Elsevier.

Smith, D. W., Blizzard, R. M., and Wilkins, L. (1957). "The mental prognosis in hypothyroidism of infancy and childhood." *Pediatrics* 19:1011.

Sonis, W. A., Spilotis, B., Maymi-Gascue, M., et al. (1987). "Maturational arrest: An experiment in nature." *Journal of the Academy of Childhood and Adolescent Psychology* 26:277.

Steinhausen, H. C., and Stahnke, N. (1976). "Psychoendocrinological studies in dwarfed children and adolescents." *Archives of Disease in Childhood* 51:778.

Taitz, L. S., and King, J. M. (1988). "Growth Patterns in Child Abuse." *Acta Pediatrica Scandinavica* (Suppl.) 343:62.

Talbot, N. B., Sobel, E. H., Burke, B. S., et al. (1947). "Dwarfism in healthy children: Its possible relation to emotional, nutritional and endocrine disturbances." *New England Journal of Medicine* 236:783.

Taylor, B. J., and Brook, C. G. D. (1986). "Sleep EEG in growth disorders." *Archives of Disease in Childhood* 61:754.

Theilgaard, A., Nielsen, J., Sorensen, A., et al. (1971). "A psychological-psychiatric study of patients with Klinefelter syndrome, 47,XXY." *Acta Jutlandica* XLIII:1. Copenhagen, Munksgaard.

Thompson, G. N., McCrossin, R. B., Penfold, J. L., et al. (1986). "Management and outcome of children with congenital hypothyroidism detected on neonatal screening in South Australia." *Medical Journal of Australia* 145:18.

Udwin, O., Yule, W., and Martin, N. (1987). "Cognitive abilities and behavioral characteristics of children with idiopathic hypercalcemia." *Journal of Child Psychology and Psychiatry and Allied Disciplines* 28:297.

Uvnaas-Moberg, K. (1989). "The gastrointestinal tract in growth and reproduction." *Scientific American* 261:60.

Waber D. P. (1979). "Neuropsychological aspects of Turner's syndrome." *Developmental Medicine and Child Neurology* 21:58.

Wolff, G., and Money, J. (1973). "Relationship between sleep and growth in patients with psychosocial dwarfism." *Psychological Medicine* 3:18.

Woodhouse, C. R. J. (1989). "The classification and management of micropenis." *Dialogues in Pediatric Urology* 12:1.

Young, W. C., ed. (1961). *Sex and Internal Secretions* (Third edition.). Baltimore: Williams and Wilkins.